Adventure Guide

Cuba

HUNTER PUBLISHING, INC,
130 Campus Drive, Edison, NJ 08818
☎ 732-225-1900; ☎ 800-255-0343; Fax 732-417-1744
www.hunterpublishing.com

Ulysses Travel Publications
4176 Saint-Denis, Montréal, Québec
Canada H2W 2M5
☎ 514-843-9882, ext. 2232; fax 514-843-9448

Windsor Books
The Boundary, Wheatley Road, Garsington
Oxford, OX44 9EJ England
☎ 01865-361122; Fax 01865-361133

ISBN 1-58843-574-1

Printed in the United States

© 2006 Hunter Publishing, Inc.

Cover photo: San Francisco Church, UNESCO World
Heritage Site, Trinidad © Almay Images

Images on pages 11, 15, 112, 119, 175, 183, 202, 251,
287, 328, 345, 377, provided by author

Index by Stepping Stone Indexing

Maps © 2006 Hunter Publishing, Inc.

1   2   3   4

www.hunterpublishing.com

 Hunter's full range of guides to all corners of the globe is featured on our exciting website. You'll find guidebooks to suit every type of traveler, no matter what their budget, lifestyle, or idea of fun.

Adventure Guides – There are now over 40 titles in this series, covering destinations from Costa Rica and the Yucatán to Tampa Bay & Florida's West Coast and Belize. Complete with information on what to do, as well as where to stay and eat, *Adventure Guides* are tailor-made for the active traveler, with all the practical travel information you need, as well as details of the best places for hiking, biking, canoeing, horseback riding, trekking, skiing, watersports, and all other kinds of fun.

Alive Guides – This ever-popular line of books takes a unique look at the best each destination offers: fine dining, jazz clubs, first-class hotels and resorts. In-margin icons direct the reader at a glance. Top-sellers include *The US Virgin Islands, The British Virgin Islands* and *Aruba, Bonaire & Curaçao.*

One-of-a-kind travel books available from Hunter include *The Best Dives of the Caribbean; Cruising Alaska* and many more.

Full descriptions are given for each book at www.hunterpublishing.com, along with reviewers' comments and a cover image. You can also view pages and the table of contents. Books may be purchased on-line via our secure transaction facility.

Dedication

This book is dedicated to Paige Lougheed Pedersen, a travel writer in training.

Acknowledgments

I would like to thank my husband, John Harris, for his never ending vigilance in finding errors in grammar and spelling. It seems like a monumental task, one of which I am certain he tires.

I thank Paige Pedersen for her assistance in the research of this book. She did things I would never do even when exploring a new place.

Barbara and Arturo Castillo Rubio were a tremendous source of support and help. Without their help and humor I could never have known as much as I do about Cuba.

Joy McKinnon is my personal navigator. She can read a map, a road sign in Spanish and tell me what to do faster and better than anyone I know.

As for the people of Cuba, your love of life will get you through any difficulties that may lie ahead. I thank everyone who helped me from the taxi driver who found a new *casa* to the workers in the tourist offices who answered all my questions.

Contents

■ Maps

Maps

Introduction

Cuba is a jewel, a sparkling diamond surrounded by the blue-green waters of the Caribbean. Like all Caribbean Islands, it has palm trees dotting the white coral beaches. It has trade winds cooling the effects of the tropical sun. It has classy hotels and first-rate restaurants. But you can get that anywhere in the tropics.

Where Cuba is unique is in its culture. In fact, Cuba is music. You can travel nowhere on the island without hearing the beat of a drum or the strum of a guitar. To accompany the music, locals indulge in the pleasure of dancing from the time they can walk until the time they die. A Cuban without music is like a drunk without booze.

Although tourism plays a big role in the economy of Cuba, tourists in the past have been confined to the all-inclusive resorts where contact with the people was restricted. Now, however, visitors can stay in *casas particulares*, homes that have been inspected by the government so standards are acceptable, and can order meals at *paladars*, selected homes that are permitted to feed up to 12 customers, including foreigners, at a time. Tourists can travel on public transportation or rent cars so they can visit some of the farther reaches of Cuba.

At the time of writing, a new law forbade any kind of personal interaction between Cubans and foreigners, although this would be impossible to monitor in the *casas* and *paladars*. Those working in the tourist industry at the all-inclusive resorts are required to turn in their tips and they are permitted to speak with tourists only if a government official, who could censor the conversation, is present. Breaking the law is punished harshly in Cuba.

But Cubans have lived through harsh and unreasonable laws before and they seem to come out better in spite of it all. Although they suffer fear during oppressive times, they find ways to work and play within the regime's restrictions. By the time this book goes to print, the situation may swing to more liberalism again.

The intermingling of Cuban people and foreigners makes for an interesting vacation. During the day it is fun to sit on a balcony of a *casa particular* and watch children play on the streets. They will unabashedly entertain you for hours (especially if they know you are watching) playing baseball with a stick and stone covered in string or performing a symphony with imaginary instruments. I watched one group pretend that they were New York fashion models. It was more fun than watching any American sit-com. The kids' script was original.

Talking to Cubans is also a treat. One reason is that they are educated. Youngsters know where Belgium or Canada is located and will come up with questions that may stump you. Adults like to exchange information or discuss politics (at the moment, yours not theirs). They love to compare cultures and show off their country. They love to poke fun and laugh.

Cuba has been under an American embargo since the 1960s and this has forced even more creativity into the people. Instead of Kentucky Fried Chicken they have Rapid Dart, instead of Ford they have Mitsubishi, instead of Michael Jackson they have the Buena Vista Social Club. When spices were unobtainable, the people grew them. When auto parts were unavailable, they made them. When they wanted Coke to go with their rum, they brought it in from Mexico.

When you go, by all means stay in a resort and enjoy the luxury of a first-class hotel. While there, or before you go, check out the latest rules about tourists and then do whatever is allowed to get out and meet the people.

History

 7000-3500 BC. The first known humans on Cuba, the **Ciboneys** (see-bone-AYS) and **Guanahacabibes** (gwan-nuh-uh-kuh-BEE-bais), nomadic hunter-gatherers and fishers, settle in caves in western Cuba.

1250 AD. **Tainos**, descendents of the Arawaks of South America, settle in Cuba.

1492. **Columbus** arrives in Cuba and calls the island Juana. He claims it for Spain.

1494. Columbus returns to Cuba and reports that the island is part of the mainland.

1508. Spanish explorer **Sebastian de Ocampo** circles Cuba and proves that it is an island.

1509. Columbus's son, **Diego**, becomes Cuba's first governor.

1512. **Hatuey**, a local Indian who rebelled against the Spanish, is burned at the stake.

1514. **Havana**, called San Cristobal de Habana, is established by **Panfilo de Narvaez**.

1520. Three hundred **slaves** arrive to work in the Jaugua gold mine.

1522. **Amador de Lares** brings the first slaves to work on the plantations.

1533. First **slave uprising** occurs at Jobabo Mines. With the help of disgruntled slaves, the French pirates burn Havana.

1554. **Pirate Peg Leg le Clerc** attacks Santiago de Cuba.

1555. **Pirate Jacques de Sores** attacks Sanitago de Cuba. City's people move inland to Bayamo.

1586. **Castillo del Morro** in Havana harbor is completed.

1607. **Havana** is named capital of Cuba.

1708. Slaves who may now purchase their freedom are called *cortados*.

1717. Cuban **tobacco production** falls under government monopoly.

1717-1723. **Vegueros** revolt against government tobacco monopoly.

1727. Slave revolt at sugar mill in Quiebra-Hacha (west of Havana).

1748. **University of San Jeronimo** is opened in Havana.

1762. **Britain** captures Havana.

1763. English and Spanish trade Florida for Havana.

1776. **Teatro Principal** is opened.

1777. Cuba's government changes to an independent colonial administration.

1784. Only trade between Cuba and Spain is legal.

1790. The first newspaper, the **Papel Periodico**, is published.

1793. **Trade** with the US begins.

1795. **Nicolas Morales**, a free Negro, joins with whites in an uprising for equality.

1796. **Trade** with US severed.

1803. Poet **José Maria Heredia** is born in Santiago de Cuba.

1812. **Constitution** inaugurated.

1816. **José Cienfuegos** becomes Captain General (commander in chief or military governor).

1819. **Carlos Manuel de Cespedes** is born in Bayamo.

1820. Constitution of 1812 reinstated.

1821. **Nicolas de Mahy** becomes Captain General.

1823. Heredia and José Francisco Lemus promote independence from Spain. Monroe Doctrine states that the Western Hemisphere is under US influence.

1824. The **Battle of Ayacucho** in Peru results in Spanish being driven from the Americas except for Puerto Rico and Cuba.

1825. US prohibits Mexico and Venezuela from helping liberate Cuba. US does not want slaves freed.

1832. **Mariano Ricafort** becomes Captain General.

1833. **Cuban Academy of Literature** is founded.

1834. **Miguel Tacon** becomes Captain General.

1842. Freedom fighter **Antonio Maceo** is born in Majaguabo, San Luis.

1848. President Polk offers Spain $100 million for Cuba. Spain refuses.

1851. **Narciso Lopez**, an advocator for the union of US and Cuba, is executed in Havana.

1853. Poet **José Martí Perez** is born in Havana. **Marquis Juan de la Pezuela** becomes Captain General of Cuba and frees slaves.

1854. Request sent to the US for **troops** to prevent emancipation of slaves.

1863. **Slaves freed**.

1898. Cuba gains **independence** from Spain, Teddy Roosevelt and the Rough Riders defeat Cubans at San Juan Hill and Cuba is then administered by the US.

1902. Cuba gains **independence** from the US.

1929. Cuba enters **depression**.

1930. **Demonstrations** result in deaths. Pay is reduced for government employees; teachers aren't paid at all.

Railway workers strike. By year's end, many cities have violent demonstrations. Schools close. Americans accuse Cubans of being associated with Moscow.

1931. Entire student directory is arrested. Rumors of a revolution spread. **Captain Calvo** is shot and killed. Both sides practice oppression and violence.

1933. Machado uses brutality to crush opposition. General strikes occur throughout the country. Machado compromises with Communists.

1933. August 12, Machado resigns and flies to the Bahamas. **Carlos M Cespedes** (son of the man born in Bayamo in 1819) takes power.

1933. September 5, **Fulgencio Batista** takes power. **Ramon Grau San Martin** becomes President. Government lasts 100 days. Guantanamo Base is left to US control. Social reforms are implemented.

1934. Women gain the **vote**.

1940. Batista wins during a democratic election.

1941. Cuba enters **WW II.**

1945. Cuba becomes a member of the **United Nations**.

1948. Cuba becomes a member of the **Organization of American States** (OAS).

1953. Fidel Castro's uprising is defeated by Batista. Constitution is suspended.

1955. Castro is given political **amnesty**. He leaves for the US and then Mexico.

1956-1958. Castro gains power and popularity.

1959. Batista resigns and Castro's provisional government is established. Five hundred and fifty Batista associates are executed.

1960. US-owned properties in Cuba are confiscated; government requests back taxes.

1961. US **trade embargo** implemented. April 17, US military under John F Kennedy **invades** at the Bay of

Pigs. US captives are traded for $52 million in food and medicines.

1962. **Soviet** missiles discovered on Cuban soil by Americans.

1965-1973. 260,000 Cubans airlifted to the United States.

1967. **Che Guevara**, Castro's aide, is executed in Bolivia.

1975. First congress of the **Cuban Communist Party** is held and new constitution is adopted.

1977. Relations between US and Cuba improve. Americans permitted to visit Cuba.

1980. 125,000 Cubans flee to the US.

1989. Castro signs **friendship treaty** with USSR. July, four officers and 10 civilians executed for drug trafficking.

1991. Collapse of the USSR and all economic subsidies end. Cuba goes it alone.

1993. Soviet troops are withdrawn from Cuba.

1994. Economic **depression** forces thousands to escape.

1996. One hundred and fifty dissidents arrested and imprisoned. Two civilian planes owned by Cuban-Americans shot down in Cuba. **Helms-Burton Act** signed, thus tightening US embargo.

1997. A **Salvadoran** confesses to planting bombs in Havana Hotels.

2002. Hundreds of **Afghan** prisoners are confined at Guantanamo Bay.

2005. Law passed forbidding Cubans to speak in private with foreigners.

Government

 The Republic of Cuba is a **communist** state (but called socialist by most) with the seat of government in Havana. Cuba obtained independence from Spain in 1898 when the US defeated Spain in the Spanish-American war. However, Cuba fell under the administrative jurisdiction of the United States until 1902 when it became an independent country and drew up its first constitution. In that document, the United States put in a series of clauses that gave them some administrative powers over Cuba and the **Platt Amendment** (part of that first constitution) guaranteed the US rights to a navel base forever. Cuba was governed by a series of dictators for the next half a century and inaugurated its first constitution under the present government in 1976, amending it twice, in 2000 and again in 2002.

Fidel Castro Ruz was President of the Council of State and the Council of Ministers from 1959 until 1976, at which time the office was abolished. He then became president and chief of state and the head of government. **Raul Castro Ruz** (Fidel's brother) was elected vice president. The National Assembly elected both men for a period of five years. The next election will be in 2008.

The **National Assembly of People's Power** is the governing body and has 601 seats. Although members are elected by the people, they must be approved by a candidacy commission before they can run for office. There are 278 local representatives, 185 provincial reps and 138 national reps. Elected members serve five years as provincial and national reps, but local reps are elected for only 30 months. There are twice as many men as women sitting in the Assembly and, of those, the majority is between the ages of 40 and 50. The National Assembly also nominates the Council of Ministers, the highest executive body.

The only political party in Cuba is the **Communist Party** and Fidel Castro Ruz is the first secretary. Everyone over the age of 16 can vote; women were granted the right to vote in 1934.

Supreme Court Judges are elected by and accountable to the National Assembly. The judges may also be part of the National Assembly. Provincial judges are elected by provincial assemblies and municipal judges are elected by municipal assemblies. The legal system is based on Spanish and American law, with some communist legal theory thrown in.

CUBA'S 14 PROVINCES

Ciudad de la Habana, Cienfuegos, Camagüey, Granma, Ciego de Avila, Guantanamo, Holguin, La Habana, Las Tunas, Matanzas, Santiago de Cuba, Villa Clara, Pinar del Rio and Sancti Spiritus. Isla de la Juventud is considered a special municipality.

The **military** consists of the army, which has about 60,000 troops, including combat and security forces. The best of these men, about 6,500 of them, are used as the Border Brigade whose job it is to defend the perimeter of the island. Cuba has fewer than 30 offshore vessels. The military is beefed up with the **militia**, a part-time force supplied with light arms that are used in controlling the general public. There is also the **Youth Labor Army**, whose main mission is to protect the environment and educate the young. The **navy** is insignificant, but the **air force** has about 15,000 members stationed at 11 bases. It is supplied with 300 planes and about 110 helicopters.

> **AUTHOR'S NOTE:** It is illegal to photograph military installations or troops.

The **police** are, for the most part, helpful and friendly to foreigners. They are not corrupt as in some Latin

American countries where officers seemingly live off bribes. The Cuban police generally don't seem to bother foreign drivers.

Economy

The purchasing power of the country is $32 billion. Exports are mainly **coffee**, **sugar** and **tobacco**, with 24% of the population employed in agriculture. Industrial production includes the manufacturing of **chemicals**, **steel**, **cement**, **petroleum** and **biotechnology**. This area employs about 25% of the labor force. The other half of the country is employed in the service industry, with **tourism** being the biggest sector. Almost one quarter of Cuba's exports go to Europe, but recently Cuba captured a small part of the constantly growing market in China. This is a great help to its economic growth. Even more recently, Cuba, Bolivia, Venezuela and Chile are talking trade.

Once the Soviet Union collapsed and stopped giving Cuba aid, the economy fell and the people suffered a severe depression. It is said that all Cubans lost about 10 pounds during this crises. After the 9/11 attack on the United States, tourism also dropped.

The **American embargo** has caused no end of economic hardships. Recently, the Bush administration decided to tighten its grip on Cuba even more by forbidding Cuban-Americans to send money or gifts to the country, whether it be by donation or through business. Cuba responded by changing its financial loyalties to the euro and Canadian dollar. The Americans then tried to dissuade European institutions from lending money to Cuba, but many European banks are ignoring this plea.

At present Cuba owes about $1.97 billion to European countries, which is about 85% of their international debt. France, Germany, Italy and Spain are the

Styrofoam boats are used by Cubans to flee their home country in search of a better life.

main contributors, although some contributions came from large Swiss banks. In its most recent purge, the American government fined contributing Swiss banks for going against the embargo. This resulted in the Swiss loans decreasing to almost nothing. Cuba responded by gaining the co-operation of financial institutions in Brazil, Venezuela, China and Middle Eastern countries. The theory is that the more Cuba owes, the less likely those countries will lean toward the American way of thinking.

CUBAN HUMOR: There is one doctor for every 40 people, one teacher for every 25 and one policeman for everyone.

■ Banks & Money

The **Cuban peso** is the official currency, but there is also the **convertible peso**. American dollars are traded at a cost of 10%, while euros and Canadian dollars are accepted at international exchange rates without a commission fee.

Money is traded for the convertible peso at a rate of one peso for one US dollar. The convertible peso can be used or traded by all Cubans. However, it is difficult to exchange this money back into any currency other than euros or Canadian dollars. Do not carry Cuban pesos out of the country as they cannot be exchanged on the world market.

> **AUTHOR'S NOTE:** Prices in this book are given in American dollars.

The **National Bank of Cuba** is open Monday to Friday, 8:30 am to noon and 1:30 to 3 pm; Saturday, 8:30 to 10:30 am. Cuba will not accept traveler's checks or credit cards that are issued by American banks.

■ Labor

 The official unemployment rate in Cuba is 2. 6% of the 4.5 million employable persons, but this is an unreliable statistic. When there are changes in trade, factory closures, agricultural ups and downs, and so on, workers are shuffled around. This movement is seldom called employment or unemployment, but rather "redistribution of workers."

The state controls any free enterprise by charging exorbitant license and tax fees. For example, the cost of running a *casa particular* is about $850 convertible pesos per month, whether the people earn that or not. Nonpayment results in closure of the establishment. Artists and farmers can't possibly pay the costs for licenses required to sell their products so free enterprise in those areas is low.

Workers can belong to the government-controlled union, **Central de Trabajadores de Cuba**, which has a mandate to defend socialism and human rights. However, even in foreign-owned businesses (mostly hotels) workers are not permitted to negotiate wages or working conditions. The government assigns workers to the jobs; foreign companies cannot hire workers independently. On payday, the government collects the money (about $100 per worker per month) and gives the worker about 100 pesos ($5). It sounds – and is – terrible, but it is still better than what professionals in general earn. More than once you will hear about qualified dentists and doctors working as dishwashers or chambermaids because they can make more money, work fewer hours and have the chance of a tip or two from tourists.

Cultural Groups

Originally, the **Taino** and **Ciboney Indians** occupied the island, but most disappeared due to disease or war. The **Spanish** started occupying the land and needed slaves to work the sugar and tobacco fields so they brought in Africans. After the emancipation of slaves, blacks and whites intermarried, creating a large mulatto group. Cuban residents today are 39% Caucasian of Spanish origin, 10% Negro, 51% mulatto and 1% Chinese. Interestingly, in 1841, African slaves numbered over 400,000 and made up 40% of the entire population. This represented about 100 different African ethnic groups.

Of the different African nations, the **Yoruba**, **Arara**, **Abakua** and **Kongo** have the biggest population. The Yoruba came from Nigeria during the mid-1800s. Once in Cuba, they became known as the Lucumi, which means "friend" in their original tongue. This group was introduced to Catholicism and mixed it with the older African religions, which developed into the **Santeria** beliefs. One of the outstanding aspects of this religion is the playing of the cylindrical Bata drums during festivals and religious ceremonies. These drums have the appearance of African gourds and are often decorated with beads and bells.

The Arara came from the Benin Republic. The most prominent western group of this origin live in Haiti and are known as the Vodun, or those who practice voodoo. They combined Catholicism with the religions of western Africa. This group, now the smallest of all the African groups, is found mainly in Matanzas province. The most distinct aspect of their music is that they clap hands and slap their bodies for percussion.

The Abakua were a secret society originating in southeast Nigeria and Cameroon. Most settled in the Havana, Matanzas and Santiago de Cuba areas. The *ireme* or the leopard-masker, also called "Diablo," is a traditional Afro-Cuban symbol dating back to 1835 that has recently been adopted as the symbol of modern African-Cuban folklore.

The Kongo group, which consists of a number of subgroups, came from as many areas of Africa. They play the Yuka drum that is made from a hollowed-out tree trunk with cow leather stretched over the ends. To the beat of this drum they danced the Danza de la Culebra (Serpent Dance) or the Matar la Culebra (Killing the Snake Dance).

Cuba has the purest American-Spanish culture in the West, mainly because of the embargo. Although there is limited American television and music available, Cubans have little access to American literature. Because their own music is so vibrant, they have little need for American music and dance, so their own stays pure. In fact, Americans copy Cubans in music. Clothing is a different matter. Clothing is mostly Western in design. The food is Ladino in flavor.

DID YOU KNOW: José Maria Heredia wrote the *Oda al Niagara* in 1824 about the world famous cataracts located in Canada and the United States. Joaquin Blez, a Cuban society photographer, in 1915 photographed the first known print of Niagara's Horseshoe Falls as seen from the American side.

Revolutionary sign.

Geography

Located just 145 km/90 miles south of Florida, Cuba and its 1,600 smaller islands and cays make up the largest country in the Greater Antilles. The main island is about 1,260 km/ 770 miles in length and between 32 and 195 km/20 and 120 miles wide. It covers 110,860 square km/ 43,000square miles. The country is shaped like a crocodile or lizard. Its shores run for 3,700 km/2,300 miles and are touched by the Atlantic to the north and east, the Caribbean to the south, and the Gulf of Mexico to the west. Cuba has almost 300 beaches.

■ Mountains

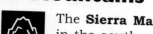

The **Sierra Maestra Mountains** are located in the south and central part of the island, with **Pico Turquino**, 1,994 meters/6,542 feet being its highest point. In the west, along the Guanahacabibes Peninsula, limestone formations shaped like haystacks are dotted with caves and decorated with orchids. The **Gran Caverna de Santo**

Tomás is the most interesting cave, running 45 km (30 miles) in length. (As a foreigner, you are not permitted to go all the way in.) These haystack-shaped hills are sitting at around 300-400 meters/980-1,300 feet in elevation. In the center of Cuba is the **Sierra del Escambray**, with **Pico San Juan** being the tallest. It sits at 1,160 meters/3,800 feet.

■ Rivers

Cuba doesn't have any significant rivers. The largest is in the southeast and is called the **Cauto**. It is about 370 km/230 miles long, but only 75 km/50 miles are navigable with small boats. Otherwise, Cuba is pretty flat, making it a desirable place for agriculture.

■ Islands & Cays

Offshore, the main islands are Isle of Youth (**La Isla de la Juventud**), **Cayo Coco** and **Cayo Romano**. Isla de la Juventud is 2199 sq km (850 sq miles) in size, with half being a nature preserve. Also, the best diving is off this island. Cayo Coco is an isolated island, popular with many of the all-inclusive tourist.

■ Parks & Reserves

Parks are classified as international, national or regional in descending order of importance. There are 275 areas in all, 79 of national importance and 196 of regional. In addition, seven special regions are set aside for sustainable development, 14 national parks, and six biosphere reserves. The term "Important Natural Elements" is used to describe those places that may be interesting but don't fit into any of the other categories. Below are the most interesting and accessible places for the average traveler, although not all are reviewed in this book. If you want to visit or get more information about specific areas, contact a Havana tour operator (page 132).

Nature Parks

Alejandro de Humboldt, Ciénaga de Zapata, Caguanes, Desembarco del Granma, Guanahacabibes, Jardines de la Reina, La Bayamesa, La Mensura – Pilotos, Pico Cristal, Punta Francäs, San Felipe, Santa María – Los Caimanes, Turquino, Viñales.

Ecological Reserves

Alturas de Banao (El Naranjal), Caletones, Cayo Coco, Cayo Francés, Cayo Largo, Boquerùn (Ote), El Salùn, Hatibonico, La Victoria – Yumurí, Los Indios, Los Petriles, Maisí, Masernillo Tortuguilla, Mogotes de Jumagua, Nuevas Grandes – La Isleta, Parnaso – Los Montes, Pico San Juan, Punta del Este, Quibiján – Duaba – Yunque de Baracoa, Reserva de San Marcos, Tuabaquey Limones, Varahicacos – Galindo.

Wildlife Sanctuaries

Bahía de Malagueta, Cayo Santa María, Cayos de Ana María, Centro y Oeste de Cayo Paredùn Grande, Correa, Delta del Cauto, Lanzanillo, Las Picúas, Plataforma Sodoriental de Cuba, Río Máximo, Saltadero.

Nature Reserves

Baitiquirí, Cerro Galano, Imías, La Coca, Las Peladas, Puriales.

Climate

■ Temperatures & Rainfall

 Cuba has a semitropical climate moderated by northeastern trade winds. Dry season is from November to the end of April and the average temperature in Havana is around 20°C/68°F, while the beaches average 25°C/77°F. However, temperatures range between 17°C/63°F to 35°C/95°F throughout the country, and there have been recordings as low as 10°C/50°F.

	Air temp (°C)	Water temp (°C)	Hours of sunlight	Rain (mm)	Rainy days	Humidity
CLIMACTIC STATISTICS						
JAN	23.1	24.6	11.0	45	3	79%
FEB	22.9	24.3	11.4	38	4	77%
MAR	24.1	24.6	12.0	48	3	76%
APR	25.1	25.3	12.6	72	4	74%
MAY	27.1	26.2	13.2	177	8	78%
JUN	27.6	27.3	13.5	216	11	81%
JUL	28.4	28.0	13.3	139	9	79%
AUG	28.1	28.5	13.0	158	10	76%
SEPT	27.6	28.3	12.4	184	10	78%
OCT	27.7	27.5	11.8	190	10	78%
NOV	24.6	26.3	11.2	79	5	75%
DEC	23.5	25.2	10.9	41	3	74%

Rainy season is between May and October when the temperatures are high and humidity runs at about 80%. The average annual rainfall is about 52 inches/ 1,320 mm countrywide, with 60% of this falling during rainy season.

Eastern Cuba is warmer than the west, but the entire country enjoys a spring-like climate and, due to some northern winter winds, you can see temperatures drop to well below the average. Temperatures in the mountains are a tad cooler than those along the beach.

■ Hurricanes

Hurricanes are common in Cuba, the season running between June and December. Storms can be frequent, up to 10 a year, and they can bring winds of up to 200 kph/124 mph. But, due to the location of Cuba, hurricanes are not as common as in Belize or Florida.

Plant & Animal Life

■ Flora

There are 7,000 to 8,000 plant species on the island, half of which are believed to be endemic. None is poisonous. About 300 belong to the orchid family and 90 to the palm family. When the Spanish first arrived, Cuba was covered with trees. Today, only 18% is forested and 80% of the flora has become rare or is threatened. Part of the problem is that people have had to return to using plants for medicinal purposes because the American embargo does not permit chemical medicines to be imported. Below are just a few of the unique plants found here.

The **cork palm** grows in the Pinar del Rio region at between 50 and 250 meters above sea level. Endemic to western Cuba, it is considered to be one of the oldest palm species on earth. It is tall (10 meters/33 feet) and has graceful, truncated leaves. Its gender-distinct, cylindrical cones that grow from the trunk top are 50-90 cm/20-35 inches long and 13-16 cm/five-six inches in diameter. They look like budding pineapples. There are about 1,000 palm species in the world.

The *corojo* and the *criollo* are first-grade tobacco plants whose leaves are used to wrap the inner smoking leaves in a cigar. The combination of these leaves helps to give the cigar its flavor. While in the field, corojo plants are kept under a cotton covering to prevent the sun from hitting the plant directly and thickening the leaves. On the other hand, criollo plants are given full sun exposure but the leaves are all picked at different times of maturity, which helps give the cigar a different flavor. It takes three months for all tobacco plants to reach maturity. The seed is planted and covered with straw to help give it warmth and moisture that aids in germination. Within six weeks, the plant has grown to about the size of a cigar. It takes another six weeks for the plant mature.

The **guanabilla**, or guava, is a hardy, intrusive shrub that usually grows to less than 10 meters/30 feet and likes a dry tropical climate. It has leathery green

leaves about eight cm/three inches long. The grayish bark of the branches peels off in irregular patterns leaving a reddish under bark. In spring, the *guanabilla* produces a white flower, but it is the yellow fruit that smells like a combination of strawberry, kiwi and something else that is the draw. The numerous seeds inside the pulpy fruit are hard, although not impossible to eat. Often, guava is used for treating stomach ailments (even amoebas), but be aware that the fruit slows down peristaltic action in the gut. If you eat too much, you'll become constipated.

The **melocactus** is a genus that includes about 40 species of **cacti** and grow from northern Mexico to the southern tip of America. The Matanzas variety, also called the dwarf Turk's cap, grows about 10 cm/four inches at maturity. These cacti are hard to grow, requiring good drainage and regular watering. However, direct sunlight like that found in Cuba is often too harsh for them. When the plants mature, they stop growing and grow a cap (thus the name) at the top that produces red or pink flowers.

The **yuraguana palm** grows in the southeast and is endemic. The fronds have long spiked leaves that form a circle and the tree usually has a number of fronds growing at the top. These are used for thatching roofs.

The **yucca**, also known as cassava or manioc, includes about 40 species, most of which grow on the mainland between southwestern United States and Mexico. However, there are a few on Cuba. The white flowers can be pollinated only by the Yucca moth, which has a special method of stuffing pollen from one plant into the stigma of a receiving plant. Without the moth, the plant will not produce seeds.

Yucca can be either a shrub or a tree, depending on the species, but it is the shrub that grows in Cuba. Its root and flower stem are roasted for food.

■ Fauna

 Cuba has about 900 types of fish (most are edible) and about 350 species of birds (one is the world's smallest hummingbird), over 4,000 varieties of mollusks, around 185 species of butterflies and more than 1,000 species of insects. I shall take only one species from each family just to give you an idea of what there is to look for.

Solenodon fossils can be found in North America dating back about 30 million years, but on Cuba and Hispañola, these animals are still walking around. This shrew-like creature is actually an insectivore that has survived here due to lack of predators. Their stout bodies grow to a foot in length and support a naked tail of equal length. Their heads, with long bristly snouts, are disproportionately large and hold tiny eyes and naked ears. Their legs are short, but the feet are huge, with five toes and large claws.

Solenodons are nocturnal and hole up in tree trunks or caves during the day. Their diet includes plants, small animals and insects as well as reptiles. Their claws and long snouts help them dig into rotting logs in search of insects. They run in a zig-zag pattern and, when really afraid, fall over their own claws. These animals have poisonous saliva that comes from the two incisors on their bottom jaw. In their arm pits and groins are glands that secrete a goat-like odor.

They reproduce only twice a year and have one to three young. The female has two teats located near her butt, which makes nursing a bit different. Between the slow birth rate and loss of habitat, this animal is now endangered.

Birds

There are recorded sightings of 338 different birds in Cuba. Twenty-five of these are endemic, like the bee hummingbird and the Cuban pygmy owl. Twenty-four of the 58 Caribbean specialty species, like the great lizard cuckoo and the olive-capped warbler, are also found on the island.

The colorful little **bee hummingbird** is about five cm/2.5 inches long, with half of that made up by the bill and tail. It weighs about two grams/0.07 oz. Because its wings move so fast (about 80 beats per second), it sounds like a bumblebee, hence the name. The bird has a bright red head and throat. The male has blue feathers on its back, wings and undercoat, while females sport green feathers. The rest of the bird is white or grey-white. This is the smallest bird on the planet and can be found in woodland shrubbery.

DID YOU KNOW: Because of their wing construction, hummingbirds can fly in any direction.

Bee hummingbirds' nests, usually perched on the fork of a branch or on a large leaf, are made of plant fibers, spider webs, lichen and moss. The female lays two eggs that, despite being 10% of her body weight, are the tiniest in the world. The eggs are incubated for 15-20 days and the young are born blind and naked. They reach maturity within three weeks.

Fish

One of the most popular fish for sports anglers is **bass**. The best time to catch bass is when the water temperatures are consistently 20°C/68°F, often in February. Cuban waters are also home to **tarpon**, **snook** (robalo), **bonefish** and **barracudas**, and **marlin** and **sailfish** are the draw around Isla de la Juventud.

In years past, the amount of pollution spewing into the waters around Cuba almost eliminated fishing entirely. However, I am told that Havana Bay is being cleaned up and the oxygen levels in the water are increasing. Because of this, fish are returning and the fishing, whether with a line or while snorkeling/diving, is getting better.

The largest common snook ever landed, caught in the waters of Costa Rica, weighed 53 lb, 10 oz. Snook are ugly fish, with lower projecting jaws on long pointed heads. The silver-gray-yellowish color is decorated with a black line along the side. Snook is an aggressive predator who loves to munch on shrimp, crayfish, crabs, anchovies, mullet and pinfish. These meals are hunted in mangrove bays, estuaries, and at the mouths of rivers. The fish readily move between salt and fresh water searching for food, but seldom swim deeper than 65 feet.

Snook is caught with either live bait or artificial lures year-round. Bait such as menhaden, sardines and mullet is used. If you catch a minnow, use it as bait over a 1/0 or 2/0 hook on an eight-15 lb test line.

Mollusks

Mollusks include squid, octopus, clams, oysters, snails, cuttle fish and cobo. They are numerous in species and are defined as living invertebrates covered with hard shells that live in or near water. Most are edible and some are quite colorful. They are fun to look for. The world's most beautiful land mollusk is the **Polymitas pictas**, which is endemic to the Oriente province and Isla de la Juventud.

Tree snails are hermaphrodites (both male and female) but must cross-copulate. Two dozen eggs are usually laid in the rainy season in soil near a host tree. In the spring, the young crawl to the trees after hatching. They live about six years and spend each winter, during the dry season, hibernating.

Butterflies

There are almost 200 species of butterflies in Cuba. The most exciting is the **green amethyst** that was first seen in Bahia Honda in 1979. The insect, about the size of a dime, is bright green with a light purple body and two eye-dots on the back wings. Before the 1930s, the amethyst was more common, found on the island of Hispañola in the Caribbean. Now, however, it is extremely rare. Prior to 2004, it had not been seen since 1979. Because of its color and size, it is hard to spot. But, it seems to like tea and coffee plants.

Insects

For professional and amateur entomologists, Cuba is a paradise, with over 1,000 insect species. There are even a few **mosquitoes**, but since Cuba is an island in a salty ocean, these are not found in large quantities.

The **Jamaican fire beetle**, or *cucujo*, holds the world record for emitting the brightest bioluminescence. It will fly into a tree and emit a white flare that can glow for up to 10 seconds. Locals like to catch this insect, put a few into a jar and use it as a lantern. The largest of the bioluminescent beetles, it measures about four cm/1.75 inches and is believed to have the greatest surface brightness in the world. The brightness is measured at 45 milli-lamberts, equaling about 1/40th of the light emitted by a candle. However, the light isn't emitted for our pleasure but rather to attract other beetles for the purpose of mating.

The Jamaican fire beetle likes to fly in forests, around dark, usually between the beginning of April and the end of June. The adults eat vegetable matter, if they eat at all, but the larva are carnivorous, biting and injecting poisonous saliva into meaty creatures such as worms and snails.

Reptiles

The **Cuban crocodile** is smaller than the American crocodile, although it is more dominant. Both the American and the Cuban versions are

less aggressive than the Columbian crock. The Cuban usually grows to about three meters/10 feet in length; females are a tad smaller.

> **DID YOU KNOW**: Crocs have been on the planet for about 200 million years and have adapted to live first on land and then both on land and water.

Like you, crocs love a warm climate. Unlike most of you, they live in fresh water swamps, have a thick skin that is yellow-green, have lots of teeth in their powerful jaws and make lots of noise by hissing and roaring. They can run fast and are one of the few reptiles that protect their young. Greatly endangered today, this croc once lived in large numbers in Cuba, the Bahamas and the Cayman Islands. Today, of the 3,000-6,000 left on the planet, the largest numbers live in the Zapata Swamp in southwestern Cuba and in the Lanier Swamp on Isla de la Juventud.

National Emblems

■ National Anthem

Pedro Figueredo is accredited with writing the music of the national anthem. Born in 1818 in Bayamo, he was a lawyer, landowner, poet and musician and first performed this piece for the public in 1868. He fought in the battle of Bayamo, which was part of the Ten Year War when the Cubans were seeking independence from Spain. Two years after the battle, Figueredo was captured and executed by the Spanish. The anthem was adopted in 1940 and the words, translated by Lorraine Noel Finley, are:

La Bayamesa

Come, O Bayamese, rush to the battle,
All our proud country's enemies defying
Do not fear valiant men for dying
For our fatherland's sake, there is life
Come, O life.
Better death than a life bound by chains,
With contempt and opprobrium surrounded
When the clarion trumpet is sounded,
Rise to arms, and take part in the strife,
Bitter strife.

■ National Flag

The flag has five horizontal stripes, three blue and two white. A red triangle with a white star in the center sits on the hoist end of the flag. The triangle is the Masonic symbol of equality and the red represents the blood shed for independence. The white star stands for liberty for all the people of the world (not just Cuba). The blue stripes are the districts into which the island was first divided, and the white stripes represent the pureness of the Cuban heart.

The flag was designed in 1848 and hoisted in 1850 in Cardenas for the liberation movement. It became official in 1902 when Cuba gained independence from Spain.

■ Coat of Arms/Shield

Cuba has had two coats of arms, the first granted by the King of Spain in 1516. It is divided in two, with the Virgin Mary on the upper half standing on a cloud and St Jacob on horseback on the bottom half. The Initials separating the two halves are: "I" for Queen Isabella, "F" for King Ferdinand and "C" for King and Emperor Carlos.

The second coat of arms was designed by poet Miguel Teurbe Tolon and adopted by the country in 1869. At the very top there is a red hat with a white star. Called a Phrygian hat, it was used in the French Revolution and in earlier times by men fighting for freedom. The hat is sitting on a sugarcane stalk, which is also seen at the lower end of the shield. The stalk is tied in a cross with a red ribbon. This symbolizes strength. Spreading to the sides of the stalk are plants; on the right is an oak branch and on the left is a laurel. The shield is divided into three sections. The bottom two-thirds is divided in two with the blue and white stripes from the flag on the left and a royal palm on the right. The palm represents the nobility and courage of the Cuban people. The top third of the shield has a rising sun over the ocean with a key below the sun and two islands at each side. The key represents Cuba's position between the Americas and the sun represents the new nation.

■ National Flower

The **mariposa**, or butterfly jasmine, is an orchid that gets its name from its appearance; it looks like a white butterfly. It is also known as the amber cane, a much less appropriate name. It was chosen as the national flower in 1936. The flower originated in Asia but managed to adapt well to Cuban soil. The whiteness of the flower represents peace as well as the purity of the ideals of independence. When in bloom, it features many flowers along a common stem. This symbolizes the unity of the Cuban people. The mariposa can be found growing along the banks of rivers and streams.

> **DID YOU KNOW:** During the wars of independence, women would carry messages hidden in mariposas, which they wore in their hair.

■ National Bird

The **Cuban trogon**, also called the *guatini*, is a very colorful bird and a close relative of the roadrunner, a flightless bird, and the quetzal, the national bird of Guatemala. The trogon is 10-14 inches (25-36 cm) in length and has blue feathers on its head, white on its chest, red on its underbelly and green on its back. It spends long periods of time sitting on its home branch in the forest and moves mainly when searching for insects or fruits. Its movements are quick and precise. During the nesting period, it makes its home in the cavities of trees. The trogon was chosen for the national bird because of its resistance to captivity. It will die trying to free itself.

■ National Tree

The **royal palm**, the most distinctive of the palm family, was chosen as the national tree because it stands so tall but can still resist hurricane-force winds, similar to the people of Cuba. The bark of the palm was used to make homes for Indians and the leaves were used for thatching. The trunk is smooth and almost white; it looks strangely artificial. The palms crown the trunk with 15-20 leaves, each with a 10-foot stem lined with rows of leaflets. Although the palms can survive dry spells, they look their best when well watered. Recently, the species has been attacked in the Caribbean by lethal yellow, a bacteria so named because of the yellowing effect the bug has on the leaves; LY can kill a tree within seven months, leaving nothing but a "telephone pole" standing. In some places, the trees are being replaced with a lethal yellow-resistant type of palm.

Top Five Destinations

■ Havana

Visit El Castillo del Morro during the evening ceremony and stay for some music. See page 113 for details.

■ Cienfuegos

Hang around the plaza and take in a concert. See pages 287-288.

■ Viñales

Go caving and hiking. See page 186.

■ Cayo Coco

Relax on the beach and drink copious amounts of rum. See page 348.

■ Isla de la Juventud

Just getting here is an adventure. Visit the old prison where Castro spent a few years during his youth. See pages 193-230.

Travel Information

Facts at your Fingertips

President: Fidel Castro Ruis, leader since the revolution in 1959.

Vice president: Raul Castro Ruis, since the revolution.

Size: 110,860 square km/42,800 square miles of land (33% arable); 3,735 km/2,320 miles of coastline (there is 29 km/18 miles along the US Naval Base of Guantanamo that is leased from Cuba).

Population:
11,309,000. Twenty percent are 0-14 years old, 70% are between 15 and 64 years old, and the rest are over age 65. Fifty-one percent are mulatto, 37% are Caucasian and 11% are Negro.

Capital: Havana.

Provinces: Ciudad de la Habana, Cienfuegos, Camagüey, Ciego de Avila, Granma, Guantanamo, Holguin, La Habana, Las Tunas, Matanzas, Santiago de Cuba, Villa Clara, Pinar del Rio and Sancti Spíritus. Isla de la Juventud is considered a special municipality.

Independence Day: December 10th, 1898, independence from Spain; May 20th, 1902 from US. Rebellion Day is July 26th, 1953.

Language: Spanish.

Education: Everyone over the age of 15 can read and write in Cuba. All education is free, although it has been reported that the relevance of the lessons in rural schools is not as specific as in urban schools. Daycare for preschool children is universal.

Life expectancy: At birth it is 77 years for males and 79.4 years for females. Fertility rate is 1.7 children per woman and abortion rates run around 35% of all pregnancies. These statistics are comparable to most developed countries.

Natural resources: About 33% of the land is cultivated for agriculture. There is nickel, chrome, copper, iron and manganese available for mining plus reserves of sulphur, pyrites, gypsum asbestos, petroleum, salt, cobalt and limestone. All surface deposits belong to the government.

When to Go

■ Seasonal Considerations

 Dry season is from November to April and the average temperatures are 20-25°C/68-77°F with cooling trade winds. This is when prices are at their highest.

Rainy season is from the end of April to the end of October. Temperatures are around 25°C/77°F, but the humidity is very high. July to October is hurricane season, when most tourists do not want to be around.

> **NOTE:** If you are in Cuba during a hurricane, know that all modern safety precautions are in place.

■ National Holidays & Other Important Days

■ JANUARY

January 1 - Liberation Day (national holiday).

January 2 - Victory of Armed Forces Day (national holiday).

January 28 - Birth of José Martí (1853), Cuba's National Hero. He fought for Cuba's freedom.

■ FEBRUARY

February 24 - Beginning of the War of Independence of 1895.

■ MARCH

March 8 - International Woman's Day.

March 13 - Attack on the Presidential Palace by revolutionaries in 1957.

■ APRIL

April 19 - Victory at Bay of Pigs, 1961.

■ MAY

May 1 - Labor Day (national holiday).

May 20 - Independence Day (national holiday).

■ JULY

July 25-27 - National Rebellion Day (national holiday).

July 30 - Day of Martyrs of the Revolution. Prayers are held at the tomb of Eduardo Chibas in honor of him, Pelayo Cuervo

Travel Information

Navarro, Juan Manuel Marquez, Frank Pais, Hchevarria, and Raul de Aguir.

■ OCTOBER

October 8 - Death of Che Guevara in 1967.

October 10 - Anniversary of the beginning of the War of Independence in 1868 (national holiday).

October 28 - Death of Camilo Cienfuego, 1959.

■ NOVEMBER

November 27 - Memorial to the death of medical students who were fighting for independence in 1871.

■ DECEMBER

December 7 - Death of Antonio Maceo in 1896.

December 25 - Christmas (national holiday).

Before You Go

■ For American Travelers

The Trade Embargo

The American trade embargo on Cuba falls under the American National Trading-With-the-Enemy Act of 1963 and its purpose is to force Cuba, through economic pressure, to abide by US governmental rules. The penalty for breaking this sanction is up to 10 years in prison and a $250,000 fine for individuals and a one million dollar fine for corporations. Besides these fines, those found guilty of breaking the embargo are subject to civil penalties of up to $55,000. If you have any dealings with a company or an individual living or working in Cuba, regardless of whether you know it or not, you are subject to these punishments.

An American citizen is not permitted to send art (including music on CDs), technology, products or services of any kind to Cuba. You may not offer consulting services to a Cuban even if he/she is not living at the time in Cuba. This is to prevent information from going to Cuba.

However, the Commerce Department of the American government can authorize sales of some things like medicines or medical supplies. This has been tightened since the 2004 legislation. NGOs with special licenses can export food to Cuba. On the other hand, if you manage to get into Cuba legally, you can bring back art, publications and any informational materials. Still, you cannot purchase any Cuban-made product in another country (such as Canada or Mexico) and bring it back into the United States.

Journalists working on a story, officials on government business, members of international organizations and professionals going to professional conferences can go to Cuba. Nationals may visit immediate families for 14 days, once every three years, or they can go for humanitarian reasons like the death of an immediate family member. Students and educators can get a special license, as can those from religious organizations. Travel agents must hold a special license to sell airline tickets to travelers heading over to the island. Those selling tickets without a license are subject to fines.

Nationals can send gifts to family members in Cuba but that too is restricted. Cubans can't even receive inherited monies from those living in the US regardless of whether it is an insurance policy or from an estate.

If by some chance you land on the island without a special license, you are forbidden to spend any money on food, travel, lodgings, visas or docking fees if on a boat. However, I believe Americans are permitted to breath Cuban air as long as it is free. Of course, nothing can be brought back to the US with you unless it is informational materials such as newspapers or other printed matter published by the Cuban government.

Despite this, according to Tracey Eaton of the *Dallas Morning News*, 79,000 Americans went to Cuba in 2001 and this did not include the 140,000 Cuban-Americans who went. However, John Kavulich, Director of Cuban Trade and Economic Council in New York claims that only 27,000 Americans went to Cuba illegally and about 137,000 authorized travelers went. Of those caught traveling illegally, 766 were slapped with fines. In 2004, 122 companies were caught violating sanction laws in the US, with most of those violations involving Cuba. Companies such as Wal-Mart, Playboy Enterprises and the New York Yankees were caught and fined a total of $1.97 million.

In final analyses, if you are concerned about being caught and fined, you should stay at home and vote for the Democrats in the next election. For details on paperwork and other required documents, see below.

■ For All Other Travelers

 There are no restrictions in Britain, Europe, Canada or any Latin American country regarding travel to Cuba, although some people do need a visa. Pack your bags, grab a fist full of money and have a blast.

■ Information Sources

Websites

 The following websites offer valuable information. Check them out as you do research for your trip.

www.GoCuba.ca

www.CUBATRAVEL.cu

www.cubanaviacion.ca

www.infotur.cu

What to Take

■ Required Documents

Americans going to Cuba must have a **Treasury Department license** in order to engage in any transactions related to travel to and within Cuba. This includes the spending of US currency. Before planning any travel to Cuba, US citizens should contact the Licensing Division, Office of Foreign Assets Control, US Department of Treasury, www.treas.gov/ofac. Those with a license require a valid passport and visa.

All visitors should have a valid **passport** that is good for six months longer than the expected stay in Cuba. A **Tourist Card** will be issued at the immigration booth upon entry, to those from Canada, South Africa, New Zealand, Ireland or the United Kingdom. This is usually valid for 30 days and it can be extended once you are in the country. Should you stay longer than 90 days you will need an **Exit Permit**. All other nationals will need to purchase a visa before entering Cuba.

Businessmen, journalists and Cuban born citizens living out of the country must apply for a **special visa** from the Cuban Embassy in their country of residence. Cubans who left Cuba after 1970 and are citizens of other countries must have a Cuban passport if they wish to enter Cuba. Journalists must report to the International Press Office for accreditation and then pay $60 US.

Everyone should be able to show a **means of transportation** (eg, airline ticket) out of Cuba within the time of the tourist card validity. Everyone must also have enough money to support themselves while in Cuba.

Travel Information

BACK UP DOCUMENTATION

Always carry – or have access to – a **photocopy** of your passport and other documents. In our technological age you can scan your passport and e-mail the scan to your traveling e-mail address (ie. Yahoo/Hotmail). This way, you always have a copy. You can also forward your postcard or e-mail address list, your medical prescriptions and even your glasses prescriptions (in the event they get lost, broken or stolen).

Upon arrival all visitors must have an **approved accommodation** arranged before they are permitted entry to the country. Staying in the home of a Cuban not approved by their government makes you liable for a $1,000 fine. Private citizens must apply to immigration for permission to have a foreigner stay in their homes. *Casas particulares* are legal and approved accommodations in Cuba. Be certain that the one you book is approved.

You cannot bring in walkie-talkies, satellite phones, hand-held GPS equipment, televisions, VCRs, DVD players, freezers, air conditioners, stoves, water heaters, electric frying pans, toasters and irons (i.e. any item that draws heavily on electricity). Fresh fruits and vegetables and pornographic material are prohibited as well. Such items are routinely seized on arrival, without compensation.

Transit visas are available and are issued for 72 hours. You must have valid documentation, an exit ticket, a hotel reservation and money.

TAX TIME

Any gift taken into Cuba must cost less than US $50 or you will be charged the full price above the $50. For example, if a gift costs $150, you will have the $50 exemption, but must pay the government $100.

■ Packing List

 Binoculars are a must if you are a birder. There is an abundance of tropical and migratory birds that are well worth scouting out.

Dress clothes should be brought for any formal evening events such as concerts and shows. Even some of the better restaurants require a skirt or dress for women and dress pants for men. These should be of light natural materials.

You'll need a **sweater** or **jacket** for the higher elevations, for some air-conditioned rooms, and for cool evenings.

A **light rain jacket**.

Pack a **loose-fitting dress** or loose blouse and skirt or shorts of light cotton for daytime wear. Men should have light shorts and baggy cotton shirts.

Shorts and **t-shirts** or **skirts/pants** are great. Everyone wears shorts. Keep your clothing loose and comfortable – the heat helps to determine attire.

> **AUTHOR NOTE:** Revealing outfits are not acceptable dress in the towns and cities. If you are a touch stodgy (like me), you may be shocked by some of your fellow tourists along the beaches. The thong is in.

Sandals are good at the beach, but **runners** or light **hiking boots** are needed for hikes, playing golf or touring the museums.

You will need at least one **bathing suit** and two would be better. A beach towel or grass matt is good for lying on the sand (the mats can be purchased along the beaches).

Cameras are a great way to record memories. Bring one that you are familiar with so that you don't make mistakes on critical images. Humidity is high so keeping the camera dry is important. Putting a camera in a plastic bag is not advisable as the moisture condenses inside. Because there is so much intense sunlight, a slow-speed film (ASA 50 to 100) is recommended (bring plenty). Bring batteries and flashes. When photographing people during the day, use a flash to eliminate harsh shadows.

UNDERWATER SHUTTER BUGS

If you're interested in underwater photography, take an introductory course before leaving home. One lady I spoke with threw out the first 100 images she took. The second hundred were great photos of sand and water and blurred sand and blurred water.

Digital cameras are popular. However, the high humidity can affect electronics.

Money belts are recommended for those traveling around. If you're staying at just one hotel, use a safe to store valuables. Belts should always be of natural-fiber, pouch-style, worn around the midriff and under clothes. Natural fiber is far more comfortable than synthetic fibers. Keep documents and money in plastic bags inside the belt so the paper won't be soaked and damaged by sweat. Always place some money and/or travelers' checks in different places, so if you are robbed you will have some mad money to live on until you get more. There are belts sold today that have zippered pockets sewn on the underside. Money must be folded lengthwise to fit into the pockets. Tiny pockets can be sewn into your clothing, in the hem of your skirt, or the cuff of your shirt. A few bills can also be placed in a plastic bag, under the inner sole of your shoe, but check this money regularly for wear. If it is worn through, no one will take it.

Daypacks are far more convenient to carry than handbags or beach bags. They are also harder to pickpocket or snatch. In cities, on buses or crowded places, wear your daypack at the front, with the waist strap done up. That way, your hands can rest on the bag while you walk. In this position, it is almost impossible for pickpockets to access the pack. Keep only the amount of money you need for the day in your daypack and the bulk of your money elsewhere, like in your hotel safe or your hidden money belt. If you keep your camera in the pack, the camera is easily accessible.

It seems to me that a map is really hard to follow if you don't have a **compass**. They are not heavy and you need not buy one that can do triangulation measurements. A simple one will do.

Diving gear like wetsuits and facemasks can be brought from home or rented from the dive shops. You will need your PADI diving certification ticket.

Snorkeling gear can be brought from home or rented in Cuba. If you plan to travel around, you may find it easier to rent.

An **umbrella** keeps off sun or rain.

Your **first aid kit** should include moleskin, Advil (hikers' Smarties), tenser bandage, antihistamines, topical antibiotic cream and band-aids. All prescription medications and things like batteries for hearing aids or extra eyeglasses should be carried. A band that attaches to your glasses and goes around your head to keep glasses from falling off is useful.

Reading material in English is sparse, although a few *casas* have book-trading services. For the most part, you need to bring books with you. Leave them behind with someone who's learning English. If you want to give someone a gift, dictionaries, "learning English" books, or magazines showing highlights of your country are always welcome.

Sunglasses and **sun hat** should be brought and worn because the intense ultraviolet light can damage your eyes. Paul Theroux, author of *Patagonia Express* and other travel books, has problems with his eyes due to

Travel Information

the damage caused by the ultraviolet rays. He often kayaked without sunglasses.

Sunscreen is necessary.

Electricity is 110 volts, 60 hertz with flat-pinned sockets, so you'll need an **adaptor**. Some hotels have both 110 and 220-volt circuits. Laptops can be brought into Cuba for personal use.

A **flashlight** is good as electricity goes off occasionally, although rarely in large resorts. Bring batteries.

Health Concerns

 Bring with you anything you might need in the way of prescriptions, glasses, orthopedics, dental care and batteries for hearing aids. Things like vitamins, bandages, antihistamines and topical creams should also be included. Anything in health care that is manufactured in the United States is difficult to obtain in Cuba. Locals use a lot of natural medicines and you may need to do the same if you don't pack it.

■ Medical Insurance

 Travel medical insurance is compulsory. If you haven't arranged it in advance, **Asistur**, Prado #208, Between Colón and Trocadero in Old Havana, ☎ 7/866-8527, asistur@asistur.cu, will provide coverage for about $3 a day, far higher than what it costs to purchase insurance at home. I have never been asked about having insurance before entering the country.

■ Treatment

 Should you become sick in Cuba and enter a hospital, you will be treated with modern techniques, medicines and equipment. There are a total of 442 polyclinics and 228 hospitals in the country. The infant mortality rate is 7.2 per 1,000 live births and the average life expectancy is 77/79 years. This is an indication of the good health care available in the country. Also, there are no inoculation requirements to enter Cuba unless you arrive from an area infected with Yellow Fever, in which case you will need to have an inoculation. As a foreigner, you will have to pay for this service in hard currency.

All tourist hotels have a **doctor** on call who can give primary care and all the major centers can give secondary medical treatments.

As North Americans wait longer and pay more for treatments at home, they are heading to Cuba for care. Laser eye surgery is as good as, if not better than, anything in Canada and the wait time is almost none. Hip replacements, breast reductions, skin disorders, nose jobs – Cuba does them all at affordable cost.

Don't expect Hyatt-style accommodations in hospitals. Cubans don't spend tons of money for building repairs and electrical outages are common. Water may need to be purchased and sheets should be brought from home. An exception is the **Cira Garcia Tourist Clinic**, a plush clinic catering to foreigners who come for nose jobs and other such repair procedures. The cost is said to be about one-third of that for the same procedure in the United States. **Clinica Cira Garcia** is at Calle 20 #4101, Miramar, Havana, ☎ 7/24-2811. Medicines can be purchased at the Farmacia Internacional at the rear of the clinic.

■ Fevers & Worse

Malaria is not a problem in Cuba. However, avoid mosquito bites as dengue fever is a problem. A prophylactic against malaria is not necessary.

Typhus may be present in areas that have poor sanitation. Vaccines against typhus are no longer available. Use mothballs or permethrin (a pesticide) for protection against infected fleas. Tetracycline is the recommended antibiotic if you should catch typhus – it kills the bacteria completely. Staying in a dirty place is highly unlikely for a foreigner.

Dengue fever is transmitted by a mosquito that bites during the day (rather than at dawn and dusk like the malaria-infested mosquito). Dengue fever causes severe headaches and severe pain to the joints and muscles. The aches are accompanied by a high fever. The disease lasts about a week. If infected, the most important thing you can do is to drink lots of water.

A first-time infection of dengue will not be the hemorrhagic kind. But a second bout increases the chances of hemorrhagic dengue occurring, making the chances of death much greater. The most notable sign of hemorrhagic dengue is small red dots on your skin. This is caused from the capillaries breaking and seeping blood. You will die without good medical care.

Extreme protection against dengue-bearing mosquitoes involves spraying or soaking clothing and sleeping gear with permethrin. Protection lasts up to three washings. The recommended dose is 20 mls of permethrin (13%) in two liters of water. Permethrin can be purchased in any garden shop that sells pesticides.

Repellents laced with DEET offer better protection. Although traces of DEET have been found in the livers of users, it is still better than getting dengue. Using a sleeping net in infected areas is highly recommended.

Routine inoculations common in your home country should be up to date. Besides these, immune globulin is recommended against **viral hepatitis** (Hep A). Signs of Hep A are nausea, upper stomach pain, tiredness and yellowing of eyes and skin. Urine will turn to a tea color while stools will become chalky. Rest is the recommended cure.

Worms and **parasites** are always present in the tropics, no matter how clean the environment. Keep your feet free of cuts and open sores so that worm larva or parasites cannot enter. Wear sandals or booties when showering and closed shoes or hiking boots when trekking in the jungles.

■ Water

In 2004 Cuba suffered a severe **drought**. As a result, water for personal use is now restricted to two pails per person, per day in some places. As a conscientious traveler, you showers should take two minutes or less. Some conservationists put the water on to get wet, turn it off, scrub down and then rinse for less than a minute. It would be a compliment to the country if you did the same.

Bottled water is available everywhere and costs less than a dollar for two liters. However, it is not served free in restaurants and if you are staying in a *casa* don't expect them to supply your drinking water.

Although **tap water** is considered safe, you should think about the age of the pipes and the material from which they were made. The water passing through old metal pipes may not sit well in your tummy.

Money Matters

■ Currency & Exchange

Cuba is having a problem deciding what to do about the American embargo. At this moment, it seems that Castro is on the winning side even though it makes things a bit difficult for the traveler. As of November 8th, 2004, the **convertible peso** became the accepted money for foreigners. The convertible peso is not the same currency as the Cuban peso used by Cubans.

You can exchange US dollars for convertible peso, (US $1=convertible peso $1), but there is a charge of up to 28% for this transaction. Most Cuban businesses no longer exchange US dollars, but are willing to exchange Canadian dollars and euros. However, the Cuban government still uses the US dollar as the measure. If the euro is exchanging for $1.30 US, you will get $1.17 in convertible pesos and you will not be charged the extra amount (up to 28%). Note that while the euro is in transition, it is accepted only in Havana and Varadero and by some (smart) *casa* owners.

In addition to convertibles, you can use Cuban pesos with street vendors and in stores that are mainly for Cubans. The Cuban peso comes in notes of one, three, five, 10, 50 and 100 denominations. Coins come in one, five and 20 centavos (100 centavos=one peso).

Money can be exchanged at the airports, at the Central Bank of Cuba and at money exchange offices called **CADECAs**.

Amigo Travel Card, ☎ 800-724-5685, www.amigotravel card.com, is like a debit card and issued in Cuba. You make a deposit of your convertible pesos and then take money out at the ATMs. This way, you will never be carrying a lot of money. There are 6,000 withdrawal locations . The card can also be used like a debit card at restaurants, hotels, gas stations and car rental agencies. If it is lost or stolen there is an eight convertible pesos charge to replace it. If you do not wish to pay this fee, you may withdraw all the cash in the account at no cost but you must go to the bank to do this. On withdrawals of more than $2,000, a two percent charge will be imposed. The 24-hour service can be reached at ☎ 7/55-4444.

You can put money into your Amigo Travel Card account through Interac Transcards that are issued through your online banking services. Each transfer to Cuba incurs a $1.50 fee. Remember, though, that this transaction cannot be done from any bank affiliated with the American banking system.

Your best plan is to take Canadian dollars or euros and change them in Cuba for the Cuban convertible peso, the official currency for foreigners. Remember that no Cuban money can be exchanged on the world market, and it is difficult to exchange this money back into your own currency. Don't exchange too much just prior to going home.

■ Travelers' Checks

Most hotels will send you to the bank to change your travelers' checks into convertible pesos. ATMs will take cards not issued through an American bank, and you can make credit card withdrawals – again, as long as it is not through an American bank. I found it easier to take cash and travelers' checks and exchange them when I needed money.

The **National Bank of Cuba** is open Monday to Friday, 8:30-noon and 1:30-3 pm; Saturday, 8:30-10:30 am. It does not accept travelers' checks or credit cards that are issued by American banks.

■ Credit Cards

Credit Cards that are issued or connected in any way to the US banks are not accepted. I have also heard that cards from other countries are often refused even though your issuing country will insist that your card is good in Cuba. My advice is to take credit cards in the event that you may be able to use them, but plan on using only cash. A good idea is to use the Amigo Credit Card (see above).

Credit cards that are supposed to be accepted are: Cabal, Transcard, VISA and International MasterCard as long as they have not been issued by a US bank or one of their subsidiaries. Cards issued by Banco Financiero, International (BFI cards), Credito y Comercio, Metropolitano, Popular de Ahorro and BISCSA (RED cards) can be used. The credit cards mentioned are accepted at some upscale hotels, restaurants, retail outlets and car rental companies. You can withdraw cash with a credit card at local banks.

■ Tipping

% Everyone in the service industry expects a tip – from the waiter to the taxi driver to the gal who washes the floors in your hotel. Five percent is usual, but 10% is always rewarded with a smile. However, a new law has been passed whereby workers in the service industry are no longer permitted to receive this money; all tips must go into the general coffers of the employer. Some restaurants add a 10% service charge. In this case, there is no need to tip.

ALTERNATE WAY TO SAY THANKS

If you feel the give-up-tip law is unfair, don't tip with money. Instead, reward good service with t-shirts, writing materials, Spanish books, pencils, razors (for men), Avon sample lipsticks (purchase the outdated ones), toothbrushes, sample shampoos, sample perfumes for men and women, balls for kids, Band Aids, over-the-counter analgesics or anything else that you can easily carry. If you belong to a club or organization, offer promotional items.

■ Planning Expenses

If you have booked an all-inclusive package, your expenses will be paid before you arrive. However, special tours will cost anywhere from $30 to $75 each. Check with your agent as to which tours are included in your package.

Those traveling on their own can expect to pay $25 for a room (2005) in a *casa* and $35 for a cheap hotel. The upper-end hotels can go as high as $300 per night. Average meals are between $5 and $10, but if you want something fancy, it will be double. Beer is around $2 per bottle and renting a car will run $50 to $100 a day. Bus travel averages $2 per hour of travel.

Dangers & Annoyances

 Every country in the world has its robbers and petty thieves, whether you are in the polite society of Japan or the northern wilds of Canada. If you hang out in the slums of a large city where you are unknown, if you are staggering drunk in a back alley, if you trust a stranger to hold your cash while you run to the washroom, if you leave your pack or camera on the seat of a bus while you run for a snack, you are going to have a sad tale to tell.

Doing anything immoral with a minor will net you 20 years in prison – no appeal. Make certain you know the age of a lady/man before getting involved. Cubans can have a romantic relationship with a foreigner but only one at a time. The motivation is usually money (not your stunning looks).

■ Commonsense Precautions

When out, **be aware** of what is around you. If it seems like you are being followed, go into a store or knock on someone's door. Make certain that expensive items like your camera or Rolex watch are out of sight. Carry only a bit of cash in your pocket and the rest in your money belt.

Be inside at night or take a **taxi** back to your hotel if you have been out late. Don't be inebriated in public. A drunk is a great target.

Although the **drug** trade is almost nonexistent, don't seek out and get mixed up in what there is of it. A mandatory sentence for possession of cocaine in Cuba is 25 years. Save booze and dope for home. If

Travel Information

you do get into trouble at home, you know the rules and you have friends to help.

Women should walk with confidence. If you appear frightened or lost, you are a target. Don't walk alone in sparsely populated places or along secluded trails.

In the event that you are grabbed or **accosted**, create a scene. Holler, scream, kick and fight with all your might. Although there is little chance that you would be accosted with a weapon, in the event that you are, then let them have it all. Nothing is of value to you once you are dead.

There are a few **pickpockets** in the larger centers, especially on the big public buses, the camels, which are crowded. The most common criminal however, is the young bicycle thief who will snatch your purse as he cycles past. Then again, if you carry a daypack, this isn't a likely problem. For the most part, you will find Cuba safe.

■ Assistance

 The **National Police Department** (☎ 116) has a Tourist Section that takes care of any problems you may encounter. They can be spotted on the streets in police uniform with an armband that states, in English, "National Police, Tourist Division."

THE BAD GUYS

Jinateros (prostitutes is a direct translation) will try to sell you anything from a room to the Brooklyn Bridge. They are a huge annoyance and the government is trying to put them down, but it is difficult. If you follow a *jinatero* to a *casa* or let them get you a car to the next town, you will pay double the going rate, if not more. Do all your own negotiating. These criminals are despised not only by tourists but by locals too.

Guides are licensed. According to the officials, you can get a guide who speaks English, French, German, Italian, Japanese, Chinese, Flemish, Russian, Bulgarian, Czechoslovakian or Hungarian. The quality of service and price of guides are regulated by the government. All guides have picture identification that they will present if requested. Hiring a guide without a license is not recommended. Guides can be hired through the hotels or the Cuban Tourist Board located on Calle 23 in Havana, ☎ 7/33-3142 or 7/34-4111, chabana@cubatur.cu.

Communications

■ Newspapers, Magazines & Radio

Granma International is the English newspaper. It is interesting to read about Latin American politics from the point of view of *Ladinos* rather than North Americans. *Granma* covers world/national news, science, economy and tourism.

There are also numerous newspapers written in Spanish. Almost every province has its own publication with specific news of the area. These are interesting to read and also to search for ads related to activities or restaurants/hotels you may want to visit.

Two national television channels broadcast throughout the country and some provinces have local stations. Satellite TV is available, most of it piped in from the US.

Radio Havana, www.radiohc.org, is offered in English, French and Portuguese on the Internet in written form. You can go back as far as May, 1999 and get the text of its broadcasts, including all of Fidel's speeches. But while you're here, and Fidel is still speaking, take the chance to listen to him live.

Travel Information

■ Real Mail or E-Mail

WWW

Internet cafés are in all the big hotels like Havana Libre and cost about $6 convertible pesos per hour. In Varadero, some privately owned cafés offer this service for half that price. The computers are hooked to satellite and are quite rapid. There are no restrictions that I know of.

Most hotels offer **postal service**. If you are staying in *casas*, ask your host where the post office is located – they are usually within a block or so of the main plaza. It is fairly cheap to send mail from Cuba to North America, about 50 Cuban pesos per postcard and 75 per letter. Purchasing stamps in the hotels costs the same, but you must buy them with convertible pesos.

If sending money to Cuba, **Transcard International**, located near Toronto, ☎ 905-305-7703, www.trans cardinter.com, has a good rate and the money arrives within a week. The cost is $12.69 for up to $250 and $16.90 for anything between $250 and $500. The other company, **Antillas Express**, based in Montreal, ☎ 514-385-9221, www.antillas-express.com, will deliver food, medicine or money. The cost is $30 for up to $300 in cash or kind being sent.

All money being sent out of Canada, over the amount of $2,000, must be registered with the Canadian government. The identification of the sender must be certified by an attorney or notary and given to the company sending the money. Trying to do this through the US can cause a lot of hassles.

■ Telephone

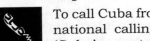

To call Cuba from any country, dial the international calling code (011 in US), dial 52 (Cuba's country number), then dial the area code (see below) and local number.

To make a call in Cuba, go to the ETECSA telephone office or purchase a phone card from local businesses or the post office and call from pay phones. These cards are good for both local and long distance calls. The smallest card you can purchase is a 20-peso card. Calling within the country is inexpensive. For example, calling from Varadero to Havana for five minutes will cost about 25 cents. Calling to the US is more, around $5 per minute.

If dialing within a city, no area code is needed. Calls to other towns and cities within Cuba will require using the area code.

Through **CUBACEL**, Calle 28 #510, between 5th and 7th Ave, ☎ 7/80-2222 , you can rent a cell phone. If using a cell in Cuba, you must dial 711 to get a line.

If bringing your own cell phone into the country it must be GSM (European) or TDMA (American) standard. The GSM must be in the 900 MHz band. For more information regarding use of European phones, contact the CUBACEL office at Calle 3-A #9402, between Ave 94 and 96 in Miramar, ☎ 7/80-2222. TDMA phones must be in the 800 MHz band. For help with TDMA phones, contact the CUBACEL that offers rentals (see above).

Culture Shock

■ Human Rights

Those who criticize or oppose the government are charged with inciting "enemy propaganda" or "rebellion" or "posing a danger" or "committing acts against the state security." Listening to foreign radio is considered an act against the state.

The right to assemble has been almost abolished. Recently, law was passed prohibiting Cubans from speaking with or receiving gifts from foreigners unless an approved Cuban official is present. The grouping for Christian Bible study is considered a crime and is punishable by imprisonment. However, listening to a communist political speech (usually given by Castro and lasting for many hours) is permitted.

All mass media is owned by the government and the production of programs is permitted only if the topic and viewpoint is approved by the government. Criticism of the government results in closure of the media and imprisonment of the journalists.

Once a charge is laid, trials are quick and sentences harsh. Crimes of rebellion often earn eight years in prison for the convicted. The evidence need not be strong and the possibility of appeal is almost nonexistent.

Prisons in Cuba are harsh and prisoners often lose 20 to 30 pounds during their incarceration period. The Inter-American Commission on Human Rights received more complaints over the conditions in Cuban prisons than the number of complaints about any other human rights violations. Generally, overcrowding, poor hygienic conditions, poor food (some has been reported to be fortified with worms), little medical care, beatings, solitary confinement as punishment, limited family visits, and non segregation of prisoners are common. There are 294 prisons and work camps in the country, with about 200,000 prisoners. There are also six high-security prisons.

■ Public Affection

Displays of affection in public are common and you will often see a couple snuggled up on a bench along the malacon or the prada. Anything beyond kissing or hugging is kept for the privacy of the home. Most sexuality is displayed through dancing and music.

■ Sexuality

Homosexuality is illegal. However, things are changing slowly. Today the universities are doing studies on the "gay problem," mostly in an attempt to combat crime and prostitution.

In 1988 the penal code was changed so that homosexuality would be punishable only if it was publicly manifested. This implies that you are permitted to be a private homosexual. If a homosexual persistently bothers others with amorous advances, a fine would be imposed. In 1993 the movie *Strawberry and Chocolate* helped turn sympathy toward gays for the discrimination they face. And in 1994 the Cuban Association of Gays and Lesbians was founded by 18 brave people. Sadly, it was shut down in 1997 when the liberal sentiment took a conservative swing.

Overall, the men are machismo and the women are "real women," sex is for heteros and anything else is perverse.

> **AUTHOR NOTE:** Some all-inclusive resorts are liberal, but this is because of the tourists, not the Cubans.

■ **Special Needs Travelers**

 People with special needs may find it difficult to get around on their own. Anyone needing to use a **wheelchair** will have a difficult time as the sidewalks are often unsafe for walking with hiking boots, never mind trying to maneuver a wheelchair. Wheelchair accessibility in hotels and restaurants is sparse, although many places have ground level entrances.

For the **deaf**, there are no communication services available. The **blind** use white canes and usually have someone helping them. Traveling with a seeing or hearing companion could make the trip an exceptional experience for the disabled person.

Traveling with **children** is always a positive in Latin American countries and Cuba is no exception. There are many playgrounds and children's entertainment

Travel Information

centers. Hotels and restaurants, for the most part, are clean and comfortable. Some even have baby-sitting services.

Seniors can have one of the best vacations of their lives here. The medical system has everything they may need in the event of an emergency. The hotels are comfortable and the food is decent. There are air-conditioned tour buses to take everyone, including seniors, to sites and the buses usually have conductors to give a helping hand to those who need it.

BEGGING

Begging is not common but an opportunist will spot a foreigner with the assumption that he is good for a buck. Don't contribute! I had one old guy shuffle up to me in Camaguay one day as I stood in a doorway waiting for the shop to open. He insisted that I give him money for coffee. I refused. He tried to guilt me out by accusing me of denying an old man some pleasure. I still refused. He then asked me if I was Cubano and I said yes. He shuffled away disgruntled at having wasted his time.

Shopping

■ Habanos (Cigars)

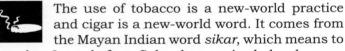 The use of tobacco is a new-world practice and cigar is a new-world word. It comes from the Mayan Indian word *sikar*, which means to smoke. Long before Columbus arrived, locals were sucking away with pleasure on a dry brown leaf rolled into more brown leaves. They addicted the early conquistadors and the habit spread quickly to the old world. In fact, the drug nicotine, found in tobacco, was named after the French ambassador to Portugal, Jean Nicot. By the mid-1700s, tobacco, once used mostly for its medicinal properties, was grown com-

mercially in North America and by 1790 the manufacturing of cigars was done in Spain, Portugal, France and Germany. By the mid-1800s, legislation had to be passed to regulate the production of cigars and an import tax was put on foreign ones. This made the cigar seem like a luxury item. It wasn't long before everyone realized that the cigars made in Cuba with Cuban-grown tobacco were the finest. By the time the American Civil War was over, smoking had become so popular that smoking cars on trains were introduced, as were smoking rooms in public establishments and private clubs. A cigar and a glass of brandy or port after dinner was, and still is, the only way to go.

There are as many brands of cigars as there are cars in the world. They come in different sizes, flavors, strengths, spices, ages, wrappings and prices. Your selection will be determined by what you like and what you can afford. It's like taking a wine tour through the wineries of France. The year of the cigar, as with wine, is important, as some years produce better leaves than others.

There are far too many brands of cigars to review here. Some of the more popular are **Cohiba**, **Monterrey**, **La Corona**, **Montecristo**, **Romeo and Julietta** and **Bolívar**. In each brand there are sub-brands. For example, Cohibas have the Panetela, the Esplendido, the Lancero and the Corona. For a good review of the many brands visit www.cigars-review.org.

THE ART OF SMOKING A CIGAR

Once you have chosen your cigar, you must cut the closed end or the cap using cutters that have fine razors. The cut should be clean and straight. Lighting the cigar with something that has no flavor, like a match (not a gasoline lighter or a candle) is important. Burn the end of the cigar with the fire before you start inhaling. Don't tap the ash off too often. If the cigar goes out, it can be re-lit as long as it is still warm. However, if allowed to cool, some of the flavor will be lost.

Sophisticated cigar smokers often choose to enjoy a brandy with their cigar. Pour the brandy into a snifter. Puff on your cigar and blow smoke into the snifter. Swirl the glass and smell the aroma, then take a sip of brandy.

Fakes

When purchasing cigars, be certain to get the real thing. There are lots of people ready to sell poor quality cigars at good quality prices. According to the Cuban government, for every authentic cigar sold, a fake is also sold. Although some of the material used to make fakes is stolen from the authentic factories, many fakes are so badly made they could make you sick. Some fake cigars found at customs were made with fill such as toilet paper and banana leaves. A few even had cockroaches in them.

To spot a fake, first make sure the box is made of thin cedar. Some boxes carrying fake cigars are made with thick plywood. If the box is heavy, see if the cigars are wrapped too tightly. Fakes are always too tight because tight cigars are easier to make. All boxes should be sealed with the green-and-white warranty stamp pasted across the lid, folded in the center with the second half pasted to the front of the box. The upper right corner of the box should have a *Habanos* stamp burned into the wood with a hot iron. Below this should be a stamp that says which factory made the cigars and when the cigars were completed.

The inside of the box should have a loose flap of paper and a thin piece of wax paper placed across the bands. The wax paper should be cut with a cutting knife, leaving no rough edges or fibers sticking out. The warranty should be on a piece of parchment sitting on the cigars. The cigars themselves should be exactly the same size and shape. The wrapper leaves should not have large veins and should not be dry or too light in color. The caps, the bands at the top and the bottom, should all be exactly uniform. Run your finger down the cigar and make sure it does not have soft or hard spots. Examine the foot of the cigar. The tobacco should be brown, fairly dark, but never really dark or green. The two layers of cigars in the box should be separated with a thin layer of cedar that almost looks like a piece of paper. At the top right corner there should be a half-moon cut out for your finger to lift the wood. This cut should be as evenly made as the paper cut for the top coverings.

While in Cuba, visit the **Casa de Habanos** in Havana for a hands-on lesson in spotting the real thing from the fake. Also, pay the price and get the real thing. I've heard that *cucarachas* taste appalling.

The **Virtual Cigar Museum**, www.cigarnexus.com, is in California. If cigars interest you, visit here before going to Cuba. Over 2,500 items on display pertain to the cigar culture.

Accessories

Cigar cutters come in almost as many sizes and shapes as the cigars themselves. The most common are single- or double-bladed. They feature stainless steel blades and sell for less than $10.

Humidors are a common purchase. Some handmade ones can be purchased in the market; higher quality ones can be purchased at the Casa de Habanos or the gift shops in the larger hotels. A good humidor has a humidifying system, a hygrometer and very well fitted doors/drawers. The inside should be lined with cedar. Some that are made of other woods may have a bug or worm in the wood. Look carefully for these bugs, because if they are found by customs you will not be permitted to take the humidor into your country.

Travel Information

■ Rum

The growing of sugarcane was traced to the East Indies, now called Indonesia. It spread to China and then India. The Persians and Arabs were the next to include cane into their diets,

but no one ever learned to do anything with it except drink the raw juice. Once explorers started going to the new world, some great mind transplanted a few shoots on Hispañola and the crop grew like a weed.

Soon, sugarcane was squeezed and the resulting juice boiled. The crystal that remained became the desired sweetener of everyone in Europe. The brown goo left after boiling sugarcane was called *melazas*, a word derived from the Spanish word *miel*, for honey. The Anglicized word became molasses and the product was soon diluted with water and left out in the sun where it fermented. It wasn't long before someone distilled the fermented molasses and came up with what we now call rum. The first reference to the drink was on the island of Barbados about 25 years after the English arrived in the mid-1600s. It was said to be a "Rumbullion" that is made of distilled sugarcane and is a "hot, hellish and terrible liquor." (Rumbullion is a gypsy word meaning strong or potent.) In spite of that assessment, the drink soon became popular in Britain, Europe and then North America.

Today rum is made from either fermented sugarcane juice or molasses. Its fermentation period can be anywhere between 24 hours and several weeks. Rum got better as the years went on due to cultured yeasts, improved maturing casks, improved filtration and eventually an improved still. Sugarcane, like tobacco, relies on the aging, care, soil in which it grows and climate for quality. Cuba has one of the best soils and climate for growing sugarcane and as agronomy became a more exacting science, the production of cane was perfected.

Rum when distilled is a colorless spirit. It is the added caramel and spices that determine some of the color and flavor. The most common spices added are cinnamon, rosemary, aniseed and pepper. Some rum is left in oak casks; as it ages, the rum takes on an oak flavor. Lighter rums are distilled in continuous columns and some are filtered through charcoal, while the dark rums are distilled in pot stills. Golden rums are a blend of the two.

Cuban rums are light-bodied, crisp and clean. **Havana Club** has the biggest factory in Cuba and is able to produce 30 million liters of rum a year. These include Silver Dry (used mostly in cocktails), Carta Blanca, Carta Oro and the seven-year-old Añeno.

There's nought no doubt so much the spirit calms as rum and true religion, said Lord Byron.

If that's too calm for you, there is always,
Fifteen men on a dead man's chest,
Yo, ho ho and a bottle of rum.

Favorite Rum Drinks

■ DAIQUIRI

☐ 1.5 oz white rum
☐ 1 oz lime juice (personally I add a bit more of this!)
☐ 1 tbsp sugar
☐ Crushed ice

Throw everything together and blend for 10 seconds or so.

■ MOJITO

☐ 2.5 oz light rum
☐ 1 lime
☐ 1 tbsp syrup - heat equal parts sugar and water to the boiling point stirring in the sugar until it is dissolved.
☐ 8 or so mint leaves
☐ Ice cubes
☐ Club soda

Place the syrup and mint leaves in a glass and grind the leaves with a spoon until you can smell them. Squeeze in the juice from a lime, pour the rum and drop in a few ice cubes. Add Club soda.

■ CUBA LIBRE

❏ 1.5 oz Havana Club (aged)
❏ Ice
❏ Coca-Cola

Pour rum over ice and add cola.

ALCOHOL TRIVIA

- "Toast," when used to mean good health, started in Rome where a piece of toast was dropped into a glass of wine.

- Anyone under 21 who carries a bag of garbage out of the house that has even one empty alcohol bottle in it can be charged with illegal possession in Missouri.

- Alcohol consumed in moderation does not kill brain cells but is thought to improve thinking. The key word here is moderation.

- In the early days of the church, alcohol was considered a gift of God. I still think it is. However, during Prohibition, members of the temperance movement rewrote the bible and removed any reference to alcohol.

- The British Navy, believing that rum was good for the constitution, provided a daily ration of a half-pint of 160-proof rum to every sailor by the 1730s and this continued until 1969. The rum was mixed with a half-pint of water and the concoction was called grog.

- Between 1762 and 1792, Cuba supplied the world market with rum.

- Everyone produces alcohol in the body as a by-product of metabolism every day of their lives.

■ Crafts

 Wood carvings of the highest quality are available in Cuba. However, these cannot be purchased in the markets – you must go to a reputable shop. The one I thought had the best carvings was in Havana: **Oviedo**, Ave Mayari #88 and Prosperidad, Arroyo Naroyo (no phone). Juan Antonio Lobato, in 2005, won first prize at the United National International contest for his carving, *The Creoles*, of two Cuban characters, one with a cigar and the other with a parasol. They stand 1.5 meters (4.5 feet) high and are made with ebony, cedar, jiqui woods.

Cars and motorcycles designed from recycled soda tins are a great little item found in the markets. The designs are copies of what you see on the streets.

DOCUMENTATION FOR ART

All original works of art must have a special document provided by the shop where the work is purchased or from the government department, Registro Nacional de Bienes Culturales, Calle 17 #1009 between Ave 10 and 12, Vedado, Havana, ☎ 7/31-3362. It is illegal for artists to sell you their work directly because the government may not get its share of the money. This does not include the things you purchase in the markets.

Travel Information

Music

 The smoke from Cuban cigars is world famous. The smoke from Cuban music is inhaled with as much sensuous appetite. Both are honest stereotypes, enjoyed with passionate zeal by Cubans in the same way that Italians love pasta and aren't afraid to admit it or the way the British shamelessly take their tea. Getting off the plane in Cuba means you are about to step into a movie – the soundtrack is provided, no matter what the scene.

It was, in fact, a film that brought Cuban music back to the world's attention. When the public had lost consciousness that the mambo and the salsa, the conga and the rumba all call Cuba mother, the film *Buena Vista Social Club* was a gentle reminder. This documentary was the music video for a nation. It was shot by feature filmmaker Wim Wenders as an aside to the album of the same name being recorded by renowned guitarist and producer Ry Cooder. Cooder fell in love with the vibrant personality of Cuban music, visited Cuba and put together a clutch of the country's best musical elders. The result was a Grammy-winning record, an Oscar-winning film and a whole new world view of the old Cuban sound.

Cuban music is not merely tunes played by Cubans. There are distinct qualities that assign it to the island, and in anyone else's hands it is mere replica. It is a rare thing for a musical genre to be absolutely intrinsic to a place, the way bluegrass is to the Smokey Mountains or Maritime Celtic is to Nova Scotia or reggae is to Jamaica. Cuba is richly endowed, with several indigenous forms of music standing as pillars on which globalized melodies are played.

The history of Cuban music follows the same navigational charts as Columbus. He landed on Cuban shores in 1492, encountering a people already skilled in music of their own. Within 50 years, however,

Spanish imperialism would brutally impose Catholic arts upon them and the rhythms of African slaves. The indigenous population was compressed to only a few thousand people through disease and genocidal policies of the day. However, a shortage of Europeans on the island meant Africans and locals were grudgingly accepted into symphony orchestras. So began the spicy stew that would brew distinctive sounds the world had never heard before. Two hundred years later, when Catholic music was made exclusive by law, a temporary British military invasion added new instruments to the island's sonic storehouse, war in Haiti brought an influx of refugees, and African slaves were rushed in by the thousand (this continued until the middle of the 1800s). This diversity of melody and beats began to mutate in dramatic fashion.

■ Musical Forms

The collision of staid European dance music and robust African rhythms are epitomized in the form of music called **Contradanza** that took shape in Cuba in the 1800s. It was groundbreaking for its day, for its borrowing from Spanish line dances and Afro-Haitian beats. It spawned the simple **Habanera** genre, which became the first Cuban musical export, finding an audience back in Europe (such as in the Bizet opera *Carmen*). It was also the forerunner to the popular **Danzon** style of music.

One of the leading musical genres rooted in Cuba is called **Son**. It is a lead soloist and a chorus of backup singers working in a call-and-response fashion. A signature bass characteristic is also present in the Son. It can trace itself back to the earliest days of Spanish conquest, to a composition in the 1570s entitled *Son de la Ma Teodora*. It is

widely accepted that Son originated in the capital region of the day, Santiago de Cuba, before it was embraced by the popular bands of Havana in the 20th century. From Son sprang other popular forms of notable Cuban music like salsa. (Salsa was technically born in New York City by expatriate Cubans and like-minded musicians in their circle.)

The other most prized development was the **rumba** dance style. It began in much the same way rap music began in modern America, as a personal art form of the black urban poor. It shaped itself out of the 19th-century lower classes and shot like a comet across the world. Rumba was almost exclusively percussion and vocal based music. It is still one of the more popular dance music styles on the ballroom floors of the world.

Another export that still tickles the dancing toes of the modern world is the **Bolero**. This catchy rhythm also insinuated itself into classical compositions of the early 1900s. It was a rich century for Cuban folk composers who also launched such phenomenon as **conga** and **mambo** and the **cha-cha**. These are still easily identifiable in films (*West Side Story*) and on pop radio (*Come on, shake your body, baby, do the cong'* by Miami Sound Machine). More Cuban flair is being applied all the time, thanks to unprecedented world encouragement and modern electric instruments. The font of music that is Cuba is still overflowing.

Americans first started to notice Cuban tastes in popular culture when a zany musician named Ricky first said "I love you" to a rambunctious redhead named Lucy. Desi Arnaz (otherwise known as Ricky Ricardo) announced his island homeland with authority on 1950s television. About the same time, mambo pioneers like Benny More and Israel Cachao Lopez were storming the post-war dance clubs from across the Straits of Florida. American music explorers like Dizzy Gillespie and Nat King Cole took a heavy interest in the time signatures and improvisations they were hearing from their Cuban friends and they injected that into the veins of jazz. Today, **jazz** is the commodity Cuba trades in most. Another expository documentary by an outside musician looking in on the Cuban scene is the film *Spirits of Havana* (directed by Bay Weyman and Luis O. Garcia for the National Film Board of Canada), which follows sax/flute great Jane Bunnett, the two-time Grammy nominee, around the island she has been recording on since the 1980s.

■ Cuban Music in the World Scene

 Long before *Buena Vista Social Club* came along, Bunnett had been putting Cuban sound front-and-center on her albums and, finally, on the big screen. What she reveals most is the way music is ingrained in Cuban society.

"That is the thing about Cuban musicians," Bunnett told San Francisco writer Julia Sewell in an interview. "Their training at the conservatories is so good, most of the people I know can play piano, play conga and also arrange. They are so well rounded and can do so much musically. Virtuosos pop up a lot. They get so much technique together at an early age. While we are out playing for an hour, watching TV, bicycling around, these guys are playing six-seven hours of music. The social scene is playing music, and this starts with 14 and 15 year olds."

Adonis Puentes grew up in that environment. He and his brother Alexis moved from Cuba to Canada in the mid-90s and brought with them a life-long musical heritage. Their father was a highly acclaimed musician and their mother a staunch supporter of their musical pursuits. They grew up across the street from a concert venue and would often host in their home such Cuban legends as Alvita Rodriguez, Carlos Zambalo, Selina Gonzales and Ibrahim Ferrer (made famous abroad by the *Buena Vista Social Club* project) singing and playing in their living room. In Canada they discovered their all-too-common Cuban upbringing made them exotic, rocketing their Puentes Brothers debut album *Morumba Cubana* up the charts. They were a little surprised by the celebrity.

"I think that because Cuba is an island, it is not accustomed to the multi-cultural environment we have here," Adonis Puentes said. "Everywhere we go, there is an audience for this kind of music. Also, sometimes we incorporate different elements with our music and we go to a different audience. Back there, Cuban music for Cubans is a little bit different. You find that certain kinds of Cuban music works only for a certain crowd and you have to respect different ways of playing the music. Here we just say we are playing Cuban music and it is more open to different crowds."

There is a thirst for Cuban music across the world, but nowhere more so than in the United States. The close geographic connections are natural in developing an ear for the music floating in from the island, and it is amplified by the many family and artistic connections made over the centuries. But politics has added a twist. Ever since Fidel Castro came to power in 1959, opinion has been as divided as the gulf between Havana and Miami. The US has, since 1961, blockaded Cuba, including the flow of musicians. Some have made their way from Cuba to America to live or tour, and some Americans have made their way down to Cuba for musical opportunities (the Havana International Jazz Festival is a renowned event), but when a Cuban performs internationally it is usually on the soil of Cuba-neutral countries like Canada, Holland or France.

Famous Cuban exiles like Gloria Estefan, Jon Secada, Arturo O'Farrill, Paquito D'Rivera and actor Andy Garcia have made massive cultural inroads outside the Cuba they love so much and, in some cases, hotly admonish for continuing to maintain Castro in leadership. But being a musician under Castro's regime is a respected state profession, like being a doctor or teacher. The nation is abundantly supplied with government-funded orchestras and radio stations that bring Cuba's musicians into everyone's homes. Groups like **Septeto Habanero**, **Orquesta Aragon**, the appendages of the **Afro-Cuban Jazz Project**, the **Afro-Cuban All-Stars** and many others have been performing together in some cases more than half a century. Sometimes the band has been handed down from generation to generation. These star-caliber musicians are not elite citizens hiding from paparazzi but instead, as characterized by the Puentes Brothers experiences, are accessible and available at street level for a casual chat or a spontaneous instrument lesson.

■ Discovering the Music

Trying to summarize the Cuban music scene is like trying to somehow describe the personality of water. Recommending the star performers of Cuba is as futile as listing the greats of American folk – once you get through Bob Dylan, Joan Baez and Joni Mitchell you run the risk of diminishing John Prine, Gordon Lightfoot and Robbie Robertson. One could check into the past works of Omara Portuondo or Compay Segundo, but one could just as easily look to Pio Leyva or Ruben Gonzalez.

Today's island is littered with powerful musical forces like Los Van Van, Jesus Chucho Valdez, Manuel Galban, Cubanismo, Juan de Marcos Gonzalez, and too many more to list. There are clubs and performance halls everywhere. There are symphonies and choral groups and chamber ensembles and rock bands and the spectrum of jazz, folk and percussion players from the top of the mountains to the seaside, and 50 miles will make a huge difference in what you are hearing.

The best way to steep yourself in Cuba's music – aside from a plane ticket – is to educate yourself first through books and film, then decide what aisles to go down at the CD store. See **Buena Vista Social Club** for starters, and don't miss **Spirits of Havana** either.

Try to find the documentary Andy Garcia made in 1993 entitled **Cachao...Como Su Ritmo No Hay Dos** on the life of Israel Cachao Lopez.

Ned Seblette recently wrote an acclaimed book called **Cuba and Its Music** that is essential reading, alongside the most famous account of the island's melody, Alejo Carpentier's **Music In Cuba**, which was first published in 1946 in Spanish but did not get an English treatment until 2005, 25 years after Carpentier died. He was then, and still is today, recognized as one of Cuba's cultural icons of the 20th century for his novels, his music, and his Cuban voice. His book has a life closely parallel to Cuban music itself. It captures hundreds of years of history and covers encyclopedic territory but nonetheless flashes sensuous artistic curves. It was almost disregarded by pop culture but at long last came pounding back to life like the syncopated heartbeat of the Caribbean. *(Reviewed by Frank Peebles of Prince George, BC.)*

Food & Drink

 I highly recommend that you eat in Cuban homes as often as possible because the food is far tastier and the portions are larger than in any restaurant. The *paladars*, homes where up to a dozen people may eat, allow more relaxed dining and the meals, for the most part, are what the cook is making that day. However, because of the government's ridiculous taxation system, most *paladars* have gone out of business. The ones that remain are usually really good (or illegal). Eating lobster is not usually possible in the *paladars*.

■ Common Meals

 The most common meals are eggs, fresh bread and fresh fruit for breakfast; rice, roasted or fried meat (pork, beef or chicken), fresh vegetables, potatoes and a dessert for lunch and dinner. Most meals cost between $5 and $10. Pizzas can be purchased on the street or in pizzerias. Juice stalls are common, offering freshly squeezed delights. Coffee is available throughout Cuba.

Moros y cristianos (Moors and Christians) are black beans and rice. The Moors are the beans (dark) and the Christians are the rice (white). Not politically correct but common in Cuba.

Yucca, or cassava, is a white root that is boiled and sometimes mashed. The flavor is very mild, almost non-existent. When not mashed, it is quite stringy.

Criolla (Creole) **meat dishes** are usually found in the south east of Cuba and are cooked with spices, garlic, onions and tomatoes. These dishes are made with chicken, pork or beef and are the most interesting (closest to gourmet) in the country.

Ajiaco is a meat, garlic and vegetable stew that, when home cooked, can be delectable.

> **AUTHOR NOTE:** Fresh veggies are difficult to come by. A salad is usually cut up tomato, cucumber and onion.

■ Beverages

 Daiquiris, **mojitos** and **Cuba libres** are the three best-known drinks available. See pages 61 and 62 for recipes.

Lemonade is readily available and well worth drinking to quench your thirst.

Coffee grown in Cuba is quite good. You can get café Americano, which is weak filtered coffee, or you can try their café con leche (coffee with milk), a very strong coffee diluted with hot, creamy milk. It is delicious.

Bucanero is probably the best tasting **beer**, a bit heavier than **Crystal**, which is very American-like in its lightness and alcohol content. **Hatuey** is the cheapest and skunkiest, while **Mayabe** is a beer that falls somewhere in the middle. Regardless of which one you drink, it will take an awful lot of beer to get a buzz because of the light alcohol content.

Selecting a Place to Stay

■ Hotels

 Cuba's many hotels are run and controlled by the government. The organizations working in the hotel business are the Cubanacan, Gaviota, Horizontes, Islazul and Gran Caribe.

Horizontes and Islazul hotels administer the middle- and lower-class ones, while the Gaviota, Gran Caribe and Cubanacan look after the four- and five-star ones. Many of the hotels are partially owned and operated by foreign companies from Spain, Italy, Canada, Portugal, France, Germany and the Netherlands. This

State hotel, with rates from $30 per night.

shared investment is beneficial to both Cuba and the visitor; the foreign investors can attract locals from their countries and the hotels in Cuba are of a standard that's familiar to the visitor.

Hotels offer everything from great rooms and pools to average rooms with few services. They can cater to the visitor interested in upper-end hotels, while lower-cost hotels are usually great for those who want to roam around and spend their money on tours or entertainment.

■ Casas Particulares

Casas Particulares are homes that have been approved by the government to rent rooms. Because the tax to operate such *casas* is so high, the room rate is seldom negotiable and varies less than $5 from place to place. However, *casas* usually include breakfast that is generally much better than anything a restaurant offers. Rates for two people sharing a room, and sometimes a bed, are about $25. Most houses are colonial buildings with big rooms, high ceilings and interesting designs. For me, *casas* are the best deal, but you should speak some Spanish to be able to take full advantage of them.

■ Camping

Camping in Cuba is my idea of resort living. The campsites usually have clean cabins, pools, restaurants, bars, and manicured grounds. The drawback is that they are seldom in the center of or close to towns.

It is best to book a room at one of the government-run tourist offices in Havana as prices are lower when booked this way. The office can also reserve a private car to take you to the camping resort. Public transportation doesn't usually go to these areas.

Tent camping is not done, although I do know of cyclists who have pitched tents wherever it was convenient and had no problems. As for regular campsites like those found in North America or Europe, Cuba has not gone this route yet.

Sewers are of the usual Latin American type and can't handle wads of toilet paper. There will almost always be a basket beside the toilet in which to throw your waste paper. Use it.

Travel Information

■ Prices & Payment

Regardless of the class of accommodation, never pay for your entire vacation before you arrive. Pay for a day or two so you have a place to land – and go from there. Talk to others and see what is available. Look around. The cost will be less and there is little chance of

PRICE CHART
Per room for two people, per day.
$ . . . . $25-$50
$$ . . . . . . $51-$75
$$$ . . . . $76-$100
$$$$ . . . $101-$150
$$$$$ . . Over $150

you being stuck without a room. Cuba has over 30,000 hotel rooms, not including *casas*. Varadero alone can accommodate around 18,000 people.

A LESSON LEARNED

I once stayed in Varadero at an inexpensive hotel. I had two rooms, a kitchenette, a private bath, a balcony, air conditioning and cable TV for $35 for two adults and a child. The rooms were cleaned daily and they were cleaned well. There was no pool (it was two blocks from the beach) and the restaurant was not for romantic dining. However, the place next door had a pool, tourist office, car rental, beautiful garden, bar, restaurant and so on. But when I saw the rooms, I thought "skid-row." The curtains were falling off the runners, the place was filthy and the hotel would do nothing about the poor condition of the rooms. Most who were staying there had paid for their entire time in Cuba before they arrived and they were stuck.

Be aware that motels, inns or *posadas* often rent by the hour and may not be too accommodating when they see you are a foreigner.

Getting Here

■ By Air

 Cuba has 10 international airports, although Havana and Varadero are the most frequently used. Recently, Holguin has also become a popular destination. Airline companies offer flights from 40 cities in 28 countries and are served by nine airlines.

Cubana de Aviacion, 1 A. Ave and Calle 55, Varadero, ☎ 7/451-3016, is not the best airline in the world but they do offer cheap tickets. They fly from many areas in Europe, Russia, Central and South America, and Mexico to Havana, Holguin, Varadero and Santiago de Cuba.

Aeroflot, Ave 23 #64, Vedado, Havana, ☎ 7/33-3200 or 7/33-3759, flies from Moscow, Chile, Ireland and Nicaragua. This airline has a dubious reputation, especially for not having a record of the reservation. You arrive at the airport after making your reservation and paying your fee to be met by a "nyet."

Aerotaxi, Calle 24 and Ave Playa, Varadero, ☎ 45/6-7540 or 451-2929, is a Cuban company that use planes according to their needs, often interchanging the military planes for commercial ones.

Aero Caribbean, Ave 23 #64, Vedado, Havana, ☎ 7/33-4543 or 7/33-5016, or Juan Gualberto Gómez Airport, Matanzas, ☎ 7/66-3016, fly from Canada, Mexico, Nicaragua, Panama, Venezuela, Columbia, Martinique, San Martin and Guadalupe in the Caribbean. This is becoming one of the better airlines in Latin America. They are trying hard.

LTU International Airways, Juan Gualberto Gómez Airport, Matanzas, ☎ 52/3611, fly direct from Dusseldorf and Munich in Germany.

Martinair Holland, Juan Gualberto Gómez Airport, Matanzas, ☎ 52/1-3016, or Calle 23 #64, Vedado, Havana, ☎ 7/33-4364.

Air Canada, Juan Gualberto Gómez Airport, Matanzas, ☎ 52/6-3016. In recent years this airline has offered excellent flying times and even better service. They are not an upscale airline.

Air Transat Inc., Hotel Mar del Sur, room 16307, Varadero, ☎ 7/66-7595 or 7/61-2731.

Aerotaxis del Caribe, Calle 24 and Ave 1A Varadero, ☎ 45/1-4807, has some flights.

In addition, British Airways, Air France, Iberia, Avianca, Copa, Mexicana, Lacsa, Taca and Air Jamaica offer direct flights from their respective countries of origin into Cuba.

■ By Sea

 If arriving by private boat, you must communicate with port authorities before you reach jurisdictional waters (12 nautical miles from the island platform). The authorities can be called by radio via channels HF(SSB) 2760 (National Coastline Network) or VHF Channel 68 on the National Coastal Network and Channel 16 for the Tourist Network.

You must have all required documents, like tourist visas and valid passports, to enter.

There are marinas along the northern shores at the Hemingway Marina in Havana, Puertosol Darsena de Varadero, Chapelin, Gaviota Varadero in Varadero, Puertosol Cayo Coco, Cayo Guillermo and Gaviota Bahia de Naranjo in Holguin province.

The southern shores have marinas at Puertosol Maria la Gorda International Diving Center, in Pinar del Rio, Cayo Large del Sur, Puertosol Cienfuegos and Punta Gorda in Santiago de Cuba.

■ Outfitters Who Do All the Work

Gap Adventures, 19 Duncan Street, Toronto, Ontario, M5H 3H1, Canada, ☎ 800-465-5600, www.gap.ca, has reasonably priced hiking, biking and kayaking trips that usually last two weeks and include things like snorkeling, Salsa dancing, birding and a tour of Havana. If high-energy travel is not your thing, GAP will also take you on a colonial tour to places like Baracoa and Santiago de Cuba, or you can do a week with them visiting the beaches of Cayo Levisa and Viñales. GAP no longer takes American dollars for payment, but will take Canadian dollars, euros, British pounds, and Australian and New Zealand dollars. I recently had friends who are very experienced in traveling use this company for a trip and they had high praise for every aspect of the services offered. One of the most important features of this company is that they use local workers as much as possible and pay the workers well for their services. As a result, the visitor gets a good trip.

Alfredo Reyes, ☎ 7/860-8930, www.westsong.com/cubatourguide/, alfredors2001@yahoo.com. Alfredo will help you get a *casa* or a hotel, find you a good restaurant, help you exchange money and plan your tours to places like Santa Clara, Trinidad or the rum and cigar factories. He can help you get theater tickets or nightclub reservations or recommend the best places to find what interests you the most. As a personal guide, Alfredo charges $25 per day and his English is impeccable. It is best to contact Alfredo by e-mail and make some plans that can be honed once you are in Cuba.

Tripcentral, Lloyd D. Jackson Square, 2 King St. West, Hamilton, Ontario, L8P 1A1, Canada, ☎ 800-665-4981, www.tripcentral.ca/trip/, offers trips for two weeks in a three-star hotel, some meals included, for $1,476 CDN, including all taxes (2005 prices). This price drops by about $200 if no meals are included. They fly to either Varadero or Holquin.

Toucan Tours, 49 Queen's Drive, Fulwood, Preston, Lancs, PR2 9YL, England, ☎ 01772-787862, www.toucantours.co.uk, run birding tours from England. However, if you are from another area, you can hook up with them in Cuba. They have excellent guides who are able to point out feathered friends like the olive-capped warblers and Cuban pewees. They start at San Diego de los Baños and visit Soroa and Cayo Coco, Cayo Guillermo and Pardeon Grande. It is the skilled guides that are the draw here.

Voyage Culture Cuba Inc., 5059 Saint-Denis, Montreal, PQ, H2J 2L9, Canada, ☎ 514-982-3330 or 888-691-0101, takes one- or two-week cycling, birding, hiking and trekking trips, as well as jazz tours. They will customize the itinerary to suit special interests and times. The jazz trip coincides with Cuba's yearly International Jazz Festival, which features musicians such as Chucho Valdes. This trip can be extended for a week so you can suck up even more jazz. The cost, staying at the classy Havana Libre, double occupancy is less than $2,000 CDN. This includes air, hotel, transportation and jazz festival tickets.

Routes to Learning Tours, 4 Cataraqui St., Kingston Ontario, K7K 1Z7, Canada, ☎ 866-745-1690 or 613-530-2222, www.routestolearning.ca, offers one- and two-week special interest tours with professional guides. For example, if you have an interest in architecture, a tour can be arranged for you to visit places of architectural interest with a professional architect and to visit those working in the profession. They also do birding, Spanish language, fine arts, music and jazz tours. This company likes to work with university, college, high school or working professional groups so it can help cross-cultural exchanges.

Getting Around

■ By Air

Cubana, www.cubana.co.cu/html/espanol/index.asp#, is the government-owned airline and the only one that provides internal flights in Cuba. You must check in one hour before flights leave and you are permitted 20 kg (44 lbs) of luggage per person. This airline does not have the best reputation for punctuality or service. However, they always seem to get there.

SCHEDULES & FARES

Prices are in convertible pesos, one way from Havana and unless otherwise stated, flights return on the same day they leave Havana. Check the website for times.

Baracoa	$133	Thursday and Sundays
Bayamo	$103	Tuesday and Thursday
Camagüey	$93	Daily
Ciego de Avila	$79	Thursday (return Friday)
Cayo Coco	$98	Two daily
Guantanamo	$123	Daily except Tuesday and Thursday
Holguin	$100	Daily
Las Tunas	$101	Tuesday and Saturday
Manzanillo	$103	Saturday
Moa	$123	Monday
Nueva Gerona	$37	Two flights Tuesday and Thursday, three every other day
Santiago de Cuba	$113	Two daily except one on Saturday

■ By Car

Car Rentals

 Driving is an easy and fun thing to do. It allows you to visit outreaches of the country and traffic is almost nonexistent, even in the vicinity of a reasonably sized city. You must be 21 years of age, have a valid drivers license or an international drivers license and have at least one year of driving experience before you can rent. You will also need a credit card not issued from an American bank. You must leave an imprint of the card or between $200 and $500 deposit for security.

Rates, depending on the vehicle, are $60-$100 per day, plus the cost of gas. Car companies accept payment with VISA, MasterCard, Eurocard, Banamex, Camet and JBC, as well as cash and traveler's checks.

There are two choices of **insurance**. Type A with $250 deductible or Type B, comprehensive. There is no coverage for the car radio or the tires. Insurance for a second driver costs about $15 per day extra if the driver is a foreigner and $3 per day if he/she is Cuban.

Driving Tips

Traffic signs are posted, but I recommend a navigator beside the driver to help translate the Spanish into English in time for the driver to react. Havana's traffic is getting heavier so driving is becoming more difficult. However, the highways are excellent, traffic lights work and traffic cops are honest.

The **speed limit** is 100 kmh (60 mph) on the highways and 60 kmh (35 mph) on rural roads, 50 kmh (30 mph) on city streets and 40 kmh (25 mph) in school and playground zones. If you receive a speeding ticket, you must pay it when you pay for your rental. Speeding tickets cost $30 for foreigners; Cubans pay $30 Cuban pesos. These fines are readily given out, although it is very difficult to speed in town areas.

If you drive on the back roads where farmers are working/living, watch for crops of corn or rice drying on the pavement. Farmers get upset if you drive over their crops.

Rental Companies

Car rental companies, located in most tourist hotels, will provide you with Guia de Carreteras, an easy to follow guide of the highways. The only drawback of renting is that demand often outweighs supply, and you may have to try a few places before you get a vehicle, especially if you want a four-wheel-drive. However, I don't recommend booking ahead for a vehicle you may never get. Check the vehicle carefully before signing the rental papers.

Cubacar, Ave 5A and 84, Miramar, ☎ 7/24-2718, www.cuba.tc/Gaviota/GaviotaCarRental.html. This company has branch offices at the following locations:

José Martí Airport, Ave Van Troy and Rancho Boyeros, Havana, ☎ 7/33-5546

Comodoro Hotel, Ave 1RA and Calle 84, ☎ 7/24-1706

Cohiba Hotel, Ave Paseo between 1A and 3A, Vedado, ☎ 7/33-4661

Hemingway Marina, Ave 5TA and Calle 248, Santa Fe, ☎ 7/24-1707

Château Hotel, Ave 1RA and Calle 60, Miramar, ☎ 7/24-0760

Bellocaribe Hotel, Ave Terrazas, Santa Maria Mar, ☎ 7/33-6032

La Pradera Hotel, Calle 17 #230, between 15A and Siboney, ☎ 7/33-7467

Tarará Residential, Tarara, Santa Maria del Mar, Havana del Este, ☎ 7/97-1696

Melia Hotel, Ave 3RA, between Calle 76 and 80, Miramar, ☎ 7/24-3236

Travel Information

Parque Central Hotel, Calle Neptuno, on the corner of Prado and Zulueta, Old Havana, ☎ 7/66-6507

Vedado Hotel, Ave O #244, between Calle 25 and Humboldt, ☎ 7/32-6501

Havanautos, Ave 5A and 84, Miramar, ☎ 7/24-2718 or 7/24-2104, www.havanautos.cu, havautos@ imagenes. get.cma.net or reshautos@cimex.com. Branch offices are located at:

José Martí Airport, Ave Van Troy and Rancho Boyeros, Havana, ☎ 7/33-5197 at Terminal 3, ☎ 7/33-5215 at Terminal 2

National Hotel, Calle 21 and Ave O, Vedado, ☎ 7/33-3192

Sevilla Hotel, Trocadero #55, between the Prado and Zulueta, ☎ 7/33-8956

Riviera Hotel, Paseo and malecón, Vedado, ☎ 7/33-3577

Habana Libre Hotel, Calle 23 and Ave L, Vedado, ☎ 7/33-3484

Neptuno/Triton Hotel, Ave 3A and Calle 74, Miramar, ☎ 7/24-1181

Servi Cupet, Calle11 and malecón, ☎ 7/33-4691

Tropicoco Hotel, Arroyo Bermejo, Santa Cruz del Norte, ☎ 7/97-1535

Villa Panamericana, Calle A and Ave Central, Cojimar, ☎ 7/95-1037

Via Rent-a -Car, Ave del Puerto, Edificio La Marina, 3rd Floor, Old Havana, ☎ 7/66-6777, www.cuba.tc/ Gaviota/GaviotaCarRental.html. Branch offices:

José Martí Airport, Ave Van Troy and Rancho Boyeros, Havana, ☎ 7/33-5155

El Bosque Hotel, ☎ 7/24-3429, ext. 611

Panautos, Calle Linea and malecón, Vedado, ☎ 7/5-3255, www.cuba.cu/turismo/panatrans/panautos.htm. Branch offices:

> José Martí Airport, Ave Van Troy and Rancho Boyeros, Havana, ☎ 7/33-0306

> Panautos, Ave Zoologico and Calle 26, Nuevo Vedado, ☎ 7/66-6226

Gasoline

Getting fuel is no problem, although you will have to pay in hard currency. Survi-Cupet gas stations can be found throughout the country. Gasoline is priced just a bit higher than it is in the United States and Canada. Most stations are open 24 hours a day.

Taxis

There are taxis for tourists and different taxis for Cubans. Tourist taxis charge in convertible pesos and the Cuban ones charge far less in pesos. There are hundreds available. I found trying to hire a taxi on the street far too expensive for my budget. Walking or taking public buses was better and until Cuba decides that not all tourists have thousands of dollars just waiting to jump out of their pockets and drop into the hands of the poor Cuban, I will continue to use public transport and leave the taxis to starve. Although the government claims that the cost should not be more than $10 for anywhere in town, in actual fact, drivers will seldom take you across the street for less than $5. There are metered taxis and the drivers are required by law to use the meters. This does not always happen. If you can force the driver to use the meter, it should start at $1. Night fares run about 20% higher than daytime fares.

You can hire a taxi for the day, but be certain to have your itinerary and price agreed upon before completing the deal. Stopping to use the bathroom could be considered beyond the agreement and cost you an extra $5.

Taxi Companies

Pana-taxi, ☎ 7/55-5555, has radio-dispatched taxi service and is reputed as being the cheapest. Their taxis are used by both Cubans and foreigners.

Habana-taxi, ☎ 7/41-9600

Taxis-OK, ☎ 7/24-1446

Taxi Transtur, ☎ 7/33-6666

Transgaviota, ☎ 7/66-6777

Turistaxi, ☎ 7/33-5539

Illegal Taxis

These are found at all times anywhere in Cuba. Fares are negotiable but a decent cost would be around $25 for the day. However, these are not licensed by the government and are less comfortable than those that are. The cars are usually Ladas or vintage cars that are not maintained well.

Classic Car Rentals

Gran Car, Via Blanca and Palatino, ☎ 7/33-5647, has vintage cars for use. You can travel in style in one of these for a city tour or to go out of town. The cost is about $15 per hour with a 20-km (12-mile) distance limit on the first hour and less distance with each additional hour. Day rates start at about $100 with a 120-km (75-mile) distance limit. If you rent one of these vehicles for longer than a day, the price drops.

■ Alternative Transportation

Cocotaxis

These bright yellow motorized tricycles charge $5 per hour for up to three people. They are available in Havana center and in most other cities. The ones in Havana and Varadero,

where most tourists are found, charge $5 for your ride and won't come down in price even if going just a few blocks. Those in other cities are less expensive and ready to bargain. Taking one, regardless of where, could be the strangest taxi you'll ever take in your life.

Horsedrawn Carts

Agencia San Cristobal, Calle Oficios #110 between Lamparilla and Amargura, ☎ 7/33-9585. Horsedrawn carts are a quaint way of traveling around the old area of Havana or the long streets of Varadero. Rates average $3 per person, per hour, with a one-hour minimum. During busy seasons, you will pay more. These carts can be flagged down anywhere along their route.

Ciclotaxis

These can be hired for around $5 per hour for two people and will travel anywhere between Old Havana and Vedado. The seats are comfortable and most have roofs for protection from the elements.

■ By Bus

 I was originally known as the Chickenbus Lady, so for me this is, and always has been, my favorite mode of transportation. There are three bus companies that service tourists. They are all good, but you must pay in convertible pesos.

Rumbos S.A Company, ☎ 7/66-9713 or 7/24-9626, operates a minibus service called the Vaiven Bus Turistico, which travels around Havana from 9 am to 9:30 pm. It passes the same stop every 50 minutes; there are 23 stops. You can get on and off as often as you wish. Tickets ($5), good for the day, can be bought on the bus or at the tourist offices in large hotels.

Camel Bus is actually a huge transport truck that pulls a trailer capable of holding 300 people. This is called X-rated travel because there is sex, violence and profanity all around. Everyone swears trying to get on and pushes and shoves to get to the back. The sex comes from rubbing so close to so many bodies. This bus can be boarded at Calle Apodaca #53 near the train station (Ave de Belgica and Arsenal) and stops at Guines, Jaruco, Madruga, Nueva Paz, San José, San Nicolas and Santa Cruz del Norte. Traveling on this is a unique experience.

Viazul, Ave 26 and Zoologico, or at the main bus station across from Revolutionary Square, ☎ 7/81-1413, 7/81-5652 or 7/81-1108, www.viazul.cu/home_eng. htm, viazul@transnet.cu, is the best bus company in Cuba and it travels to the far outreaches of the country. Each person is permitted 20 kg (44 lbs) of luggage. You'll need to visit the website to confirm schedules and prices as they are both subject to change.

Astro Buses leave from the same station as Viazul in Varadero and in Havana at the station across from Revolutionary Square. Astro carries Cubans and foreigners; Cubans pay in pesos, while foreigners pay in convertibles. Their schedules are the same as Viazul.

SCHEDULES	
Havana to Viñales	Daily. Leaves at 9 am or 2 pm.
Viñales to Havana	Daily. Leaves at 8 am, 4 pm.
Both buses, each way, stop in Pinar del Rio. The cost is $11 to Pinar and $12 to Viñales. The cost between Viñales and Pinar is $6.	
Havana to Varadero	Daily. Leaves at 8 & 8:30 am, 4 & 6 pm.
Varadero to Havana	Daily. Leave at 8 am, 4, 6 and 11:40 pm.
Both buses, each way, stop in Varadero Airport and Matanzas. The cost is $10 to Varadero, $7 to Matanzas and $6 from Varadero to the Airport.	
Varadero to Trinidad	Daily. Leaves at 7:30 am from Varadero, 10:45 from Santa Clara, 12:15 pm from Cienfuegos; arrives in Trinidad at 1:55 pm.
Trinidad to Havana (not Varadero)	Leaves Trinidad at 2:45 pm, Cienfuegos at 4 pm, Santa Clara at 5:25 pm; arrives in Havana at 8:40 pm.
The cost from Varadero to Trinidad is $20, to Santa Clara is $11.	

SCHEDULES

Trinidad to Santiago de Cuba	Daily. Leaves Trinidad at 8:15 am, Santi Spíritus at 9:45 am, Ciego de Avila at 11:15 am, Camagüey at 1:50 pm, Las Tunas at 3:50 pm, Holguin at 5:05 pm, Bayamo at 6:25 pm.
Santiago de Cuba to Trinidad	Daily. Leaves Santiago de Cuba at 7:30 pm, Bayamo at 9:40 pm, Holguin at 11 pm, Las Tunas at 12:15 am, Camagüey at 2:15 am, Ciego de Avila at 4:15 am, Sancti Spíritus at 5:35 am; arrives in Trinidad at 7 am.

The cost from Trinidad to Sancti Spíritus is $6, Ciego de Avila is $9, Camagüey is $15, Las Tunas is $22, Holguin and Bayamo is $26, Santiago de Cuba is $33.

Santiago de Cuba to Baracoa	Stops in Guantanamo. Daily. Leaves at 7:45 am and arrives at 12:35 pm.
Baracoa to Santiago de Cuba	Daily. Leaves at 2:15 pm and arrives in Santiago de Cuba at 5 pm.

The cost is $15 between Santiago de Cuba and Baracoa and $6 to Gunatanamo.

Travel Information

Havana

Cuba is music and Havana, with its 2.2 million people, is the center where a traveler could easily spend a month poking around, never seeing the same thing twice and all the while moving to the rhythm of the music. Declared a UNESCO World Heritage Site in 1982, Havana has museums, parks, restaurants, concert halls, shops and forts and other restored colonial buildings. Accenting all this is music.

The malecón, the road following the shoreline, starts across the bay from Fort Moro and borders the north shore of Havana, a city that covers 730 square km. The malecón borders Havana for just under 10 km/ six miles. This walkway, used day and night by Cubans and foreigners alike, is where you can sip on a beer and watch Cuban life watching you. The downside is that the water along this stretch is about the worst in the Caribbean for pollution. However, Cubans are starting to clean it up.

Take a city tour to give you an idea of the city's layout. Havana has 15 suburbs, winding streets and a non-grid layout. Some of the most interesting things you will see are the many old colonial homes, which have been refinished and are now occupied by local middle-class citizens. The huge old trees with their hanging aerial roots offer shade and add to the romance. The wealthy Miramar area is now where most consulates and embassies are located. The area still exudes the feeling of power.

At night, the bars and concert halls are alive with entertainment, as are the streets. Sitting along the stone benches on the Prada allows you to watch locals chatting and talking, some dancing just for the joy of being there. Going to a concert is a must, whether it be a symphony or the Tropicana. Just being able to sit in the Gran Theatro or wander the halls of Capitolio, Havana's most distinct landmark, is a privilege.

Once you have explored Old Havana with its Hemingway haunts and Central Havana with its historical National Hotel and revolutionary museum, you will want to walk farther, see more, cross the bay to the fort, and just discover. Lucky for you, Havana is one of the safest cities in the Western world.

Getting Here

■ By Air

 Landing at Havana's modern **José Martí International Airport**, you will find yourself 25 km/16 miles from the center. The cost of a taxi there is $20 convertible pesos. The tourist bus runs $8. However, if you can get three or four people to share a taxi, it will be cheaper and more efficient.

The domestic airport is at the opposite end of the runway to the international one. If you are flying directly to or from another town, you will need to take a taxi to/from the other airport.

> **AUTHOR TIP:** Change money at the airport so that you have some convertible pesos when you get to town and while you look for a bank or money exchange.

You must pay a $25 exit fee upon leaving the country. Do not lose your tourist card or you will have to re-purchase that too, at $25.

■ By Boat

There are two landing marinas near Havana. **The Hemingway Tourist Community**, Calle 248 and Ave 5, Playa Santa Fe, ☎ 7/204-1150, communication radio HF 7472m HVF 16, is a marina with 400 yacht mooring stalls, some of which accommodate larger boats. It offers electricity, fuel, telephone service, satellite TV, medical services, weather information, nautical maps, navel repair and supply shops, beauty salons and a fitness club. There is also a Customs house for those making Havana their port of entry. The Hemingway International Nautical Club, stationed here, has over 1,000 members from 44 countries. They sponsor regattas and fishing tournaments.

Puertosol Tarara Marina, Via Blanca Km 18, Havana Este, ☎ 7/797-1462, communication radio VHF 77, has 56 air-conditioned homes, each with four or five bedrooms. There is a private beach and an International Diving Center. Catamarans, windsurfing equipment, JetSkis, banana boats, and fishing and yachting services are available.

■ By Bus

There are two bus stations, one by the zoological park and another by Revolutionary Plaza. Before you arrive, determine which is closer to where you want to be. The buses stop at both locations and taxis wait for disembarking passengers. Negotiate a price to go into town. From the park it should not be more than $10 and from the plaza station to the center it should not be more than $5.

History

 1514. Havana, named after a local chief, becomes San Cristobal de la Havana village on the Mayabeque River in the south of the country. Five years later, it is moved north to the banks of the Almendares River and then finally to the port where it is located today.

1519. First mass celebrated under a cedar tree at what is now the city center. Apparently, a descendant of that tree grows on the Plaza de Armas.

1533. Pirates and slaves burn down the city. The Castillo de la Fuerza is built for protection and is now the second oldest in the Western world.

1555. Pirate Jacques de Sores attacks Havana.

1586. Castillo del Morro is completed. The fort is built to protect the city from invaders and guards can see a long way out to sea in all directions from the lookouts.

1607. Havana officially becomes the capital of Cuba.

1674. A wall is started around the city to protect it from invasion.

1728. University of San Jeronimo opens in Havana.

1763. England takes Cuba, then trades it with Spain for Florida, which Spain occupied at that time.

1774. Population reaches 73,000 people.

1776. Teatro Principal opens.

1790. The first newspaper, the *Papel Periodico*, is published.

1812. The constitution is inaugurated.

1818. Havana is given permission to trade with any city in the world. Prior to this it was allowed to trade with only seven Spanish cities.

1833. Cuban Academy of Literature is founded.

1837. Railway is built.

1844. Gabriel de la Concepcio Valdes (Placido), a mulatto poet, is executed for his participation in a slave revolt.

1848. Havana gets gas lighting.

1851. Narciso Lopez, an advocate for the union of US and Cuba, is executed in Havana. The telegraph is brought onto the island.

1853. Poet José Martí Perez is born in Havana. Marquis Juan de la Pezuela becomes Captain General of Cuba and frees slaves.

1862. Public transportation is introduced.

1869. Poet José Martí is sentenced to six years in prison for opposing the government.

1873. The last slave ship arrives in Cuba.

1876. Cementario Cristobal Colón is established. It now holds about a million graves.

1890. Electricity and telephones arrive in the city.

1893. A proclamation declaring equal status for blacks is signed.

1895. War of Independence results in Cuba being under the control of the US.

1898. US battleship *Maine* explodes in Havana Harbor.

1902. Cuba becomes a republic and the national flag flies over Havana for the first time.

1904. Alejo Carpentier, a novelist, is born in Havana.

1908. The first black political party, Partido Independiente de Color, is founded in Havana by Evaristo Estenoz.

1910. José Lezama Lima, a writer and editor of numerous literary magazines, is born.

1912. Rene Portocarrero, a painter, is born in El Cerro, Havana.

1920. Alicia Alonso, a ballerina, is born in Havana.

Havana

1928. Julio Antonio Mella leads uprisings against General Gerardo Machado.

1929. Capitolio is built.

1933. Fulgencio Batista becomes president of Cuba.

1950. National Ballet of Cuba is founded by Alicia Alonso.

1952. After losing power, Batista leads a military coup against President Carlos Prio.

1953. Fidel Castro leads a military attack on Moncada Garrison in Santiago de Cuba. Castro is captured and sent to prison.

1954. Students demonstrate in Havana and José Echeverria, comrade of Castro and Guevara's, is seriously wounded.

1955. Castro is released from prison.

1956. The yacht *Granma* lands at Las Coloradas in the east carrying revolutionaries from the US.

1957. The Presidential Palace, occupied by Batista, is attacked by students. It later becomes the Revolutionary Museum.

1959. Fidel Castro overthrows the Batista regime and becomes president.

1961. US attacks Cuba at the Bay of Pigs. Many American prisoners are taken.

1962. The Second Declaration of Havana is delivered in February. Cuba adopts the communist ideology.

1982. Old Havana is declared a World Heritage Site.

1991. Russian aid discontinued.

1998. Hurricane Georges destroys about 100 homes in Old Havana. Pope John Paul II visits.

Services

■ Useful Numbers

National Police: ☎ 7/782-0116

Fire Department: ☎ 7/781-1115

Ambulance: ☎ 7/204-2811

Cardio Vascular Emergency Dept.: ☎ 7/204-2811 or 204-2814

Airport: ☎ 7/745-3133

> **AUTHOR NOTE:** You do not need to dial the city code (7) if you are calling from within Havana.

■ Communications

TELEPHONE: See page 52 for details on calling cards and ETECSA offices. If you go to hotel lobbies to make a call, they will charge you 40 cents for the call. You must pay in dollars (convertibles), but you will receive change in Cuban pesos (worth less than a nickel).

If you need to activate a cell phone, contact **Cubacel Cell Phone Co.**, Calle 28 #510, between Ave 5 and 7, Miramar, ☎ 7/880-2222. The activation fee is $3 and the rates are anywhere from 50-75 cents per minute for use, depending where you are calling to or from.

MAIL: For the most part, mail is reliable. I have sent many parcels to Cuba with almost no problems. Mail sent out of the country takes at least two weeks to arrive at its destination.

There are **post offices** in Old Havana at Calle Obispo and Bernaza and in Vedado at Calle 27 and L, ☎ 7/733-6097. Most hotels have a postal service at the check-in desk.

Havana

COURIER SERVICES: You have two options in town. **Cubanacan Express**, Ave 5 #8210 between Calle 8 and 84, Playa, ☎ 7/733-2331 and **DHL**, Ave 1 and Calle 40, Miramar, ☎ 7/204-1578 or 7/733-1876.

INTERNET ACCESS: Internet services are either state-owned or foreign-owned firms who have special licenses. Telephone Internet service costs the individual $260 convertible pesos per month. Private corporations must pay $600-$800 a month. This cost is passed down to you, the Internet café user and usually runs $3-$6 an hour.

Havana and Varadero have Internet cafés. Access can also be had through some hotels, as well as all the ETECSA telephone offices. They usually sell Internet access cards for $15 (good for five hours), which usually but not always, can be used in any increment you want. These cards are good for most ETECSA offices except in cities like Pinar del Rio or Santiago de Cuba. Without a card, ETECSA charges $8 an hour.

The most convenient place to access the Internet is at Hotel Havana Libre. There are about six machines, each in a separate cubicle so you have privacy. The cost is $9 per hour or $3 for 20 minutes or any portion thereof. This is expensive, but one pays for convenience. The ETECSA office in Havana is on Calle 23 and Ave P.

MUNICIPALITIES

Havana is both a city and a province. The city has just under three million people, 28% of the total population of the country. Of the 19 municipalities in the province, 15 are part of the city of Havana. They are La Habana Vieja, Centro Habana, Plaza de la Revolución, Cerro, Playa, Marianao, La Lisa, Diez de Octubre, Boyeros, Arroyo Naranjo, San Miguel del Padron, Cotorro, Guanabacoa, Regla and Habana del Este.

■ Laundry

 Hotels have laundry service and most *casas* will be able to accommodate a wash and iron for a price. Hotels charge by the item; homes charge by the load. The best way to deal with laundry is to pack plenty of clothes and give them away as they get dirty. Cubans appreciate them – for many, these items are not available. If you plan to wash clothes in the shower, bring soap and a clothesline of sorts.

■ Maps

 Guia de Carreteras is a good map of Cuba's roadways, printed in foldout pages in book form. It gives distances, villages and gas stations. Published by **Havanautos**, it costs $6 and can be purchased only in Cuba. Outside of the country, the most reputable map is put out by the **World Mapping Project**. This map is printed on both sides of waterproofed and rip-proof paper, in full color on a scale of 1:850,000. It features most tourist attractions. Other maps I can recommend are published by **ITMB**, 530 West Broadway, Vancouver, Canada, ☎ 604-879-3621, www.itmb.com, and the Geographical Map of Cuba published by **Geografico General de Cuba** in Havana. It is on a scale of 1:230,000 and was updated in 2003. It sells for about $3 in any bookstore in the downtown area. The same company puts out a good map of Havana that includes city maps of Cayo Coco, Playa Estes and Varadero (basic).

■ Medical Centers

Clinica Cira Garcia, Calle 20 #4101, Miramar, ☎ 7/724-2811. Medicines can be purchased at the Farmacia Internacional at the rear of the clinic. This is a plush clinic catering to foreigners who come for nose jobs and other such procedures, which are said to cost about one-third of the

Havana

cost in the United States. If you become ill, you can go to this clinic.

Hospital Fajardo, Calle Zapata and Ave D, (Plaza de Revolución) Vedado, ☎ 7/755-2452. This is a general hospital.

Instituto Superior de Ciencias Medicas de la Habana, Calle 146 and Ave 31, Playa, ☎ 7/721-8545, www.sld.cu/instituciones/iscmh/index.htm. This is the oldest and largest medical school in the country. It is a teaching hospital, so it may have some up-to-date equipment that other general hospitals do not have.

Frank Pais International Orthopedic Scientific Complex, Ave 51 #19603, La Lisa, ☎ 7/721-7755, is an orthopedic hospital.

Hermanos Amejeiras Clinical Surgical Hospital, San Lazaro #701, Central Havana, ☎ 7/777-6043, is used for those needing surgery.

Julito Diaz Orthopedic Hospital of Rehabilitation, Ave 243 #19815, Fontanar, Boyeros, ☎ 7/745-4857 is another orthopedic hospital.

International Clinic of Playas del Este, Ave las Terrazas #36, Santa Maria del Mar, ☎ 7/797-1032, specializes in helping visitors. You will most likely be able to find someone who speaks your language.

William Soler Cardiocentro del Pediçtrico, Ave San Francisco #10112, corner of Peria in Boyeros, ☎ 7/744-3621, specializes in care for children with heart problems.

Most hospitals have a drugstore attached to them so you can obtain medicines your Cuban physician may prescribe. However, bring any medications you are already taking with you when you come to Cuba as those specific drugs may not be available in the country.

Festivals

In addition to Mother's Day, International Women's Day, Guevara's death and José Martí's birth, and the usual celebrations revolving around revolutionary attacks, Havana has some fun events that you should try to attend. For all festival tickets, see the tour offices in the big hotels.

■ Events & Celebrations

The **Habano Cigar Festival** has been held every February since 1998. It is organized by Habanos S.A, the company that manufactures Habanos cigars. The national non-smoking ban is lifted during this event. Each year the festival specializes in a different aspect of cigar making, selling or history. The organizers bring in well-known artists and dance groups and the closing dinner is a popular event. The organizers have an auction of the best in cigars or equipment; humidors are occasionally signed by Castro and put up to the highest bidder. Part of this festival is held in Pinar del Rio.

International Jazz Festival is held for four days, usually every other year, in early December. It is organized by Chucho Valdes, a famous Cuban pianist, and it includes concerts, jam sessions and a grand concert on closing night. So far, the participating countries are Argentina, Brazil, Canada, Trinidad, the USA, Tobago, Spain, South Africa, England, France, Germany and Japan. Featured stars are people like Kenny Barron, Cedar Walton, Steve Turre and Harry Belafonte. The event is held in many venues around town, such as the Casa de la Cultura, Jazz Club Irakere and Hotel Havana Libre.

The **International Ballet Festival** has been going since 1960 and is one of Cuba's oldest festivals. It takes place in late October/early November and past

Havana

performances have included around 60 of the world's best companies representing 58 different countries. Just sitting in the National Theater watching one of these performances is worth the trip to Cuba.

The annual **International Percussion Festival** (PERCUBA) in April lasts for five days and the concerts take place in the National Theater. Theoretical and practical workshops are offered, as is the opportunity for exchanges, especially between musicians. There are performances in classical, popular and traditional music styles, and exhibitions of instruments. The organizers (PERCUBA) welcome any professionals involved in percussion performances or teaching to join in, but for this the Cuban government charges $50 to soloists and $150 to groups. If you need a pianist, you'll pay an extra $25. The cost to watch/listen is $80 for the four days.

Cubadisco takes place at the end of May each year and is sponsored by record/CD producers. This event attracts performers from around the world, including places as far away as Japan (which was featured in the 2005 event) and Germany. During the opening ceremonies, awards are presented to exceptional musicians or those who have contributed to the world of music in an exceptional way. Winners may be from any country. The presentations are followed by music and more music. Many record companies bring along promotional material about their own music. Most of the events are held in the Theater Auditorium and the cost for spectators is around $100. To enter a performance, the cost is $130-$150. Tickets for performances may be obtained at Havanatur.

The **Havana International Film Festival** has been held every December since 1979. It has given awards to films such as *Strawberry & Chocolate* (Cuba), *Whiskey* (Uruguay), and *Garage Olimpo* (Argentina/France). Visitors can watch up to 200 films made in Latin America and you can be present when the overall winner is announced. This is a must for film lovers.

Visit www.habanafilmfestival.com for exact dates, times, entries and nominations. The International Film and Television School, located in San Antonio de los Baños, has famous people such as Gabriel Garcia Marquez, Francis Ford Coppola and Agnes Varda involved in teaching and administrating. Thousands of students from over 35 countries have come here to study film since its inauguration and some of the films produced have gotten international recognition.

Orientation

Old Havana, a UNESCO World Heritage Site, is the historical center. Alongside old buildings and museums are trendy restaurants.

Vedado. The word means forbidden, but it is not forbidden to you as a visitor. It was originally the greenbelt of Havana, where foliage was left to flourish. This, of course, has since changed as it is now wall-to-wall concrete and a thriving residential area. It also holds hotels, restaurants, clubs (many great jazz clubs) and theaters.

Miramar is a wealthy residential area that also accommodates some of the embassies and consulates, the Karl Marx Theatre and the International Conference Center.

The **Arroyo Naranjo** suburb is now the city's greenbelt – moved out a ways from Vedado. It holds the Botanical Gardens, the National Zoo and Expo-Cuba.

Playas del Este has the closest beaches to Havana. Just a few kilometers from the center, it features hotels, marinas, restaurants and a few residential buildings. The beaches, running west to east, are **Bacuranao**, **Megano**, **Santa Maria del Mar**, **Boca Ciega** and **Guanabo**.

Ave de los Presedentes between Calles 17 and 27 has monuments to presidents and heroes of Latin

America. At Calle 27 is the statue of Major General José Miguel Gómez, president of Cuba between 1909 and 1913. At Calle 23 is a statue of Chilean president Salvador Allende, which was sculpted by Monica Bunster. Between Calles 17 and 19, is a statue of Benito Juarez, who is credited with leading revolts to free Mexico from Spanish rule. He became president of Mexico. The statue was presented to Cuba by a Mexican delegation. The final statue, near Calle 17, is that of Simon Bolivar, the man who is credited with freeing South America from Spanish rule. He became the first president of Bolivia and his statue was presented to Cuba by Hugo Chavez, president of Venezuela, where Bolivar was born.

Prado Promenade, in Old Havana, is a tree-lined street with the promenade running along the center. It is lined with stone benches where you can watch Cuban life unfold. Often there are kids practicing fencing or playing a ball game; musicians will play while other folks snack on a lunch. The marriage center is part-way down this street; often, you can watch a modern Cuban wedding here. This street was built in 1777 and has never lost its popularity.

The **malecón** is a strip of road between the city and ocean. There is a seawall along the malecón where locals sit during nice weather and chat, drink beer, gawk at tourists and enjoy the day (or evening). The malecón starts at the Castle de la Punta and goes west through the city to the Almendares River in Vedado. The tower of La Chorrera is the famous symbol at the end of the road. It was constructed in 1646 as a sentry post used for protection against invaders coming up the river. The malecón as we know it today was completed in 1921. At present, the waters along the malecón are badly polluted, but attempts are being made to clean it up. It is a slow process.

China Town in central Havana has restaurants, Chinese Society groups, businesses and shops dedicated to Chinese culture. First occupied by Chinese workers

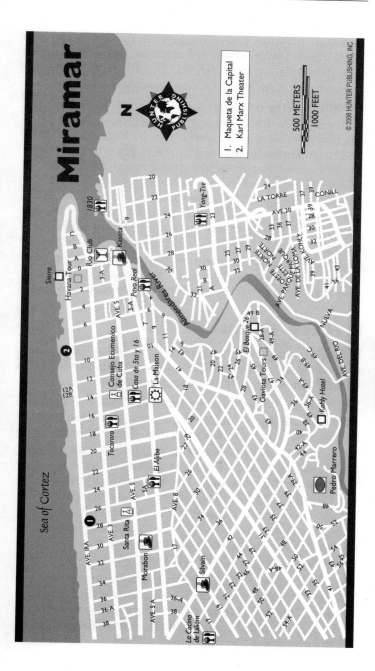

Miramar

N

HUNTER PUBLISHING

1. Maqueta de la Capital
2. Karl Marx Theater

500 METERS
1000 FEET

© 2006 HUNTER PUBLISHING, INC

Sea of Cortez

Havana

Almendares River

Sierra
Rio Club
Kasta
Havana Tour
Poyo Real
Consejo Ecumenico de Cuba
Casa de 5ta y 16
La Maison
Tacororo
Santa Rita
Morabon
El Aljibe
Silvain
La Cocina de Lilliam
Yang-Tse
El Bosque
Gaviota Tours
Kohly Hotel
Pedro Marrero
Nueva
LA TORRE
CONILL
AVE 20
AVE. PARQUE PROA
AVE. DE LA LOMA
OESTE EL NORTE
ESTE NORTE
AVE. DEL RIO

1830
3-A
AVE. 5
5-A
AVE. 5A
AVE. 3
AVE. 1RA
AVE. 5
5-A
AVE. 8
AVE. 5A
AVE. 5
36-A

in 1858, this area saw its high period between the 1930s and 1960s. This splendor is returning again, only this time for the tourists. The Chinese Cemetery is nearby at Ave 26 and Calle Zapata in Vedado.

The **University of Havana** was opened in 1728 in the Convent of Santo Domingo. It was moved to its present site on Colonia Universitaria in Vedado in 1902. The huge stairway leading to the main entrance is often occupied by students doing what students the world over do – exchanging ideas, making romantic dates, listening to music or reading poetry. This is the university that Fidel Castro attended to obtain his degree in law. The last time I was there I was not permitted entrance, so I went around back and found a way in. I am sure if the guard had found me I'd have been thrown in prison for trespassing. However, I am told that visitors can go into the university if they wish.

■ City Tours

Taking a city tour is recommended, to give you an idea of the layout of the city and the most important places to visit.

The **Vaiven Tours** city excursion will take you to the different districts of Havana, the old Hemingway house, the cigar factory and the Gran Theatro. The tour is by bus and dress is casual. Purchase your ticket on the bus. You can get on and off at will – your ticket is good for the day. The bus stops at places like the Capitolio, Revolution Square and University Hill. Tours run daily starting at 9 am and cost about $5 per person; entry tickets to different places of interest or museums are extra. Two places where the bus stops are at Hotel Riviera and Hotel Deauville. ☎ 7/724-3688.

The "Specialized City Tour" from **Havanatour** (see below) is a bit more organized, takes longer and provides a guide. This tour stops at Fort Morro, Plaza de Armas and the Cathredral, and travels down Obispo Street while telling you the important places you are seeing.

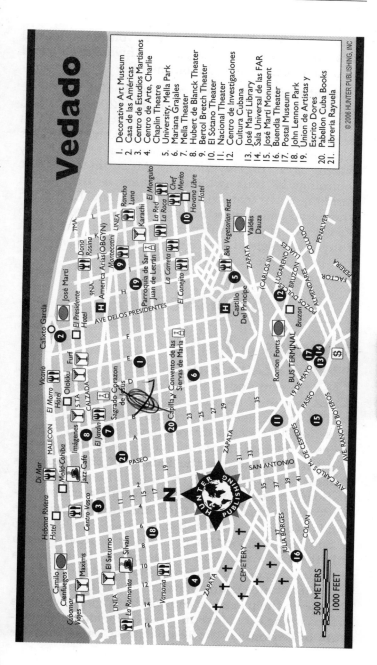

Vedado

1. Decorative Art Museum
2. Casa de las Américas
3. Centro de Estudios Martianos
4. Centro de Arte, Charlie Chaplin Theatre
5. University, Mella Park
6. Mariana Grajales
7. Mella Theater
8. Hubert de Blanck Theater
9. Bertol Bretch Theater
10. El Sótano Theater
11. Nacional Theater
12. Centro de Investigaciones Cultura Cubana
13. José Martí Library
14. Sala Universal de las FAR
15. José Martí Monument
16. Buendia Theater
17. Postal Museum
18. John Lennon Park
19. Union de Artistas y Escrito Dores
20. Pabellon Cuba Books
21. Librería Rayuela

© 2006 HUNTER PUBLISHING, INC

500 METERS
1000 FEET

It stops at the Museum of the Revolution, Central Park, Gran Theatro, the Capitolio, University Hill, and the José Martí Memorial monument.

Havanatour, Calle 1 between Ave 2 and O, in the Edificio Sierra Maestra, Miramar, ☎ 7/204-7541, also offers a city tour with an English-speaking guide. You are picked up at your hotel and taken to various points of interest. They also offer a full- or half-day walking tour of Havana, the Museum tour, the Hemmingway tour (which includes a drink at la Floridita, a bar/eatery), or a Sugarcane Excursion (where you will visit a mill and the Hershey Garden and get part of your transportation by local train). Ask at any of the bigger hotels – the National or Havana Libre – or visit the Havanatour office.

Sightseeing

■ Plazas & Parks

 PLAZA DE ARMAS: This park, on Ave del Puerto and Calle O'Reily, is in Old Havana, south of the malecón but still along the water. This is the oldest square and was a military focal point for Old Havana. It was paved in wood cobblestones at the request of Antonio de Cespedes (see below). On the square is the **Palace of the Captains General**, built between 1776 and 1791, which housed the Spanish governors. Later it became a prison. Today it plays host to the **City Museum**. The palace stands where an old fort, built in 1538 by Hernando de Soto, once stood. There is also the **Real Fuerza** with the famous bronze statue of the La Giraldilla weather vane, one of the most beloved symbols of Havana. Her stance is one of defiance (the Cubans say). The one on the plaza is a copy of the original, which is located in the City Museum. Inside the fort is the **Museum of Ceramics**. The Temple (the Chapel) and the

Santa Isabel Hotel are also on the plaza. **El Temple** was built in 1828 and is in the spot where the first mass was held. That mass took place under a cedar tree (see History section). Inside El Temple is a huge painting by Juan Bautista Vermay, founder of the San Alejandro Academy of Fine Arts. The present tree on the square was planted in 1959 to replace the original that was cut down in 1754 and replaced with a memorial column.

> **AUTHOR NOTE:** Tradition has it that if you can walk around the tree three times without saying anything, you will get a wish granted.

At one side of the tree is the **Carlos Manuel de Cespedes monument**. He was a plantation owner and lawyer, born in 1819 in Bayamo. He is often called the "Father of the Nation" because he started the Ten Years War of Independence against Spain. He issued the famous Grito de Yara from his plantation in 1868, declaring Cuba's independence. He then freed his slaves, led a few more revolts and became head of government for Cuba. He was later deposed by other revolutionaries and, in 1873, caught by the Spanish and executed.

PLAZA DE LA CATEDRAL: Cathedral Plaza, at Calle Empedrado and San Ignacio in Old Havana, is where you will find the city's main cathedral. Inside are paintings by the French artist Juan Bautista Vermay, sculptures and gold works by Italian artist Francesco Bianchini, and frescoes by Guisseppe Perovani. There is also the funerary monument to Christopher Columbus; this is where he was laid in state. Next to the church is the **San Carlos and San Ambrosio Seminary**, which dates to the early 1800s. Construction of the square (and the church) was completed in 1777. The plaza was originally called Zanja Real, or the royal swamp, because it was here that the public bathhouse was located. On the western edge is where a cistern was placed to hold the water. There is a hole in the wall with a commemorative plaque indicating where the water flowed from the area into the sea. In the 18th century, wealthy families built mansions near the square and promenaded on Sundays.

The oldest house on the square, the **House of the Count of Casa Bayona**, has the **Victor Manuel Art Gallery** and the **Museum of Colonial Art**. The house was built in 1720. The Count of Casa Bayona is known for humbling himself before his slaves and inviting them to dinner after he had washed their feet. The slaves took advantage of this and set fire to his mill. As punishment, their heads (separated from their bodies) were placed on spikes along the road.

El Patio restaurant, Calle San Ignacio #54, on the plaza's northwest corner, is in the **House of the Marqueses of Aguas Claras III**, who resided here 1751-1775. The elegant house was built by Antonio Ponce de Leon, a descendent of the first explorer to set foot in Florida. On the plaza's eastern edge is **Casa de Lombillo**, pre-1750. This is where Havana had its first post office; it now holds the Dept of Education.

PLAZA VIEJA: Located on Calle San Ignacio, between Ave Teniente Rey, Mercaderes and Muralla, in Old Havana. On Old Square are the **Photography Library, The Cuban Arts and Crafts Foundation**, and the **Visual Arts Development Center**, all set in the **House of the Count of Jaruco**. Construction of the plaza was started in 1587 and not completed until the mid-1700s. It was originally called the New Square, but its name changed after newer plazas were built. It has also been called the Royal Square, the Major Square, the Vegetable Square, the Juan Bruno Ayas and the Julian Grimau Park. The center of the plaza was once the location of the Mercado de Cristina, named after Queen Cristina of Spain. The market was replaced by a park in 1908 and the underground parking was put in later. The fountain in the center with its four dolphins is made of marble.

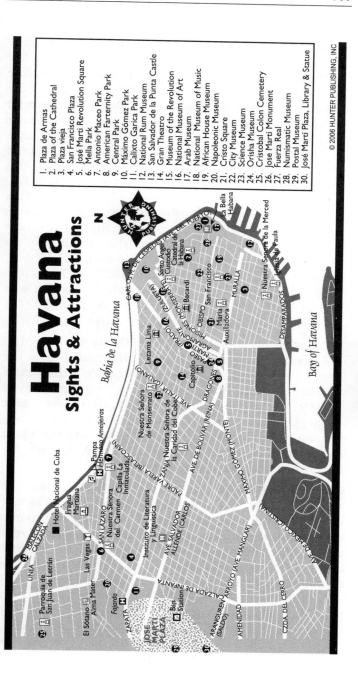

Havana
Sights & Attractions

N

Bahía de la Habana

Bay of Havana

La Bella Habana

1. Plaza de Armas
2. Plaza of the Cathedral
3. Plaza vieja
4. San Francisco Plaza
5. José Martí Revolution Square
6. Mella Park
7. Antonio Maceo Park
8. American Farternity Park
9. Central Park
10. Máximo Gómez Park
11. Calixto Garica Park
12. National Rum Museum
13. San Salvador de la Punta Castle
14. Gran Theatro
15. Museum of the Revolution
16. National Museum of Art
17. Arab Museum
18. National Museum of Music
19. African House Museum
20. Napoleonic Museum
21. Cristo Square
22. City Museum
23. Science Museum
24. Orisha Museum
25. Cristobal Colon Cemetery
26. Jose Martí Monument
27. Fuerza Real
28. Numismatic Museum
29. Postal Museum
30. José Martí Plaza, Library & Statue

© 2006 HUNTER PUBLISHING, INC

Havana

Hotel Nacional de Cuba

HUNTER PUBLISHING

SAN FRANCISCO PLAZA: This plaza, at Calle Oficios and Ave Mutalla, is just two blocks from the Sierra Maestra Terminal where cruise ships dock. The plaza, the second to be built in the city, features the **Convent and Lesser Bascilica of San Francisco de Assisi** (Iglesia y Convento Menor de San Francisco de Asis), built in 1719 and remodeled in a baroque style in 1730. Its bell tower is 125 feet high and inside the church is a Tiffany clock. The church is now used as a concert hall, but inside you can still see the tombs under sections of the floor that were tiled in glass. This church was home to Friar Francisco Solano, who was canonized by the Catholic Church. A figure of Francis of Assisi once stood at the top of the building, but a hurricane that blew through in 1846 took off his head. The rest of the figure was removed. San Francisco Plaza also housed the city's first convent, which was built in 1591 and was a working convent until 1841, at which time it became a military barracks.

Also on this plaza is the **Lonja del Comercio**, the original stock exchange built in 1907 that now houses the foreign film offices. The marble fountain in the center was the first fountain in the city and was carved in1836 by Giuseppe Gaggini of Italy. On the west side of the plaza is a Benetton outlet, one of the first international retail stores in Cuba. At one time the plaza was famous for the San Francisco Festival, when everyone in Havana came to gamble.

CRISTO SQUARE: Set at Calle Brazil and Ave Villegas near the Capitolio, Cristo Square is where Wormald from Graham Green's *Our Man in Havana* was "swallowed up among the pimps and lottery sellers." Today the square isn't the greatest attraction, but its dullness will change with restoration. The **Convent and Church of Good Voyage** (Buen Viaje) was built in 1755 for sailors who needed a place to pray. In 1932 the church was expanded. Check out the monument to Gabriel de la Concepcion Valdes, commonly called Placido, a mulatto poet born in Ha-

*Above: This sign indicates there are rooms for rent;
a similar sign in red means the rooms are for Cubans only.*

Below: Moto-taxis are cheap on gas, although the ride can be uncomfortable.

Above: Fewer old cars are still running because needed parts are not avail...

Opposite: The Capitolio, Havana.

Below: Buses offer comfortable but basic transportation.

THE WHITE POWER 1958

Above: Havana Harbor and maleçon.

Opposite: Casablanca, across the harbor from Havana.

Below: Colorful Havana street.

Above: Housing, Havana.
Opposite: Part of the old city wall that was built in the 1500s.
Below: Fort at Cojimar.
Following page: Monument to Ernest Hemingway, Nobel Prize winner.

vana in 1809. He was quite young when he became famous throughout Latin America as a revolutionary poet. His writings brought him a jail term and then execution, along with 19 of his buddies who were accused of conspiring in the Escalada Conspiracy of 1844.

JOSÉ MARTÍ REVOLUTION SQUARE: This well-known square is surrounded by Ave Boyeros, Ave Manuel de Cespedes and Ave 20 de Mayo. It is dominated by the huge monument (shown at right) to Cuba's National hero, a poet, playwright and activist against colonialism. José Martí was expelled from Cuba at the age of 17 for his actions against the Spanish, but returned eventually to fight for freedom. Obviously, he was better with pen than gun. He died at the age of 42 just moments after entering his first battle. At the base of the monument is a museum dedicated to him and inside are documents and photos commemorating this man's life. As might be expected, all of Martí's writings speak against any type of tyranny or dictatorship and promote freedom of individual thought. Take the elevator to the top of the monument to get a view of the city from its highest vantage point. The National Library and Theater are near the square, as is the Ministry of Information and Communication, which houses the **Postal Museum**, which specializes in stamps of Cuba (see below). The **Palace of the Revolution** (headquarters of the Communist Party) is behind the monument. Across from the square is the bus station and to one side is the huge face of Che Guevara, made of wrought iron and pasted onto the side of a military building. This is a gargantuan open square where many travelers enjoy the flavor of Havana. It has seen the most rallies and

Havana

demonstrations held in support of the revolution, and it's where Castro gives his May Day speech to revitalize the spirit of the revolution. I'd suggest missing that one as Castro's speeches are known to last for hours.

CRISTOBAL COLÓN CEMETERY: Features over a million graves, tombs and mausoleums. At the entrance is a 22.5-meter (75-ft) replica of the Arch de Triumph with the inscription, "The pale death enters both the cabins of the poor and the palaces of kings." The cemetery, at Calle Zapata and Ave 12, Vedado, was designed by Arellano de Loira, a graduate from Madrid's Royal Academy of the Arts. He won a contest run by the Spanish government to build a new cemetery and it became one of the most famous in the world. The place is so big that it is divided into quarters and there are named streets and avenues; street signs allow visitors to find specific graves. This is where photographer Alberto Korda shot the famous photo of Che Guevara with his tam and squinted eyes that is seen on many T-shirts today. There is a $1 entrance fee.

El Cementario, Havana.

MELLA PARK: This park serves as a memorial to Julio Antonio Mella, a dissident born in Havana in 1903 who also became the founder of Cuba's Communist Party. He was assassinated in Mexico in 1929 under the orders of General Gerardo Machado. His ashes are entombed in this park, which is located at Calle San Lazaro, opposite the university's main steps.

ANTONIO MACEO PARK: Here you will see a statue of Major General Antonio Maceo, the *Bronze Titan*, riding his horse. The marble statue was designed by Italian artist Domenico Boni and was erected in 1916. Maceo was a hero in Cuba's fight for independence. He died in San Pedro, Bauta, on December 7, 1896, along with his aide Captain Francisco Gómez Toro. There is another monument to Maceo at the site of his death. The park is on the malecón at Calle San Lazaro. Next to it is the **San Lazaro Fortified Tower** (also called La Chorrera), built in the 16th century so Cubans could detect danger coming up the river.

AMERICAN FRATERNITY PARK: This tiny park has a multi-cultural silk-cotton tree that was planted in 1928 in soil brought from 21 countries with delegates for the Sixth Pan American Conference. There are statues of Simón Bolívar, San Martin (liberator of Argentina, Chile and Peru), Benito Juarez (liberator of Mexico) and Lincoln (liberator of the slaves) on the site. Located on the Prado, Calle Reina and Amistad, behind the Capitolio.

CENTRAL PARK: This is where the old and new parts of Havana are divided. There is another statue of José Martí here, designed by Cuban Vilalta Saavedra. It is the oldest statue of Martí in the city. Cantral Park is on the malecón and Calles M, N, 9 and 11.

MAXIMO GÓMEZ PARK: Located on the malecón and Ave de las Misiones in Old Havana, this park has a statue of Gómez designed by Italian artist Aldo Gamba (1836-1905). It was inaugurated in 1935 on Gómez's birthday, November 18th. Gómez was born in Santo Domingo (Dominican Republic) and at the request of José Martí became the Supreme Commander of the Cuban Liberation Army. Gómez teamed up with Maceo and fought for freedom.

CALIXTO GARCIA PARK: Named after a strategist who worked during the struggles for independence between 1868 and 1898, this park is on the malecón at Calle G, in Vedado. The statue of Garcia on a horse stands 30 feet high and was designed by Americans Felix W de Weldon (sculptor) and Albert Peets (architect) in 1959. In the center of the square is a five-pointed star made of black granite with a pedestal holding the country's coat of arms.

GARCIA HISTORY

Garcia's grandfather was the first in the family to choose a military life. He fought as an officer in the Spanish army at the Battle of Carabobo in Venezuela in 1821. He later took exile in Cuba and was imprisoned for demanding freedom for slaves there. The younger Garcia followed his grandfather's desire for fairness and freedom but fought against the Spanish from 1868 to 1898. After the war he moved to Washington and died at the age of 59. He was buried in Arlington Cemetery.

JOHN LENNON PARK: This became a gathering place for rock and Beatles fans, so it was dedicated to one of the Beatles, John Lennon. The statue of Lennon, sitting on a park bench with his arm over the backrest, was designed by Cuban artist, José Villa. The park, located along Calles 17, 15, 6 and 8 in Vedado, was opened in December of 2000.

LENIN PARK: Calle 100 and Ave Cortina de la Presa Arroyo Naranjo, ☎ 7/744-2722. This nice 1,700-acre park has a plethora of things to do, like swimming, visiting the art gallery, drinking rum or eating at the restaurant. The outdoor stage often has live entertainment. At the entrance is a huge arch with a larger-than-life carving of Lenin. There is also a riding school, ☎ 7/744-1058, where you can rent horses.

Baragua Swimming Pool, ☎ 7/797-4221, and Reinaldo **Paseiro Cycling Track**, ☎ 7/797-3776, Ave Monumental Km 4.5, Villa Panamericana, Havana del Este, is an Olympic-size pool that accommodates swimming meets, Olympic diving, water polo and synchronized swimming. It has sidewalls made of glass so that synchronized swimming can be watched from the bleachers below water level. The cycling track is home to Havana's team, which races in the Vuelta, a five-day endurance race held in stages around the province of Havana. Stage 1 goes 120 km/75 miles around Guayaba, while another stage has 18 six-km/four-mile laps and a one-km/.6-mile uphill climb. The other big race in Cuba is the Tour de Cuba. Call ☎ 7/797-2121 if you are interested in any of the racing events There are also tennis courts available.

■ Forts

Fuerza Real on the Plaza de Armas, Ave del Puerto and Calle O'Reily, is south of the malecón at the entrance to the bay. Built between 1558 and 1578, it was the city's first fort used for strategic purposes. The need for protection was realized in 1538, when locals watched as two French pirate ships came into the harbor, burned the palm-thatched huts and demanded 600-ducat ransom before they would leave. They sailed away with the Spanish ships in hot pursuit, but the Spanish flubbed that chase and the French returned to loot and pillage again. The result of this fiasco was the building of the fort. The first one, built in haste, protected only the seaward side of the city. Pirates soon spread the word that Havana was easy to enter and rob from the back. One such pirate was Jacques Sores who came to Havana in 1555 and for a month robbed, killed and burned everything in sight. Finally, King Felipe II of Spain ordered the fort to be rebuilt so that it could truly defend the city. The fort protected many governors living within its walls before the Palace of the Captains General was built. On its northwest corner is a statue of a woman showing a bit of leg. She is called La Giraldilla and she represents Doña Isabel de Bobadilla, wife of Governor de Soto. He died on the banks of the Mississippi River, and she is supposed to be looking out to sea for her husband's return.

El Castillo del Morro was built between 1589 and 1610 and guards Havana's harbor. It was considered the optimum in security, but the British tore this myth down in 1762 when they sailed past the fort undetected and entered Havana from the east. The **Bacuranao Tower**, built where the Bacuranao River enters the Caribbean, is where the British hit shore back in 1762. The fort next to El Morro, called **San Carlos de la Cabaña**, was constructed as added protection after the British left. The lighthouse at the point was built in the 1900s and is still used today to guide sailors into the harbor. The fort is open daily, 9 am until late. You should time your visit to see the changing of the guard, the firing of the canon, and the raising of the chain across the mouth of the bay. The cannon announces the closing of the city's gates for the night. If you go around 6 or 7 pm, you will have time to visit the shops, and tour the buildings and museum before getting a good vantage point from which to see the events. After the firing of the cannon (*cañonazo*), a band often plays in the parade grounds and young and old dance together until the guards decide it is time for everyone to leave. This is usually before 11 pm. It is amazing to sit on the walls of the fort or on the rocks below at the entrance to the bay and watch the activities of the harbor.

Castillo de San Salvador de la Punta is across the bay from El Morro and along the malecón where the tunnel is located. This was supposed to do what El Morro and San Carlos forts eventually did – protect the city from invasion. This fort was built between 1590 and 1600. Little remains of the fort. Shortly after it was completed, the city erected a protective stone wall around its center because the fort itself did not offer enough protection. As the city grew, the walls were torn down and today, only a few corner and sentry posts can be located.

■ Museums

 There are far more museums in Havana than those I have listed here. There are museums dedicated to things like playing cards, history of perfume or Islamic influences. If you would like to explore more museums, visit one of the tourist offices (see page 132) and get a complete list. All in all, there are 289 museums in Cuba, 68 of them dedicated to history, 14 to art, seven to science and technology and four to archeology. There is bound to be something for almost everyone.

MUSEUM FEES

The cost of entry to any museum in Havana is, unless otherwise stated, between $1 and $5. Taking photos will cost an extra $1-$3 for still cameras and $5-$10 for videos. Locals pay the equivalent in pesos.

MONEY SAVER: *Occasionally, locals will purchase your ticket in pesos and split the difference. Since pesos are worth so little, that means you get the entry ticket for just over half-price.*

AUTHOR'S PICK

El Capitolio, Paseo del Prado in Central Havana, is not actually a museum even though walking through it is like visiting a museum. You must leave your daypack at the counter. The building is open 10 am to 4 pm and is a replica of the Capitol Building in Washington, DC. Before the revolution it was used to hold sessions of the senate and the legislative assembly. El Capitolio was constructed in 1929 as the parliament building. Outside, a majestic stairway made of granite and bordered by two bronze statues was designed by Zanelli. The steps lead to two impressive bronze doors with 60 bas-relief images portraying important events in Cuban history. The main hall, known as the Lost Steps Hall, features two important pieces. The first is a diamond, inlaid into marble, which once belonged to King Alexander of Russia. This diamond marks point zero from which all distances are measured in Cuba. The second important piece, standing under the main dome of the building in the central axis, is the second-largest bronze statue in the world under cover. The statue was built in Rome by the Italian sculptor, Angelo Zanelli, and shows a young woman with a helmet and a spear. She stands 142 meters/465 feet high,

weights 49 tons and is covered in 22-karat gold leaf. Above her, on the roof, is the national coat of arms with the six provinces that originally formed the country. Continue walking along the main halls and peer into a few of the side chambers. Eventually, you will find an gallery where high-quality artworks can be purchased. El Capitolio is a very impressive place and a must-see while you are in the city.

MONEY SAVER: *If you wish to return to El Capitolito and shop at a later date, keep your entry ticket and you will not have to pay again.*

Façade of the Gran Theatro.

Havana

Gran Theatro, Paseo del Prado, across from the Capitolio, costs $2 to enter and this includes a guide, though our guide knew little about the building, which was in shambles. Watch your step as the floorboards are rotting in some rooms. When the theater was built in 1838 it was quite beautiful. Some of the items in the main halls are still spectacular, but need care and repair. Artists who are anxious to sell their wares have taken over some areas. Although I love this building from the outside, I would only go inside again if I had tickets to a performance. Ask at the Tourist Office or check the notices outside the building for details on current performances.

AUTHOR'S PICK

Museum of the Revolution, Calle Refugio 1, between Calle Monserrate and Calle Zulueta in Old Havana, ☎ 7/ 762-4091, is open Tuesday to Saturday, 1 pm to 6 pm and Sunday, 10 am to 1 pm. It is in the old presidential palace that was occupied by Batista when the country was overtaken by Castro. Three floors feature items salvaged from the revolution, with everything from Guevara's hair to blown-apart water canteens. Many revolutionary documents have been preserved and become tedious reading after a few hours. There is a bigger-than-life caricature of three important rulers; Batista as a Nazi, George W Bush dressed as Caesar, and Regan as a cowboy. Across from the museum is the *Granma* Memorial, which holds the boat in which Castro and 80 of his buddies returned to Cuba from exile so they could continue the struggle for control of the country. The boat can be seen through the windows from the museum or you can enter the memorial building and see it up close.

National Museum of Art, Calle Trocadero between Zulueta and Monserrate, ☎ 7/761-1864, is open Tuesday to Saturday, 9 am to 5 pm, and Sunday, 9 am to 1 pm. The collections are located in two buildings: the Palace of Fine Arts, which contains Cuban works from colonial times to the present; and the Austrian Center, which has international art ranging from early Greek, Roman and Egyptian pieces to European paintings and Asian silk works. Pre-arranged guided tours are available, and a gift shop sells books, art reproductions, postcards and silk-screen prints.

Arab Museum, Calle Oficios between Obispo and Obrapia in Old Havana, ☎ 7/861-5868, is open Tuesday to Saturday, 2:30 pm to 10 pm, and Sunday, 9 am to 1 pm. This is the only place in Havana where those of the Islamic faith can pray. A Koran is available for study. The rest of the museum is dedicated to a collection of pieces dating back to the nomads of the Sahara Desert up to the Moorish art that was popular in Spain before the 1600s. Probably what happened was the Spanish got rid of the Moors and then wanted to get rid of the old art, so they sent it over to the New World with the explorers and early colonists. Some of the hand-made inlaid pieces are exceptional.

Numismatic Museum, Calle Oficios #8 between Obispo and Obrapia in Old Havana, ☎ 7/761-5857, is open Tuesday to Saturday, 1 pm to 8 pm, and Sunday, 9 am to 1 pm. It holds coins from as early as the 1600s, war medals, notes, vouchers, lottery tickets and things like coupons that were handed out to sugar-mill workers in place of money. There are about 1,500 pieces in all, a few of which are solid gold. Some items are from Europe and South America.

Hemingway Museum, Finca La Vigia, San Francisco de Paula, ☎ 7/791-0809 or 7/733-5335, is open Wednesday to Saturday, 9 am to 4 pm, and Sunday, 9 am to 1 pm. It is not open during rainy season. There is a $3 entry fee. This museum is in the country house that Hemingway occupied during his stay in Cuba. The house has some of the mounted animal heads of which the writer was so proud. They stare down at his books, typewriter and ice bucket that was always near the whiskey/rum bottle. Also here are documents and photos, furniture and souvenirs that Hemingway treasured. To get here, take city bus M-7 from Calle Industrias between Ave Bolívar and Dragones.

National Museum of Music, Calle Carcel #1, between Aguilar and Habana in Old Havana, ☎ 7/761-9846, is open Tuesday to Saturday, 10 am to 6 pm, and Sunday, 9 am to noon. This museum has some unique and rare instruments, sheet music, records and music-related items dating as far back as the 16th century. The library here has books and magazines specializing in music.

African House Museum, Calle Obrapia #157, between Mercaderes and San Ignacio in Old Havana, ☎ 7/861-5798, open Tuesday to Saturday, 2:30 pm to 6:30 pm, and Sunday, 9 am to 1 pm. This is not only a museum with items from 26 different African countries, but also a research center where those studying African culture, especially Afro-Cuban history, can

Havana

bring their works for critique and display. The museum has pieces from Castro's personal collection.

Ethnographic Museum (House of Fredi) in Pueblo de Madruga, La Havana (55 km/34 miles southeast on the main highway), is for those interested in the Santeria religion practiced first by African slaves. The museum is in a temple where priests initiate those wanting to become followers. On September 12th, the village holds a procession of priests and believers that is colorful and tons of fun. Music, of course, is the big draw. This is considered a spiritual place and quiet respect for the religion is expected. The museum is open daily, 9 am to 5 pm, and is full of sacred objects that include necklaces, bracelets and altar pieces, some of which are said to hold the power of early priests.

Postal Museum, Ave Rancho Boyeros, between Calle 19 de Mayo and 20 de Mayo, Plaza de Revolución, ☎ 7/770-5043, is open Monday to Friday, 10 am to 5 pm. The big draw is the "one-penny black," the first postage stamp used in Cuba. This was in 1840. The museum also has ledgers and cancellation stamps. A shop here sells stamps and other philatelic accessories.

Museum of Sciences, Calle Cuba #460, between Ave Amargura and Brasil in Old Havana, ☎ 7/763-4824, Monday to Saturday, 8 to 11:30 am and 1:30 to 5 pm. This museum is named after the Cuban doctor, Carlos Finlay, who discovered the cause of yellow fever. There is a 19th-century pharmacy and laboratory, personal belongings of the doctor's and a library with over 9,500 books. Among the collections is the printed speech given by Einstein when he visited Cuba. Opened in 1874, this was Cuba's first museum.

The Orisha Museum, Paseo del Prado #615 between Ave Monte and Dragones, Old Havana, ☎ 7/763-5993, (call for hours). This fairly new museum holds 32 terra cotta deities from the Yoruba region's Orisha sect, a group of African slaves from Benin and Nigeria. Each image has a description of its religious significance.

National Rum Museum, Ave del Puerto #262, on the corner of Calle Sol in Old Havana, ☎ 7/761-8051, no admission charge. Watch the magic of the sugarcane juice turn into something worth drinking. The Havana Club Rum distillery was built in 1919, and rumors abound that people like Al Capone visited. The tour starts with the making of rum barrels. It continues with the pressing of the cane, the fermentation process and the filtering systems used, finally ending with the blending of different rums. The on-site shop sells the finished products.

Museum of Decorative Arts, Calle 17 #502 between Ave D and E, in Vedado, ☎ 7/732-0924, is open Tuesday to Saturday, 11 am to 6:30 pm, and Sunday, 9 am to 1 pm. It is housed in a colonial mansion previously owned by Countess of Revilia de Camargo. The most impressive of the treasures are Wedgewood, Meissen and Sevres porcelain pieces that sit beside valuable and unique cut crystals. A writing set that once belonged to Marie Antoinette is displayed. Inlaid cabinets and brocade-upholstered furniture pieces are all decorated with oriental ceramics. The most valued piece is a handmade rug woven in 1772 by Francis Carolus Romanus.

Napoleonic Museum, Calle San Miguel #1159 and Ave Ronda in Central Havana, ☎ 7/779-1460, is open Monday to Friday, 9 am to noon and 1 to 4 pm, and alternate Saturdays, 9 am to noon and 1 to 4 pm. This is considered the most complete collection of objects of war, art or personal belongings of Napoleon Bonaparte outside of France. It is all housed in an old Venetian-style house and exhibits are displayed in chronological order. Three paintings of note are the *Bonaparte in the Bois de Boulogne, Return from the Island of Elba* and the *Battle of Waterloo*. I thought the death mask of Bonaparte, brought here by the doctor who attended him, was most interesting. The collection was purchased by a Cuban politician, Orestes Ferrara, and is housed in Ferrara's old mansion.

Havana

City Museum, Tacon #1, between Ave Obispo and O'Reilly, Palace of the Captains General, Old Havana, ☎ 7/761-2876, open from Tuesday to Saturday, from 11:30 am to 5 pm, and Sunday, from 9 am to noon. This museum is housed in the original Governors' Palace that was built in 1791. The palace was the seat of power until 1898 and later became City Hall, where the City Governors held office. The museum protects many of the city's original treasures, while reproductions are left at the original sites. A good example of this is the weathervane that is the symbol of the city. The Flag Hall has the original flag flown in Cuba for the first time in Cardenas by Manuel de Cespedes in 1868. There is also a large collection of art.

■ Leisure Clubs

Havana Golf Club (called Diplo Club), Carretera de Vento, Km 8, Capdevila, Boyeros, ☎ 7/733-8820 or 8918, has a nine-hole, par 35 golf course, five tennis courts, a racquetball court, a bowling alley, billiard tables, a swimming pool and video games. There is also a restaurant and souvenir shop on site. The club is open Tuesday to Saturday. Clubs and caddies are available.

Habana Club, Ave 5 between Calle 188 and 192, Reparto Flores Playa, ☎ 7/204-7500 or 3300. There is a marina, a sports club, dining and bar facilities, and a pool. The main building was built in 1928 as the Havana Biltmore Yacht Club. In the clubhouse are photos of the club when it was patronized by the Cuban bourgeoisie prior to the revolution. A bit of irony? Today it seems to be doing much the same thing, with a fitness center, gym, sauna, games room, day care and other bourgeois entertainment. If this is above your budget, at least poke around, maybe use the Internet and get a feel of Cuban high society before Castro.

Almendares Club, Calle 49C and the corner of 28A, Reparto Kohly, Playa, ☎ 7/204-4990 or 5162, is accessible by public transportation. Located on the River Almendares, there is a pool, mini-golf, souvenir shop and restaurant serving reasonably priced meals. This club is known for its historic role in Cuban baseball when members played against the members of Habana Club. The most famous game occurred in 1947, when the entire country stopped to listen or watch or argue as to who should/would win. There was dancing in the streets and many fist fights, some fans even moved to shooting rival fans.

BASEBALL HEROES

Baseball was first introduced to Cuba in 1864 by an American-educated youngster named Nemesio Guillot. He brought the rules of the game along with some equipment when he returned to Cuba, and the fever started. By 1871, Steve Bellan was so good he could play third or second base along with the outfield and he quickly became the first Latin American major league player. By 1874, the first organized tournament was played in Matanzas when Havana beat out that town with a score of 51 to nine. Yikes!! By 1878, Havana had its first league, making it the second-oldest professional baseball organization in the world. (The oldest is the National Baseball League in the US.) Today there are about 2,000 baseball fields in the country.

Adventures in Nature

National Aquarium of Cuba, Ave 3 #4508, and Calle 62 in Playa, ☎ 7/203-6401, has about 70 saltwater species from the Caribbean Sea and the Gulf of Mexico living mostly in tanks. See such things as corals, turtles, eels, seahorses and lobsters. When I was there, I watched a lobster eat the shell of his tank mate. (He probably ate the mate before I got there.) An entertaining dolphin show is performed three times a day. You can watch it from below water level through the glass tank. This visit should not take longer than two hours, one for the show and one for poking around.

The **Botanical Gardens**, Ave 5 and 68, Miramar, ☎ 7/754-9170, is set on 1,500 acres and houses 4,000 different plant species, including 500 orchids. The Japanese garden was designed by Yoshikuni Araki in 1989. The first botanical garden in Havana (now moved) was at Fraternity Park; it was opened in 1817 under the care of José Antonio de la Ossa. He worked at the park for seven years, collecting and caring for many species. When Castro realized the value of some endemic plants found on his island, the new gardens were opened and more plants added. There is a waterfall, small lake, cafeteria and washrooms.

Adventures on Water

■ Scuba Diving

 Cuba has 40 diving centers that employ about 150 certified guides. All offer trips to numerous sites.

POPULAR DIVE DESTINATIONS

The main destinations are in Havana, Varadero, Isla Juventud, Maria la Gorda, Trinidad, Santiago de Cuba, Cayo Levisa, Cayo Largo, Jardines de la Reina, Cayo Coco and Cienfuego.

Shelves step down from the northern shores of the island into the Atlantic to depths of more than 35 meters/115 feet. Each depth offers different challenges for the diver, and diving schools can teach the skills needed to go deeper. All divers must carry their PADI (or equivalent) cards with them.

From Havana, 72 sites are accessible along 100 km/ 65 miles of Cuba's northern shore. Good diving areas reach out about three km/two miles from shore. There are sunken ships and flower and brain coral along this stretch. Blue chromis, squirrelfish, blackbar soldierfish, grunts, jeniguanos and tangs are among the more common fish found closer to land. Farther out you will find turtle, nurse shark, blue marlin, tuna and swordfish. The most popular diving areas are **Playa el Salado**, which has 15 diving sites; Havana, where there are 23; **Tarara**, where there are 16; and **Puerto Escondido**, where there are seven. The area from Mariel to Puerto Escondido is considered the best of the best. All of these areas can be reached during a day-trip from Havana.

Scuba Outfitters

Scuba Diving Center, Ave 7 #4403 between Calle 44 and 46, Miramar, ☎ 7/202-1075, hola@habanasol. com, is operated by Eva Martínez and Ernesto Travieso. They offer professional diving trips with certified divers to depths of 35 meters/125 feet. Shipwrecks, small coral reefs, caves and tropical fish are among the highlights found in these 24°C/75°F waters. The boats take eight divers at a time and all equipment is included in the price. The company offers courses for beginners and advanced divers. The cost of a single, one-tank dive in Miramar is $25; two dives at La Aguja site in the Hemingway Marina is $65. The second trip includes tanks; other equipment can be rented.

Caribbean Diving Center, Casa #4, Marina Tarara Habana del Este, ☎ 7/796-0201, www.caribscuba. com, offers everything from three-hour dives to liveaboard trips lasting a week. They also run snorkeling or fishing trips. You can select from 15 sites near Havana and the company supplies all equipment.

La Aguja Scuba Diving Center, Residencial Turistico Hemingway, Ave 5 and Calle 248, Santa Fe Playa, Havana, ☎ 7/729-7201, has boats that can take eight divers and offers a choice of 30 sites. They will go to a maximum depth of 35 meters (125 feet) and do both day and night dives. They also offer courses by instructors who have CMAS, ACUC and IDEA certificates. Rates include all equipment.

■ Trips on the Canimar River

 A Canimar River trip goes through an estuary where birding is good. It heads to an area where snorkeling is fairly good.

If kayaking is your thing, talk to **Gap Adventures** (page 77) about their 10-day kayaking trip that includes this river. **Travel2Cuba**, Ave 5 #6604, ☎ 7/204-2489, also offers this trip for a full eight-hour day for $45 per person with a minimum of four people.

Adventures on Foot

■ Hiking

 The **Hemingway Trail** could be a two-day excursion – one day to Cojimar (the setting for *The Old Man and the Sea)* and the other to Finca La Vigia in San Francisco de Paula, now the Hemingway Museum (page 121). Start in the morning at El Floridita on Calle Obispo, Old Havana and have your photo taken with a daiquiri in hand, sitting on the stool in front of the Hemingway photo. Old Papa is given credit for making this drink known to the world.

From there, visit Hotel Ambos Mundos, 5th floor, where there is a room (often closed but insist on seeing it) where Hemingway stayed. Often, during the mornings, he wrote there. If it is lunchtime, head over to the Cathedral and go to La Bodequita del Medio for a fried pork lunch with yucca and a mojito. Hemingway used to say, *Mi daiquiri in El Floridita y mi mojito in La Bodequita,* which loosely translates to, "I'll have my daiquiri at El Floridita and my mojito at La Bodequita."

Now hop on a bus near the tunnel and head out to Cojimar, where Hemingway used to park the *Pilar*, his fishing boat in which he used to take people looking for marlin. In fact, a marlin tournament named in his honor is hosted by the Hemingway Marina in Havana (Ave 5TA and Calle 248, Santa Fe, ☎ 7/724-1707). You can visit La Terraza in Cojimar where Gregorio, the hero from *The Old Man and the Sea,* used to get free coffee, and later, $10 from tourists wanting his autograph.

> **MONEY SAVER:** *I suggest eating at the little place across the street and just watching the action at La Terraza because their prices are so outrageous.*

As you walk in or out of Cojimar you'll see a small park with a bust of Hemingway across from the ruins of the fort. The park has seen better days. Return to your hotel in Havana and flop. The Hemingway trail takes a full day and, if you act like him, lots of drinks.

The second day could start like the first with a daiquiri followed with a mojito and then a bus out to La Vigia Ranch in San Francisco de Paula. This is where Hemingway did most of his writing. There is a refreshment bar at the ranch where you can have another mojito or daiquiri. Return to your hotel and take an aspirin and read *The Old Man and the Sea.* (I found the story dragged when Gregorio was in the ocean trying to get back to shore. In the opinion of this humble travel writer, Hemingway needed to cut even more than he did.)

To get to Finca la Vigia, take bus M-7 from Calle Industrias between Ave Bolívar and Dragones. To get to Cojimar, take bus number 58 from Ave Independencia and Calle Bruzon.

Havana

Casablanca is across the harbor where the huge statue of Christ, visible from many places in Havana, is located. Take a ferry from the docks in Old Havana. On the opposite side, walk up the steps and then follow the road to your left even farther up the hill. The only reason to come here (besides paying homage to Christ) would be for the view of Havana.

Cultural Adventures

■ Learning Spanish

Speaking Spanish is essential if you are going to get anything out of the country other than smoking cigars, drinking rum and dancing the salsa at a tourist resort. Taking language courses in Cuba is possible. However, you should know that Cubans speak very quickly and they don't always finish their words. For example, I say, *mas o menas*, while most Cubans will say, *ma ho men* to mean the same thing. So finding teachers who speak clearly and slowly is crucial, especially for the beginner.

Language courses in Cuba are expensive; often four or five times more than the same thing in Guatemala or Bolivia. However, if you decide to take a course while here, you will be forced to speak the language all the time, which is an advantage. There is very little English out of the main tourist centers. If learning in Guatemala or Bolivia, you will find a lot of English spoken throughout the country, so you may not be forced to practice your Spanish.

My advice is to book lessons for only one week. Take a room with a family that will give partial board (breakfast and supper) and be prepared to move on if you are unhappy. Paying for two or three weeks means you are stuck, even if you are unhappy with either the school or the host family.

Language Schools

Language Courses Abroad Ltd, 67 Ashby Road, Loughborough, Leics, LE11 3AA, England, ☎ 01509-211612, www.languagesabroad.co.uk/cuba.html, offers courses for one or more weeks. You stay with a host family that provides food and a private bedroom. Courses costs between $773 and $1,174 for one week; between $1,229 and $1,612 for two. This school offers many options. If you have the 20 lessons per week plus five extra private lessons, the cost increases to $1,248 for one week and $1,718 for two. They also offer things like music or dance lessons, field trips, and cultural events. The cost to register is $71 per person and students must be 18 years old or more.

Learn Spanish in Havana, 413 Ontario St, Toronto, Ontario M5A 2V9, Canada, ☎ 800-219-9924, http:// study spanishincuba.com. The school is in Miramar and students stay in Hotel Residence, which has a pool, private beach, restaurants, bars, games room, Internet access and medical care available. Some of the cost depends on whether you share a room. There are usually no more than eight students in each class and a lesson lasts just under an hour. There is free transportation from the hotel to the school. Classes run Monday to Friday; all start on Monday, and you are expected to arrive on Sunday so that you are ready to work the next morning. Your accommodations are booked from Sunday to Saturday and the package, excluding meals, airport pick up, entertainment and laundry, is $525 to $650 per week, depending on the options. The school operates all year. Minors (those under 18) must have a waver signed by their parents; the school does not take anyone under age 16. There is a $200 non-refundable deposit required at registration.

ENFOREX (no address; they are based in Spain), ☎ 866-607-7246, www.enforex.com, offers courses throughout the Spanish-speaking world. The advantage of studying with them is that you can transfer your course work from one country to another as you

Havana

travel and as your language develops you will be promoted according to their lesson plans. The usual program is four hours of study a day, five days a week, in classes of fewer than five people. They offer home-stay programs. A $100 process fee includes your placement test. This fee is paid only once per year, which means that if you travel from Cuba to another country within the same year, your second, third etc. placement is included. The courses run around $350 (20 hours) to $475 (30 hours) per week and rooms cost $245 for a single and $315 for a double per week.

Tour Operators

 Cuban tourist services are operated similarly to those in any country. You talk to the operator, decide on your trip and let them look after the details. Some specialize in transportation, some in hotels and others in events. Look around. With the following operators, I try to include a website so you can see for yourself what they seem to offer. Note that I say "seem." Be careful. Your best bet is to take the recommendations of someone whom you know. I have used some of Cuba's tour operators and have never been disappointed. For the most part, the workers are polite and helpful and eager to show you their country. Cuba also has tour operators for special groups such as a sports team, tourist operators, business groups or those wanting to invest in Cuba. For those specialized operators, contact Infotur (below).

■ Specialty & General Outfitters

 Infotur, Calle 5 and 112, Miramar, ☎ 7/204-7036; Calle 28 #303, between 3 and 5, Miramar, ☎ 7/204-0624; Ave Obispo between Calle Bernaza and Villegas in Old Havana, ☎ 7/

863-4586; at the cruise terminal on Ave del Puerto, Old Havana (no phone); or at either airport terminal. The airport offices are in service to give you information, help you rent a car or book accommodation. You can also purchase books on Cuba and postcards, CDs or videos, posters and maps from them. The convenience of this company is that the workers can speak English – if you need information and your Spanish is rusty or nonexistent, they are a good resource. The offices are open daily from 8:30 am to 8:30 pm except for the airport, which is open 24 hours a day.

Cubamar Viajes, Calle 3 between the malecón and Ave 12, Vedado, ☎ 7/866-2523, www.cubamarviajes. cu, offers cycling, birding and camping trips (some with small motor homes) around the country. They stay in Cuba's rendition of a campsite, which to me is first rate (see page 73). These campsites include a small cabin with private bath and a swimming pool in the main areas. This is a far cry from camping in North America, which usually means a tent.

Gaviota Tours, Ave 47 #2833, Kohly, ☎ 7/204-5708, www.cuba.tc/gaviota/gaviotatours.html, offers city tours for groups or individuals. Group costs can be as low as $18 for an all-day tour; if you want the tour to yourself, you'll pay as much as $40. Gaviota also has tours to Viñales, Guama, Varadero, and Cañonazo (Fort Morro) or a Hemingway tour complete with drinks. An overnight to Cienfuego and Trinidad will run around $129. Gaviota does a good job, especially in the transporting of passengers.

Havanatur, Calle 1, between 2 and 0, Edificio Sierra Maestra, Miramar, ☎ 7/204-7541, or Calle 23, corner of Ave M, Vedado, ☎ 7/755-4082, www.cuba.tc/ havanatur.html, can arrange trips to some of the cays and beaches, book hotel rooms (three- to five-star) in places like Cienfuegos or Trinidad, rent cars and confirm flights. From places like Isla de Juventud or Varadero, Havanatur can also arrange diving trips or catamaran rides.

Havana

Where to Stay

 Hotels and *casas particulares* vary in price; some hotels are as cheap as *casas* and some *casas* are more expensive than cheap hotels. *Casas* require that you interact some with your host family, while hotels give you privacy. All-inclusive resorts keep you from having much contact with Cuban people. There is everything available to satisfy almost everyone's vision of a good place to stay.

Some hotels have an inviting entrance and the image on the Web makes booking a must, but be careful. Rooms can be horrid and in low-class, trashy joints. If you are booking on your own, make reservations for only a few days so that you have the option of changing. Most rooms in *casas* are clean and comfortable. Some even have air conditioning, and almost all include breakfast.

Cuba likes to push all-inclusive resort vacations. If this is your choice, I strongly suggest you get out and explore the island and Havana. The people are friendly, the cities are safe and there are fun places to visit.

I have reviewed establishments of all types, but I have not by any means included all the places because the list is far too long. Havana has something like 75 hotels and just as many *casas particulares*. Ask friends or people you meet while in Cuba where they are staying, what they are paying and how much they

PRICE CHART
Per room for two people, per day.
$ . . . . $25-$50
$$ . . . . $51-$75
$$$ . . . . . $76-$100
$$$$ . . . $101-$150
$$$$$ . . Over $150

are getting in the way of services and comfort. I highly recommend *casas particulares*. They are not the Hyatt by any imagination, but they are interesting, safe and fun. Often, they cost a quarter of the price of a hotel room. You will also find the *casas* to be far more accurate accountants when it comes to billing. Finally, if you really want to explore off the track, some places have only *casas*.

THINGS TO NOTE

- Don't call **long distance** from your room. The cost, even if you don't make a connection, is around $4 per minute. If you do make a connection, even the ringing of the line is charged for.

- Check all your **bills**. Cubans are famous for charging for things not considered part of the package. For example, although many rooms have safes, they often cost extra if they are used. Some restaurants have bathroom services where you must pay for your toilet paper (even if you don't use it). Always check your restaurant bills because you will seldom receive one that is accurate. Until Cubans are taken to task for this practice, it will continue to be a problem.

- Be aware that a *jinatero* (hawker selling, mostly, hotel rooms) may follow you to a room and, once you take it, demand the commission even though they did nothing to earn it. The last time I was in Cuba they were so bad they looked like they were collecting protection fees reminiscent of the old Capone days. The *casa* owners seemed too scared to do anything about it. One thing that can be done is telephone the *casa* ahead of time and agree on a price. That way, all the *jinateros* in the country can follow you but they won't get paid.

Havana

Havana
Places to Stay & Eat

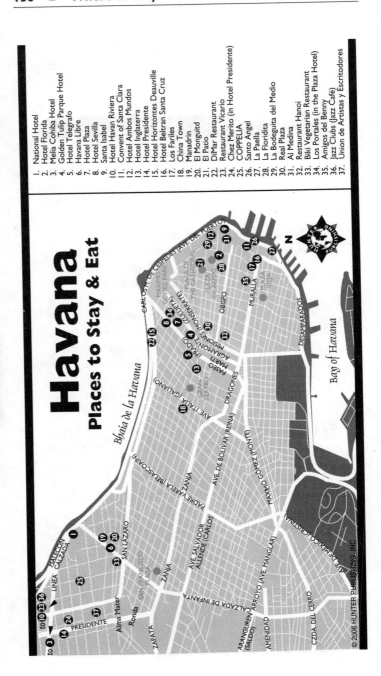

1. National Hotel
2. Hotel Florida
3. Melia Cohiba Hotel
4. Golden Tulip Parque Hotel
5. Hotel Telegrafo
6. Havana Libre
7. Hotel Plaza
8. Hotel Sevilla
9. Santa Isabel
10. Hotel Havan Riviera
11. Convent of Santa Clara
12. Hotel Ambos Mundos
13. Hotel Inglaterra
14. Hotel Presidente
15. Hotel Horizontes Deauville
16. Hotel Beltran Santa Cruz
17. Los Farîles
18. China Town
19. Manadrin
20. El Monguitd
21. El Patio
22. DiMar Restaurant
23. Restaurant Vicario
24. Chez Merito (in Hotel Presidente)
25. COPPELIA
26. Santo Angel
27. La Paella
28. La Floridita
29. La Bodeguita del Medio
30. Real Plaza
31. Al Medina
32. Restaurant Hanoi
33. Biki Vegetarian Restaurant
34. Los Portales (in the Plaza Hotel)
35. Amigos del Benny
36. Jazz Clubs (Jazz Café)
37. Union de Artistas y Escritodores

Bahía de la Havana

Bay of Havana

© 2006 HUNTER PUBLISHING, INC.

■ Hotels

National Hotel, Calle 21 and O, Vedado, ☎ 7/733-3564, $$$$$, is by far the most historical and interesting place to stay in Havana. It has been in business for over 75 years, and has been upgraded. Its 426 large rooms have cable TVs, radios, mini-bars and personal safes (that you must pay extra for). However, repair and touch-up are sometimes lacking so you may see chipped paint or find a tap not working. There is a swimming pool, gym, business center, babysitting service, and so many restaurants, bars and coffee shops that you probably won't be able to try them all. The grounds are huge and well maintained. However, rooms are not as grand as the grounds and main public areas. The cave on the property is interesting as it was used as a bunker during the Revolution. Now the cave is a tiny museum filled mostly with photos. Famous people like Frank Sinatra, Winston Churchill, Nat King Cole and Errol Flynn have stayed at this hotel – what else does one need for recommendation?

Hotel Florida, Calle Obispo #252 and Ave Cuba, Old Havana, ☎ 7/862-4167, $$$$$, has 25 rooms on three floors set around a courtyard. If you want to stay in a high-end place, this is a very good deal. Rooms are large and comfortable, with elegant furniture, high ceilings and wood floors. Bathrooms are huge, mostly marble, and clean. It is a treat to be on Calle Obispo, within walking distance of the greatest sites.

Melia Cohiba Hotel, Ave Paseo, between Calle 1 and 3, Vedado, ☎ 7/733-3636, $$$$$ (over $200), is a clean hotel with good service, but away from the center. A taxi runs about $7 each way to and from Old Havana. The rooms are fairly well maintained. They have mini-bars, cable TVs, radios and personal safes. There are numerous expensive eateries, but the hotel is close to other less-expensive eateries where food is equally as good. There is a pool, gym, massage room, hair salon, sauna, and business center, as well as tennis courts. The shops sell better quality T-shirts and some women's clothing. There is also a children's area and a lovely fountain. You will find that the air conditioning is tepid, rather than super cold.

Golden Tulip Parque Central Hotel, Calle Neptuno between Prado and Zulueta, Old Havana, ☎ 7/860-6627, $$$$$, is across from the central park, next to one of the city's many theaters. The 277 rooms are large and clean, and the beds are big enough for a party. Too bad Cubans aren't permitted entry to your room. There are sitting areas, too. The clean bathrooms are huge, with both tubs and showers. There are room safes, mini-bars, cable TVs and fluffy towels. The rooftop pool is a great draw, as is the central location. However, the best thing seems to be **El Paseo Restaurant**, which serves exceptional meals with outstanding service and reasonable prices. The bar, on the other hand, should be avoided. This hotel is wheelchair accessible.

Hotel Telegrafo, Prado #408 and Ave Neptuno, Central Havana, ☎ 7/681-1010, $$$$$, has 63 rooms, some wheelchair accessible. The hotel is centrally located and modern, with excellent security. The triple-glazed windows keep street noise out of the large and well-decorated rooms.

Havana Libre, Calle L, between Ave 23 and 25, Vedado, ☎ 7/733-4011, $$$$, is almost as historically interesting and quite a bit cheaper than the National, above. The 574 rooms on 25 floors have cable TVs, radios and safes. There are restaurants and bars along with a business center, pool, sauna, massage room, gym, hair salon, money exchange, solarium, baby-sitting service, Jacuzzi and shops. There are different reports on rooms; some are fairly good while others stink. If your room is not to your liking, complain. The food in the dining room is okay, but far overpriced. Instead, go to local eateries where you'll get much better food for much less money.

Hotel Plaza, Calle Ignacio Agramonte #267, Old Havana, ☎ 7/860-8583, $$$$, is a beautiful old hotel with stained glass windows, antiques in the halls and 188 grand rooms, each with cable TV, a personal safe, and air conditioning. There is a bar and restaurant, a tourist office, car rental and business center.

Hotel Seville, Calle Trocadero #55, between the Prado and Ave Zulueta, ☎ 7/860-8560, $$$$, is a colonial building filled with antique furnishings and photographs of historical figures such as the colorful Al Capone, the great Caruso and the mighty Joe Louis. There are 188 rooms with mini-bars, cable TVs, antique furnishings, large beds and tiled bathrooms. The rooms are spacious, with high ceilings and air conditioning. Construction of the building was started in 1880; it was designed as a replica of the Alhambra Palace in Granada, Spain. There is a pool, sauna, gym, massage parlor and a line of shops that sells gifts, cigars, snacks, clothing and postcards. The bar and restaurant are both good for relaxing, but it is the central location that is the hotel's biggest draw.

Santa Isabel, Calle Baratillo #9 between Ave O'Reilly and Narciso Lopez, ☎ 7/860-8201, $$$$, has just 27 rooms located in a colonial building that was first opened as a hotel in the mid-1800s. The central courtyard, rooftop restaurant and great location all add to the appeal. The terrace overlooks Plaza de Armas, so it's great for people-watching. There are safes and cable TVs in the rooms. Some rooms have antique furniture but others have some pretty cheap pieces. There is a business center.

Havana Riviera, Paseo and malecón, Vedado, ☎ 7/733-4051, $$$$, is classed as a five-star in Cuba but stay away. There has never been a good report about this 1950s-styled hotel except for its saltwater pool, which is reported to be excellent. I have not stayed here. The large foyer has modern art that has been accented with chips and dirt, and their Copa Room charges $25 entry fee (this includes one drink). A tour operator attached to the hotel offers excursions at the going rates.

Convent de Santa Clara, Calle Cuba #610, Old Havana, ☎ 7/861-3335, $$$, has a garden that makes the nine nun's cells used for rooms more appealing. The rooms are much bigger than you might expect and the place is certainly comfortable. I did not stay here, but I do understand that it is quiet as long as students aren't staying in the dorm beds (they also have first preference). There is no air conditioning, but each room has a ceiling fan.

Hotel Ambos Mundos, Calle Obispo and Ave Mercaderes, Old Havana, ☎ 7/860-9530, $$$, offers 52 rooms in a colonial building that was once the home of Hemingway. That alone would be an attraction; if you are a real fan, visit room #501 to see his "stuff." However, do not stay in the rooms facing the courtyard as they are second-rate (one good reason to pay only for one night if booking from home). Rooms facing the streets are larger, brighter and better furnished. Each has cable TV, a private safe and mini-bar. The rooftop restaurant has an excellent reputation.

Hotel Inglaterra, Paseo del Prado #416, between Ave San Rafael and San Miguel, Central Havana, ☎ 7/860-8595, $$$, is just down from the Capitolio, which makes it convenient to many attractions in the city. There is a whole strip of sidewalk cafés on the street below the hotel. The rooms themselves have cable TVs and personal safes, but they are nothing special.

Hotel Presidente, Ave Calzada and Calle G, Vedado, ☎ 7/755-1801, $$$, has 160 rooms in a lovely old building that has all the modern conveniences like clean beds and hot water in the tiled bathrooms. Each room has cable TV and a safe. There is a babysitting service and breakfast is included with the price. The food is excellent and dinner, too, is recommended. The halls and foyer are decorated with antiques and the staff is very helpful. Hotel Presidente is conveniently located.

Hotel Kohly, Ave 49 and 36A, Miramar, ☎ 7/204-0240, $$, has 136 clean, comfortable rooms. Although this is some distance from the center, the difference in price from places in Old Havana will easily cover bus fare. There is a restaurant, pool, gym and sauna, along with a pool hall and bowling alley.

Hotel Horizontes Deauville, Calle Galiano #1, between the malecón and Ave San Lazaro in Central Havana, ☎ 7/733-8812, $$, has 144 rooms that border on basic, with cement floors and drab décor. Supplies like soap and toilet paper are pretty sparse and seldom replenished. Eating at the restaurant is definitely out. This hotel is fairly inexpensive when compared to others, but it is only for the tougher traveler.

Beltran de Santa Crus, Calle San Ignacio #411 between Ave Sol and Muralla, Old Havana, ☎ 7/860-8330, $$, is difficult to find because you approach the entrance from what looks like a side street. This is a colonial building with 11 large rooms around a central courtyard that is decorated with wrought-iron furniture and potted plants. The rooms have tiled floors, twin beds, air conditioning, cable TVs and windows overlooking the courtyard. The place is quiet, clean and safe and one of the more pleasant places to stay in this price range.

Los Frailes, Teniente Rey #8 between Ave Oficios and Mercaderes in Old Havana, ☎ 7/862-9383, $$, has 22 rooms in a mansion once used as a monastery. Although it has been redone, the monk motif has been preserved. The 22 rooms are very small with no windows facing the street, but the place is clean and the "monks" offer good service. The bathrooms have antique furnishings and hot water. There is no restaurant, so you'll need to go down the street to eat.

■ Casa Particulares

Casas are the best option if you want inexpensive, clean rooms. Don't forget that you will need to practice your Spanish, no matter how poor your vocab. Rates are between $30 and $40 (in 2006) for a double, although you can still find the odd one for $25. The owners can't lower the prices because of the high tax imposed by the government, so don't haggle. *Casas* are safe and clean, and the families are proud to welcome foreigners into their homes. I have never seen an uncomfortable, dirty or small *casa* room. Breakfast is usually included in the price. I list only a few options here, but there are many more. If you receive a recommendation from someone, even a Cuban, don't be afraid to try it out. If an e-mail address is included, I suggest you book in advance.

> **AUTHOR NOTE:** Please do not book and then not show up as it hurts homeowners to lose a night's rent. And if they are all forced to close, it will be to the detriment of the visitor.

A CASA FOR YOU

A blue-striped triangle sign (measuring no more than six inches) on a door indicates that legal rooms are available. If the sign is red, it means that the rooms are for Cubans only.

Visit www.particularcuba.com/cristo.htm for room recommendations. The website offers e-mail contacts.

Jorge Coalla Potts, Calle 1 #456, Apt 11, between Ave 23 and 21, Vedado, ☎ 7/832-9032, jorgepotts@ web. correosdecuba.cu, is one of the most popular *casas* in Havana. The place is spotless, there is air conditioning and the owners are friendly. If they are full they will phone around to find another place that they recommend.

Villa Jorge Luis, Calle Soledad #161, between Ave San Lazaro and Jovellar in Central Havana, jvelaz@informed.sld.cu, has just one room in the very center of the city. The location is good.

Hostal Coatzacoalcos, Calle 6 #316, apt 1, between Ave 3 and 5, ☎ 7/203-7719, is clean and comfortable with air conditioning. It offers private bathrooms and hot water is available all day. Breakfast is included and there is safe parking available. This is a good place. They also have rooms in Trinidad.

Conchita Garcia, Calle 21 #4, between Ave N and O, 7th floor, Apt 74, Vedado, ☎ 7/832-6187, conchita garcia23@yahoo.com.mx, has two large, nicely decorated rooms joined by a bathroom that is shared by the two rooms but not with the family. There is a telephone and television available.

Maria Moreno Arias, Calle 21 #4, between Ave N and O, 7th floor, Apt 73, ☎ 7/832-6293, has one room with a large fridge. It is across from Conchita – so if one is full, the other may not be.

Lilliam de la Osa, Calle 21 #4, between Ave N and O, 4th floor, Apt 24, ☎ 7/832-5361, solangel.ruano@ infomed. sld.cu, has two rooms that share a bath. The rooms are large and clean and the hot-water shower is excellent. Lilliam speaks English. Of all the *casas* within this building, I found Lilliam's to be the best.

Casa Maria Elena, Calle 21 and Ave O, Apt 12, ☎ 7/ 832-7457, has two rooms with private bathroom. The house is a tad battered, but the owner is pleasant and the room is spotless. There is a nice sitting area.

Clara Aniuta, Calle 21 #4, Apt 51, 5th floor, between Ave N and O, ☎ 7/833-5813, 8907887@sms.sbacel. com, has two rooms joined by a bathroom. The rooms are large and a bit tacky in décor, but comfortable enough. The host will make meals if you ask.

Casa Raquel, Calle Mistad #417, Apt 2, between Ave Dragones and Barcelona, Central Havana, ☎ 7/867-8626, has an apartment for rent with private bath and hot water. It is central, comfortable and private. The rate here is higher than for a simple room.

Casa Sandra, Calle G #301 and Ave 13, 13th floor, Vedado, ☎ 7/832-4021, sandravigil76@yahoo.com,

Havana

has a lovely place that is less expensive than many. The place is sparkling clean and full of antiques, and the bathroom has hot water. You need not hang out in your spacious bedroom; rather enjoy the comfort of the house. She has two bedrooms available.

Aparment Marta, Calle 25 #415, Apt 3, between Ave J,Y and K, Vedado, ☎ 7/832-4914, has a room for rent with private bath and hot water. There is air conditioning in the apartment.

Casa Ines, Calle 2 #559 between Ave Ayestaran and Ayuntamiento, Plaza de la Revolución, ☎ 7/870-0237, canaines@casaines.com, has two rooms with kitchenettes, double beds, color TVs, air conditioning and private bathrooms. Ines supplies toilet paper and soap and keeps her place exceptionally clean. If full, she will send you to either Casa Ernesto or Casa Manolo, both of which are within walking distance. Ernesto's and Manolo's also have lovely rooms, although not with kitchenettes. They do have air conditioning and private bathrooms.

La Superabuela, Calle 1 #355, Apt 2, 2nd floor, between Ave 17 and 19, Vedado, ☎ 7/832-3033, la_superabuela@hotmail.com, has two double rooms with air conditioning, double beds, private baths and some use of the kitchen area. The name of the *casa* means "super grandmother," so I imagine they have a sense of humor and that grandma has a lot of energy. You can rent mountain bikes for $5 per day with a $150 refundable deposit.

Frank and Zaida, Ave San Juan de Dios #153, between Calle El Villagas and Aguacates, Old Havana (no phone), has two sleeping rooms with private bathrooms and hot water. You can use the kitchen or take a room without kitchen privileges and have some (or all) meals made for you. I was told that Frank's breakfasts are the best in Havana.

Casa Antigua, Calle 28 #258, between 21 and 23, Vedado, ☎ 7/833-5175, encuba@casantigua.com, is set in a lovely colonial building. The private rooms are decorated with antique furniture and a balcony is open to guests. The owners speak English and can help with your traveling needs. This is a friendly place peppered with that great Cuban hospitality and fun.

Where to Eat

There are hundreds of restaurants in the downtown area of Havana. Many are expensive, while others serve horrid food. Those following in the trail of Hemingway will need a lot of cash as Cubans have learned to exploit his memory almost as well as that of the revolution itself. I prefer to save the money and eat in Cuban restaurants that are not being "promoted" by the government.

Paladars are private homes where residents can serve up to 12 guests. Most *paladars* are reasonably priced, but because of the high taxes imposed by the government and the hard work it takes to make one successful, these are disappearing. If you do manage to find one, you will usually be offered a limited menu but the quality and quantity of the meals excellent.

Peso **shops** along the streets are clean and I would not hesitate to eat at most of them. You must pay in Cuban pesos at these shops and in markets selling food. Market food is fresh and mostly "organic." Because of the embargo, Cuba is unable to purchase many insecticides so they have gone back to growing plants in combinations that help prevent diseases.

AUTHOR TIP: Ask other travelers about places to eat. Those listed below are ones I have tried or have had recommended to me. But things change, restaurants like La Floridita get cocky and others open hoping to attract customers.

Havana

Chan Li Po, in Chinatown (there are only a couple of streets) at Calle Zapata and Galiano or Rayo and San Nicolas. Chan Li Po is usually patronized by locals so that's an indication of the quality. The meals are cheap and exceptionally delicious. Spring rolls and the chop suey special are recommended, as is the seafood soup. The cost, without drinks, is around $5 for a full meal. Some of the waiters speak English. On the same street is the **Mi Chin Tang**, which serves good Chinese food and even better pizza! The third place along this strip is **Los 3 Chinitos**, known for their shrimp cocktails. Chung Shan Los Dos Dragones on the first floor serves some of the freshest, cheapest and most delicious food in this area.

The Mandarin, Calle 23 and M, Vedado, ☎ 7/832-0677, opens noon to 11 pm daily and serves Chinese and Cuban dishes that are fairly good, fairly large and fairly cheap. When I was there, they charged in pesos, but that probably has been stopped. The entire menu was not available, but what they did have was okay.

El Monguito, Calle L, between Ave 23 and 25, Vedado, (no phone) across from Havana Libre, is a tiny place with three or four tables. Their Cuban tortillas (like an omelette rather than a flat bread) with banana are worth waiting for. The dish comes with rice and beans and costs about $7.

Restaurant Tocororo, Calle 18 #302, corner of 3rd, Miramar, ☎ 7/733-4530 or 7/733-2209, is open from noon to 11 pm daily except Sunday. It was the chef Erasmus who made this place famous, and since he left to work at El Rancho Palco (see below), some of the fame left with him. It is expensive even by North American standards – a meal costs $30 and up. The restaurant can seat over 100 people and features a lovely garden eating area. The house appetizer is *pechitos de camarones* (deep-fried shrimp) and the dish of the house is lobster.

El Patio, San Ignacio #54, on the Plaza of the Cathedral in Old Havana, ☎ 7/733-8146, is open from 11 am to 11 pm daily and is recommended for an average lunch. You will be sitting in the courtyard of a 17th-century colonial building that was owned by the Marques de Aguas Claras, or on the street watching the action. A sandwich and beer cost $7 or so, while a full meal runs around $20.

DiMar, malecón and Calle Paseo, is air-conditioned and open 24 hours a day. It offers seafood for a reasonable price. The décor is pretty plastic. On my visit, a *camarone* cocktail was $2.10, fries 35 cents and a fried fish dinner was $1.80. Not a bad deal!

Restaurant Vicario, malecón and Calle E (one street west of Boyeros), has good Cuban food such as a salad for $1, fish dinner for $7.50, pork chops for $5.50 and a sandwich for $3. An espresso machine sits in the shop, although I never saw it used.

La Cocina de Lilliam, Calle 48 #1311, between Ave 13 and 15, Miramar, has great snapper or grouper, oven baked with all the trimmings, for less than $10 per serving. This is a small place with a Cuban flavor.

Restaurant Chez Merito, Calzada #110, and Ave G, Vedado, ☎ 7/755-1801, in El Presidente Hotel, is open from noon till 3 pm and 7 to 11 pm daily. The atmosphere is inviting and the food is excellent. The specialty is spaghetti with Italian tomato sauce for $7. Lobster runs at $23.

Paladar La Guarido, Calle Concordia #318 between Gervasio and Escobar in Central Havana, ☎ 7/762-4940, is located up three flights of stairs in an old building; it was made famous when it was used in the award-winning film *Fresa y Chocolate* (*Strawberries and Chocolate*). The atmosphere is what will bring you to this romantic place. However, the food is good too, with the Gazpacho soup one of the favorites.

Coppelia, Calle 23 and Ave L, Vedado, open daily from 11 am to 10:30 pm, is an ice cream haven near Havana Libre that is popular with locals. So popular, in fact, that the shops (there are several) take up al-

Havana

most one square block. Many of them sell in pesos, but offer a limited selection, while the shops selling in Cuban converts have dozens of flavors. The area has benches and picnic tables and lots of trees so the atmosphere is cool and relaxing. The ice cream in Cuba is safe to eat.

Santo Angel, Calle Teniente Rey on the corner of Ave San Ignacio, Old Havana, open from 11 am to 11 pm daily, is across from the Plaza Vieja and offers international cuisine. Because of governmental advertizing, its prices are high ($20 for a meal).

La Paella, Calle Oficios #53, between Ave Lamparill and Obrapia in Hostal Valencia, Old Havana, ☎ 7/867-1037, noon to 10 pm daily. The dish of the house is paella; both the chicken and seafood versions are recommended. At one time this was a great bargain but word is out and an average-tasting dish runs around $15 while the seafood paella costs $25.

El Aljibe, Ave 7 between Calle 24 and 26, Miramar, ☎ 7/204-1583, open noon to 11 pm, serves traditional Cuban food such as chicken in garlic sauce, Moors-and-Christians, fried plantains, and fried potatoes all for about $12. This large open-air restaurant is a favorite spot for the nouveau-riche and expats (many who are working at the consulates).

La Floridita, Calle Obispo #557 and corner of Ave Monserrate in Old Havana, ☎ 7/867-1300, is open 10 am to midnight. This is one of the Hemingway rip-off joints where you can get a $7 daiquiri (mine was watered down, I suspect). Eating here is far too expensive for barely passable food. The rooms are full of Hemingway memorabilia, and when you are given the menu you will also receive a catalogue of overpriced Hemingway souvenirs. After ordering a drink or meal, and before you even get your change, the waitress will hold her palm out looking for a tip. Obviously, I didn't like this place. You are far better off going around the corner to La Bodeguita or elsewhere and getting really good daiquiris for the same price or much less.

La Bodeguita del Medio, Ave Empedrado #207, between Ave Cuba and San Ignacio, Old Havana, ☎ 7/867-1374, open 11:30 am to midnight daily. This is the home of the mojito and is another Hemingway hotspot – which translates into expensive exploitation, although I didn't find it as crass as La Floridita. Originally, this was a grocery store and later became a favorite bohemian hangout (remember, bohemians like cheap), full of folks who liked to sip on mojitos, nibble jerk beef and solve the world's problems.

Real Plaza, Calle Zulueta, and Neptuno, Old Havana, in the Plaza Hotel, ☎ 7/860-8583, is open from noon to 10 pm and serves the best pizza I found in Havana. The service matched the quality of the food. The atmosphere is 1920s and the air conditioning works like a charm. I returned often.

Al Medina, Calle Oficios #12 between Calle Obispo and Obrapia in Old Havana, ☎ 7/863-0862, 9 am to midnight, is located in a colonial mansion. It serves Middle Eastern foods such as falafel and couscous salad. What a treat.

El Rancho Palco, Calle 140 and Ave 19, Playa, ☎ 7/208-9346, open from noon to midnight, is some distance from the center but the one place you may be encouraged (by others) to visit for that special night out. Expect a meal to cost around $50 per person, not including drinks. The wine list is short. The restaurant has a romantic forest setting and the meals are supposed to be prepared under the direction of Erasmus, a famous Cuban chef. Those are the official reports. Erasmus might have been taking an upgrading course when I was in Cuba. Steak and seafood are the recommended dishes but, sad to say, this place is not up to its reputation. However, on the same property is the **La Finca**, a small house with tables inside or out on the patio. This restaurant has a cozier atmosphere and food that is a bit better.

Restaurant Hanoi, Calle Teniente Rey and Ave Bernaza, Old Havana, ☎ 7/867-1029, open daily from

Havana

11 am to 10 pm. It is in a house that was once called the house of vines – the vines are in the courtyard. Built in 1640, the restaurant at one time served very inexpensive, traditional foods but now the same meal – Vietnamese or Creole, an odd combo – costs more here than in Canada.

Vegetarian Restaurant Biki, Plaza Mella, Calle San Lozardo,(no phone), open Tuesday to Sunday, 11 am to 7 pm, is one of the few places that specializes in vegetarian foods. They serve Cuban dishes, buffet style and charge in pesos. Do not pay in dollars.

Los Portales Restaurant, in Hotel Plaza, Calle Ignacio and Ave Agramonte #267, ☎ 7/860-8583, is an Italian restaurant that has great pizza for $4, lasagna for the same price, and ice cream for $1 to $2.50 depending on what you have. There is air conditioning but no music (the place was peaceful!).

Nightlife

Havana is a safe city and going out at night is a must. Try at least one Tropicana show (or reasonable facsimile) and visit a jazz bar. One evening at El Castillo del Morro for the closing of the gates is a requisite (see page 116 for details). Otherwise, ask the locals where the best bars are and follow them.

SAFETY

Havana is safe, but don't go out at night with all your money and passport hanging out of your pockets. Do not get plastered and expect no trouble. Do not walk home late at night down dark alleys. Do not get caught up in the dope trade. Take a taxi (mark down his number) when it is late. If you follow these suggestions, you may still get robbed but the odds are lower.

■ Live Performances

 Most good jazz clubs are on Ave 23 in Vedado, just a block from the malecón. If you don't recognize the musician playing at La Zorra (see below), stand around and see where the Cubans are going and follow them.

La Zorra and El Cuervo, Ave 23 between N and O, Vedado, ☎ 7/766-2402, is the home of Cuban jazz. The cover charge is $5 and the club opens around 9 pm. It is the most famous club in Cuba and the entertainment is excellent. It is managed by Tony Orlando, an energetic guy who also writes reviews in Cuban magazines, hosts a Sunday night show on the radio, and MCs at the club.

Amigos del Benny Café, Calle Mercaderes and Ave Teniente Rey, Old Havana, ☎ 7/861-1637, open 11 am to midnight, was the first café in the country, established in 1772. It has been remodeled to look like a 1950s place and honors the Cuban jazz musician Benny More. There is live entertainment after 10 each evening and the salsa dancing is great. Beer is less than $2 and sandwiches are not much more.

Tropicana, Calle 72 between Ave 41 and 45, Marianao, ☎ 7/766-1717. The show starts at 10 pm daily. Tickets can be purchased at any large hotel desk in downtown Havana. They cost $70 per person with one rum drink or $80 with a rum drink and hors d'oeuvres; taking photos will cost you another $5. This is probably the most famous of the cabaret shows in Cuba. It started back in 1939. It is under the stars and if the stars are put out by rain so is the show. This is a professional show with beautiful and talented performers dressed in rich costumes and dancing to first-class brass bands. It is a delight to be here.

Salon Rofo, Calle 21 and Ave N and O, Vedado, (no phone), is open during the day for meals but the cabaret seems more attractive. It starts at 10 pm and the $20 fee includes two drinks and the floor show. Salon Rofo is patronized mostly by Cuban businessmen and is part of the Capri Hotel (closed for restoration), which played a role in Havana's gambling days before the revolution.

Jazz Café, Calle 1 and Paseo, Vedado, ☎ 7/755-3302, open noon to 3 am daily except Sunday, is located on the third floor of a shopping mall. This is a glitzy café that sports a lot of big names like saxophonist Cesar Lopez, trumpeter El Greco, flutist Javier Zalba, and guitarist Elmer Ferrer. Entertainment doesn't start until 11 pm. There is a cover charge of $5.

Gran Theatre of Havana, Paseo del Prado, between Ave San Rafael and San José in Central Havana, was opened in 1838 and still offers performances from the National Ballet of Cuba, the Pro Lyric Art Center and the Havana Spanish Dance Company. Stop by and get a ticket to see at least one show. You will not be sorry and for my buck, I'd prefer this to the Tropicana. The cost will have to be covered in dollars rather than pesos and can be anywhere from $25 to $50 for a show.

Karl Marx Theatre, Calle 1 and Ave 10, Miramar, ☎ 7/723-0801, can hold almost 9,000 people in its main hall. The theater is famous for presenting the rock group Manic Street Preachers to Fidel Castro in 2001. It often offers public concerts – watch for signs pasted on walls or ask at the information desk of your hotel.

■ Movies

 Charles Chaplin Theatre, Calle 23, between Ave 10 and 12, Vedado (no phone), specializes in Cuban film, some of it very risqué. If you can speak even a smattering of Spanish, I suggest you take in one of their films. They have presented controversial movies such as *Strawberry and Chocolate, Guantanamera, Alice in Wonder Village* and *Suite Habana*, a very honest look at ordinary life in post-revolutionary Cuba. Watch the local newspapers for information on what is playing while you are here.

■ Dance & Art

 Union de Artistas y Escritodores (Writers and Artists Union), Calle 17 and H, Vedado, has excellent events that include live music, dance performances and reading events. The cost for foreigners is $5 for the evening. This is a lively place, patronized mostly by university students and those heavily into art. I like hanging out with these people, hoping some talent and inspiration will infect me.

Shopping

 There are shopping malls around the city with stores that specialize in items such as perfumes, jewelry, clothes, shoes, and personal goods like shampoos. Then there are the high-quality art stores that sell things a foreigner might want as souvenirs. Cigar and rum shops abound, and both items are popular purchases for foreigners.

The government would like you to spend your money in the hotel shops or one of their specialized stores. However, I do urge you to also look at the little markets like the one behind the **Havana Libre** on Calle 23, between Ave M and N. It is open from 9 am to 6 pm and illegal items like black coral jewelry, turtle shell belts or armadillo instruments will often be offered from behind a curtain or pulled out from under a counter. Best to avoid that stuff.

Cathedral Plaza, Calle Tacon and Emedrado, Old Havana, is open from 9 am to 6 pm. This is where barter-

Havana

ing can and should be done. All sale items are made by local artists. One of the neat things that can be purchased is hand-formed and painted clay made in the shape of ladies with cigars in their mouths. These are actually incense burners. When the incense is smoking, the smoke comes out of the cigar.

The painters have moved from Vedado to Parque Luz Caballero, toward the harbor and near the San Cristobal Cathedral. Study some of the old artworks before purchasing. Cuban art is known for its flat, miniature figures on paintings, which are often *campesino* scenes. Of course, modern work is anything the artist wants to paint, but the more traditional Cuban style is unique.

> **AUTHOR TIP:** Remember that original art must have a document provided by the shop where the work is purchased or from the government department, Registro Nacional de Bienes Culturales, Calle 17 #1009 between Ave 10 and 12, Vedado, Havana, ☎ 7/731-3362. I have never had a permit nor have I ever had my stuff looked at when leaving, but that doesn't mean it won't happen to you.

■ Large Stores & Malls

Villa Panamericana Shopping Mall, Carretera Central, Villa Panamericana, Havana del Este, is open from 9 am to 7 pm every day except Sunday. A mini-village that should be visited at least once by shopping enthusiasts, it is located close to Cojimar, the setting for the Hemingway novel, *The Old Man and the Sea*. Besides being a shopping mall, it is a hotel, with swimming pools and tennis courts. There are restaurants, discos, pharmacies and a gym at the villa as well.

Harris Brothers Department Store, Calle Monserrate between Ave O'Reilly and San Juan de Dios, Old Havana, ☎ 7/873-1615, open 9 am to 9 pm daily. It is located in a four-story building that has been modernized and is considered the biggest complex within the city limits. It has stores, markets and coffee shops.

■ Arts & Crafts

Oviedo, Ave Mayari #88 and Prosperidad, Arroyo Naranjo (no phone), has wood carvings done up in modern designs that are worth a look. The pieces are not expensive, considering the hardwoods being used and the time to carve and polish them. An average piece standing about 18 inches tall starts at $100.

Center for Alternative Art, Calle 6, between Ave 25 and 27, Vedado, ☎ 7/730-2147, is in the home of graphic artist Sandra Ceballos. She has a tiny gallery that holds the works of a number of artists. Stop in.

Gallery Casa Joben, Ave de los Presidente and Ave A, has postcards and black-and-white photos produced by those studying at the gallery. Often, words of wisdom are printed under the photos.

Habana 1719 Perfume Shop, Mercaderes #156 in Old Havana (no phone), is open 10 am to 6 pm daily. Try shopping for Sparkling Tiger or Jungle Zebra. I'm sure your mate will love Cuba Jungle Snake or Cuba Sparkling Snake.

■ Music & Books

Longina Music Store, Calle Obispo #360 in Old Havana, ☎ 7/862-8371, is open 10 am to 9 pm daily. It has about the best collection of Cuban music in the city. The store is large and some of the clerks speak English but there are few bargains. Prices are the same as what you would pay at home.

The advantage of buying here is that you can buy tunes that you may not find at home.

Libreria Abel Santamaria, Calle Conte and Cardenas in Old Havana,761-3738, is open from 9 am to 5 pm, Monday to Friday. They have a good supply of Spanish literature as well as a notable second-hand book selection. They also trade.

Pabellon Cuba Books, Calle A between Ave 19 and 21 (no phone), has new and used books. I found many guides in English here that were not available elsewhere. Prices are high – books are a luxury in Cuba.

Libreria Rayuela, Paseo and Ave A (behind the tourist office in Vedado), has some books in English and some photo books of Cuba. The average cost is $20-$30 per book.

■ Cigars & Rum

House of Habanos, Mercaderes #222, in Old Havana, ☎ 7/862-9293, is open from 10 am to 5 pm. If you would like to do a tour of this shop before buying your cigars, it will cost $10. Buying your cigars from Habanos will guarantee the best quality. If buying from the *jinateros* standing outside waiting like vultures, you may end up smoking unmentionables. A good cigar like a Cohiba will cost you around $20 and small packages of excellent cigarillos run around $4.

House of Rum and Cigars, Calle Obisop and Bernaza, Old Havana, ☎ 7/733-8911, 9 am to 9 pm daily, offers a large selection of rums and cigars. They will even tell you which ones go best together. The best rum is, of course, the seven-year-old stuff, but if you want some for mojitos, purchase a clear rum. However, it is cheaper to purchase a bottle of rum at the local corner store. (The House of Rum charges $15 for a bottle of seven-year-old, but the price is about half that at a corner store.)

Western Cuba

Playas del Este

The beaches east of Havana are patronized mostly by Cubans. The hotels are okay, the beaches are okay and the food is okay.

This strip, commonly called the **Blue Circuit** (perhaps because of the sea color), runs for nine km/5.5 miles along the north side of the island, starting about 20 km east of Havana. Traveling from east to west, the beaches are **Guanabo**, **Playa Tarara**, **Boca Ciega**, **Santa Maria del Mar**, and **El Megano**. Going farther east, there is a strip of rocky shore without beaches and then there is the **Jibacoa** area.

Santa Maria or Guanabo are your best bets for things like doctors, post offices or telephone offices.

■ Getting Here

BY BUS: Take any bus going east from the center of Havana and get off at the beach of your choice. Buses run along the main highway both ways; if you are at one beach and want to move along to the next one, jump on the bus. Going back to Havana can be arranged with one of the hotel shuttle buses.

BY TAXI: A taxi will not cost more than $12 each way from Havana to Santa Maria so if there are a few people to share the cost, it is often the best choice.

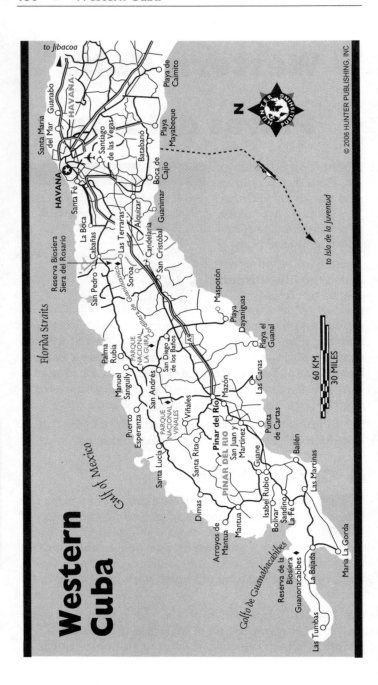

HITCHHIKING: It is illegal for trucks to pass you by if you are hitching a ride. This is another option for getting to the beaches. If you hitch, have a gift to give the driver (disposable razors are good).

Guanabo

This is a rather quiet village where Cuban life goes on unaffected by tourism. It is also definitely safe from crime. The brown-sand beaches are dotted with seaweed (instead of Styrofoam cups) and often deserted. There are some restaurants and many *casas*, making beach living here a bit cheaper than in places that have resort hotels. In fact, there are so many *casas* that you should never be without a place to stay, even if you do not book ahead.

■ Services

Post office, Ave 5, between Calle 490 and 492, Monday to Saturday, 8 am to 6 pm.

Telephone Office (and Internet), Ave 5C between Calle 490 and 492, open daily 9 am to 10 pm.

■ Places to Stay

Hotels

Villa Playa Hermosa, Ave 5 and Calle 470, ☎ 7/796-2774, $, is a one-star hotel with double beds in small bungalows. The baths and cable TVs are shared. There is a small pool. The rooms do have a few chips around the edges. Be sure not to pay for more than one or two nights so that you can look around if you are not satisfied. This is a popular place for locals, who like to party most of the time – but especially when on vacation.

Hotel Gran Villa, Ave 5 and Calle 462, ☎ 7/796-2271, is a fairly small hotel very close to the beach.

The 10 tiny and basic rooms all have air conditioning, cable TV and private bathrooms, but the place is not spit-polished. There is a restaurant and bar.

Casa Particulares

Some places do not have telephones so if you must have a place booked before you arrive, write to them.

Casa Doña Carmen, Calle 5 C #49808, between Calle 498 and 500, ☎ 7/796-4334, has an apartment with a separate entrance, air conditioning in the bedroom, fully equipped kitchen, private bathroom and hot water. The house is secure and there is a small patio at your disposal. This place is a real gem.

Casa Alberto and Neisa, Calle 500 #5008, between Ave 5 and 7, is close to the beach and has one room with a private entrance, a private bath and a fridge. There is a pleasant furnished patio in the back yard and meals can be prepared for you.

Casa Salustiano, Ave 7 #46204, is a lovely two-story house with two rooms for rent just a couple of blocks from the ocean. The upstairs room has a private bath, and the downstairs one has shared. The clean rooms have double beds and tiled floors. The big attraction is a small private pool in the backyard. This is a very good deal.

Casa Sol Mar, Calle 1 #50017, between Ave 500 and 504, has two nicely decorated rooms, both with air conditioning and private entrances. Guests can use the terrace that overlooks the ocean.

Casa Miram Trujillo, Ave Quebec #55, between Calle 478 and 482, ☎ 7/796-3325, is comfortable and clean and the owner loves kids. This is also a dog lover's home, the place to stay if, like me, you're crazy about canines. Someone here can always speak English or French.

Casa Armada, Ave A #50025, between Calle 500 and the BEACH! This is a lovely home with a walled yard, clean amenities, pleasant owners and the most comfortable patio in Guanabo. Meals can be arranged. The room has two beds, a private bathroom and a/c.

■ Places to Eat

 I suggest booking at your *casa* as that is where you will get the best meal for your buck. There are a few restaurants on Ave 5 where you can eat or just sit and enjoy the peacefulness of the village while sipping on a drink.

Cappalia, Ave 5 between Calle 478 and 480, is the place to go for ice cream; they often have a dozen flavors. They also offer snacks like salads or chicken and are open 24 hours. Just up the street between Calle 472 and 474 is the **Parriada**, another good place for a snack. A hamburger will cost around two bucks.

Playa Tarara

Playa Tarara has a marina offering boat fuel and minor repairs. You can have your laundry done, load up on grub, get information from the tourist office, or eat a restaurant meal. There is also an **International Diving Center**, ☎ 7/797-1462, commercial@tarara. mit.tur.cu. Many people come to this beach specifically to snorkel and/or dive.

■ Adventures in Water

 Diving, snorkeling and fishing can be arranged at hotel tour desks. Cubanacan is the most popular tour operator in this area. Cubatur and Havanatur also have desks in some of the hotels, but they don't do the watersports.

■ Places to Stay

Tropicoco Hotel, Ave del Sur and Calle Las Terrazas, ☎ 7/797-1371, $, is run by the Horizontes chain (which means it is inexpensive) and has 188 rooms – doubles, triples and a few junior suites. The hotel has been renovated recently and features air conditioning. It is close to the ocean and has an outdoor garden, an inside pool and a disco, which was closed at time of writing but may open by the time you arrive. There's a sauna, three bars, a beauty salon, gift shops and a massage parlor.

PRICE CHART
Per room for two people, per day.
$ . . . . $25-$50
$$ . . . . . . $51-$75
$$$ . . . . $76-$100
$$$$ . . . $101-$150
$$$$$ . . Over $150

Villa Armonia Tarara, Calle 8 and Ave 1, ☎ 7/797-1616, $$$, has 45 villas near the beach that are great for families, and there are over 200 standard rooms in the main buildings. The villas can sleep four comfortably and have fully supplied kitchens. All rooms have air conditioning, cable TVs, hairdryers, safes and daily maid service. The hotel center has a restaurant, pool with swim up bar, gym, souvenir shop, massage parlor, tourist office and Internet café. You can use their muscle-powered watercraft free of charge.

Club Atlantico, Ave Las Terrazas between Calle 11 and 12, ☎ 7/797-1494, $$$, Santa Maria Beach, is an all- inclusive hotel located in a three-storey building almost on the ocean. Each standard suite has two twin beds, air conditioning, private bath, full kitchen, cable TV, safe and balcony. Two- and three-bedroom apartments are also available. On the premises is a pool, Jacuzzi, children's play area, games room, restaurants, tour office, nightclub, beauty salon, tennis courts and souvenir shop. Club Atlantico offers laundry service, live entertainment and beach equipment. This is one of the more popular resorts in this area.

Boca Ciega

This beach has a long straight stretch of yellow sand shaded with some palms. Aside from the beautiful sandy beach, there isn't much here except for the one hotel.

■ Place to Stay

The one huge all-inclusive, **Club Arenal**, ☎ 7/797-1272, $$$$, is on Laguna Itabo, just a short walk from the beach between Santa Maria del Mar and Boca Ciega town site. It is just half an hour from Havana and offers a private shuttle to take you back and forth. Rates are anywhere from $100 to $150 a day, depending on the season and which package you purchase. There is every amenity you could possibly want, including wheelchair accessibility. The décor is quite attractive, and the rooms are huge, with separate sitting areas. The activity coordinator is reported to be very enthusiastic, so much so that he often joins in on the games. However, the evening entertainment is bad and the drinks are often non-existent. This hotel is also far quieter than those in places like Varadero or some of the cays.

Santa Maria del Mar

Santa Maria del Mar is the main beach of the Playas del Este, and has numerous hotels and restaurants. It can be busy during the Cuban vacation period, July and August. The nightlife at the hotels is lively and fun, especially for those who can muddle their way through a bit of Spanish.

■ Adventures on Water

The **Nautical Center**, ☎ 7/797-1339, at the east end of the beach, rents paddleboats and kayaks. There is a lake close by where you can take a motorboat (provided by the nautical center) and tootle around the mangroves looking for wildlife. Paddleboats cost $3 an hour; motorboats are $25 for the trip to the mangroves (you stay on the lake for about two hours).

■ Places to Stay

Hotels

Gran Caribe los Pinos, Ave las Terrazas #21, cubacon@enet.cu, (no phone available) $$$$/$$$$$, has 68 rooms in cabins dotted throughout the gardens close to the beach. Each accommodation has air conditioning, a kitchen, twin beds, balcony or terrace, fridge and cable TV. The more expensive rooms have private pools. There is a pool, gym, sauna, restaurant and bar. The hotel supplies non-powered watercraft at no extra charge and there is a tennis court, games room and business office.

Hotel las Terrazas, Ave del Sur between Calles 9 and 10, ☎ 7/797-1344, $$/$$$, has fully supplied apartments with one, two or three bedrooms. They also have standard rooms with air conditioning, cable TV and kitchenettes (some). There is a pool (with a separate children's pool), a restaurant, a bar and a tourist office. Non-powered water vessels are available free of charge.

Casa Particular

Villa Juanita, Pastora #601, Cayajabos, just before you come to Las Terrazas, is a lovely house, with two clean rooms that share one bath located on the second floor of the house. The food is great and the owners friendly. They welcome cyclists.

■ Places to Eat

Open-air **La Caleta**, Ave Las Terraza, has fairly decent seafood meals for under $10 and various beef dishes for around $6. This is a large place, convenient to the beach and open from 7 am to 10 pm daily.

Pizzeria mi Rinconcito, Ave de las Terraza and Calle 4, near Los Pinos, opens from noon until about 9:30 pm (depending on how many customers). This is the best pizza joint you will find until you reach Santiago de Cuba. The crust is thin and the toppings are thick. The price is good, around $3 for a medium.

■ Nightlife

Nightlife options change often here. Check with your hotels to see if they have live entertainment. In this environment, I usually prefer a beer on the beach (never more than two, as a hangover in the sun is pure hell). Shaking around a dance floor in that humidity just isn't fun to me either, but inquire locally about discos.

Jibacoa

The Jibacoa area is halfway between Havana and Varadero and accessible from Matanzas or Havana. If you are taking a bus or hitching, you must walk the two km/1.2 miles to the water from the Via Blanca Highway (the main highway), as there is no transportation. Then you can walk east to the *campimento* (camping) or west to some of the hotels.

■ Adventure on Wheels

Mirador de Bacunayagua has the best view of the bridge that spans the Yacuma and Bacunayagua Valleys. The bridge is 18 km/

11 miles east of Havana on the Via Blanca Highway. Built between 1956 and 1960, the bridge was designed by Luis Saenz Duplace. It measures 313.5 meters/1,000 feet long, is suspended 110 meters/361 feet above the river and has an arch span of 114 meters/374 feet. From the Mirador, the bridge looks impressive, as does the entire valley. All vehicles traveling between Varadero and Havana must cross the bridge. A stop at the Mirador requires taking a tour or having your own car, as public buses do not stop here.

Two large factories can be seen from the road along this stretch. One is the **Havana Club rum factory** at Santa Cruz del Norte, which now produces 30 million liters of booze a year. Factory tours must be taken with a tour company. The other factory is the **Central Camilo Cienfuego Sugar Mill**, built by the Hershey family in the mid-1800s. The family also constructed a rail line, which services the mill and is still operating, but just. Again, a tour of the mill must be done with a company.

LIQUID GOLD

Between the Mirador and Havana are many oil pumps drawing black gold from the ground. The Cuban government has reported that Varadero is sitting on so much crude that the government may close the resorts and replace them with oil wells, which are much less of a nuisance than tourists.

■ Adventures on Foot

 To hike in the area, you need to reach the hills that backdrop the *campimentos*. **El Abra** (see next page) can arrange for horse trips into the hills (much easier than walking in the heat) that cost about $10 for a couple of hours. The length of your trip will depend somewhat upon how much the guide likes you.

■ Adventures on Water

Snorkeling is the thing to do and it matters not whether you are staying in an upscale hotel or at the *campimento*. Snorkeling gear is available, usually from your hotel, for about $5 per day. If they do not have any, ask where the equipment can be rented.

The **lava cliffs** along the shore are great hiding places for things like sand crabs and barnacles. The cliffs are also fun to climb. They form a shelf into the water where, just a few feet from shore, the snorkeling is best. The trail along the shore goes for about five km/ three miles to **Villa Tropico**, an Italian all-inclusive resort where an armed guard will turn you back. The beach beyond the fence is theirs.

To get here, take the bus that runs between Havana and Matanzas and ask to get off at the trail that leads to El Abra (or Hotel Breezes Jibacoa). Walk north toward the beach. Once there, turn right (east) and follow the trail. You will come to some huts and pass a couple of farms before reaching El Abra.

■ Places to Stay

El Abra, about five km/three miles along the beach road, ☎ 7/928-3344, $, is my favorite place between Varadero and Havana. The huge grounds are well kept, the cabins clean and comfortable – and the toilets have seats! There is no air conditioning or TV – another bonus – but there is a large pool, a pizza bar and a restaurant that serves excellent meals. The staff is friendly and the ocean is about 30meters/100 feet from the fenced grounds.

Breezes Jibacoa, ☎ 7/928-5122, $$$$, cubacon@ enet.cu, is an all-inclusive village featuring 250 large rooms with patio doors leading to a balcony or deck, and 18 acres of lush vegetation on the grounds. Jungle hills form a backdrop. Each room has two beds, night tables, a private bathroom, hairdryer, coffee maker, iron, air conditioning, and a mini-bar. You can swim in their huge pool surrounded by deck chairs or you can head out to the beach where there are 300 meters/1,000 feet of raked and cleaned sand. Or, you can sit under a

PRICE CHART
Per room for two people, per day.
$. $25-50
$$. $51-75
$$$. $76-100
$$$$. $101-150
$$$$$. . . . . over $150

palapa hut and have a waiter bring you a drink while you read a book. There are restaurants, bars and snack shops conveniently placed around the resort. **Martino's Restaurant** serves good Italian food. There is a gym, Jacuzzi, tennis court, volleyball (in or out of the pool), and basketball hoops. There are also exercise classes you can join, table games, kayaks, and bicycles you can use. If upscale is what you want, this may be the place. The tour office can arrange to take you into Havana for a day or to the caves in Matanzas.

Breezes Jibacoa is past El Abra, and its guests will be picked up either at Havana or Varadero airport. No children under 16 allowed.

Villa Loma de Jibacoa, at the mouth of the Jibacoa River, ☎ 7/928-5316, $, economia@jibacoa. esihabana.cu, has a number of little cabins with private bathrooms, TVs, fans and daily maid service. This is equal in standard to El Abra except Loma overlooks the bridge and is a little farther from the beach. There is a restaurant serving international meals, a pool, a bar, and a currency exchange desk. Deposit boxes are located in the rooms and some muscle-powered sports equipment is available for guest use.

To get to Villa Loma, ask the taxi driver to let you off so you can walk up the trail to this *campimento*, which is accessed from a different side road and is closer to the main highway than El Abra.

■ Places to Eat

When you leave the grounds of El Abra, turn left up the hill. Walk for 30 to 45 minutes and you will come to a *paladar* that serves excellent food. There is a sign. The most interesting thing about this place is the owners have fighting cocks and they love to show their guests how the birds are trained. Of course, all the *campimentos* have places to eat, but eating at a *paladar* offers a change, not necessarily in food but in setting.

West of Havana

Both Soroa and Las Terrazas can be visited as day-trips from Pinar or Havana. However, they both have hotels, in the event you want to stay.

Las Terrazas

Las Terrazas is a tourist complex, 65 km/40 miles west of Havana, which has adopted the catch-phrase "eco-tourism center," where "sustainable tourism" is promoted. The hotel has been built with modern materials like polished tiles and white plaster and the entire complex is tucked into the mountain vegetation so that it is non-intrusive to the eye. The government encourages visitors to explore the remains of old coffee plantations nearby and to go birding in the replanted forest. All the hiking trails are maintained and easy to follow, with most taking less than two hours – in the heat, that seems to be enough.

> **AUTHOR TIP:** Be certain to carry water when walking the trails.

Western Cuba

The town was built in 1971 with reforestation/eco-tourism as its main purpose. There are about 1,000 local people living here, many working at the hotel. A visitors center in the village provides maps of the trails and will also provide a guide if you are hesitant to travel through the jungle on your own. Guide services run $20 for the morning – that's per person.

If you are traveling independently, the cost is $2 to access the village, although if you are staying at the hotel, there is no fee.

■ Adventures on Foot

 La Serafina is the longest trail in the park and the best for birders. Because it goes up quite a distance, the birds vary. There are reported to be over 75 species in the forests here at any given time. Going with a guide will increase your chance of seeing the more elusive birds.

Las Delicias starts at the same place as the route to the Buenavista coffee plantation but turns off and heads uphill to a good view of the valley. This hike is about three km/1.8 miles.

El Taburete is the easiest of the hikes. It starts by the road that leads to the village (near the turnoff for the hotel) and goes around the hills before returning to the hotel.

Take time to tour the restored **Buenavista Estate**, which is within walking distance from Las Terrazas. Follow the hiking trail for 2.5 km/1.5 miles from the town center to the estate.

El Contento Farm is also close to Las Terrazas. The round-trip hike is seven km/four miles through the ruins of an old coffee estate that once belonged to William Orse, a British settler who lived and worked here during the 1800s. The walk ends at the San Juan River, where you can swim before walking back to the hotel.

■ Place to Stay

Moka Hotel, Km 51 along the National High-way between Havana and Pinar del Rio, ☎ 7/ 387-8600, $$$/$$$$, is in Las Terrazas tourist town on the Loma del Salon (a hill). It is taste-fully tucked into the surrounding jungle vegetation, its colors non-intrusive. The hotel is spacious, yet its 26 rooms are small. They are equipped with private bathrooms, cable TVs, mini-bars and air condition-ing. There is also a restaurant, bar, tourist office, swimming pool, and bike/motorbike rentals. You can have all your meals included in the room rate or pay for the room only and purchase your meals at the res-taurant or snack bar. The main reason visitors stay here is to explore and hike in the region.

At the lake below the hotel is a two-bedroom house with two air-conditioned rooms, a kitchen, bar, and television. Those renting the house have the option of using all the services of the hotel. This is a good deal for larger groups and those who like to make some of their own meals. Contact the hotel for reservations.

Soroa

Soroa is a tourist complex much like Las Terrazas. It is in the Sierra del Rosario region, 70 km/44 miles west of Havana and six km/four miles north of the main highway.

It is best to come to Soroa by car or on a tour booked from your hotel in the city because there are no buses, and public transportation (hitching) could be slow.

■ Sightseeing

One of the attractions is a **botanical garden** with an orchidarium that has 350 orchid spe-cies and 11,000 ornamental plants, some of which go to reforestation programs. Bird-viewing stations are interspersed around the gardens, and trails go for about 0.5 km/.3 miles. The gardens were first built by Tomas Felipe Camacho, who left Havana in 1943, just after his daughter died. He came to this peaceful spot to try to live without his beloved child. He was hit with a second tragedy when his wife died shortly after. He then dedicated his life to building the gardens. Tomas died in 1960 and shortly after, the new Castro government took over. The gardens are open from 8 am to noon and from 12:30 pm to 4 pm daily. The cost to enter is $3 per person.

■ Adventures on Foot

 El Salto walk runs a short way along the river to a waterfall that drops 20 meters/66 feet into a pool; swimming is allowed. The waterfall isn't really much to see, especially during the height of dry season. The cost to walk this trail is $2.

You can walk up to **El Mirador**, which is at the top of a hill in town. Signs close to the hotel indicate the way. The walk takes half an hour or so, along the dirt trail. Other trails lead off the main one. Part-way up is a massage hut where you can sit in a hot spring, have a massage and pretend you've been up to the top. The cost for the dipping is $2.

To do any of the other treks in the area, hire a guide ($6 per person) at the hotel.

■ Places to Stay & Eat

 Hotel Soroa, Km 8 Carretera de Soroa, $$/ $$$, has cabins with air conditioning, cable TV, kitchen facilities in 10 of the cabins and private bathrooms with hot water. Six cabins are designed for the luxury traveler and have their own swimming pools and butler service. For the peasants, there are a few cabins where you must fend for yourself. The hotel has a number of restaurants and bars. For outdoor entertainment, you can rent a horse, have a massage, or swim in the large pool (not the one attached to your cabin). This is a great place to stay.

Casa Pepe, $, Carretera Km 5 on the road into Soroa, is a little house with one room for rent; it includes a bathroom. It is a lot cheaper than the hotel.

■ Leaving Havana Province

 West of the province of Havana is the province of Pinar del Rio, mostly an agricultural area. Arriving in the city of the same name you get the feeling that you've hit the Wild West. The population is sparse and the landscape is wild. You expect to see a *gaucho* riding up on his horse.

The countryside is famous for its haystack mountains, with caves and underground rivers that attract spelunkers or hikers. Thermal baths and beaches in are not difficult to reach for health spa and sun lovers.

> **AUTHOR NOTE:** *Mogotes* is the local name for the haystack mountains seen between Pinar del Rio and Viñales.

San Diego de los Baños

San Diego de los Baños was discovered by a sick slave during slaving days. The medicinal waters of this spa resort have been popular with Cubans for over 300 years. About 20 km/12 miles off the National Highway between Havana and Pinar, it is difficult to reach. You can get a ride on a truck from Pinar del Rio or bring your own vehicle. If you come by truck, you must stay at least one night in the village. With your own car, you should be able to get back to Pinar for the night.

The baths are located in a village building beside the river, from which some of the water and mud are obtained (the spring that feeds the thermal pool in the spa has its source near the river). The spa is open from 8 am to 5 pm daily and there are medical staff on duty at all times to see what kind of program they can put you on to cure whatever you may have – and even some things you may not realize you have, like wrinkles or psychological problems. When I was there, the doctor was quite convinced that I had some psychological problem and insisted on talking with me in an attempt to identify it. A serious consultation will cost $25; this includes recommended treatments. A 15-minute dip in the hot springs deep in the bowels of the building costs $5. There are changing rooms and lockers where you can leave your belongings. The spa also provides lovely large towels. You are not permitted to stay in the water longer than 15 minutes because of the dangers of heat exhaustion. If all your problems aren't solved, there are numerous "doctors" in the village who can sell you mud to cure all the ailments you couldn't cure while at the springs. The mud is packaged in nice containers and costs anywhere from $10 to $100 depending on its purpose.

BIRDING BUFFS

Parque la Guira is just outside the village of San Diego. You can walk to it in under an hour. Go to the gas station on the edge of town and turn right (the village should be behind you). Continue until you see a huge stone gate with what was once a beautiful garden enclosed. The wild vegetation at the park draws birds and offers good camouflage for you. Maybe the odd spider or iguana will cross your path. This is a pleasant walk.

If you have to stay overnight in San Diego de los Baños, you have a few options. **Hotel Mirador**, ☎ 8/ 2387-8338, $$, is in the village, just beyond the spa building. The 30 air-conditioned rooms are average size with bamboo furniture, soft beds and hot-water showers. There is a restaurant, pool and bar. There is little to do in town besides visit the spa and drink around the pool. You can book trekking trips at the hotel's tour desk.

There are very basic *casas* in town. Ask the gentleman who runs the restaurant across from the school.

Pinar del Rio

■ History

Before Columbus arrived in Cuba, Indians lived in the Viñales area hunting and gathering. Some left records of their existence by painting on cave walls. These paintings are now a tourist attraction.

The Spanish settlers called the area (all the land from the Los Palacios River to the San Antonio Cape) Nueva Filipina. When the provinces were reorganized in 1778, the name was changed to Pinar del Rio for the pine forests surrounding the Guama River, where most people lived.

Murals, Pinar del Rio.

Development of the area revolved around tobacco growing and cattle ranching. The tobacco industry took a huge financial leap when the Francisco Donatien Cigar Factory opened in the early 1800s. This resulted in most of the land being used to grow the plant and also led to a railway being built to service the island's most western point.

■ Services

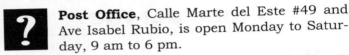

Post Office, Calle Marte del Este #49 and Ave Isabel Rubio, is open Monday to Saturday, 9 am to 6 pm.

ETECSA, Calle Gerardo Medina and Juan Gómez, has Internet cards for $6 per hour. You use only whatever portion you need until the hour is used up. There are three machines; the connection is dial-up, but the speed is fairly rapid.

Medical Hospital, Carretera Central (2.5 km/1.5 miles from the center), ☎ 82/75-4443.

BUYER BEWARE

The *jinateros* are a piss-off here. They meet your car on the outskirts of town and insist on tagging along with you. They cannot be shaken off. Many people refuse to stay in Pinar for this reason. You might want to telephone your *casa* or hotel ahead of time so the *jinateros* don't get a commission.

■ Getting Here & Away

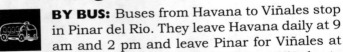

BY BUS: Buses from Havana to Viñales stop in Pinar del Rio. They leave Havana daily at 9 am and 2 pm and leave Pinar for Viñales at 11:30 am and 4:30 pm daily. The bus from Viñales to Havana departs at 8 am and 2 pm and leaves Pinar at 8:50 am and 2:50 pm. The fare from Pinar from Havana is $11; from Pinar to Viñales is $6.

■ Festivals

 The **Tobacco Festival** has been held every December since 1998 to celebrate the growing of tobacco. You must be a cigar-lover to go to this festival as these are smoked, tested, exchanged and enjoyed by all who attend.

■ Sightseeing

 Francisco Donatien Tobacco Factory, Calle Maceo Oeste #157, ☎ 82/387-8122, makes Vegueros, originally a coarse cigar not made for export, but one that was kept for the Cuban smoker. However, this is no longer true; in 1961 the Castro government changed the factory's policy. Now, Veguero cigars are made for export. They are good-quality cigars, with a mild grassy flavor.

It is interesting to go to the factory and see how cigars are carefully rolled, inspected and boxed before being sold. The man I spoke with had no teeth at the front; lost to smoking! The factory is open from 8 am to noon and 1 pm to 4 pm Monday to Friday, and Saturday till noon. There is a charge of $3 for the tour. You can purchase some cigars here or go across the street to Habanos, where you can drink coffee and buy cigars from most factories in Cuba.

IT'S A WRAP

Alejandro Robaina, an 84-year-old tobacco farmer, is reputed to grow the best cigar wrapper in the world. On the Vega Robaina plantation, Alejandro plants his seeds during a certain phase of the moon (he won't say when), tends and picks the plants by hand so the leaves are not bent or torn, inspects them regularly for the blue mold to which they are prone and keeps the plants under a tenting material so direct sunlight doesn't cause the leaves to become thick and brittle. When it is time to harvest, he knows the day, or almost the hour when this should be done.

Of all tobacco wrappers exported to Havana, 30% come from Alejandro's crops. This wrapper is used only in hand-made premium cigars, one of which is called the Vegas Robaina, named in his honor. Alejandro was given a car by Castro in appreciation for his knowledge and love of the plant.

La Guayabita Brandy Factory, Ave Isabel Rubio Sur #189, between Calle Ceferino Fernandez and Frank Pais, (no phone), was previously called Casa Garay. Brandy has been hand-produced in the small rooms of this factory since 1906. The liquor has been awarded prizes at the Havana Fair since the factory opened, and in 1921 it won the Rome Fair Medal. It is interesting to tour the factory, get the smells, see the bottling process and finally purchase your souvenir bottle. The tours are ongoing and in English, from Monday to Friday, 9 am to 4 pm, and the cost is $1 per person.

Cathedral de San Rosendo, Ave Maceo Este #3 and Gerardo Medina, ☎ 82/283-2430, was built in 1883. You can visit the church during services. Its two bell towers might be of interest to some, but the church itself has little to draw visitors.

Teatro José Jacinto, Ave Martí and Calle Colón, was built in 1883 and is considered one of the most beautiful buildings in Cuba. It has been going through restoration since 1991 and the work is still incomplete. If there is a performance while you are here, considering buying tickets. Visit the tourist office for information.

Museums

The province of Pinar del Rio has 20 museums, one in almost every municipality. I did not visit them all. If you happen to be in a small municipality with some

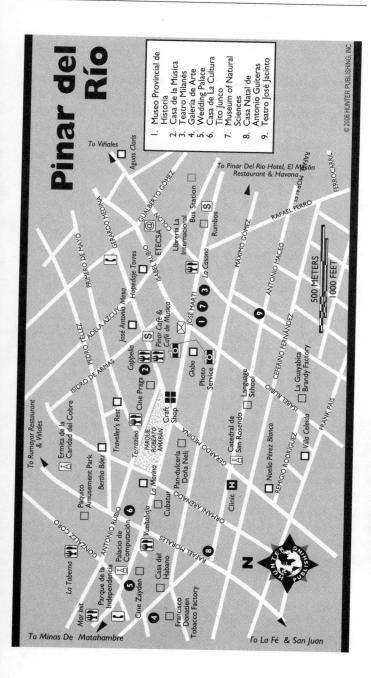

Pinar del Río

1. Museo Provincial de Historia
2. Casa de la Música
3. Teatro Milanés
4. Galería de Arte
5. Wedding Palace
6. Casa de La Cultura
7. Museum of Natural Sciences
8. Casa Natal de Antonio Guiteras
9. Teatro José Jacinto

© 2006 HUNTER PUBLISHING, INC

To Viñales

Aguas Claris

To Pinar Del Río Hotel, El Mesón Restaurant & Havana

GERARDO MEDINA

PRIMERO DE MAYO

PEDRO TELLEZ

ADELA AZCUY

ISIDRO DE ARMAS

GUALBERTO GÓMEZ

ISABEL RUBIO

ETECSA

Bus Station

Librería La Internacional

La Casona

Rumbos

MÁXIMO GÓMEZ

RAFAEL FERRO

ANTONIO MACEO

CEFERINO FERNÁNDEZ

ISABEL RUBIO

FRANK PAIS

FERROCARRIL

MORACELE RAFA

José Antonio Mesa

Pinar Café & Café de Musica

Coppelia

Cine Praga

Traveller's Rest

Bertha Báez

Terrazina

PARQUE ROBERTO AMARÁN

Craft Shop

JOSÉ MARTI

Globo

Photo Service

Language School

Catedral de San Rosendo

La Guayabita Brandy Factory

Villa Celeida

Noelia Pérez Blanco

REMIGIO RODRIGUEZ

GERARDO MEDINA

ORHANI ARENADO

Pan-dulcería Doña Neli

Clinic

Cubatur

La Marina

Vueltabajo

Palacio de Computación

Casa del Habano

Parque de la Independencia

Cine Zayden

Francisco Donatien Tobacco Factory

Ermita de la Caridad del Cobre

Paquito Amusement Park

ANTONIO RUBIO

RAFAEL MORALES

GONZÁLEZ CORO

La Taberna

Mar Init

To Rumayor Restaurant & Viñales

To Minas De Matahambre

To La Fé & San Juan

500 METERS
1000 FEET

N

HUNTER PUBLISHING

spare time, by all means ask about their local museum.

Museum of Natural Sciences of Sandalio de Noda, Ave Martí Este #202 between Ave Com Pinares and Hermanos Saiz, ☎ 82/382-2206, is located in a beautiful building, the first concrete one built in the country. It is called the Guach Palace. A palace may be a misnomer; the building is an eclectic mansion with ornate, cement exterior arches reminiscent of a sultan's home, separated by Doric columns and accented along the roof with spiked decorations. There is also an Ionic frieze and a Hindu portico inside. The palace was built by Dr. Alvarez Guasch, in honor of his wife.

The displays, located in eight rooms, try to illustrate evolution from ancient marine fossils that were found in the Viñales Valley to the more recent species like butterflies and animals (no stuffed humans yet). The most famous and oldest fossil ever found in Cuba is that of the *Lactophrys trigonus*, a trunkfish that changed little through the years. The second most famous fossil is the plesiosurus, an ancient reptile that lived during the late Jurrasic period, 200 million years ago. The evolution of plants is also explored, although I found this far less interesting. The museum is open from Tuesday to Saturday, 2 pm to 6 pm, and Sunday, 9 am to 1 pm. The cost is $1.

Provincial Museum of History, Ave Martí Este #58 between Calle Colón and Ave Isabel Rubio, ☎ 82/382-4300, has a wide range of displays, including items that belonged to Enrique Jorrin. He is famous for being the man who first played the cha-cha in the hotel Rumayor (now closed, although the restaurant and bar are still open to the public) just outside the city limits on the road to Viñales. The historical displays start with the early Indian people living at the front of a cave, then move on to colonial times, with a few items relating to slavery and the development of tobacco. Other rooms are dedicated to art, both colonial and modern. Famous painters who have displayed their work here are Pedo Pablo Oliva, Tiburcio Lorenzo and Domingo Ramos, the man who made the Viñales area famous with his art. One room contains crystal, porcelain and pottery. The museum is open from Tuesday to Saturday, 2 pm to 6 pm, and Sunday, 9 am to 1 pm. There is a $1 fee to enter.

Casa Natal de Antonio Guiteras Holmes, Ave Maceo Oeste #52 and Ormandi Arenano, ☎ 82/275-2378, is in a house built during the 1800s. It holds personal items that belonged to Guiteras, a student of pharmacy and an opponent of Machado during the 1930s. Guiteras led an unsuccessful uprising in Santiago de Cuba in 1930 and was sent to prison for a year. He formed the Revolutionary Union with socialism in mind. After the fall of Machado, he became a member of the government and opposed US intervention in Cuba. He seized the American-owned electrical company, turning it into a Cuban operation. After Batista came to power, Guiteras went underground. Then, while attempting to leave for Mexico, there was a scuffle with Batista's henchmen and Guiteras was killed. He was 28 years old. Open 9 am to 4:30 pm; Saturday until noon; closed Sunday. Free.

■ Adventures in Water

Maria la Gorda

 This tiny island is the most western part of Cuba, along the Guanabacabibes Peninsula and inside the **Ensenada de Corrientes Nature Preserve**. You can either stay at the only resort on the island or go back and forth from Pinar.

FAT MARY'S INN

The village was named after legend. Apparently, a Venezuelan woman, named Maria la Gorda, (Fat Mary) was captured by pirates and abandoned here on the beaches. To survive, she started feeding any sailors/pirates who came to the area. She was so successful that eventually she opened an inn. And so Maria la Gorda's place came into being.

Diving is popular here. Shallow dives (five meters/16 feet) feature coral formations that house some of the smaller fish and crustaceans. At about 10 meters/32 feet, you will start to see chains of hillocks cut with channels and places where walls fall quite steeply. These have great tunnels and caves where black coral is starting to form (it grows one cm/a third of an inch per 100 years!). Occasionally you will see barracuda and stingrays and during the right time of year (usually December), those with a tremendous amount of luck will see a whale shark.

This popular resort area has a total of 39 good dive sites close by; some of them are exceptional. The only resort on the island is run by Gaviota Hotels, ☎ 82/77-8131, www.gaviota-grupo.com, $$. It can also be booked through the Ministry of Tourism in Pinar del Rio, Macea #117, between Galiano and San Juan. The resort has comfortable, air-conditioned cabins with good views. There is nothing special about the cabins, some even have shared bathrooms, but those coming to dive spend little time inside so it doesn't matter much. There are also some fairly large rooms in the main section fo the hotel that have private bathrooms and air-conditioning. The International Dive Center is located at the hotel. The center supplies boats and equipment and a two-dive trip will cost $50-$75.

■ Places to Stay

Hotel Pinar del Rio, Calle Martí and the highway, $$, ☎ 82/385-7074, is a big 1960s-style hotel. It has 135 large, comfortable rooms with private bathrooms and hot water all day. Each room has a balcony, cable TV, twin beds, and a dresser. Rooms are cleaned daily and the hotel is in good shape. However, the elevators are a bit dodgy and often not working at all. There's an on-site restaurant and a few small snack bars that are open at odd times, some during the day, some at night. The popular swimming pool in the back is patronized by many Cuban families and music is played on huge ghetto blasters until about 9 or 10 pm every evening. The disco across the street from the hotel closes at midnight – don't expect to sleep before that. At the time of writing, this is the only hotel in town accepting foreigners.

Aguas Claris, road to Viñales, ☎ 82/385-2772, $$, about five km/three miles from the center of town, has cabins with air conditioning, hot water, balconies, cable TV and glass patio doors. Getting to and from the center can be done by taxi ($5), public bus (slow) or hitching. Walking isn't that bad either. I loved

PRICE CHART
Per room for two people, per day.
$ $25-50
$$ $51-75
$$$ $76-100
$$$$ $101-150
$$$$$ . . . . over $150

Lily pond, Aguas Claris.

this place. The swimming pool is large, the grounds are immaculate and there is a frog pond full of lilies near the restaurant. You must book ahead with Cubamar if you want a room.

Tanya and Rodrigo, Calle Colón #167, between Mariana Grajales and Labra, ☎ 82/375-3359 or 82/375-3875, has two rooms in the house, one with a private bathroom, the other without. The rooms are large and lovely and the breakfast is exceptional. The kitchen sitting area is between the two rooms and can be used as a gathering spot. This is a good place, but do not let Rodrigo arrange anything for you as he will take a hefty cut for himself.

■ Places to Eat

La Casona, Ave Martí and Calle Colón, ☎ 82/387-8263, is in the center of the city and can hold about 50 people. They serve both Cuban and International cuisine for about $10 per dish. Open from 11 am to 11 pm daily.

Restaurant Rumayor, Km 1 on the road to Viñales, ☎ 82/276-3051, is a large rambling place with stone walls and open patios that offer some privacy. The meal to order is *pollo ahumado* (smoked chicken). It costs $10 but is one of the best meals in Cuba. There is a cabaret downstairs ($5) where you can dance the cha-cha (which originated in this hotel (now closed).

Hotel Pinar del Rio, Ave Martí and the highway, has a good restaurant. A good-size portion of fish or chicken with salad and drink costs about $3 per person. They offer the main meal of the day between 11 am and 2 pm (when Cubans eat theirs). If you don't join that, you will have to eat off-premises.

■ Nightlife

Café Pinar, Calle Velez Caviedes Norte #34, ☎ 82/387-8199, is the only hopping spot in

Pinar, with live music from 10 pm until 2 am almost every night. If you come for a meal (good spaghetti, I am told) before the music, you do not have to pay the $2 cover charge.

Café de la Musica, Calle Velez Caviedes Norte (no phone), is across from Café Pinar and costs only $1 to enter. It has a nice patio from which to listen to their nightly entertainment. The hours of operation are 9 pm to 2 am nightly.

Disco Azul, Calle Martí and the highway, across from Hotel Pinar, is a rocking place. If you're staying in the hotel, you may as well join the fun because you won't be sleeping before the place shuts down at midnight.

Cabaret Rumayor, Km 1 on the highway to Viñales, ☎ 82/386-3051, is a Tropicana show, albeit much smaller than those in Havana or Matanzas. The show is performed daily from Tuesday to Sunday at 11 pm. You can eat here prior to the show. The restaurant is known throughout the region for its smoked chicken, a truly delicious feast (see above).

Viñales

The trip to this village and its nearby caves can be done as a day-trip from Pinar or as an overnight excursion. Viñales is a nice little place – far cozier than Pinar, but more expensive too. The landscape is nicer and the atmosphere at most *casas* and hotels is intimate.

■ Getting Here & Around

 BY BUS: A bus from Havana passes through Pinar before finally arriving here. It travels from Havana (9 am, 2 pm) to Pinar del Rio (11:30 am, 4:30 pm) and on to Viñales 50 minutes later. The bus from Viñales leaves for Havana at 8 am and 2 pm; it leaves Pinar at 8:50 am and 2:50 pm.

The cost to Viñales from Havana is $12; the cost from Pinar to Viñales is $6.

BY TAXI: You can hire a taxi in Pinar to take you to Viñales at a cost of $20 a day. The driver will take you to the caves, stop for lunch, head on to the miradors and bring you back to Pinar. If there are four people sharing, this is a good deal. The best taxi I found was Humberto Suarez Morejon, Calle B #21, Km 3.5 Carretera to Luis Lazo, ☎ 8/277-9633. Humberto speaks English and is an excellent driver. If he is busy, ask at the taxi stand outside the bus station in Pinar; there are lots of drivers waiting to take you.

■ Sightseeing

 El Mural de la Prehistoria is a 180-meter/ 550-foot painting on the side of a haystack mountain (*mogote*). Commissioned by Castro and painted by Leovigildo Gonzalez Morillo, the mural depicts the evolution of humans from early on to the early Indians of Cuba. Castro decided to have the work done when he was sitting near the mountain. The surroundings are much more interesting than the painting itself. I suggest you take a photo from outside the fence and save the $1 entry fee; it is not worth entering unless you are desperate to sit and have a drink at the restaurant. You must take a taxi to get here.

■ Adventures on Foot

Caving

 Cueva del Indio is eight km/five miles north of Viñales. This cave takes about half an hour to go through and includes both walking and riding in a boat. There are some nice rock formations, but nothing spectacular. Partway through, you will climb into a boat and travel for another five minutes to the exit of the cave. Good shoes are required. Outside the cave you can watch an Indian dance-and-drum

performance or you can ride on an ox; the Indian
dance is free, the ox ride is $2. The cave is open from
9 am to 5 pm and costs $5 per person to tour.

Cueva de Santo Tomas, beyond the village of
Moncada, is one of the largest caves in Cuba. The interconnecting rooms go for almost 50 km/31 miles
and drop five levels; visitors are only allowed to go
2 km/1.5 miles. Some rooms have names indicating
what you might see inside, like the chaos room, dark-
ness room or the incredible room. This cave has not
been "developed," so you must have headlamps, good
shoes and a guide. Book this tour in Viñales or Pinar
and allow yourself half a day. It is well worth your time
and money. It is open at 8 am until 6 pm. A short one-
hour tour costs $8 and a half-day is $17.

Climbing

Climbing is a new sport here, and if you wish to partake, bring gear. This region has many overhanging
faces on 300-meter/1,000-foot crags that ascend stalactites and tufa columns overlooking a valley full of
mogotes (haystack mountains) beckoning to be
climbed. For information on climbing, go to www.
cubaclimbing. com and follow the routes, advice, and
information there. Worth reading is the site's section
about the history of climbing in Cuba. Contact José
Millo Gómez, Calle Rafael Trejo #108; or Ana Maria
Cruz Mitjans, Km 1, Carretera to la Ermita, in Viñales
if you need a Cuban guide.

> **AUTHOR TIP:** Assuming you will
> pack your own gear, try to bring some
> that you can leave. This will always
> win you a friend in Cuba.

■ Adventures on Wheels

Motorbikes are available for rent from a
shop on Calle Salvador Cisneros, the main
street in Viñales. They cost $20 a day. The

bikes are 50 cc Suzukis; larger ones cost a bit more. There are no helmets and gasoline is extra.

■ Adventure in Water

Cayo Juitas is 90 km/55 miles from Pinar along the Minas de Matahambre road on the north side of the island and five km/three miles past the village of Santa Lucia. It is the perfect place for a day-trip from Viñales – be sure to take your favorite book.

> **AUTHOR NOTE:** A 3.2-km/two-mile causeway goes from the mainland to the island. You must have your passport and pay $5 per person to drive across the causeway.

Cayo Juitas offers nothing but a lighthouse and a small concession that rents watercraft (pedal boats or kayaks) and sells hamburgers, sodas, beer, etc. The island has seven km/four miles of white sandy beaches, few people and no hotels (although I hear they are going to build one soon). You should have your own transportation or hire a taxi for the day. You can camp on the island if you rent a tent (you are not permitted to use your own).

HEALTHY REEF MAY NOT LAST

Cayo Juitas has one of the healthiest reefs in Cuba, according to the Reef Relief Organization, which studied it in the late 1990s. However, they did find evidence of black-band disease, identified by a ring-shaped bacterial mat, which infects coral and leaves it dead within a short time. The bacteria belong to the Phormidium family. It is believed that warmer waters and human sewage contribute to the presence of the bacteria, but the actual role of the sewage in the reef's deterioration has not been established. The reef is located on the western side of the island and its drop-offs offer great snorkeling. However, no sea urchins or large game fish swim in or around these reefs. If those are what you are looking for, take a boat and go farther west, where the coral is home to large parrotfish and snappers.

Mangroves on the north side of the island have good birding, while the south has shrub and grasses, attracting different birds. Most common are hawks, hummingbirds and woodpeckers.

The island's lighthouse was built over 100 years ago and is still in operation. Its keeper is probably one of the last real lighthouse people in the world. Day-trips can be arranged from the tour office in Hotel Pinar del Rio. They cost $50 a day, which includes transportation and a meal. Independently, you can hire a taxi in Viñales for about $50 for the day.

Cayo Levisa and its hotel of the same name, **Hotel Cayo Levisa**, $$, is where divers station themselves at the western end of Cuba. The cay has about three km/two miles of white-sand beach and one resort (all-inclusive is optional) with two dozen cottages set along the beach. They have cable TV, private bathrooms, two double beds, tiled floors and air conditioning. Each cottage has either a balcony or a patio.

Divers can expect to see star and brain corals and tons of sea fans waving in the currents. Fish include ocean sturgeons, grunts and Bermuda chubs. Of the 15 diving sites near the cay, **St. Carlos Crown** is the most popular. Equipment and one dive will cost about $50; a two-tank dive will run $75. Diving during peak seasons, from December 15 to the end of April, requires booking and full payment at least three weeks in advance. The hotel has equipment for rent and offers day and night dives.

To get here, take a public boat from Palma Rubia Sea Port, just northwest of Viñales. Levisa is about 20 km/12 miles northwest of the port. The boat leaves the Sea Port at 10 am and 6 pm daily, returning from Levisa at 9 am and 5 pm. You can also hire a water taxi for $10 per person.

■ Spas

St. Vicente Spa, Km 33, Carretera Puerto Esperanza, ☎ 8/93-6201, $$$, is just five km/three miles from Viñales, on the banks of San Vicente River. The river waters are supposed to have medicinal properties and when you combine the water with the mud, you'll be cured of things you don't even know you have. There are 30 lovely rooms, some in tiny cottages. Each room has cable TV, twin beds, air conditioning, a balcony and tiled floors. The spa is a true retreat, and I heard that the mud facials are great. The gardens are well kept and the restaurant serves good food, although the variety is limited. The tour office here offers horseback riding and river tours. You need not stay at the hotel to have a mud bath or a horse tour, but non-guests pay more.

■ Places to Stay

Hotels

Hotel Los Jasmines, Km 25 on the road to Pinar, ☎ 8/93-6205, $$$, is a large complex with two apart-ment-like buildings, done up colonial style, towering over the swimming pool. They also have some cab-ins for rent. Most rooms look out to the Viñales Val-ley, which is dotted with *mogotes*, the lovely lime-stone haystack mounds that give the region its fame. The rooms have air

PRICE CHART
Per room for two people, per day.
$. $25-50
$$. $51-75
$$$. $76-100
$$$$. $101-150
$$$$$. . . . over $150

conditioning, private bathrooms, balconies and mini-bars. Rates include breakfast. The tour desk offers trips to the caves and the islands, as well as horse treks through the valley. There are two restaurants and a number of bars, a massage parlor and a souvenir shop. Although a bit outside the center of town, this is a lovely place to stay. Tour buses stop at the viewpoint above the hotel so visitors can take photos.

Hotel La Ermita, Km 1.5 on the Pinar road, ☎ 8/93-6071, $$, is closer to town than Jasmines and every bit as comfortable. The 62 rooms are large, some are wheelchair accessible and all are located close to the swimming pool. The grounds are lush with vegetation and attract many birds.

Casas Particulares

Nena's, Calle Cienfuegos #56 (no phone), has two rooms with fans and a private bathroom. Meals can be arranged. The husband works on a tobacco farm and will teach you how to roll cigars or show you how tobacco is grown.

Mario Arteaga Gonzales, Salvador Cisneros Interior #1, Edificio Colonial apt. #9 (no phone), is close to the bus station and just behind the hospital. The apartment is owned by an older couple who rent one room without private bath. This is not a party house. There is a porch where you can sit. Meals can be arranged and are very good. The prices here are lower because of the shared bath.

Villa El Panchon, Calle Joaquin Parez #27 (no phone), is just a two-minute walk from the main street in the center of town. Owner Gladys Acosta Calzadilla has one spotless room with a private bathroom. Meals can be arranged and there are special rates for longer stays.

■ Places to Eat

 Casa de Don Tomas, Calle Salvador Cisneros #140, ☎ 8/93-6300, is on the main street in town in a blue colonial house with two covered porches. It is the oldest house in the area and the front and back patios are always full of foreigners eating or drinking. Although the food is not the very best in the village, and it runs a bit higher in cost than most ($10-$20 per meal), the atmosphere is the draw. The drink of the house consists of rum, pineapple juice and honey. It is delicious. The restaurant is open from 10 am to 11 pm daily.

Jurasico, Pons Road, five km/three miles from Viñales, ☎ 8/93-3223, offers international food but their specialty is chicken in orange sauce for $12. This is a nice restaurant with tables on an outside porch overlooking a pool, tablecloths and efficient waiters.

■ Nightlife

 Nightlife in Viñales is pretty much what you make it. There are some quiet bars on the main street or you can make yourself a rum cocktail and drink it while sitting at your residence. There is also the choice of going to the disco that is located in a cave (highly overrated) at El Palenque (see below). **Artex Bar**, on the main street (Salvador Cisnero) in town, has nightly entertainment and no cover charge; this is where most foreigners go. It opens at 5 pm and closes around midnight.

El Palenque, Km 36 on Carretera Puerto Esperanza, ☎ 8/93-6290, is the cave disco where your eardrums can be pounded out. It is also a restaurant with a roasted chicken specialty ($10). There is a cabaret in the early evening and the disco is open till 2 am. You will need transportation. If your hotel is in St. Vincente, this is a good form of evening entertainment. The entry fee is $5 if you are not having supper.

Isla de la Juventud

The Island of Youth, 100 km/62 miles south of Havana and 114 km/70 miles west of Cayo Largo, is the largest of the 672 Canarreos Islands in this archipelago. It covers 2,200 square km/850 square

miles and has a population of 72,000. The island is second in size only to the main island. It is designated a "Special Municipality," with its own capital.

The capital of the island, **Nueva Gerona**, was founded in 1830 and named Reina Amalia after the wife of King Ferdinand VII of Spain. During colonial times, the island was used as a rest area for the Spanish military. Prior to that it was the temporary home of pirates such as Captain Morgan and Frances Drake. In recent times, it became a penal colony housing famous men like Fidel and Raul Castro and José Martí.

The island's beaches are pristine, many untouched. The diving is so good that the island hosts one of the world's largest international underwater photography contests. If you are learning to dive and don't want to put out a lot of bucks going to the main diving centers, there are calm waters and interesting diving spots near Nueva Gerona, where skilled masters give lessons.

Juventud also has botanical gardens, historical museums, nature preserves and a general easy swing to its atmosphere. There are mineral springs, pine forests, a few caves, marble quarries and wetlands for birders.

Besides tourism, the island's economy depends on marble quarries, fishing, and the growing of citrus fruits and vegetables. In fact, so much food is grown here that during times of crisis island residents never suffer food shortages like those on the main island.

Geography

Isla de la Juventud is split into two fairly distinct topographical sections dissected by a large swamp called **Cienaga de Lanier**, which runs closer to the southern portion of the island than the north. The north consists of flat, dry farmland, although there are a couple of hills near Nueva Gerona – **Sierra de Caballo** stands at 280 meters/920 feet and **Sierra de Casa** is 235 meters/770 feet. Northern beaches have mostly black sand. The southern part of the island has wetlands and swamps that are good for birding and crocodile farms. The areas that are not swamp are home to some wild animals and the beaches, usually deserted, have white sand.

History

1494. Columbus discovers and names the island Evangelista. The island is inhabited.

1800. Spain sends colonizers and re-names it Reina Amalia. Pirates such as Frances Drake, Captain Morgan and John Hawkins use the southern part of the island, where the settlers are not living, as a refuge between raids.

1830. Nuevo Gerona is founded and the island becomes known as the Island of Exiles. It has also been called the Isle of Treasure and the Isle of Parrots prior to this. Locals become totally confused as to its real name.

1898. Island is ceded to the US.

1903. Japanese settlers establish the community of Jacksonville.

1907. US courts decide that the island actually belongs to Cuba, not the US, because the island's name was omitted from the Platt Amendment.

1914. Island is named the Isle of Pines.

1928. Modelo Prison is constructed by dictator Machado.

1953. Fidel and Raul Castro are jailed on the island.

1955. Young revolutionaries are given amnesty. Many leave the country.

1978. The name is changed from Isle of Pines to Isla de la Juventud.

Getting Here

■ By Ferry

 You must purchase your ticket at least a day in advance at the Naviera booth (7 am to noon daily at the Astro Bus Terminal in Havana, across from Plaza Revolución). Alternately, you can reserve a ticket at ☎ 7/878-1841. The $11 each-way fare includes the bus ride to Batabano on the south shore of the main island (Cuba), 1½ hours from Havana. You could take a taxi to the terminal for about $20. Your return ticket must also be booked a day ahead (and that fare will, again, include the bus ride).

> **AUTHOR NOTE:** It is possible to get a ticket for the ferry at Batabano Terminal, but there is no guarantee that you will get one for the day you want. If you need to stay over, there are some very basic homes that may give you a room, but I wouldn't be too sure of it. Better get your ticket in Havana.

Isla de la Juventad

You must show a passport before entering the ferry terminal station. Security will check your ID numerous times, and you will pass from one queue to another until every bit of baggage is checked and rechecked. You must turn in things like Swiss army knives, nail files, camp fuel and anything else that could be classified as a weapon. These items are taped into plastic bags and held until you land on Juventud. The atmosphere is similar to US Red-Zone security wrapped up in total confusion. My immersion heater (used to make coffee) caused a lot of trouble.

The ride to Isla de la Juventud takes five or six hours, depending on how often they have to fix the boat. Boats leave at 8 am and shortly after 2 pm. The hydrofoil is no longer running. The ferry dock in Nuevo Gerona is a five-minute walk from the center of town.

■ By Air

 There are two and sometimes three flights a day to Gerona from Havana, leaving at 6 am, 2:50 pm and 8 pm. Each flight takes about 40 minutes. Be at the airport a minimum of two hours before your flight. Flights rarely leave when they are supposed to and that means that they could leave early or not at all. The planes are old and decrepit but, so far, they always get to their destinations. Read a book. The cost is $22 each way and it is advised to purchase your return flight in Havana as the planes are often fully booked. For an extra $10 you can fly VIP, which means you get a special waiting room where you receive a free rum drink and you are the first to enter the plane and pick your seat. Return flights leave at 7 am, 3:50 pm and 9 pm daily (if there *are* three; but check with the airport first).

In Havana, purchase air tickets at the **Cubana de Aviacion** office, Calle 23 and Ave Infanta, Vedado and in Gerona at Calle 39 and Ave 18 in the Hotel Cubanita.

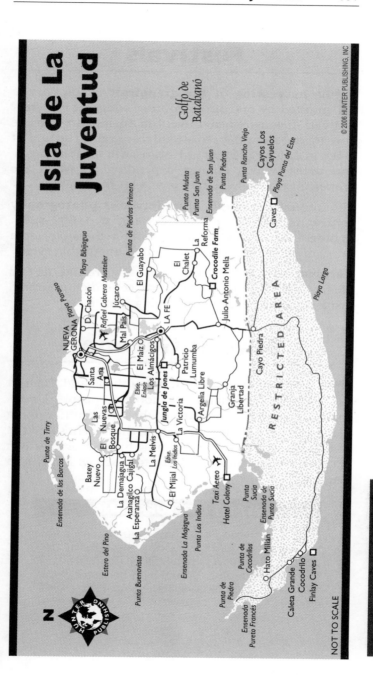

Isla de La Juventud

NOT TO SCALE

© 2006 HUNTER PUBLISHING, INC.

Festivals

The **harvesting of the grapefruit** in January is marked by one of the country's biggest and best festivals. If you are near Juventud during this time, be sure to save a few days to attend this event. The tourist office in any large hotel in Havana will be able to give you dates, which change depending on when the grapefruit ripens, which depends on the weather.

The annual international **underwater photography** contest is hosted by Hotel Colony, ☎ 4/639-8282. Photographers may want to contact the hotel or a tourism office for more information about this event.

Carnival is held every spring, usually around the end of March to mid-April. There is street dancing, eating, drinking, parades and interesting costumes.

Nueva Gerona

This tiny village is the capital of the island. It has a population of just a few thousand people. Everything, including one of the beaches, is within walking distance in the town. Buses go to the beaches and the prison museums, or taxis can be hired. Horse-drawn carts can take you from place to place within Nueva Gerona.

PLANT LIFE SUFFERING

You'll see that royal palm, guava, avocado and papaya trees are dying throughout the island. No reports are available about what is really happening. Don't let this deter your visit – so far it isn't extremely obvious.

AUTHOR CAUTION: There is a well-known *jinatero* on the island by the name of Zoraida. Be careful. She is slick and experienced and will arrange all your needs at a price that is probably double what other *jinateros* charge (which is almost double what you would pay working on your own).

■ Services

Post office, Calle 39 #1810, ☎ 45/332-2600, open 9 am to 6 pm daily, except Sunday.

Telephone office, Calle 41 and Ave 28, open 9 am to 9 pm daily, except Sunday. There is no Internet service at this office.

Internet service is available at the Guide Center on Ave Martí in the center of town. The cost is $6 per hour.

Immigration, Calle 34 and 35, open Monday and Wednesday, 8 am to 5 pm, with an hour off at noon.

Hospital General, Calle 39A, ☎ 45/332-3012, has a decompression chamber for divers. There is also an emergency room.

Banco de Credito y Comercio, Calle 39 #1802, at Ave 18, is open 8 am to 3 pm weekdays. They will change your traveler's checks or allow you to withdraw money on your non-American credit card.

■ Getting Around

BY BUS: Public buses go to the beaches.

BY CAR: You can rent a car, but they are not permitted south of the Crocodile farm or Colony Hotel unless they are four-wheel-drive and carrying a guide ($8 per person in the car!) There are just a few car companies on the island, and getting a car can be a problem. I dealt with **Havanautos**, Calle

Isla de la Juventad

32, open 7 am to 6 pm. They told me they had a small car reserved but when I arrived they had only a large one. They would not give it to me at the cheaper price. A small car costs about $50 a day with $10 a day insurance, plus gas. A 4x4 costs $70 a day, plus insurance. **Mi Car**, Calle 3, 4 between Ave 37 and 39, ☎ 46/12-6185, is open 8 am to 6 pm daily. They are cheaper, but usually out of stock.

GUIDE SERVICES: You can hire a guide at the Guide Center on Ave Martí in the center of town (same building as the Internet office.) A guide costs $8 per person.

Rumbos, Calle 39 between Ave 22 and 24, ☎ 46/332-3947, is the official government tourist office. They are good for information on the island's south end where you can't visit without a guide and 4WD car.

BY TAXI: A good taxi driver is **Alfredo**, ☎ 46/332-1216. He charges $30 a day for touring, $25 to go to the Crocodile farm. His car is not new, but it will get you to and fro.

■ Sightseeing

Central Plaza, called Parque Julio Antonio Mella, has the provincial museum (see below), the church of Nuestra Señora de los Dolores and St Nicolas de Bari, (open only weekdays in the mornings and, ironically, never open on Sunday) and to one side, the Fondo de Bienes Culturales (cultural center), where you can watch young ballerinas practicing their art on weekdays. Except in rainy season, this plaza is dry and hot and without a single green spot. The church isn't much either, except for its bell tower, which can be seen whether the church is open or not. On the other side of the plaza is the cinema. I never found it open.

The **El Pinero**, Calle 24, beside the river. This old boat is painted black and white. Although you can't enter it, photographers will enjoy its qualities. The boat was used from the early 1920s until the mid-1960s to ferry people from Juventud to the mainland. It is also the boat that took Castro and his buddies from prison on this island to freedom.

Museums

El Abra Farm Museum, Siguanea Highway, Km 2, open Tuesday to Sunday, 9 am to 5 pm, $2. Follow the road to the marked turn off at Km 2 and the farm is about a kilometer in. This attractive place was once the home of José Sarda, a friend of José Martí's father. Martí had been sentenced to six years in prison in Havana after being convicted of sedition. In prison, doing hard labor, the 16-year-old Martí rapidly lost his health. Because his father had a bit of influence, Martí's sentence was changed so that he could spend the time at the Sarda farm.

It was here that he wrote his famous *El Presidio Politico en Cuba*. The poem was repeated by revolutionaries during the struggle of the 1950s. Shortly after Martí regained his health, he was banished to Spain.

The farm has been declared a National Monument. Its rooms house documents that once belonged to Martí, along with an old bed and some shackles that apparently were taken off his legs when he arrived. Unless you are a huge Martí fan, this isn't really a worthwhile excursion. Most of the valuable items from Martí's life are in Havana.

Leaving the farm, follow the Siguanea Highway a little farther south and you will come to a driveway with two white pillars. Enter and drive to **El Abra Restaurant**, perched at the side of a lake about a kilometer down the driveway. There are signs along the way indicating where to go. This is a good place to have a beer and watch for birds/insects or eat a good meal ($7). The lawns are well kept and have modern rock sculptures for decoration.

Model Prison Museum, Chacón neighborhood, ☎ 46/12-5112, is open from Tuesday to Sunday, 8 am to 4 pm. Admission is $3 per person. Follow the road that goes to Bibijagua Beach and turn off at the sign indicating the Reparto Chacón, about two km/1.2 miles from the center of Nueva Gerona. Follow that road to the prison.

Constructed as the model prison between 1926 and 1931 by the former president and dictator Gerardo Machado, this imposing institution is a replica of Joliet prison in Illinois. Just looking at its circular walls painted a ghastly yellow scared me silly. I can imagine the depression that would befall a prisoner as he is led through the gates and up the steps to his new home. Prisoners could never escape from here, as much of the surrounding land is swamp and there are no islands within swimming distance.

Model Prison.

The four circular buildings of the institution were designed to hold 6,000 inmates. There are five storys to each building and each floor has 93 cells that were to hold two inmates. When it opened, 24 prisons around the country were downsized and all the prisoners who had received a sentence of more than 180 days were sent here. The mess hall alone will seat 5,000. The

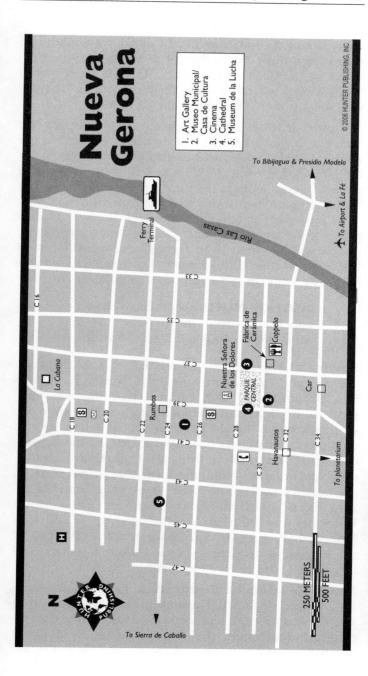

Nueva Gerona

1. Art Gallery
2. Museo Municipal/ Casa de Cultura
3. Cinema
4. Cathedral
5. Museum de la Lucha

© 2006 HUNTER PUBLISHING, INC

To Bibijagua & Presidio Modelo

To Airport & La Fé

Ferry Terminal

Río Las Casas

C 16

C 33

C 35

C 37

C 39

C 41

C 43

C 45

C 47

La Cubana

C 18

C 20

Rumbos

C 22

C 24

C 26

C 28

C 30

C 32

C 34

Havanautos

Car

Nuestra Señora de los Dolores

Fábrica de Cerámica

Coppelia

PARQUE CENTRAL

To planetarium

To Sierra de Caballo

N

250 METERS
500 FEET

Isla de la Juventad

most famous inmate was Fidel Castro, who spent two years here after his storming of the Moncada Barracks in Santiago de Cuba in 1953. He lived in cell 3859. This is where he wrote the famous line, "History will absolve me!" The prison closed in 1967.

A wander through the halls and cells will make you appreciate your freedom. The museum, located in the hospital block, holds documents and some photos of life in prison during the 1930s. The most interesting part of the museum is the dorm where Castro and his buddies spent two years serving time and planning their moves after they were released. Each bed has a photo and a small bio about the prisoner the cell held. Castro and his men were segregated from the rest of the cells because of the danger of them soliciting more followers from the general prison population.

> **AUTHOR NOTE:** Robert Louis Stevenson set his well-known story, *Treasure Island*, on Isla de la Juventud.

Provincial Museum, Central Plaza, Ave 30, between Calle 37 and 39, is open Tuesday to Sunday, 9 am to 6 pm, $1 entry fee. This colonial building was constructed in 1830 and still looks imposing despite the chipping paint. Inside there is the usual archive of documents written by revolutionaries. The most interesting are the artifacts from pre-Columbian inhabitants and art reproductions from **Cueva del Este** in the island's south. The latter objects are from the pirate days when men like Frances Drake, John Hawkins, and John Baskerville used the island as a hideout between raids on Spanish ships. The rest of the items give a glimpse of more recent events. The large relief map is very interesting.

Museo de la Lucha Clandestina, Calle 24, between Ave 43 and 45, open Tuesday to Sunday, 9 am to 4 pm, $1 entry fee. This museum is dedicated to the underground struggle the Cuban people underwent against Batista. It was called the M-26-7, or the Movement of July 26th. There are tons of documents, mostly unreadable unless your Spanish is exemplary. However, there are other things to look for, like the paraphernalia used to smuggle messages to other revolutionaries during the 1950s.

Museum of Natural History and Planetarium, Calle 41 and Ave 52, Tuesday to Saturday, 9 am to 5 pm, $1. This museum is a 10-minute walk from the center of town, going toward the main highway. It has a sad collection of taxidermy specimens and the round-roofed building is the planetarium. Neither is worth the visit unless you need a place to get out of the sun.

■ Adventures on Foot

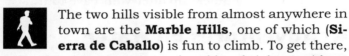

The two hills visible from almost anywhere in town are the **Marble Hills**, one of which (**Sierra de Caballo**) is fun to climb. To get there, follow 22nd Street to its end and head right. Avoid going up the hill that is being mined. The path is marked by two concrete posts. The journey to the top takes less than an hour. Bring water as it is hot and there are no shops along the way. You will have the best views of the town and surrounding ocean from here. It's fun to watch the many raptorial birds seen here.

At the bottom, walk to the left and see a set of stairs leading into a cave, **Cueva el Agua**. You can go about 100 meters (300 feet) in, but you must have a light and it is not advisable to go too far without a guide.

You must hire a guide for each person in the car ($8 per person) and a 4WD vehicle to enter the island's **Restricted Area**, in the southern part of the island. You can take these tours with Rumbos if you book a day or two in advance. There is a military checkpoint at Cayo Piedra, 18 km/11 miles south of Santa Fe. You can go no farther without both a guide and 4x4.

Finlay Cave is on Caleta Grande, south of Frances Point (near Hotel Colony) and inside the restricted area. There are about 14 black-and-white pictographs

Isla de la Juventad

here that are similar in design to those at Punta del Este. First explored in the 1970s, these paintings are believed to go back about a thousand years.

Cueva de Punta del Este offers the best cave pictographs. It has about 250 drawings in the six accessible caves; some date back a thousand years. This cave system has been called the "Sistine Chapel" of indigenous art because of its possible religious importance and because of how well done and preserved some paintings are. Have your guide show you the most significant caves and paintings. Otherwise, you could be here for the entire day and still not see the best pieces. Even so, you will spend at least three hours looking around. There is a beach where you can have lunch and a quick dip after your cave tour.

■ Adventures on Water

 Santa Fe, 19 km/12 miles south of Nuevo Gerona, is locally called Fe. It once had the Cotorra Mineral Baths to boast about. However, the baths were closed for renovations and, at the time of writing, had yet to open. At one time, the hot water was said to cure up to 300 different ailments.

Beaches

Public buses leave from the center of town for **Playa Bibijagua** at 8 am, 11 am, 12:30 pm, 3 pm, 4 pm. It takes half an hour to travel the six km/four miles. The last bus returns at about 6:30 pm. A taxi out here will run $5 each way, while the bus fare is 20 centavos.

Bibijagua is a black (actually dark brown) beach with lots of palms and picnic tables. There are hawkers selling everything from crocodile skin souvenirs to coconut milk, but they are non-intrusive. If you say no once, you won't be bothered again. This beach is not overcrowded and is a great place to lie in the sun and read a book. However, the water, in season, does have water fleas that bite like hell.

The bus stops at **Ana Molata's Paladar**, next to the beach. For $5 you can get a fish or chicken dinner complete with rice, salad, bread, fried platanos, dessert and coffee. Beer costs a buck a bottle. A camping compound called **Arenas Negras**, ☎ 46/32-5266, was partly open when I visited. The 30 four-person cabins are one-storey plaster places, neatly kept and available for Cubans first. There is a pool. I would not count on getting a room, but it's worth a try if this beach is to your liking.

EVANGELINA COSSIO CISNEROS

A heroine of the island, Cisneros was a beautiful Cuban woman living here in late 1896, during the Spanish-American War. She was charged with enticing a Spanish general into an ambush. If you have noticed the beauty of Cuban women in general, this should not come as a surprise. For her misdeed, she was imprisoned.

Just previous to this, William Randolph Hearst and Joséph Pulitzer had started publishing newspapers in New York that were in fierce competition with each other. Both men changed facts to draw readers. When Hearst heard of the imprisonment of Evangelina, he followed her story regularly, showing the horrors of Spanish prison life. Finally in 1897, Karl Decker, a reporter working for Hearst, was sent to Cuba to plot Evangelina's rescue. He rented a house across from her cell, placed a ladder between the two rooms, cut her bars and removed her. She quickly made her way to the United States with the help of the reporter. After her arrival, she married a general in the US army. Great controversy arose as to whether it was all a prank to get her into the US.

Isla de la Juventad

The first bus for **Playa Paraiso** leaves from town at 8 am and the last returns at 6 pm. You pay in Cuban pesos. A taxi is about $5 each way and will return to pick you up if you book it ahead of time.

The area has golden sandy beaches interspersed between the rocky outcrops, offering privacy. **Isla Mono** (Monkey Island) juts out about a mile from shore and the waters near it offer good diving. At one time, monkeys inhabited the island but it is now deserted. This is the beach where you can come for short diving lessons or some snorkeling.

Playa Paraiso has a restaurant and bar open noon to 6 pm daily. It specializes in fresh fish served with condiments for $6. You may find a hawker selling coconuts (with milk) for $1. However, most locals believe he should be selling the stuff for half that.

Diving

Evaristo Barrero Romero, Calle 18 and Ave 37, ☎ 46/332-4065, offer one-tank dives at Playa Paraiso for $25, transportation and equipment included. If you want to dive Monkey Island, you will have to go on the two-tank dive for the entire day. Evaristo is also an instructor; he is good, especially with children. Snorkeling equipment is available for rent; a set of flippers and snorkel goes for about $5 a day.

WATCH THE DOUBLE-BUBBLE DIVE

Be aware that a common practice is to book you for a morning dive and for the driver to arrive late. By the time you're out, the water is choppy and the dive isn't as good. The dive master will then try to talk you into booking two dives. Of course, the cost doubles. If this happens, cancel and book for the following day at the time you wish. Serious divers should go to Hotel Colony.

Hotel Colony, end of Siguanea Highway, 46 km/28 miles south of Nuevo Gerona, ☎ 46/339-8181, is set on the white-sand beach of Siguanea, across from Punta de Francis where all the great diving is located. There are 77 rooms in the main building, which was built during the 1950s for rich Cuban vacationers. Newer bungalows cost just $2 more and are far more spacious and comfortable. Their bathrooms have been upgraded with new showers and tiled walls. All rooms, both in the hotel itself and the bungalows, have air conditioning, private bathrooms, radios, telephones and TVs. There is a pool outside the main foyer. If you come for the day, the cost is $3 per person to swim; if you have a room, it is free. There is a gym, bar, tennis court, tour office and a couple of restaurants. A room costs $42 for two with breakfast and $54 with dinner . Beverages are extra. It is cheaper to arrive and pay for a room than it is to book ahead.

The shallow beach here is good for kids and there is lots of sea life right near shore to keep them occupied. The dock is not usable, but it is attractive, and the hotel grounds are well maintained, with lots of trees for shade during the midday sun.

Serious divers make this their base. A wreck dive is about $20 and a night dive is $40. Depending upon who you talk to, there are about 55 good dive sites in Punta Frances National Marine Park, which runs for about six km between Punta Pedernales and Punta Frances. These sites have corals, sponges and gorgonians tucked in between the tunnels, caves and sharp ledges. You should see tarpons, spadefish, jacks, grunts, schoolmasters, snappers, groupers, parrotfish, helmets, spiny lobsters and barracudas. You will also see turtles, rays and sharks. The best sites are the Tunnel of Love, Blue Cave, Stone Coral, Pirate's Anchor, Small Kingdom, Hidden Passage, Black Coral and Sunken Ships. These dives start at 10 meters (33 feet) and go for well over 35 meters (115 feet). If you are lucky enough to have more time, ask

Isla de la Juventad

the dive master if he'll take you to places most tourists don't get to see. It is in this area that one of Cuba's modern-day heroines, diving record-holder, Deborah Andollo, has trained.

If you are not diving you can snorkel. The cost is about $8 for half a day. All equipment for diving and snorkeling is available at the diving center in the hotel.

You must travel 25 km (15 miles) from the hotel to the diving sites. Most boats go each morning at dawn and offer two dives. There is a decompression chamber at the diving center and they claim to have a doctor on site all the time in the event of a breathing problem.

You can fly to the nearby airport from Havana or Nuevo Gerona and have a hotel van pick you up (let the hotel know in advance). A bus leaves Nuevo Gerona at 8 am daily and costs $3 each way. It meets the boat going to Punta Frances. This makes it possible for you to stay in town and commute for diving.

> **AUTHOR NOTE:** An underwater photo contest is held each year. Ask at the desk if you want to enter.

■ Adventures in the Air

Paragliding

An official, government-recognized paragliding club has about 30 members. Gliding on the island is an experience that is second only to gliding at Guantanomo. However, this area has exceptional scenery and the landing spots are softer. July and August are the best months, but between the seasons (dry and wet) are also good. The best take-off place is **Sierra de Caballos**. Because of its height, the hill collects the strongest winds on the island. Most gliders in Cuba don't have much extra money or extra gear, although all club members do have their own equipment. It is best to bring your own and leave any that you can spare. The contact person for the club is Andrius Torres Taudiaux, Calle 51 #5016, between Ave 50 and 54. He has no phone, but if he is not home you can visit Casa Elena's on Calle 54, #4500, ☎ 46/32-3992. Andrius glides for pleasure and also takes students to practice or learn.

■ Adventures on Wheels

Cycling

Although it is hot, travel by bike is a great way to get around some of the places that are close to the center of town. The two prisons are a good example. **Evaristo Barrero Romero**, Calle 18 and 37, ☎ 46/32-4065, has heavy mountain bikes with just a few gears that he rents for $3 a day.

■ Adventures in Nature

AUTHOR NOTE: Be aware that you are not permitted to drive on your own past Fe to the south or past Hotel Colony on the other side of the island. You must have a 4WD and a guide, who can be hired from the Guide Center on Ave Martí ($8 per person).

Granaja de Cocodrilos, Km 37 on the Fe Highway, about five km/three miles on a secondary road (turn left at the sign). It costs $3 to enter and the tour takes about an hour. Display pools show crocodiles in their different stages of development from kid to king. Cuban and Columbian crocs are here, but you won't see any American crocs at the farm. The eggs are collected from the wild in May and incubated. It takes 80 to 90 days for the critters to hatch. The second pool holds the really young ones. All the following pools hold crocs in different stages of development until they reach the one-year stage. You can also view five-year-old crocs. You can hold the very young ones – the older ones are too dangerous. We were told that the Cuban crocs are the most dangerous. Farther out are larger swamp areas where the Columbian crocs hide from visitors. Tour operators work 24 hours a day looking after their charges. They change staff every week. These workers are educated in their field and a few speak English quite well.

Jungla de Jones, is 13 km/eight miles west of Santa Fe along the road to Hotel Colony. This is a botanical garden that has things like 100-year-old bamboo groves, one of which has even been made into a coffee shop. Thick vegetation surrounds the perimeter of the park, keeping peering eyes and noise from the road (as if there is much!) to a minimum. There are many species of mangos, bamboo, palm and other exotic plants interspersed around the yards. The gardens are well kept, extensive and worth a stop.

The history of the gardens goes back to the beginning of the last century, when Helen and Harris Jones, American botanists, decided to build them. They collected plants from around the world and nurtured them like they would their own children. When Harris died in an accident in 1938, his wife was left heartbroken. However, she decided to mend her sorrow by continuing with the gardens until she too, met a tragic death at the hands of two escaped prisoners from Modelo. Thinking there might be money at the Jones farm, they killed her and set fire to the home.

The gardens are open Tuesday to Sunday all day. It costs $3 to enter. ☎ 46/19-6246.

> **AUTHOR NOTE:** There are plans to rebuild the Jones house and do some extra work on the gardens. This may take awhile to happen.

■ Places to Stay

Visitors most often stay in one of the three-dozen *casas particulares*, each with one or two rooms for rent. They are comfortable and most have air conditioning and private baths and include breakfast. A *casa particular* is a good way to see old Cuban culture. Juventud has not enjoyed the tourism that the main island has, so the people here are still untainted by our odd and demanding ways. Most places will cost $25 for a double. Be aware of the *jinateros*, who can increase your prices with their large cuts. One of their tricks it to isolate you from other Cubans except for the ones who give them a commission.

PRICE CHART
Per room for two people, per day.
$ . . . . $25-$50
$$ . . . . $51-$75
$$$ . . . . . $76-$100
$$$$ . . . $101-$150
$$$$$ . . Over $150

Casas Particulares

Casa Jorge Luis Mas, Calle 41 #4108, between Ave 8 and 10, Apt #7, ☎ 46/32-3544, has lovely rooms. The family is not intrusive and offers a good place to stay. The meals, I have heard, are excellent. The *casa* is also very conveniently placed in the center of town.

Casa Elena Richardson Fredrich, Calle 54 #4500 between Ave 45 and 47, ☎ 46/332-3992, henry44@ web.correos decuba.cu, has one room that is often booked. Elena makes some of the best meals in Cuba so her place is in demand. There is a nice patio out back where guests can sit and much needed air conditioning is available in the room. The only drawback is that the house is a 10-minute walk from the center – on a hot day, it seems like a long way to go to purchase more beer.

Nery de los Angeles, Calle 41 #1804, Apt 5, between Ave 18 and 20 North, ☎ 46/332-4311, has a clean and comfortable air-conditioned room for rent in an apartment fairly close to the center. Breakfasts are included.

Yosvany Damaso, Calle 22 #5103, between Ave 51 and 53, ☎ 46/332-2876, has two nice rooms with air conditioning and private baths. Dinners can be arranged (highly recommended). Yosvany also has bicycles for rent; guests get first dibs. They go for $3 per day.

Villa Choli, Calle C #4001, between Ave 6 and 8, ☎ 46/332-3147, has two rooms with private bathrooms, air conditioning, and soft beds. Meals are available. This is a good spot.

Villa Pena, Calle 10 #3710, between Ave 37 and 39, ☎ 46/332-2345, magui@ahao.iju.sld.cu, has two rooms on the main floor with air conditioning and private bathrooms. There is a terrace and a well-kept garden to enjoy. It is a great deal. The house is right in the center of town, close to all the action. Meals are available and the owners can tell you all the places to visit that aren't included in this (or any other) book.

Casa Gloria, Calle 18 and 37, ☎ 46/32-4065, has two rooms with private bath and air conditioning. You have free rein to sit in the living room or the balcony if you wish. Gloria is a biologist who can give you the names and interesting uses of the plants around the island. Her husband is a diving instructor. They have bikes and snorkel gear for rent.

Casa Gerardo and Anita, Calle 20 #3518 between Ave 35 and 37, ☎ 46/332-6560, anagall@web. correosdecuba. cu, is in the center. There is a private entrance. The room has a private bathroom, small fridge, fan, telephone and terrace. You can order meals to be eaten with the family. Recommended.

Casa Elda, Calle 43 #2004, between Ave 20 and 22, ☎ 46/332-2774, janet@ahao.ijv.sld.cu, is run by a retired lady who loves to have company. She has half a house for rent so you can have your own kitchen, living room, bath and bedroom. There is also a big back-yard where you can rest or play badminton. She told me her house is intimate and quiet.

Casa Villa Daili, Calle 8 #4932 between Ave 49 and 53, ☎ 46/332-2972, is in the northern part of town, close to the hospital and bus station. There is one room with private bath and you have use of the living room and terrace. The food is good and the owner has a taxi for hire.

Villa Viviana, Calle 32 #4110, between Ave 41 and 43 (no phone), is a lovely two-storey house decorated with marble. The two rooms are comfortable and clean with a private bath. Meals can be arranged.

Hotels

There isn't much from which to choose in Gerona. **The Cubana**, Calle 39 #1417 and Calle 18, ☎ 46/332-3512, is right in town but is for Cubans only. If things got really tough, I'd suggest trying them but don't count on getting in.

Villa Isla de la Juventud, Km 1 La Fe Highway, ☎ 46/332-3290, $$, is also called Villa Gaviota. This is probably the best hotel in town. It has 20 rooms with fridges, private bathrooms and comfortable beds. The rooms border a small pool. The grounds are pleasant, set right on the river. There is a tour office at the hotel that will arrange trips to places around the island.

Motel Rancho del Tesoro, Km 2 La Fe Highway, ☎ 46/332-3035, $$, is a two-star but it isn't bad. There are private bathrooms, telephones, cable TV, tiled floors, a coffee shop and taxi stand outside. There are also a few places to sit outside. This hotel is a little farther away from town than Villa Gaviota.

■ Places to Eat

I always suggest eating with your family if staying in a *casa* (which I also recommend). However, there are times when you want

Isla de la Juventad

some good old restaurant grub. On this island, there are a few places that are worth a visit.

> **AUTHOR NOTE:** Ask whether the price is in pesos or convertibles (equivalent to US $) before you order.

Pizza Parlor, Calle Martí and Ave 23 (no phone), is in the center just up from the Cuchinero Restaurant (below). The pizza is excellent and the patio, trimmed with bougainvillea, is set in a lovely garden with a dry-rock fountain (one without water). A medium pizza costs $3 and is plenty for a good-sized lunch.

The Gondola, on Calle 30 and Ave 35, is far more expensive than the Pizza Parlor. A tiny order of fries is almost two bucks.

Cuchinero Restaurant, Calle Martí and Ave 24, ☎ 46/332-2809, open noon to 11 pm, is a good place and the food is passable if sometimes a bit sparse in quantity. But the meals end up being far too expensive unless you are paying in pesos.

El Dragon, Calle Martí and Ave 26, ☎ 46/332-4479, open noon to 9 pm, is a Chinese restaurant in name only. The food is always a bit greasy. This is one place that, if they charge in pesos, the price is good. But if they want converts, the price is way out of line. The best part of this restaurant is the paper dragon hanging from the ceiling.

Coppelia, Calle 37 between Ave 30 and 32, ☎ 46/332-2225, 10 am to 10 pm. Ice cream, while you are in Cuba, is a must. This shop is part of a chain with a much larger Havana store. It is always busy.

■ Nightlife

Nightlife is always along the lines of a beer in the backyard or on your patio after strolling up and down the streets, chatting with locals. The **movie theater** may be showing something in

Spanish, or the **Casa de la Cultura** on the other side of the plaza might have an event.

Discos

You could hit **Disco la Movida**, Calle 18, a lively dance spot where locals flock to meet other locals and enjoy a few hours of exercise. Your other option is to head out of town to the disco next door to Villa de la Juventud. It's called **Super Disco**. Music starts at 10 pm. One of the advantages of being on this island is that it is fairly safe to walk home after dark. Super Disco is about a kilometer from the center of town.

■ Shopping

 Cupit Cimex, just off the plaza, has the cheapest beer in town. It costs 70 centavos for a cold bottle. Stock up!

Galeria de Arte Gerona, Calle Martí and Ave 26, is a local art gallery that has, among other things, art by Kcho (Alexis Leyva Machado), an artist born in the town in 1970. He now works and lives in Havana but his first exposition was here in 1986 when he was just 16. There are also a few pieces by Nelson Dominguez, another famous very modern artist.

Cayo Largo

This is one of Cuba's most popular islands with its 26 km/16 miles of glistening white-sand beaches along the south and mangrove swamps along the north. The island allows access to coral reefs just a few hundred meters from shore. There are eight resorts, dozens of discos, bars, and restaurants, and two nature preserves. You will find that most guests speak English, German, Italian or French. Other than the hotel workers, few people on the cay speak Spanish.

Men and women can and will bathe topless, bottom-less or just about anything in between, although it is only **Playa Paraiso** that is truly a nude beach. There, naturism makes its Cuban home. Naturism is a way of life that is in harmony with nature characterized by the practice of communal nudity with the intention of encouraging self-respect, respect for others and for the environment.

CAYS, CAYES, QUAYS OR KEYS?

Cayo in Spanish means shoal, rock or barrier reef. *Cay* or *Caye* in old French means sandbank or bar and that word originated from the medieval Latin word *Caium*. The *Oxford Etymological Dictionary* states that in 1707, in his book *Jamaica*, Sir Hans Sloane claimed that the Spaniards used *Cayos*, which led to the corrupted English word *Cayes*. Falconer in the *Dictionary Marine* (1789) claims the word *Caies* means a ridge of rocks or sandbanks, commonly called, in the West Indies, keys.

Cayo Largo is 120 km/ (73 miles) southeast of Juventud and the most easterly of the islands in the Canarreos Archipelago. The weather is generally a tad warmer than Havana, but the seasons are the same, with a dry season from November to May and a rainy season (hurricane season) from June to October.

The island is shaped like a boomerang. It is less than 30 km/19 miles long and never more than three km/ two miles wide, so walking is the way to travel.

From the main village and marina, the road (highway) goes south toward the resorts. The most western beach on the island is at **Playa Sirena** and next to it is **Playa Paraiso**. From those beaches or from your ho-tel, you can walk, cycle, motorbike or drive past half a dozen resorts and arrive at Playa Lindamar at the eastern end of the strip. As you continue east you will come to **Playa Blanca**, **Playa los Cocos** and **Playa Tortuga**. There are no resorts – yet – beyond Barcelo Cay Largo Beach Resort. The road goes only as far as Playa Blanca.

Because few people live here, many iguanas, turtles and birds make it their home. There are a number of iguana species; some are huge while others are fairly small. All are lovely to watch and photograph.

■ Getting Here

 BY PLANE: You can fly from Havana directly to Cayo Largo's small airport. The daily flights cost $100 return, $75 one-way. You can also fly direct from Canada; check with a travel agent. The cost is $500 CDN, round-trip, from Toronto or Montreal before taxes ($100-$160 CDN).

An exit tax of $25 must be paid in cash (euro, Canadian or American dollars, or convertible peso). If using American dollars, a 10% fee will be added to this tax making the total $27.50.

SMART MONEY

You should bring Canadian dollars or euros to Cayo Largo. You will be charged a 10% tax to exchange US dollars. You must spend converts or use credit cards not connected to a US bank. People run into problems using credit cards; I would avoid them. There are no ATMs on the island.

■ Adventures on Water

Beaches

 Walking the beach is a favorite pastime. The most beautiful of the beaches is **Playa Sirena**, where tour boats sometimes bring visitors from the main island. Boats from hotels on Cayo Largo will take you to the beach for $25. You can also take a free shuttle from your hotel to the village marina and take the ferry ($2) to the beach. The ferry goes three times a day. Departure times may change so check at your hotel.

The sparkly white sand of Playa Sirena, set between tiny rocky coves, is the best on the island. The water is often calm here when it is rough at the other beaches and there is some snorkeling near a little cove on the sheltered side. The beach and bay are home to conch, starfish, sand dollars and, occasionally, jellyfish. There are some palm trees for shade, a few palapas and one restaurant where you can get refreshments.

> **AUTHOR NOTE:** There is a $500 fine for taking things like starfish or conch shells off the beach.

Playa Paraiso is the official nude beach, but there are others where clothes are optional. I don't know if you *must* take your clothes off when you are on this beach; I didn't visit. Punta Tiempo, on the east side, offers good snorkeling as well as a bar where you can get a much-needed beer. On calm days, the snorkeling is good all along the beach.

Playa Lindamar is where most hotels are located. Lounge chairs and umbrellas are set up along the beach and you can also get bar service. A coral reef in front of Hotel Lindamar and Isla del Sur offers good snorkeling when the sea is calm, and fish (including barracuda) are often seen. Some parts of the beach are very wide, while other sections have lovely rocky outcrops. Often topped with a bit of vegetation, these outcrops provide private and cozy coves.

Playa Blanca is the longest of the beaches, with some rocky sections that come right down to the water. To get here you can walk or rent a scooter, buggy or jeep and drive to the end of the road where there is a tower.

A sign not far past the tower says "no motorized vehicles beyond this point," which means you have to walk from there.

Playa los Cocos has, of course, coconut palms shading parts of the beach. Not far into the water a shipwreck can be seen. The sand is glistening white.

Playa Tortuga is where green turtles come to lay their eggs, usually between June and October. It is not advisable to go to watch their laying as your presence disturbs the female. Since she carries her eggs until they are ripe (they swell and the shells harden), she can't go back into the water and wait for privacy. If the eggs harden too much, she can't lay them. I'd suggest leaving this beach to them during laying time.

Boat Trips

Cayo Iguana can be reached by booking a tour at your hotel. The island has a white lighthouse that is still in use, although it is not the kind one can enter. Cayo Iguana is full of iguanas of all sizes and colors; most are tame and come up to you begging for food. You will see them outstare each other trying to master intimidation so the winner can get the rest of the free food offered by the visitors. You could shoot a dozen rolls of film on these delightful creatures. There is a small hut on the island and a few mangroves around for those interested in birds. There is also good snorkeling here; the surrounding waters have a sunken ship as well as coral reefs that are home to large and small fish.

The following cays have enough variety to give you an idea of what to see off the island. Every hotel has its tourist desk; tours are about $75 a day and well worth the money. I have listed Cayo Iguana above because it would be the first one I would choose to visit due to the rarity, quantity and tameness of the animals.

Hotels also have kayaks, catamarans and pedal-boats that you can play around in. Some have sailboats but you must go with a Cuban captain. The bigger (more expensive) vessels cost extra to use.

Isla de la Juventad

Cayo Pajares is a mangrove island with a rocky shore along one side. The island has many birds, including the booby, and is a must for birders.

Cayo Cantilles has a monkey sanctuary. The monkeys are fairly tame and, of course, look for handouts from soft-hearted tourists.

Cayo Rosario is just 32 km/20 miles west of Cayo Largo and a good destination for those wanting to sail. The diving near Rosario is good, with coral hillocks that go down about 20 meters/66 feet. The water is clear and visibility is excellent.

Diving

The International Diving Center (no phone), cuban connection@yahoo.com, at the marina in the village and Playa Sirena, can take divers to 32 different sites where there are reefs, ships, caves, and tunnels. You will likely see turtles, barracuda, whale sharks (during the full moons of March, April and May), and hundreds of tropical fish. The best time is from mid-December to the end of March, when the largest varieties of fish are around and the waters are calmest.

IDC can take a total of 24 divers per day – 12 in each boat. The boats are 41-foot yachts with a capacity to hold 19 people. They have 36 regulators and jackets and 32 diving suits for rent. Tanks and weights are included in your diving costs. The six instructors, available every day, are all SSI and/or PADI certified. You must have your card with you if you wish to dive.

Water temperatures are around 24°C/75°F year-round and the tides are mild with no strong currents. There is little pollution and the coral is well preserved.

The diving area near the main island has coral and barrier reefs with ridges and channels that go down 20 meters/66 feet and a few slopes that go to 35 meters/115 feet.

IDC's main dive sites are Las Rabirrubias (eight meters/26 feet); Canal de la Barracuda (seven meters/

24 feet); Punta de Barrera (six meters/20 feet); El Ballenato (13 meters/43 feet); and Las Cuberas (10 meters/33 feet). Some of the coral mountains are comprised of brain, pillar and leaf coral. There are also star coral, feather coral and sea fans. For wildlife, you will see snapper, grunts, turtles, eagle ray, sting-ray, lobster, crabs and morays.

> **AUTHOR NOTE:** The turtle's shell makes its ribs immoveable. In order to breath, turtles either swallow air or they kick their legs and pump the air into their lungs.

To explore walls, you will have to sail almost 50 km/ 31 miles to the cays northeast of Cayo Largo. Here, walls drop off sharply to a depth of 15 meters/50 feet and go farther down to 200 meters/650 feet where tube, basket and branch sponges are seen. It's at this depth that black coral is found. The most common fish at this site are snapper, barracuda and spadefish.

Diving near Cayo Rosario will give you views of coral hillocks, house black groupers, cubera snapper, dog snapper, jacks, grunts, black margates and porkfish.

The cost to dive is $40 for a one-tank dive and $70 for a two-tank dive. If you book 20 dives, the cost is about $450 and each night dive (lights are extra) costs $50 per person. Be aware that, because of electrical prob-lems, there are often delays in the diving times. (With-out electricity, they can't fill the tanks.)

■ Adventures in Nature

The **Turtle Farm** is at the village near the plaza. Open daily from 8 am to 6 pm with an hour off at noon for lunch. Entry fee is $1, which includes entry to the tiny museum.

TWO PLUS ONE MAKES THREE

Two species of turtle can be seen here, the **green** and the **hawksbill**. Actually, a single leatherback named Maria makes for three species. The **leatherback** is very rare and about 300 years old. She may have returned to her natural waters by now, but her legacy lives on.

The preserve is under the care of the University of Havana and was opened in the 1980s. Workers obtain eggs that have been laid on Turtle Beach and bring them here for safe hatching. This takes two months. The turtles are looked after for an additional three months before being released into the ocean to fend for themselves. This added time spent in care makes them stronger and less vulnerable to predators.

KNOWING YOUR TURTLES

Green turtles are so named because of the color of their fat. The **black turtle** is a subspecies of the green. This slow grower does not reach sexual maturity until 20 years of age and some are believed to wait for 50 years. The green turtle will grow to about one meter/39 inches and weigh about 330 lb/150 kg. However, in the recent past these creatures would grow to twice that size. Today, we harvest them so rapidly that they no longer have time to grow.

The green turtle is vegetarian and likes to graze on meadows of sea grass that grow in warm ocean waters. However, immature greens are known to eat a bit of meat. The females nest once every two to four years. Each nesting season results in two or three breeding sessions about 14 days apart. The female lays around 100 eggs each time and the young hatch about 60 days later.

Leatherback turtles are in great danger of extinction, but there is one at the farm on Largo that seems to have gotten lost and landed on Turtle Beach. She didn't want to leave, so the workers took her in. The leatherback is the largest recorded living turtle, 270 cm/110 inches in length and weighing 2,000 lb/900 kg. It is so named because it has a flexible shell. There is no separation from the sides of the shell and the underbelly, so it appears barrel-shaped. Leatherbacks are known to exist worldwide. Almost half of them nest on Mexico's western shore. However, some travel to Japan and, when the young hatch, the sea currents return the babies to the western shores of America.

Hawksbill turtles are endangered due to the commercial value of the shell, meat and eggs. Recently, their presence has drastically declined in the Caribbean and Atlantic Oceans. The hawksbill is different than other turtles in that it has a beak-like mouth and two claws on each flipper. It grows to around 87 cm/34 inches and weighs 80 kg/175 lb. However, the biggest ever found weighed in at 127 kg (280 lb). The hawksbill can nest over a span of six months, between July and October. During this period the female nests four or five times, allowing a 14-day interval between each nesting. She lays around 140 eggs, which hatch about 60 days later. At birth, each hatchling weighs 12-20 grams (less than an ounce). Generally, hawksbills eat sponge from around a reef and use the reef's ledges for resting spots. However, garbage like plastic and Styrofoam has been found in the stomachs of these creatures. This decreases the amount of nutrition they can absorb and weakens them.

■ Places to Stay

All-Inclusive Resorts

There are seven all-inclusive resorts on Cayo Largo. All are luxury places that serve typical Cuban meals. This means for some the food is exceptional, while for others the food is not edible. Included in prices are breakfast, snacks, lunch, dinner, national non-premium alcoholic drinks and soda or juice. Meals are served buffet-style or, with reservations, as a sit-down à la carte meal.

Most hotels offer volleyball and basketball courts, a gymnasium, sauna, Jacuzzi, children's activities, games rooms with table tennis and pool, kayaks, windsurfing, pedal boats, and snorkeling gear. Evening entertainment is included and usually consists of live performances. There are other things like dancing lessons or organized pool games.

Internet service is available and costs about $6 an hour at all the hotels.

Sol Club Cayo Largo, ☎ 45/24-8260, is on Playa Paraiso, 15 km/nine miles from the airport and the most westerly of the chain of beaches. It belongs to Sol Melia Hotels, a European group that offers four-star accommodations. There are about 300 air-conditioned rooms in two-story buildings a little back from the water. They have satellite TV, hot water, telephone, mini-bar, hairdryer, safe, terraces with lounge furnishings and daily maid service. A standard room can have either one king-size bed or two three-quarter ones (smaller than a double and bigger than a single). There are also junior suites and two rooms that have been equipped to accommodate handicapped persons. The well-kept grounds have a fairly large salt-water pool, deck chairs, bar service at the pool and a catamaran that can be rented. A shuttle will take you from the hotel to Playa Sirena each morning and bring you back in the evening.

The best snack foods are at the pool bar. The service is excellent throughout the hotel and things are clean. This is one of the top destinations on the island and is occasionally overbooked. Confirm your reservations!

Sol Pelicano, ☎ 45/54-8333, is on Playa Paraiso, next to Sol Club, and is operated by Sol Melia Hotels from Europe. The rooms are located in two- or three-story buildings done in a colonial motif. Pelicano was renovated in 2002 so everything is in pretty good shape. The hotel has the usual amenities; standard rooms have either two single beds or one queen-sized bed. The huge grounds have lovely gardens, a salt-water pool and a children's pool that has playthings reminiscent of Disneyland. The hotel is smaller than Sol Club and the buildings are closer to the beach but, perhaps surprisingly, package prices are usually cheaper. Snack bar **Zun Zun** has the best coffee at this resort, so after breakfast head over there. À la carte restaurant **La Yana** has excellent service; reserve early. Meals here are not included in your package. The best bar is **Ranchon** near the beach, both for booze and light snacks. Beach volleyball and tennis are popular, as are the hammocks, scattered throughout the grounds, which offer shade and privacy. The downside of this hotel is that the food is not so hot and they often run out before all the guests are fed.

For about $75 you can take the catamaran (the same one that's used by Sol Club) to the beaches west of the hotels and out to Iguana Island. This is an all-day excursion. Another trip (this one by plane) offers a day in Havana, although many tour agents don't recommend it. I do, of course. The planes are not very modern, but small planes are so safe that I wouldn't worry. If you have an extra couple of bucks and would like to see some Cuban culture, don't skip Havana.

Villa Lindamar, ☎ 45/34-8111, tucked up in the bay between Playa Paraiso and Playa Lindamar, is the third hotel along the strip. It is considered three-star in quality, although I really liked the rooms and would

Isla de la Juventad

rate them higher. This is a small resort with only 50 thatch-roof cabañas located close to the water. Each hut has a porch with a hammock, one king-size or two three-quarter size (smaller than a double) beds, a private bathroom with shower, air conditioning, telephone, satellite TV, a safe and a mini-bar. The huts look across the bay toward Pelicano. Seclusion is the selling point at this resort. There are fewer restaurants/buffet rooms than at the bigger resorts, but there is a pool bar and some watersports equipment available, as well as a tourist office and souvenir shop.

Villa Soledad, ☎ 45/34-8111, comes next as you head east along the beaches. It offers simple rooms in duplexes or six-plexes that are two-star in luxury. At the time of writing, Villa Soledad was being renovated. It is run by the Cuban company Gran Caribe, with rates that are far lower than other hotels. There is no pool, restaurant or bar, but you are free to visit the other hotels and use their facilities. The rooms are clean and comfortable, the beach nice and the service excellent. Bathrooms even have bidets and, for the ecologically conscious, solar paneling is used for electricity. If you want quiet, this is the place.

Villa Coral, ☎ 45/434-8111, has 60 large, comfortable rooms located in several two-story, Spanish-style buildings painted bright pink so you will never have a problem finding them! Accenting the pink is bougainvillea growing around the property. The buildings, some close to the beach, are very nice, and each room has a balcony, air conditioning, a king-size or two single beds, bath with shower, TV, safe and mini-bar. There is a small pool and a swim-up bar and an Italian restaurant. The hotel is on the beach, where there are lounge chairs and palapa huts.

Hotel Isla del Sur, ☎ 45/434-8111, was the first hotel built on the island and is located at the tip of a peninsula. This is a three-star hotel with 57 rooms located in a two-story building painted bright tropical colors. The building faces the ocean. There is a pool, kid's pool, buffet, snack bar, and an all-night bar. You can play tennis, change money, shop (though there isn't much for sale), get rid of the kids at the babysitting service, or get your hair done at the beauty salon. Horseback riding is also available. Each room has either a king or two single beds, TV, fridge, safe, telephone and balcony. I really liked their bar, Medusa's, a place that can make everyone feel like they have snakes coming out of their heads in the morning.

Barcelo, opened in 2003, is the last hotel at the east end of the string of beaches. It is a four-star belonging to the Barcelo Group in Europe. Rooms are in two-story buildings, each containing 12 rooms. There is also a choice of bungalows and about a dozen junior suites. Because of the nightlife, this hotel draws a younger crowd. The beach is tiny and you must climb over two sand dunes and some rocks to reach it. However, each spacious room has air conditioning, cable TV, tub and shower. Some rooms are equipped with handicap facilities and all have balconies. There are restaurants and bars galore. Organized activities are offered, along with tennis courts, football, basketball, volleyball courts, an adults-only pool and a children's pool, a sauna, a Jacuzzi, and a gymnasium. There are bicycles and non-powered water vessels. There is live entertainment each evening and the bar can be quite lively. The modern murals around the main floor of the reception area are very interesting. The hotel has been having phone problems; contact it through one of the other island hotels.

■ Nightlife

The nightlife is what you make of it. There are bars and discos in almost all the hotels, but the best one for the young crowd is at **Barcelo**.

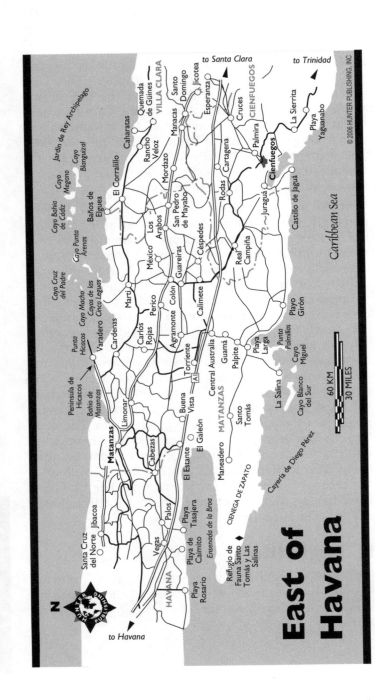

East of Havana

East of Havana
Provinces of Matanzas & Cienfuegos

The province of Matanzas has **Varadero**, one of the most popular resort areas in Cuba, with 20 km/ 12 miles of beach and the **Zapata Peninsula**, now a national park, where millions of birds stop on their way north and south during their migrations. The city of Matanzas has about 120,000 residents and is supported mainly by industry.

The name Matanzas means "mass murder" in Spanish and there are two theories about its origin. First, the name may have been given after the Spaniards came and killed many of the indigenous people living here. The other theory is that a lot of domestic animals in the area were killed before being shipped elsewhere for consumption.

Matanzas

Matanzas city is the provincial capital, and it is no longer a place where mass deaths occur. Today, it has a prominent artistic presence. The concert hall has hosted such figures as Ana Palova, Sarah Bernhardt, Fanny Elssler and Adelina Patti, one of the best sopranos of all time. Even Louis-Philippe de'Orleans, who later became the king of France, was here. And although many come just to see the caves (page 240) or the Yamuri Valley, which is totally justified, they forget the rest of the area. That is a pity. I like the Matanzas. It is a city of bridges, their supports decorated with murals. A place where children, spiffed up in school uniforms, stop to ask about your country.

■ History

Founded in 1693, Matanzas was a sleepy town that chugged along until the 1800s, when sugar production created a boom. This continued until the mid-1900s when the sugar prices fell. A port was built to help facilitate international trade and this boosted the economy again.

Prior to the sugar boom, the salt mines of Varadero kept ships stopping once every six months or so when passing between Havana and the Old World. Because of this shipping trade, the port at Varadero was built. Varadero (which means place of dry-dock) also became the stopping place for boats that needed repair.

Matanzas was the birthplace of many artists, such as the poets José Jacinto Milanes, Augustin Acosta and Bonifacio Byrne. Also born here was the famous Carilda Oliver Labra, considered the most passionate of Cuban poets. Frank Dominguez, a romantic musician, and Damaso Perez Prado, who created the mambo, hail from Matanzas. Concert performer Nilo Menendez and composer José White credit the area for their beginnings. It must be something in the earth that creates such a high number of talented persons.

■ Getting Here & Away

BY BUS OR TRAIN: The bus and train stations are at the same location, at the Estacion de Omnibus, on the main highway between Calle 272 and 171. Between the hustle and bustle of the station, where sounds and smells attack your senses, there are taxis and horse-carts to take you anywhere in the city. Keep a tight hold on your belongings and another hold on your sanity. You can easily get tickets for Havana or Varadero or to the

Zapata Peninsula. There are buses about every hour between Matanzas and Varadero.

NAMES & NUMBERS

The streets all have two names, thus causing some confusion; the old names are what the locals use and the new names (the numbered ones) are what the locals understand but the tourists use.

Contreras is Calle 79

Daolz is Calle 75

Maceo is Calle 77

Medio/Independencia is Calle 85

Milanes is Calle 83

San Luis is Calle 298

Santa Teresa is Calle 290

Zaragoza is Calle 292

(Santa Teresa, Milanes and Zaragoza are seldom used either by locals or tourists.)

■ Services

ETECSA Telephone Office (and Internet), Calle 83 and Ave 282, is open from 9 am to 9 pm daily.

Tourist Office, Calle Milanes and Santa Teresa, ☎ 52/5-3551, infotur@asimtz.colombus.cu. This is one of the better offices in the country, and the staff speaks English well.

Post Office, Ave Medio, between Calle 288 and 290, is open from 9 am to 6 pm, Monday to Saturday.

DHL Courier Service, Calle Medio #62, between Ave Santa Teresa and Ayuntamiento (no phone).

Faustino Perez Hospital on the Carretera Central, ☎ 54/5-2629, about a kilometer from the town center, is the newest medical service in the area. They specialize in cosmetic surgery but are equipped to handle most medical needs.

■ Festivals

 La Colla de Monserrate, May and December, is a music festival featuring traditional Cuban dance.

Baile de las Flores, a Danzon (Afro-Cuban music and dance, explained below) festival held in May. *Baile* means "dance."

Baile de la Guingaz, is another *danzon* (Afro-Cuban music and dance style, also the national dance) festival held in June.

Baile del Trebol and Quema del Muñeco de San Juan, June 23rd and 24th. A music festival featuring traditional dance and music.

The **Danzon Festival** is held every odd year in November and is sponsored by the Matanzas Provincial Center of Music. Check with the tourist office or at your hotel for information about the event.

THE DANZON

The *danzon* was first performed on January 1, 1879 in Matanzas. It was the work of Miguel Failde. At that time, the aristocracy thought the dance obscene. However, the young people liked the Afro-Cuban beat and used the dance as a weapon against other foreign music. Like all dances and music, the popularity of the *danzon* changed over the years. In 1910, José Urfe brought the dance into the spotlight when he produced *El Bombin de Barreto*. It was later refined by Aniceto Diaz in 1920s. The 1930s brought the mambo by Israel and Orlando Lopez and, finally, in the 1950s it was the cha-cha-cha, created by Enrique Jorrins that became popular. These changes in popularity continue today with performers like Van Van, Buena Vista Social Club and José Valdez.

■ Sightseeing

The **bridges of Matanzas** have given the city the name The Venice of Cuba. Five bridges cross the San Juan River, which runs through the city's center. They are: Concordia, built in 1878; Tirry, built in 1897; San Juan, 1904; Sanchez Figueras, 1916; and Canimar, 1957. Some of the pylons have been decorated with murals at one end, while others have attractive towers. From the bridges you can often see fishers working the river, throwing their nets from their boats.

Monserrat Hermitage, Calle 63 and malecón, was completed in 1875. Inside this building are four marble statues representing the four regions of Catalonia: Lerida, Gerona, Barcelona and Terragona. The view from the Hermitage, which overlooks Matanzas Bay, the city and the Yumuri Valley, is the best you will get. There is no charge to enter.

Fort San Severino Castle, Carratera del Puerto, Zona Franca, on the western side of the bay, open 9 am to 5 pm daily, $2 entry fee. This fortress was completed in 1734 for defense against pirate attacks. At that time, it was considered the largest fortress in the Americas. Since then it has been used as a slave trading post and a prison. Now a national monument, it offers a great view over Matanzas Bay.

Museums

Matanzas Provincial Museum, Calle Milanes, between Ave Magdalena and Ayllon, Plaza de la Vigia, ☎ 52/4-3195, is located in the small and rather simple Junco Palace that was built in 1838. Fire damaged the palace in 1845 when the entire neighborhood went up in flames. Restoration was started and the palace was lived in until the revolution but all repair wasn't completed until the 1970s.

Nineteen rooms contain collections of art, weapons that were used for war and slave control, and archeological and ethnological items dating back 1,000 years. At one time there were very rare books here, but rumor is that many have been sold to help support the government during financially difficult times.

Pharmaceutical Museum, Calle 83 on Plaza Libertad, ☎ 52/4-3179, $2 entry fee, open daily from 10 am to 5 pm, is a splendid chemist's shop set up in 1882 by French doctors Dr. Triolet and Dr. Juan Fermin de Figueroa. Three years after the revolution, the new government made it into a museum. There are old books and labels, bottles, and other items needed for a dispensary. There is even an old lab where distillation of water took place, with heat coming from a fireplace under a caldron of water, and copper pipes where the cooling occurred. Other items include glass syringes and ancient blood pressure cuffs. This is an excellent display, all contained in the

original building with the original desks, counters and display cases. The museum's collection is considered second in the world for being complete. (France has the best in the world.)

Museum of Miguel Failde Perez, Calle Velarde #95, is the home of the first person to play the *danzon*, Cuba's national dance. It developed from the Spanish Contradanza, which was itself a rendition of English country music of the 16th century. Using a trombone, two clarinets, two violins, kettledrums and a now-ob-

East of Havana

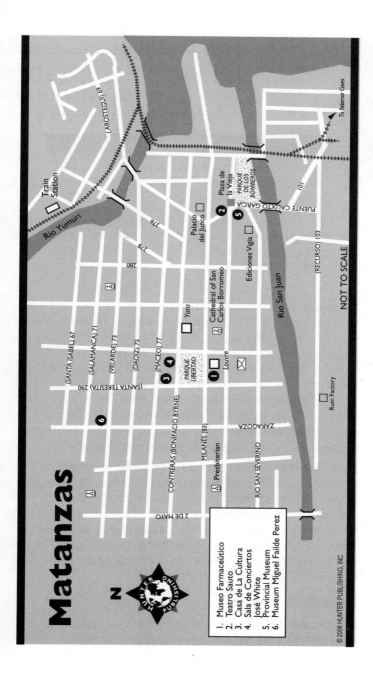

Matanzas

N
HUNTER PUBLISHING

1. Museo Farmacéutico
2. Teatro Sauto
3. Casa de La Cultura
4. Sala de Conciertos
   José White
5. Provincial Museum
6. Museum Miguel Failde Perez

© 2006 HUNTER PUBLISHING, INC

Train Station
Rio Yumuri

(AROSTEGUI) 69

Plaza de la Vieja
PARQUE DE LOS BOMBEROS
PUENTE CAUXTO GARCIA
Palacio del Junco
Ediciones Vigia
Rio San Juan

101
(RECURSO) 103
NOT TO SCALE
To Belomar Caves

276
278
280

(SANTA ISABEL) 67
(SALAMANCA) 71
(VELARDE) 73
(DAOIZ) 75
(MACEO) 77
(SANTA TERESITA) 290

Yara
Cathedral of San Carlos Borromeo
PARQUE LIBERTAD
Louvre
Rum Factory

CONTRERAS (BONIFACIO BYRNE)
MILANES (83)
Presbiterian
ZARAGOZA
RIO SAN SEVERINO
2 DE MAYO

solete instrument called the ophicleide, Perez wrote and conducted the piece of music called *Las Alturas de Simpson* (Simpson was a neighborhood in Matanzas). This was in 1879, and it was the first Cuban rendition of the *danzon*. By the 1920s it had become one of Cuba's most notable styles of music.

THE OPHICLEIDE

An ophicleide is a horn or bugle of sorts that was invented in the 1800s. The first ones were made with nine keys, while later models had 11 or 12. The name means "keyed serpent." The ophicleide replaced the more difficult instrument called the serpent, an oddly shaped horn with numerous curves and hard-to-reach keys.

Museum of Art of Matanzas, Contreras #36, 10 am to 6 pm daily, $2. This museum has numerous pieces worth seeing, including works by Antonia Eiriz who graduated from Havana School of Fine Art in 1958. Others who have had temporary showings here are American Phyllis Ewen, whose work was on display in 1993; Williams Carmona, who now lives in Puerto Rico but was born in Cuba; and Abigail Gonzalez, a Cuban photographer who has had works displayed in Canada, France, Japan, Germany and Mexico.

Sala White, Calle Contrera #28805 between Ave Ayunta- miento and Santa Teresa, was named after Cuban violinist José White, who won the Great Conservatory Paris prize in 1854. This is where the danzon was first performed. Today, Sala White is the home of the Matanzas Symphony Orchestra. Ask at your hotel or check the posters outside the building for information on performances.

Plazas & Parks

Plaza de la Vigia, Calle Milanes between Ave Magdalena and Ayllon, was built, along with a build-

Above: Playa del Este.

Below: Museum in Varadero.

Above: Image of Che Guevara in Matanzas.

Opposite: Caves near Viñales.

Below: Hills near Viñales.

Above: These rock paintings near Viñales were commissioned by F

Below: Tobacco farm near Pinar del Rio.

Above: Playa Bibijagua, Isla de la Juventud.

Below: Crocodile teeth for sale, $5 each.

Above: Castillo Jagua, Cienfuegos.

Opposite: Fantastic plants at Cienfuegos' Botanical Gardens.

Below: The castle viewed from afar.

Above: Flowers in the Botanical Gardens near Cienfuegos.

Below: Rubin Martinez Library, Sancti Spíritus.

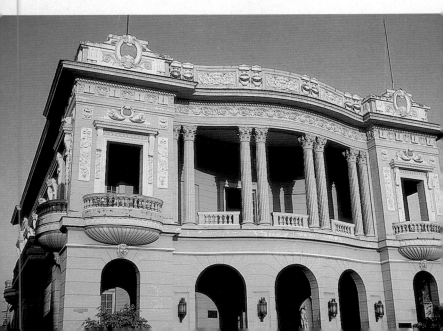

ing on one side, in 1693 and the city just grew around it. On the square is the **Fire Brigade Station** that shows the historical development of fire brigades through time. The **Junco Palace** houses the provincial museum (see page 235), which once had the famous book, *Libro de los Ingenios*, illustrated by Laplant. The book "mysteriously" disappeared. Across from the palace is the old **Customs Office**, open to the public during regular office hours. Finally, on the plaza is the **Sauto Theatre**, ☎ 52/4-2721, which was designed by architect Daniel dal'Aglio in 1863 and is still used for cultural events because of its exceptional acoustics. A guided tour is available Tuesday to Saturday, 9 am to 8 pm ($2). There are often concerts, ballet, opera or symphony performances held here. Call for current schedule.

Plaza Libertad, Calle 286, between Ave 83 and 85, is just five blocks from Plaza de la Vigia and is flanked on one side by the **San Carlos Cathedral**, built in1736. It became a cathedral in 1915.

■ Adventures on Foot

Hiking

San Miguel de los Baños was at one time a world-famous health spa with healing minerals in its hot spring. Located just 32 km/20 miles south of Matanzas city, in the hill country similar to the hills at Viñales, the sulphurous waters were said to cure everything from cancer to gout. To get here you must leave the main highway; from Matanzas, pass Limonar (see *Adventures in Culture*, below) and turn south just before Colseo. It is best to travel in your own car. Miguel, now almost a ghost town, has about 3,000 residents who will be glad to sell you all the mud laced with medicinal waters you could possibly use. One method of cure that I heard about is to put some of this mud into a microwave, warm it up and place it on arthritic joints. Sure cure!

All that remains of the spa is ruins, but they are very photogenic and the hike up Loma de Jacan, near the springs, to a view of the valley is worthwhile. The pilgrim path follows about 400 steps along the stations-of-the-cross to the crucifix at the top. To get here by bus is difficult; hitching could be fun as long as you have a lot of time as the last eight km/five miles does not have much traffic. With bad luck, you might have to walk that stretch.

Caving

Bellamar Cave, Finca La Alcancia, ☎ 52/5-3428, on the road leaving town to the southeast, about five km/three miles from the center, 9 am to 6 pm. You must have a guide. Groups go down every hour on the hour. The cost is $3; you can rent a camera at extra cost.

This is the one natural attraction in the province visitors should not miss. It features about three km/two miles of halls, passages and huge galleries decorated with stalactites and stalagmites, as well as several underground springs. (My favorite was the bed of penises.) The first section is well lit and no flashlight is needed. Going beyond the first huge room needs special permission from the government. To get that, you must be a scientist and be able to dedicate lots of time to negotiate with the Dept of Natural Sciences in Havana. This should be done at least six months prior to your visit.

The caves were first found in 1861 but it was not until more recently that studies have been done of the 28 rooms that descend to 50 meters/165 feet. Fossils and prehistoric paintings have been found in some rooms and it is believed that indigenous people, long ago, used the caves as a home.

Outside the cave are several *tiendas* serving refreshments. Chicken is the big draw.

Santa Catalina Cave is at Predios de Camaroica, four km/2.5 miles east of Carbonera, on the Matanzas-Varadero Highway, 20 km/12 miles east of Matanzas.

There is a $2 entry fee and the caves are open from 9 am to 6 pm daily. The big attractions are huge rock formations resembling mushrooms, some that stand over a meter tall. There are 11 km/five miles of underground passages that, like the Bellamar Cave, contain pictographs from indigenous groups.

■ Adventures in Culture

Limonar is a village famous for its struggle against slavery. It has an active Afro-Cuban religious group and a Monument to the Rebel Slave that was erected in 1991 to commemorate the slave rebellions of 1843. The other tribute here is the Ignacia Monument that commemorates independence fighters Gualberto Gómez and Antonio Lopez Coloma, who took up arms against Spain in 1895. Otherwise, this is a dusty little town that will give you an idea of what the "real Cuba" is all about. To get here, travel south from Matanzas about 19 km/12 miles. The village is right on the main highway.

■ Places to Stay

Casa del Valle Health Spa is at Km 2 on the highway to Chirino, just five km/three miles west of Matanzas, ☎ 52/5-4584, $$$$. It's a good place to come for the treatment of specific disorders, and the Faustino Perez Hernandez University Hospital in the city sends foreigners who have had cosmetic surgery to this spa while they are recovering.

The spa offers a sauna, massages, physiotherapy, psychotherapy, hypnosis, magnet therapy, acupuncture, nutritional programs, ozone therapy, anti-stress programs and treatments

PRICE CHART
Per room for two people, per day.
$ . . . . $25-$50
$$ . . . . . . $51-$75
$$$ . . . . $76-$100
$$$$ . . . $101-$150
$$$$$ . . Over $150

for asthma, obesity and hypertension. I believe it could be referred to as old-age or geriatric tourism. There is a minimum of seven days' stay here so assessment can be properly completed and treatments recommended. The 40 rooms in the two-storey buildings flank a large pool that has lounge chairs and sun umbrellas around the deck. Each room has air conditioning, cable TV, private bathroom, refrigerator and radio. There are also pool tables, a sauna, horseback riding, mopeds for rent and a gymnasium. If a standard room is not to your liking, consider one of six tiny cottages around a little lagoon. The hotel is 60 km/37 miles from the airport in Havana, 45 km/28 miles from Havana and 75 km/46 miles from the region's public beaches.

Hotels

Hotel Velasco, Calle Milanes, Plaza Libertad, ☎ 52/5-4074, $, is on the square and can be noisy. This was and may still be a Cuban hotel. But even if they refuse you a room, they will suggest a *casa particular*. The Velasco is an old hotel that has had some remodeling in the last five years. There is a fan that stirs up the air in the foyer and a wooden staircase leading to the rooms. At one time locals sat in the foyer and stared at foreigners until they become totally unnerved. This has changed. However, the hotel is simple and offers fairly basic accommodations.

Canimao Hotel, Carretara de Varadero, Km 3.5, is on the Canimao River, ☎ 52/6-1014, $$. The 120 air-conditioned rooms have private bathrooms, cable TV and modern décor. There is a restaurant on the premises. The hotel is on a hill tucked into lush jungle vegetation and close to both the river and the beach. Amenities include a pool, taxi service, a gift shop, and bar. Medical services are available if needed. This is not a bad deal if you want to be away from the tourism of Varadero but still want to stay in the area.

East of Havana

Casas Particulares

There are dozens of *casas* in Matanzas. If the ones I list below are full, or have closed, have no fear, someone will phone around for you and find just what you need. A room should not cost more than $30 for two, with breakfast.

Casa de Marianela, Calle 95 #29402, between Ave 294 and 298, ☎ 52/4-3634, has a lovely room in an old colonial building. There are two double beds, tiled floors, and a table with chairs. The place is clean and the bathroom is huge.

Casa Evelio and Isel, Calle 79 #28201, Apt. 3, between Calle 282 and 288, ☎ 52/4-3090, has a room with a double bed, a small fridge, television and private bathroom. The building was completed in the 1960s, so it is fairly modern. You may use the main part of the house and meals can be arranged.

Casa Vistamar, Calle 129 #14224, between Calle 143 and 144, ☎ 52/6-1364, has a room in a lovely home with a nice yard and a balcony. There is a well-decorated dining room available for your use. The owners will go out of their way to make you feel welcome and comfortable.

Villa Montelimar, Calle 129 #21808, between Calle 218 and 220, ☎ 52/6-2548, is just a kilometer from Bellemar Caves. It is in a quiet neighborhood that is safe to walk around after dark. The single room is large, the house clean and you have the use of a lovely garden. There is a private bathroom.

■ Nightlife

Caminao Discotheque, Hotel Caminao, ☎ 52/1-1014, is reported to be a good place to enjoy yourself if staying in Matanzas.

El Jaguey Night Club, Ruinas de Matasiete, Calle Luis Cuni, Viaducto, ☎ 52/5-3387, open 10 pm to 6 am. This is another recommended place to go swinging. However, it is a bit out of town so getting to and from means hiring a taxi. If you stay until closing, you may be able to get an early morning bus home.

Varadero

The name means "place of dry-dock." This port was where ships stopped for repair while on their trips between Spain and Cuba. The name stuck. Today, this strip along the Hicacos Peninsula, 22 km/14 miles long and less than a kilometer/.6 miles wide, has resort after resort dotting its white sands – enough rooms to accommodate 18,000 people.

Just a few kilometers away, along the Via Blanca between Havana and the entrance to the peninsula, are the oil pumps pulling crude out of the ground. During certain wind patterns, the smell of the oil wells can be "enjoyed" throughout Varadero. There are rumors that the entire peninsula is loaded with crude and that the government will consider moving the hotels to another region so they can drill.

Directly across the sea is the United States, a mere 180 km/112 miles away.

■ Getting Here & Around

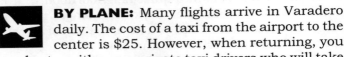

BY PLANE: Many flights arrive in Varadero daily. The cost of a taxi from the airport to the center is $25. However, when returning, you can barter with some private taxi drivers who will take you for around $20.

MONEY SAVER: A bus services the airport. If your departing flight is a bit later in the day, you can stay in Havana, take the bus to Varadero for a few dollars, and get off at the airport, thus saving the taxi fare.

BY BUS: You can purchase tickets for Havana, Viñales, Trinidad or Santiago de Cuba at the bus station, Calle 36 and the Autopista. See pages 86-87 for schedules. If traveling from Varadero to Havana, the bus stops at El Piñon, where a cappuccino costs $1.75 and a dry sandwich is $2.50. You're better off bringing your own snack and something to drink.

BY TAXI: Taxis cost around $5 no matter where you go on the peninsula. You can take a moto-scooter for slightly less. Public buses are also available. Fares can be paid in either convertibles or pesos.

ALTERNATIVE TRANSPORT: Horse-drawn carts or open-air buses charge less than taxis.

■ Services

Varadero International Clinic, Calle 61 and 1, ☎ 45/66-8611 or 45/66-7711, has 24-hour medical service. They also offer an anti-aging program for those who, unlike me, need or want it. People who enter these programs are the same people who purchased the Brooklyn Bridge.

Poli-clinico, Calle 27 and Ave Playa, ☎ 45/61-3484, is the municipal health center and is concerned mainly with treating acute ailments.

Police are found on every corner, at every bank and at some larger restaurants in the city. If you have a problem, just run into the street screaming "police" and you'll get attention within seconds.

Post Office, Ave 1, Calle 36, is open daily, except Sunday, from 9 am to 6 pm.

Internet access is available at **DITA**, Ave Playa, between Calle 41 and 42. They have about 12 machines and charge $3 an hour. You pay for an hour (or more if you wish), get a name and password put into the main terminal, and then use it as you need it. There is air conditioning and customers seem to move through fairly quickly. It is the most popular (and the best) Internet place in Varadero.

ETECSA, Ave 1, Calle 30 charges $6 per hour with a minimum of 30 minutes. The machines are average. The workers at this office will help you make a call or operate a computer.

Cubacel/mobile telephones, Edificio Marbella, Ave 1 between Calle 42 and 43, ☎ 45/80-9222, is the place to contact for a mobile phone connection.

Immigration Varadero, Ave 1 and Calle 38. If you need to extend your visa, come here. However, Spanish is necessary.

CANADIAN VISAS

Be aware that Canadians are permitted to stay for 90 days, even if the visa says 30. Going to immigration will make no difference. They won't change your visa but they won't throw you in jail if you stay more than the 30 days stamped on your passport.

■ Sightseeing

Organized Tours

The **City Tour** is offered by most hotel tour offices. It is a two-hour excursion with transportation by mini-bus. However, there is really not much to see in Varadero besides another hotel. The center, which can be reached easily by public transportation, has a few interesting buildings, as well as **Josone Park**, which can easily be visited on your own. I'd save my money and head into Havana (on my own) or Cardenas (with a tour) and see some historical sites.

A tour to **Havana** is offered by every hotel on the peninsula that has more than 10 rooms. However, Cubans living in Havana know the tour route and the beggars are relentless. (One lady, when she saw that I wasn't about to part with any cash, pulled out a bag from under her dress to show that she really wasn't pregnant.) If you want to tour Havana, take a bus into the city and, at your own pace, visit the places you want. Do not listen to all the warnings about the dangers of the big city. Havana is one of the safest cities in the world. The *jinateros* (hawkers selling everything from bus tickets and taxi rides to rooms and rum) will drive you nuts – but just tell them to buzz off and keep going. The cost of a Havana tour from Varadero is anywhere from $100 to $200 for the day. If you travel on your own and stay in a *casa*, you can do it for a lot less, see more and get a far better feel for Cuba.

Independent Touring

Casa de Al, Ave 1 and Calle 1, ☎ 45/566-7090, is at the southwest end of the trolley circuit in Old Varadero. This estate, sitting near the water overlooking the coast, was once Al Capone's mansion. Today it is a restaurant. Like many of Al's enemies, the car he drove has been laid to rest in cement. The building is beautiful, made of stone for coolness with fountains on the property and lush vegetation hiding some of the sitting nooks. There are numerous rooms (many not open to the public) that are worth a peek. If you eat here, try the paella, the specialty of the house.

Varadero Museum, Calle 57, between Ave 1 and Playa, ☎ 45/566-3850, was built in 1923 by the Dupont family from the US. They lived in it until 1959 when they fled the country during the revolution. The property, along with the Xanadu Mansion that is now a hotel, was confiscated by the present government and offered back to the Duponts if they paid their back taxes. The Duponts refused. At the time of the revolution, they owned the entire peninsula. The house, probably considered a humble dwelling to the Duponts, was used as a summer cottage. It is a wooden two-story dwelling with wrap-around porches on both levels. The upper porch gives visitors a good look at the bay. Inside the building, some rooms are furnished with old furniture and dishes that were left behind when the Duponts fled. The archaeology room features the body of an aboriginal man who died around the age of 20-30 years and was buried on the peninsula. The sports room has a few shirts, shoes and trophies from Cuban heroes. The mansion was restored in 1980 and, shortly after, developed into a museum. There is a $1 entry fee and the building is open 10 am to 5 pm with an hour off for lunch starting at noon. It matters not if you come when the building is not open as the yards are lovely to roam around and the beach is just in front. Often, this museum is supposed to be open but you will find it closed.

Santa Elvira Church, Ave 1 and Calle 47, is open from 9 am until 9 pm daily. This simple church, made mainly of wood and stone, was completed in 1938 and has little to boast about in the way of riches. The altar is plain with few plaster statues and the pews are unadorned wood. But it does have an irregular floor plan; more like a modern evangelical church than a traditional Catholic cross-shaped design. The red tiles of the roof rest on wooden beams.

San Miguel de los Baños, is 40 km/25 miles from Varadero. One of the oldest and most famous of Cuba's spas, San Miguel has medicinal water containing bicarbonate, sulfide and magnesium-silicate. This is not an operational spa. What you really come for is to get a bit of mud and to visit different surroundings. The muds are said to cure or at least alleviate osteo-muscular ailments, osteo-arthritis, degenerative and post-traumatic rheumatoid arthritis, and skin and respiratory ailments. Back when the Spanish first discovered the baths, there were 48 people living here. By 1948, there were over a thousand.

There are places to stay in San Miguel but it is better to visit as a day-trip. It is 12 km/7.5 miles from Limonar, 25 miles from Varadero and 45 km/28 miles southeast from Matanzas. To get here you have to come by car or bus, or take a tour. If taking a bus, an overnight trip might be in order as getting there and back would take longer than a day.

Dolphinarium, Autopista del Sur, Km 11.5, ☎ 45/566-8031, has shows starring local dolphins. Those with some extra loot can stay after the show and swim with them (I believe this runs $60 over and above the $10 show price, for a mere half-hour). A photographer will take your photo with one of the smiling sea creatures for another ten bucks.

■ Adventures on Foot

Golf

 Varadero Golf Course, Carretera de las Americas, on the road to La Torre, ☎ 45/566-7750, is the first professional golf course built in Cuba. It is an 18-hole, par 72 course designed by Canadian architect Les Furber. The 6,850-yard freeway has an easy bogey and a difficult par caused by islands, sand traps, lakes and natural obstacles such as wind. There are five par five holes and five par three holes. The remaining eight holes are all four-par. The first nine holes are easier than the second and the 15th to the 18th are considered difficult.

There are two practice putting greens and a 300-meter/958-foot driving range along with a pro shop, caddie house and a snack bar. But best of all, the clubhouse is the Villa Xanadu Mansion, built by the Dupont family and taken for back taxes by the present government when they won the revolution. You can stay there.

Green fees are $70 for 18 holes and $48 for nine. Bags, balls and carts are available ($30 for carts and bags and $6 for a bucket of balls). Nine-hole games, starting after 5:30 pm, cost $25 per person. All fees have a 10% service charge!

Tennis

Deportiva, Ave 1, Calle 37, has hard-surface tennis courts that are free and open from 9 am to noon and 2 pm to 6 pm daily. You'll meet a lot of Cuban sports enthusiasts here.

■ Adventures in the Air

International Parachuting Center, Via Blanca, Km 139, ☎ 45/566-7256, skygators@cubasports.itgo.com or at Barracuda Dive Center, Ave Primera, between Calle 58 and 59, ☎ 45/566-7072, ventas@aqwo.var.cyt.cu, is run by Cubanacan and offers training courses or tandem jumps, low-altitude jumps and ultralight flights. The club is enthusiastic and offers the "Thriller" that is only for the courageous. If you think you fit into this category, ask about it. The center also has a cafeteria, a bar and five basic rooms with air conditioning, so you can stay the night. Space is available on a first-come first-served basis. The cost of a basic jump is about $150.

■ Adventures on Wheels

Enjoy **Go-Cart Racing**, located on the Autopista on the way to the airport, about five km/three miles from the bridge. The track is open daily from noon till 6 pm.

■ Adventures on Horseback

Center Hipico, Via Blanca, Km 31, ☎ 45/566-7799, will take you horseback riding on a short trip down the beach or for a full day into the Yumuri Valley. The costs vary depending on where you go and how long you stay, but most start at around $10 per hour.

The **Cuba Star Travel Company**, based out of Germany, offers riding trips in different parts of Cuba for a week or 10 days. Prices vary depending on how long you ride. For more information, visit www.cubastar travel.com and contact them from home.

■ Adventures in Nature

Josone Park, Ave 1 and Calle 56, covers nine hectares of manicured grounds, which can be explored on foot, bike or horse-drawn carriage. There is a pool and a small man-made lake where you can take a rowboat out or swim (lockers for your gear are available for a fee). A huge stone mansion, located at the back of the property beyond the footbridge, is decorated with carved woods and stained glass. It was completed in 1942.

There are four restaurants, Antigüedades Retiro, Dante and La Campaña specializing in international cuisine, and a bar, La Gruta, on the shores of the lake. The bar often has live entertainment. However, nothing is cheap: a dish of ice cream (not a big one) costs $4.50. On the other hand, for those with lots of bucks, the Italian restaurant has a large wine cellar (that actually is not in the cellar).

An attractive bridge goes over the lake at Josone Park.

Hicacos Point Natural Park, on the northeastern tip of the peninsula, was declared an ecological preserve in 1974. Besides exhibiting lots of birds and plants that are natural to the area, the 312-hectare park has Ambrosio Cave, Mangó Lake, El Patriarca Cactus and La Calavera Salt Works ruins. To get here take any bus along Ave 1 to the eastern end or take a taxi for about $10. **El Patriarca Cactus** (free to photograph) is believed to be 600 years old. It stands well over 20 feet and has numerous arms pointing in every direction like the snakes on Medusa's head. The fruit of this endangered plant is the wild avocado. The highly perfumed white flowers at the end of each thorny arm look somewhat like dahlias. **Ambrosio Cave** ($5 to enter) has prehistoric paintings dating back about 3,000 years when it is believed the first settlers discovered the island. They were fishers and gatherers and their life is (sort of) depicted in the six drawings found in the cave. This is one of the 15 archeological sites on the peninsula and the easiest one to reach. The cave is 250 meters/750 ft long and has five interconnecting galleries. It contains 72 drawings, which makes this one of the largest collections of Indian pictographs in the Caribbean. During the colonial period, runaway slaves used to hide here. Mangó Lake (free to walk around) is the largest body of fresh water on the peninsula and is home to 31 bird species, 19 of which are migratory. There are 24 varieties of reptiles. The maintained walking paths are easy to navigate; most stretches are in the shade. **La Salinea la Calavera** (salt works; $3 to enter) is thought to have been the first salt mine worked by the Spanish in the Americas. It is believed that even Sir Francis Drake partook of salt from this mine. There are just a few artifacts here.

Canimar Park, Via Blanca, Km 106, ☎ 45/526-1516. Visiting includes an 11-km/seven-mile ride on a double-decker boat through jungle. The river here is located between Varadero and Matanzas and the setting has been developed (or not) so visitors can learn about plant and bird life in the area. The park opened in 1994. The tour includes a lunch of old-fashioned Cuban food and not so old-fashioned drinks. There is a reproduction of local life before modern technology displayed under a thatch-roof hut. Options for the tour are to either ride a horse or row a boat. Or you can swim or just relax on a hammock and look for birds.

There are plans for the not-too-distant future to present cockfights and rodeos. Brochures at almost every hotel tourist desk attempt to lure you into a visit.

For this trip you must get tickets from the Cubamar Travel desk, Calle 54 and the Autopista, ☎ 45/566-8000 or 45-525-3189, or from a hotel that works with Cubamar. The park is at Km 106 on the Via Blanca. If visiting independently, take a bus going to Matazas and ask the driver to let you off at the park.

■ Adventures in Water

Day Sails, Snorkeling Excursions & Submarine Trips

There are four marinas in Varadero and most boat tours start at one of them: **Puertosol Darsena**, Carretera Via Blanca Km 31, ☎ 45/566-8060; **Aquaworld** (Marina Chapelin), Carretera de Las Morlas, Km 12.5, ☎ 45/566-7550; **Gaviota Marina**, Carretera de Las Morlas, Km 21, ☎ 45/566-7755; and **Aqua Puetosol**, Ave Kawama #201 between Calle 2 and 3, ☎ 45/566-8063. If you go on your own, the cost for your excursion will be the same as if you paid for it at a hotel tour desk and gotten transportation to the marina. (That is unless you can talk the captain into letting you on for less and paying him directly without anyone else seeing. I've never been successful at this trick in Varadero.)

VaraSub, is a modern, 44-ft semi-submarine that has reinforced glass windows that make peering at the bottom of the ocean comfortable. The Japanese-made boat can hold 48 people. It has air conditioning and an open bar that serves soda or rum. The trip takes an hour and a half and there are six trips a day, the first at 9 am. The boat leaves from the harbor at Super Club Puntarena near the entrance to Varadero. If you'd rather not go in the sub, opt for the glass-bottom boat called *Nautilus* that has 56 sheets of thick glass through which you can peer at the bottom of the ocean. On this trip, you also get free drinks. Note that this boat does not have scheduled trips but is used only for private hire.

You can purchase tickets for the above trips, as well as transportation to the harbor, at the Buro Tour and Travel Office, Ave Playa between Calle 36 and 37, ☎ 45/566-7027 or 45/566-7589 or at Ave de Las Americas and Calle 65, ☎ 45/566-7203. The cost is $65 for adults and $55 for children under 12 if you include transportation to the boat. Otherwise, the cost is $35 for adults and $25 for children under 12.

Mundo Magico is a mini-submarine that descends about 35 meters/115 feet so you can observe ocean wildlife. This vessel can carry 46 passengers and the ride takes about 55 minutes. It leaves from Puertosol Harbor. You can purchase your ticket at the harbor or from hotel tourist desks.

The **Dolphin Swim** is a popular eight-hour excursion by catamaran that holds up to 60 people. The four boats leave from Gaviota Marina, ☎ 45/566-7755, at different intervals during the morning and make three stops a day. The $75 ($53 for kids) includes transportation to and from the dock. There is a swim and snorkel stop near a cay, a lobster lunch stop at Cayo Blanco, and, finally, the all-important swim with dolphins.

The mammals are held in a fairly large underwater compound and come out to swim with the visitors. Children love this. Guides make certain suntan oil or insect repellent is not transferred to the animals; you will be asked to wash before entering the water.

A loaded catamaran, Varadero.

However, the snorkeling stop is hardly worth going into the water for. There are a few fish swimming around and the odd brain or fan coral, but that's about it. Lunch is passable but certainly not great and it takes about two hours.

On the plus side, the boats are large and comfortable, the bar never goes dry and the waiters try hard to entertain. A net at the front of the boat allows tanners to lie in the sun. Be certain to take sunscreen. This tour is offered from every hotel in the city.

The two-hour **Jungle Tour** goes on a Sea-Doo through mangrove canals to a small island zoo. Tours start at 9 am daily, with the last tour at 3 pm. The mangroves house many tropical birds such as tanagers, blackbirds and kingfishers, and the small zoo has crocodiles, iguanas and other lizards. The $40 cost includes the two-person watercraft, life jackets, dry bags for camera and a soft drink at the zoo.

The tour departs from Marina Chapelin, Carretera las Morlas, Km 12, ☎ 45/566-8441. However, there are rumors that the business was for sale so things could change.

Sailing Seafari leaves from Puertosol Darsena at the south end of Varadero, ☎ 45/561-4453. This all-day trip on a sailboat goes to Cayo Piedras off the northeast end of the peninsula, where you will be served a seafood lunch and given a couple of drinks. You can also snorkel. The boat returns to the dolphin pool in Varadero in time to watch their suppertime show. This is an excellent trip, where neither the bar nor the waiters are ever dry.

Scuba Diving

About 30 diving destinations are packed between the **Piedras del Norte Cay Underwater Park** in the Bay of Matanzas at the western end of the peninsula and the **Jardines del Rey** at the eastern end of the strip. Visibility usually runs 30 meters/100 feet and the water temperature is about 24°C/75°F.

There are sunken ships, underwater cliffs, coral reefs and wildlife. The main diving attraction in the area is the Hoyo Azul Ojo del Mégano, a 70-meter-wide (225-foot) cave that has walls, reefs and fish galore. The other highlights are *Las Mandarinas* and *El Barco Hundido,* both sunken ships. The Piedras del Norte Park has scuttled ships, planes and trucks here to create an artificial reef. This is a good area for both diving and snorkeling. One of the sights divers enjoy is the green moray that hangs around a "secret" spot (you can be taken there by request). There is a decompression chamber in Varadero.

The Barracuda Club, Ave 1 and Calle 59 (near Josone Park), ☎ 45/566-7072, has professional divers who can take you down or give you your first lessons. They also have equipment for rent. A two-tank dive costs about $75 per person, with equipment. The other place to hire dive masters is the **Aqua Scuba Diving Center** at the Puertosol Darsena de Varadero Marina, Carretera Via Blanca Km 31, ☎ 45/566-8060, at the eastern end of the peninsula.

CORAL FAST FACT

Stony corals such as the brain coral and star coral, the main builders of reefs, are found exclusively in warm waters no deeper than 25 meters/80 feet. Stony corals are arranged in multiples of six polyps to each tentacle.

■ Places to Stay

 There are enough rooms to hold 18,000 people in Varadero. Most of the hotels are large, impersonal institutions that prefer you to book an all-inclusive stay from your home country. I find these spots quite boring. I have reviewed only a few hotels along the town's 22-km/14-mile strip because there are so many, and after the first 10, it would make for pretty dull reading.

There are no *casas* in Varadero. The government was forced to clamp down to ensure that the hotels got the business, and even the old stand-bys no longer take the risk of renting a room. Any local caught breaking this law will receive a fine of up to $3,000 and spend a few years in prison.

ALL-INCLUSIVES

The food at all-inclusive buffets is usually rated as bad. Often, guests are not permitted to eat at the à la carte restaurants. Drinks are watered down and wine gets better only with quantity. People often get stomach problems. If you have paid for an all-inclusive, that means you don't get to try any foods elsewhere unless you pay more on top of your package. Be very careful before you book. Visit www.tripadvisor.com on the net and see what others say about being there before you make a decision to pay for it all.

Hotels

All prices in Varadero drop by almost half after March 15th and go up again in October. I have quoted prices in high season.

PRICE CHART
Per room for two people, per day.
$. $25-50
$$. $51-75
$$$. $76-100
$$$$. $101-150
$$$$$. . . . . over $150

Hotel Turquino, Ave 3, Calle 34, between 3rd Ave and the Autopista, ☎ 45/561-3796 or 2012, $, has two-room apartments with double beds, private bathrooms, balconies, air conditioning in the bedrooms, and cable TV in the living rooms/kitchenettes. The apartments are also supplied with fridges (no stoves) and great room service. There is a small restaurant/bar on premises but there is no pool or garden, although there is lots of vegetation around the courtyard. If a cheapie is what you need, this is the place.

Mar del Sur, Ave 3, Calle 33, ☎ 45/566-7482, mardelsur@horizontes.hor.tur.cu, $/$$, has an inviting atmosphere, lovely gardens, a large swimming pool, a pleasant bar and a restaurant. However, the rooms are trailer-trash quality, with ripped curtains and cheap, chipped furniture that has been painted a ghastly purple or brown. It is filthy and not worth $10 per night, never mind what they ask. The guard looking after the yards is careful that no one enters who should not be there, so security is good. On the other hand, the maids constantly beg for handouts. Avoid this place at all costs. Next door is the Turquino, which is much cheaper, cleaner and better kept.

Palma Real, Ave 2 and Calle 64, ☎ 45/561-4555, $$, has 466 rooms in two large buildings just a block from the hotel's private beach (with bar). This hotel is an all-inclusive. Each room is large and has a private bathroom, cable TV, balcony and sitting area. There are four restaurants, a few snack bars, a disco, a beauty parlor, a kids' pool, a massage parlor, sauna, tennis courts, a tourism office and a car rental. There are five pools in all, with a bridge between two. This is a middle-of-the-road hotel. The greatest draw is the location, in the center of town not far from the Josone Park. The reception area seems to be the place to hang out until you head off for dinner. The beach is narrow and not exceptionally attractive and the palapas are on a vegetated hill up from the sand.

Villa Tortuga, Calle 9 between Bolevar and Ave Kawama, ☎ 45/561-4747, $$, is at the west end of town but within walking or local-bus distance from the city center. The air-conditioned rooms all have private bathrooms with lots of hot water, tiled floors, small sitting areas and cable TVs. There is a pool and restaurant on site. If you are looking for a cheap place with not too many frills, this is a good choice. The gardens are all well kept and quite pretty and the hotel is not far from the beach. This is not a party hotel.

Sun Beach, Calle 17, between Ave 1 and 2, ☎ 45/566-7490, $$, has almost 300 large rooms, half of which have balconies. They have private baths, cable TVs, tacky furnishings, sitting areas, mini-bars (upon request), and tiled floors. This is an older hotel that is showing a bit of wear but it is conveniently located and not too expensive.

Coralia Cuatro Palmas, Ave 1 between Calle 60 and 61, ☎ 45/566-7040, $$/$$$, is in the middle of Varadero in a convenient location. If you can get in without paying for an all-inclusive, you could be ahead of the game, but they often refuse to do this. The Coralia is not a resort but rather a second-rate hotel that's a bit shabby around the edges. Some call this character. Being close to the city's best beaches and places offering good food (usually better than what is offered at the all-inclusive) is what makes this hotel a draw. Each room has a safe that works with the same card as the one for your door, cable TV, a balcony, two twin beds and a fair-sized bathroom. Do not take a room facing the street unless you can sleep through a lot of noise; the bar across the road plays until the last drunk leaves. There is a pool, restaurants, a bar and live entertainment each evening.

Arenas Blancas, Calle 64 between Ave 1 and the Autopista, ☎ 45/561-1086, $$$, is the best place to stay if you want to party. The 450 rooms, some wheelchair-accessible, have twin beds, cable TVs, private bathrooms, air conditioning and tiled floors. The one basic complaint is that it is noisy. The biggest draw is the maid service, but this is usually good all over Cuba. The staff that looks after everything else is often lacking in speed. The pool is average but clean and the grounds are very pretty. The beach is excellent and close by, although you must get there early if you want a chair and umbrella.

Hotel Pullman, Ave 1 between Calle 49 and 50, ☎ 45/566-7161, $$$, was built in the 1950s and has a castle/fort appearance, with a garden that has stone statues near fishponds, plus a fairly large pool where guests enjoy the odd rum and coke. There are 15 average-sized rooms with fans, TVs, tiled floors and private bathrooms. There's a small restaurant and bar, and parking is available for a fee. This popular place is clean and just a block from the beach.

Los Delfines, Ave la Playa between Calle 38 and 39, ☎ 45/566-7720, $$$, is an old stone colonial-style building right on the beach in the town center, close to everything. The 47 rooms have private bathrooms, satellite TV, comfortable beds, and tiled floors. Breakfast is included. This is a wonderful building that gives an aura of intimacy often lacking in monster hotels. Amenities include a pool (and separate children's pool), two restaurants (average), two bars, laundry service and a tour desk. This property and the Pullman are good deals for the independent traveler.

Hotel Varadero International, Ave Las Americas, Km 1, ☎ 45/566-7038, director.hint@gcinter.eca.cma.net, $$$$, has been around for 40 years and boasts many distinguished guests. Its 163 rooms are large, each with a balcony, double or king-size bed, writing table, dresser, private bath, tiled floors, air conditioning, satellite TV, hairdryer, safe and daily room service. There is a tennis court, swimming pool, well-kept garden, children's playground, live entertainment, restaurant, bar and disco. The hotel is wheelchair accessible, has a games room, scooters for rent, tourist office, gymnasium and car rental service.

Paradisus Varadero, Rincon Frances, ☎ 45/566-8700, paradises.varadero@pvaradero.solmelia.cma.net, $$$$$, is an all-inclusive monster hotel with a total of 421 rooms located in 28 two-story buildings. All the amenities of a five-star hotel are offered, including iron, hairdryer, fridge, bathrobes, coffee makers, sitting areas and balconies or patios. However, the air conditioning works too well and wool blankets are needed for comfortable sleeping. Eating in the buffet is not all that pleasant, and trying to get into the better restaurants at the hotel is difficult. There is a limit to the number of times you are permitted to eat in the restaurants. There are three pools, two for kids and one for adults that is probably the biggest pool in Varadero. If you can't get a seat at the pool, head to the long beach where the water is great for wading. There is a sauna and Jacuzzi, fitness room, exercise class, scuba diving (not included in price), beauty salon, tennis, volleyball, shuffleboard, kayaking, windsurfing, and a spa. If that's not enough, you can use a bike and cycle to town, shoot an arrow into a board or play soccer. You can take dance lessons or just wait until your entertainment specialist takes you off to do something fun. There are some souvenir stores and lots of entertainment, some of it very amateurish.

If you would like to get married here, you will have some extras thrown in to help the romance blossom. These include late housekeeping service, a bottle of sparkling wine, separate rooms the night before the wedding (for the price of one room), bride's flowers, wedding cake and breakfast in bed the day after the wedding. If you want a quiet wedding, the witnesses and translator can be arranged and all the documents for the ceremony can be taken care of.

Superclub Puntarena, Ave Kawama and Final, ☎ 45/566-7120, direccion@riparad.gca.cma.net, $$$$$, is at the west end of the beach where the canal comes in. The hotel's two high yellow towers, which can be seen from everywhere in Varadero hold 532 rooms. This popular, all-inclusive place is busy and noisy in the main reception areas. I understand that the rooms are just as noisy because of the old air conditioners, water pipes, etc. Be aware that you must pay $10 deposit for every towel in your room. If it disappears, so does your deposit. There are nice gardens and the beach is fairly decent, but the pool is a constant source of complaints. It is divided in two by a concrete slab and you are allowed to swim in the pool that is on the side of the building where your room is located. The two sides shall never mix (or meet)! Why they did this is beyond me. Even worse, if you are on the non-bar side, you are not permitted to go to the bar side and ask for a drink. As for food, the best advice I can give is to bring "Tums" unless you are lucky enough to eat all your meals in one of the restaurants where the food is far superior to that served in the buffets. But things change. A few bad reports and the Cuban government may do something, so check www.tripadvisor.com occasionally to see what the most recent reports are.

Tryp Peninsula Varadero, Parque Natural Punta Hicacos, ☎ 45/566-8800, dir.ger@t.p.solmelia.cu, $$$$$, is located at the very tip of the peninsula, about 14 km/nine miles from the center of the city. It has 591 rooms and is probably the most luxurious place in Varadero. The large rooms have everything, including air conditioning, cable TV, separate shower rooms and bathrooms, private safes, coffee machines, sitting areas, mini-bars (always full) and lots of fluffy towels. Some rooms also have Internet connections, which is very new for Cuba. The staff is helpful and serves drinks quickly without watering them down. The meals have had all kinds of reports from horrid to okay. There are six or seven wedding locations at the resort, and the coordinator does a top-rate job. The beach in front of the hotel is raked daily and the large pool with many arms and curves has a swim-up bar. The hotel is wheelchair accessible. Use of all non-motorized water vessels (like pedal boats and kayaks) is included; baby-sitting is extra. Amenities include a Jacuzzi, sauna, massage, tennis, badminton, beach volleyball, shooting range, and more. If you are a game person, there is something for you. This is a fun place.

Hotel Kawama, Calle O, Kawama, ☎ 45/561-4416, $$$$$, has 235 attractive, large rooms with king-size beds, tiled bathrooms and air conditioning. They are located in rustic villas dotting the property. Each room has a balcony or patio. The curvaceous pool has lots of chairs and palapas and the well-kept gardens have palms, bougainvillea and oleanders. The entrance and bar are spacious and not crowded. The beach attached to the hotel is super and use of a mini catamaran, windsurfing boards and paddle boats is included in the price. This is not a party hotel but rather for those wanting a quiet vacation.

Hotel Melia Las Americas, Autopista del Sur, ☎ 45/566-7600, $$$$$, is the crème de la crème of hotels in Varadero, just eight km/five miles from the center of town. It has 230 rooms and 90 junior suites. The rooms are large, with windows on two sides, balconies, tiled floors, huge soft beds, coordinated décor, and marble bathrooms that never seemed to run out of hot water. The sitting areas have love seats and comfortable rocking chairs. The large closets have full-length mirrors, the TVs have cable connections, and the irons and hairdryers work. The rooms are in two-story bungalows/condos with vegetation surrounding the walkways between the buildings. The lobby is as nice as the rooms, with a skilled piano player most evenings. There's a huge pool just off the beach, and romantic gardens that are full of exotic plants interspersed around little man-made streams that are crossed by tiny bridges. The gym is great, with all the various machines working as they should. The bars, restaurants and snack shops are clean and the food is good, but the service can be slow or, in some cases, non-existent. However, the food at this hotel's à la carte restaurants is superior to the food served at the Xanadu Mansion next door. Within a short walk of the hotel are a shopping mall and the golf course at the Xanadu Mansion. This hotel caters to the golfer/middle-aged guest.

■ Places to Eat

 Every hotel has at least one restaurant, and there are hundreds of independent eateries from which to choose. Be aware that some places run out of just the thing you are looking for like, say, ketchup. But this is Cuba and no matter how much you kick and scream you won't get what you want if they don't have it.

Vicaria, Ave 1, Calle 36 (no phone), has the cheapest meals in town, served under palapa huts with soft music playing. The food is good but not exceptional. Chicken is the mainstay meal. This is a popular place with both locals and foreigners.

Xanadu Mansion, Autopista del Sur, Km 8.5, ☎ 45/566-7388, open 7 am to 7 pm, is the old Dupont house where the food is nothing to rave about but the charges are. Water, buns and butter are all extra, even if you don't eat them. Once on the table, the price is on the bill. You are better off going into town and getting something more reasonably priced.

El Toro Steak House, Ave 1 and Calle 25, ☎ 45/566-7145, has the best steak in the city cooked to perfection. Cuba must import meat from Argentina because there isn't enough land here to raise cattle. For us foreigners, this is good because Argentinean beef is exceptionally tender and flavorful. The price of a steak with trimming is about $15. Order a drink and enjoy the atmosphere, as it will take a minute – or several – to prepare your meal.

El Meson del Quijote, Carretera de Las Americas, ☎ 45/566-7796, is where the hero Quijote and his faithful follower Pancho Sanchez can be seen walking the endless plain of eastern Varadero. Even if you don't eat here, be certain to see the metal statues of Cervante's heroes. I have no idea how good the food is or how expensive as I never made it to the restaurant, nor did I run into anyone who could tell me about it.

Islazul Restaurant, Ave Playa and Calle 42 (no phone), is across from Hotel Ledo. They boast of having lobster pizza in season but I'd be skeptical. The spaghetti is actually alpha-ghetti with cumin. Cost per meal is around $3.

La Bodegona de Varadero, Ave Playa and Calle 31 (no phone), has diced chicken with soy and olives for $5. 50. Sooo good. Or try the pan-fried beef with onions and garlic for $8. Servings are generous.

El Carbiño, Ave 1 and Calle 30 (no phone), is a sidewalk snack bar and café open 24 hours. It is very popular in the morning for those who need an eye-opening beer. Later, it is nice to sit at the table, sip on a cool one, and watch the street action (as long as you can avoid the characters who start practicing early for their more inebriated performances later at night). Beer is cheap, so that is probably the attraction.

Lai Lai Chinese Restaurant, Ave 1 and Calle 18, ☎ 45/561-3297, is a Chinese restaurant decorated with red vases and silk pictures. They have spring rolls for $1 and stir-fried cabbage for $2.50. The place looks lovely from the outside, but the waiters are sullen and the small portions are very bad. Stay clear of this place; it has put all its efforts into decoration and none into service or food quality.

La Dragon, Ave 1 and Calle 55 (no phone), noon to 9 pm daily except Sunday, is across from the park and serves the best Chinese food in Varadero. It doesn't matter what you order, you will find that it is good. The service is equal to the food and the price is about $2 per dish (although each dish is on the small side).

Restaurant Calle 43, Ave 1 and Calle 43 (no phone), is under a huge thatch roof and serves tasty fish or chicken served by pleasant waiters. Prices are average. There is live entertainment in the evenings.

Restaurant Idilio, Ave 1, Calle 31 (no phone), has great hamburgers on fresh bread, served with fries for $3. The fries are interesting and look more like the potato chips one gets in a bag. However, sprinkled with lots of salt and a bit of ketchup they are really good.

Restaurant Guamaire, Ave 1, Calle 29 (no phone), has an outdoor patio with tables and an inside dining area with linen tablecloths. The beef and the melanesa dishes are both recommended, but we found the *mojitos* a bit on the light side. Stick to beer.

La Gruta, Ave 1 between Calle 58 and 59, in Parque Josone, ☎ 45/566-7228, is a dark little restaurant that has a long wine list (with most bottles in stock). A beef dinner with rice, bruschetta and a shared bottle of good red wine is about $30 per person. The meat is good and the service elegant.

■ Tour Operators

The Barracuda Club, Ave 1 and Calle 59 (near Josone Park), ☎ 45/566-7072, has professional divers who can take you down or give you your first lessons. They also have equipment for rent. A two-tank dive costs about $75 per person with equipment. The other place to hire dive masters is the **Aqua Scuba Diving Center** at the Puertosol Darsena de Varadero Marina, Carretera Via Blanca Km 31, ☎ 45/566-8060, at the eastern end of the peninsula. In addition to its diving amenities, this marina has 112 moorings, three for large yachts. All amenities for sailors, including immigration and customs, are located here. There is another dive center at **Hotel Sol Club Coral**, Carretera Las Americas and K, La Torre, ☎ 45/566-7240.

Buro Tour and Travel Office, Ave Playa between Calle 36 and 37, ☎ 45/566-7027 or 45/566-7589, or Ave de Las Americas and Calle 65, ☎ 45/566-7203, offer many excursions.

Cubamar, Calle 54 and the Autopista, ☎ 45/566-8000 or 45/525-3189, is where you must make arrangements for the Canimar River trip (see page 128).

Mopeds/Bike Rentals, Ave 3, Calle 31, has mopeds (M550) in very good condition for $8 per hour, $11 for two hours, $22 for 24 hours. They also have the larger (M55E) bikes for $1 per hour more. Gasoline is extra.

■ Nightlife

More than 100 discotheques, bars and cabarets are available on the peninsula so you are bound to find something to your liking. Many hotels have discos or piano bars with live entertainment, but it is also fun to explore, so poke around. Varadero is very safe at night, but if you are leery about going home late, cabs are always available.

Below is a review of the Matanzas Tropicana that is offered by every hotel's tour desk in Varadero. It is the same as the one in Havana only a bit cheaper. I would suggest seeing the show at least once in your lifetime.

Matanzas Tropicana Night Club, Km 4.5 Autopista del Sur, ☎ 45/526-5380, open daily 8:30 pm to 2:45 am. This is a copy of the original Tropicana held in Havana since the 1950s. Due to the popularity of the show, the government felt that a second venue would be appropriate so they built this one just out of Matanzas. The club interchanges the dancers with those in Havana, so the quality is the same at both open-air theaters. The theater can hold over 400 people for dinner and drinks. The dancers shake to the rhythm of everything from Afro-Cuban *danzon* to salsa to son to bolero to tango. There is a souvenir shop, cigar shop and flower service. Photos of you sitting here can be taken by a photographer. Reservations are recommended.

You can travel to the club on your own and purchase tickets at the door for $35. This gives you just the show and a couple of rum drinks. Or you can book at the desk of any hotel in Varadero. The cost of going with a guided tour is higher, around $70, but this includes transportation and dinner.

When you factor in your dinner, your taxi to get there and the cost of the seat, you are no better off on your own. Also, the seats are generally much better if going with a hotel group than if traveling independently. All tickets include some Cuban rum. If there is rain, the show will be cancelled and a refund will be forthcoming.

Continental Cabaret, Hotel Varadero International, Ave Las Americas, Km 1, ☎ 45/566-7038, brings Cuban variety shows and performers to its stage, Tuesday to Saturday. Some big names who have performed here are Frank Sinatra, Nat King Cole, María de los Angeles, Santana and Rosita Fornés. Going to the Continental is an all-night event. Have a gourmet dinner, watch the show and, at the twitching hour, kick up your heels with the disco crowd. However, you will pay a lot for your night. There is a cover charge of $10, and drinks are at North American prices.

Casa de la Cultura, Ave Primera, no phone, offers everything from poetry readings to the Saturday night rumba event where you dance to Afro-Cuban music. Check on the door for a listing of events, concerts and groups performing. There is no admission charge and many things also go on during the day, between 9 am and 6 pm. As an example, an hour of dance class during the day costs $2.

FM 17, Ave 1 and Calle 17, ☎ 45/561-4831, is in the center of town and is popular with locals. The bar is open 24 hours a day and there is wheelchair access. You can purchase food like hamburgers and fries from a kiosk just outside the bar and entertainment is usually offered at night. A similar bar, the **Arboleda**, is one block up at Calle 18 (no phone), where the tables are on the street. The only downside of this bar is you may be hassled by the odd drunk.

Habana Café, Sol Club las Sirenas Hotel, ☎ 45/566-8070, is a fairly famous club for foreigners. It plays the music of the '50s and '60s and recreates the atmosphere of that era with photos of old VIPs and copies of old advertisements. They even have an old car in the bar. Drinks here are "all-you-can-drink" for the cover charge ($15, but this price changes depending on the season). Don't confuse this place with **Casa Habanos**, Ave 1 and Calle 39, an elegantly decorated bar where you can purchase cigars, coffee or alcoholic drinks. The atmosphere is relaxing, the prices average and the refreshments first class. Open 9 am to 8 pm.

Cueva del Pirata (Pirate's Cave), Autopista Sur, Km 11 (no phone), has its bar/disco in a natural cave. It's a long way to go for atmosphere and many people feel claustrophobic when inside. All the gossip I was able to pick up said not to bother going to this one.

Bar 62, Calle 62 (no phone), in central Varadero, has Cuban music every night between 9 and midnight. Everyone dances, sings, laughs, drinks and generally has a good time. This place is highly recommended; I was told about this by a taxi driver and later heard from others about how good it was.

■ Shopping

Bazar Varadero, Ave 1, between Calle 44 and 46, ☎ 45/561-2329, is a large artists market with attractive wood carvings. The artists do not work every day. If you see something you like but want to think about it, ask when your artist will be back again so that if you do decide to purchase that item, you can return to the same artist.

QUICK FRIENDS, FAST ENEMIES

When bartering for anything in Varadero, be aware that many Cubans will have no problem betraying a friend to earn a foreign buck. Be careful in whom you trust.

At **Raudilio Fleitas Government Store**, Calle 34, between Ave 1 and 3, you can buy cheap beer (50 cents/bottle). It is sold at room temperature, so be sure you have a fridge in your room. You must return the bottles, as they are worth more than the beer in Cuba.

House of Habano Cigar, Ave Playa and Calle 31, ☎ 45/561-1430, or Ave 1 and Calle 63, ☎ 45/566-7843 or Ave 1 between Calle 39 and 40, ☎ 45/561-4719. For cigars, for sampling cigars, for coffee, for atmosphere, this is the place to go. You can sit and enjoy a rum drink or a coffee and try a brand of cigar before you purchase. You know you are getting the real thing when you shop here.

Purchase your bottles of **rum** at any *tienda* along the strip. It is cheap and there are no imitations. Or go to **Casa del Ron**, Ave 1 and Calle 63, ☎ 45/561-4659.

Sol y Mar Art Gallery, Ave 1 between Calle 34 and 36, ☎ 45/561-3153, has local art that is quite good and a bit different from what you will find in the markets. Study up a bit on Cuban art and, if you like it, then come to this market to find the good stuff.

Cardenas

Cardenas is a peaceful town where bicycles and horse-drawn carts are more popular than cars. It was here, in 1850, that the first national flag was raised and, more recently, where the child Elian Gonzalez was returned to his father after a custody battle between the father and his Cuban-American relatives, that was reported around the world. For those unfamiliar with the case, the Cuban father won the battle and the child was returned to Cuba.

At the entrance to the city, when you come in from Varadero, is a 15-ton cement crab. Erected in 1996, it has become the symbol of the city.

■ Getting Here

You can visit Cardenas as a day-trip from Varadero. It is about 10 km/six miles south of Santa Marta at the western entrance to Varadero. You can hitch (easy, fun) or hire a car/taxi. Once you get to town, there is so much to see that you will be busy all day. Give yourself enough time to get back to your lodgings. The other option is to stay in the village and get away from the touristy places.

■ Festivals

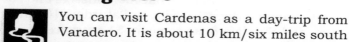

Toque de la Diana Mambisa - March 1. A religious celebration commemorating the dead who fought for Cuba's freedom. Toque de la Diana Mambisa is the playing of a hymn on a bugle.

Parranda Guajira - May 1-8. This festival honors two musical styles and the *campesinos* who played them.

Fogata de San Juan - June 21. Locals light a bonfire and celebrate the unity of other countries that helped Cuba in its fight for independence.

■ Sightseeing

Electric Power Station Ruins, Calle Linea and Velazquez, are the ruins of the country's first power station, which went into operation in 1889. It was replaced by the new plant in 1925.

San Martin Railway Station, Calle Concha and Vives, was built in 1875 and was, for a time, the largest in the country. Cardenas was the second city to become part of the rail line in Cuba. Today, the line is still used but rail travel is slow and tedious. Only die-in-the-engine railroaders should travel by rail.

Museums

Oscar Maria de Rojas Museum, Calle Calzada #4 between Echeverria and Martí, no phone, is a military building constructed in 1863, a year that saw a tremendous amount of development in the area. There is an odd combination in this collection: insects and colonial weapons. Open Tuesday to Saturday, 10 am to 5 pm, and Sunday, 8 am to noon. $1 entry fee.

José Antonio Echeverria Museum, Calle Genez, between Calzada and Coronel Verduga, no phone, is the house where Echeverria was born. He is the man who planned the attack on the presidential palace during the revolution. The house is an example of old colonial architecture. Open Tuesday to Saturday, 8 am to 4 pm, and Sunday, 8 am to noon. $1 entry fee.

Museum of the Battle of Ideas, Calle Vives and Colonel Verdugo, no phone, is located in what was once a fire hall, dating from 1872. The house holds documents and newspaper articles about the historic fight over the guardianship of Elian Gonzalez, who escaped from Cuba with his mother. She died en route, while Elian made it to the States. There, his American relatives laid claim to him and wanted to raise him in the US. However, his father, who lives in

Cuba, fought for custody and won. Elian was eventually returned to his father in Cuba. The building has a library and temporary exhibitions. Open Tuesday to Saturday, 9 am to 5 pm, and Sunday, 9 am to 1 pm. There is a $2 entry fee and a guided tour costs $2 per person.

Churches

San Antonio Church, Ave Calzada and Lopez, was founded by Mother Teresa of Calcutta and is dominated by the 26-meter/75-foot steeple towering above the front entrance. The church is the Cuban headquarters of the Sisters of Charity.

The Trinitarian Priests School and Church, Ave Calzada and Calle Real, features the church directly in the middle with classrooms to each side. The ones to the right of the altar were added later, while the ones to the left were built at the same time as the church. However, before this was a church, it was the Isla de Cuba Hotel, built between 1905 and 1906.

Plazas & Monuments

Plaza Colon is where the first building was constructed in Cardenas around 1828, and the Christopher Columbus bronze statue, designed by José Piquer, is the first one erected in the Americas. Hotel La Dominica is also on the plaza. This was where in 1850, after independence, the first national flag was raised.

Plaza Spriu has a statue of Echeverria in its center and some of the best-preserved colonial buildings in the city surrounding it. It was built in 1861 and was the second public square in town. The plaza was named after a Catalan trader.

Plaza Malakoff was originally a market square that was built in 1859 to house those selling wares to locals. It was restored in 1996.

Bicycle Square, Calle Cespedes and Ave 26, has a bike mounted on a pillar to mark the significance of this mode of travel, often used by local people.

Monument to Mothers, Calle Calzada and Ave Saez, is another monument made of cement; this one has a lady wearing a long skirt walking with two kids hanging onto each side of her. It's easily identified, even if you don't read Spanish. Every mother in the world can relate to the clinging of kids to the skirts.

Monument to the Flag, Calle Cespedes and Ave Litoral, was erected in 1945 to commemorate the raising of the first flag in Cuba. The hotel where the flag was raised is called La Dominica.

Monument to the Martyrs, Calle Salud and Ave Calvo, is a tribute to local independence fighters, called "mambises." This mausoleum dates back to 1900. This is where the Toque de Mambisa festival is held every March.

Zapata Peninsula

Zapata means "shoe" in Spanish. However this peninsula is not shaped like a shoe, nor does it produce shoes. It was named after the first owner, who received the land from the King of Spain in 1635. The area is interesting because it was never a slave-worked region. Rather, Spanish men and women came and took mates from the local population. They established farms that are still working today. Being basically "back to the land" people, they worked the farms, fished, cut wood, kept bees and sold crafts to survive.

It wasn't until after the 1959 revolution that the area became accessible to the rest of the country. Then the people received electricity, roads, schools, doctors and, finally, tourists. Two of the first tourists to ever visit were Jean Paul Sartre, from France, and Graham Green, the British novelist who wrote a few stories about Cuba. Prior to these men, Frances Drake and Gilbert Giron were rather unwelcome tourists who plundered the coasts and robbed Spanish ships. Rumors still circulate claiming there are treasures hidden in the lands around these farms.

There are three places where tourists can stay: Playa Larga, Guama or Playa Giron. All have attractions of interest to nature lovers although Guama is the least comfortable or interesting of the three. This is a very unpopulated area and is recommended only for adventuresome travelers.

■ Getting Here & Away

BY CAR: If traveling by car you will have no problems following the pot-holed roads that take you through the area.

BY BUS: If traveling by bus, you have two options. To get to Playa Larga, you must take the Viazul bus to Jaguey. From there you can reach Playa Larga just 20 km/12 miles south by hitching. You can also fly into Playa Larga. The other option is to take a bus going to Cienfuegos and get off at Real Campiña or Yaguaramas, and then hitch down the 25 km/16 miles to Playa Giron. There are two buses from Havana every day that travel along this main road, and one from Varadero.

The two towns on the bay are about 30 km/19 miles apart. Playa Larga is at the northwestern end of the Bay of Pigs, while Playa Giron is at the entrance or the southeastern end. For any exploring of the parks and viewing of wildlife, you must stay at either of the two places.

> **AUTHOR TIP:** No matter where you go, be certain to bring insect repellent. This is a swamp!

■ Sightseeing

 Bay of Pigs Museum, at Playa Giron, has historical details (from the Cuban point of view) about the horridly botched attack on Cuba by the Americans during the Kennedy administration. From what I understand, the invasion came out of an initiative from Richard Nixon, the flawed planning of Dwight Eisenhower, and the failed implementation of John F Kennedy. What a team!

On April 17th of 1961 about 1,300 Cuban-Americans landed at the Bay of Pigs hoping to get the sympathy and help of the local population to overthrow the government. What really caused this attack was that, after Castro took control of Cuba, he also took control of American oil refineries on the island. The Americans retaliated by refusing to purchase any more sugar. Castro responded by taking possession of all American businesses in Cuba. The two boys, Castro and Kennedy, were like kids playing in the sandbox, which resulted in Kennedy feeling that he had no other choice but to hit with a stick. Castro seems to have had the bigger stick because he managed to capture 1,197 American troops within a couple of days and sent the other 103 packing.

The museum has a number of maps and photos, an aircraft and two tanks, but there's not really much to see for the $2 entry fee. Open daily from 10 am to 5 pm with an hour off at noon. $, ☎ 45/9-2504.

■ Adventures in Nature

 Montemar National Park is 5,000 square km/2,000 square miles of wetland, making it the largest wetland preserve in the Caribbean. It houses some of Cuba's most interesting wildlife in its swamps, lagoons and rivers of clear water that flow into reservoirs. There have been more than 900 species of plants found here, 115 of which are endemic to Cuba and five that are found only in this area. Hidden around are over 150 species of birds, including the smallest, the Cuban humming bird. The Zapata rail, Zapata sparrow and Zapata wren, all endemic to the island, have been seen in this park, which is home to 12 different mammal species (not counting humans), 31 reptiles and five amphibian species. Insects? There are tons. The Cuban crocodile, in danger of extinction, is here, as is the *manjuari*, a prehistoric fish. Manatee swim in the salt waters off the shores of the peninsula and mongoose roam the higher ground, looking for snakes. To visit the park, it is best and easiest to take a tour.

PREHISTORIC FISH

The *manjuari* is a primitive skeletal fish that first appeared during the Paleozoic era, about 27,000 centuries ago, when reptiles first appeared. It is the earliest known evolutionary link between fish and mammals. The body of this lizard-like creature can grow up to six feet in length; its green skin features spots, rather than scales. The skin is covered in natural oils, thus assisting in its rapid movement through the water. Its flat head has external bones and its mouth has three rows of sharp teeth that make it look a bit like a cousin to Jaws. Neither the fish nor its eggs are edible, and it is a protected species.

Birding guides are available at **Playa Larga International Bird Watching Center** by the Playa Larga hotel. You are far better off taking a guide than going alone as they know where the different species can be found. They can also identify many of the birds you may not be familiar with. Visiting Montemar National Park is exciting, like going down the Congo River deep into the jungle.

Laguna del Tesoro, at La Boca, is a 900-hectare lake that is the largest body of fresh water in the country. It is a pool you'd rather be in than look at from May to

October, when the temperatures are around 30°C/ 86°F and the humidity is 85%. There is a small island on the lake inhabited by Taino Indians. The lake's information center rents boats so you can go out to the islands and observe the Indians going about their daily life. If you'd rather fish, trout, carp, shad and biajaca (*Cichlasoma tethracantha*) are common.

> **ENVIRONMENTAL ALERT:** The biajaca is an endemic fish that is protected under the Convention on International Trade in Endangered Species of Wild Flora and Fauna (CITES), a treaty of which Cuba is a signatory. But the lake is still being indiscriminately fished for local consumption and for export.

The lovely sculptures, mostly of indigenous women, dotting the grounds around the lake are designed by Cuban artist Rita Longa.

Built on this group of islands linked by wooden bridges is Guama, the tourist hotel. Rooms here are in thatch-roof huts built on stilts. See below for details.

Hatiguanico River is one of the best places for birding as the river meanders through mangrove and mahogany forests dotted with hundred-year-old oak trees, in a northwest direction from the Zapata swamps to Batabano on the Caribbean. Some of the birds are woodpeckers, egrets, cormorants, jacanas and American bitterns. The Zapata rail, Zapata sparrow and the Zapata wren are usually found near the headwaters of this river. Always be on the lookout for the bee hummingbird, the smallest in the world and Cuba's national bird.

The river starts as a freshwater spring and is a good place to do a bit of fly fishing for tarpon and snook. For this you will need a guide, obtainable at the hotel in Playa Larga.

The river trip can be done with Gap Adventures (see page 77) as a kayak trip that includes other interesting rivers in Cuba.

MANGROVES WITH A PURPOSE

Mangroves are often found parallel to coral reefs. The plants like brackish, nutrient-rich water, and they clarify it for the coral, which needs clear, nutrient-poor water. Some mangroves (there are red, black and white that like different conditions) are able to filter the salt water through their root system, while others release the salt through pores on their leaves.

In addition to offering a protected environment for hundreds of fish, mangroves provide a home to birds and land animals. They also keep soil erosion to a minimum and absorb some of the harsh wave action caused by hurricanes and storms. The wood from the trees is used to make traps and nets and it can also be burned for fuel.

Cave of the Fish is 15 km/nine miles from Playa Larga and from Playa Giron, which puts it smack dab in the middle between the two beaches. There is a restaurant and a tiny sign that says "Cueva del Pesces" leading to a path from the road to the cave. The cave entrance looks like the earth has split in two, with thick vegetation surrounding it. Fish and underwater wildlife can be seen in the brackish water. The split is 75 feet long and 20 feet wide and 500 feet from shore. The most amazing thing about this split, which is actually a cave whose ceiling has caved in, is that it goes down about 300 feet, with a freshwater layer on top and saltwater about 10 feet down. While swimming around, you will share the waters with colorful tropical fish. There is a $1 charge to enter.

CAVE SEARCHING

Caves and splits like the Cave of the Fish can be found all along the coast of the Bay of Pigs. Some of the ground covering the openings has fallen, making the caves into what the Maya called cenotes, which were often used for ceremonial purposes. When exploring this area, it is fine to look for the caves, but be very careful if entering alone as you don't know what's inside. For underwater exploration (diving with tanks), see the tourist desk at Playa Larga Hotel.

La Salina Wildlife Refuge is a large saltwater lagoon that's home to 165 bird species, some of which are migrant. This includes huge colonies of flamingos, cranes, cormorants, egrets, herons, sandpipers, terns, plovers, spoonbills and ospreys – those huge raptors that are similar to eagles. The most common birds in this area are migratory. The refuge is best reached from Playa Larga and you must either have your own car or go on a tour. For specific driving directions, ask at your hotel or the car rental office.

Santo Tomas Wildlife Refuge holds three rare species of birds in its forests. They are the *ferminia*, which is endemic to this area, *cabrerito de la cienaga* and the very rare *galinuela de Santo Tomas*. The refuge, about 30 km/19 miles from Playa Larga, has a permanent population of 200 people. Anything that you can contribute to their economy would be appreciated. This refuge can be reached either by your own car or by tour. Again, you'll need to ask at your hotel or the car rental office for specific driving directions.

La Boca de Guama Crocodile Breeding Farm at Lake Tesoro has almost 10,000 crocs in every stage of development from egg to grandpapa. There is a lookout point where you can watch the adult crocs wallow in mud. It takes a long time to see them actually do anything, and while you're watching the smell you'll detect is Oscar de la Crocodile. The crocs raised here are released into the huge Zapata Swamp when the wild population needs upping. The *tienda* here prepares some croc meat for visitors to purchase. Some believe that the meat has aphrodisiac qualities. I am told that they cook only the old and dying crocs.

■ Adventures on Water

 Diving and **snorkeling** can be done from shore but the farther out you go, the better the wildlife. A ledge drops dramatically, forming a wall for sponges and other corals a short distance from shore. The best samples of elkhorn and brain coral in Cuba are in this bay. There are over 40 species of coral that house 70 species of mollusks, probably the most extensive number in the Caribbean.

■ Tour Operators

Octopus International Diving Center, Playa Larga, ☎ 45/9-7294, has all the equipment to take divers out to the coral reefs south of the peninsula. The cost is $50 for a one-tank dive and $75 for a two-tank dive.

Giron Beach Diving Center, Hotel Playa Giron, ☎ 45/9-4118, has equipment, boats and dive masters.

■ Places to Stay

Hotels

 Playa Larga Hotel, Playa Larga, ☎ 45/9-7225, $, is in Montemar National Park. It has 68 rooms, 41 of which are in small bungalows with sitting areas, private bathrooms, air conditioning, twin beds, cable TVs, small fridges and balconies or patios. The cottages are spotless and comfortable, although not five-star. Most parking places are close to the cottages. There is a pool on site and the gardens are well kept. The hotel has bikes and motor scooters for rent, plus some cars. You can also hire a horse and guide for the day. This is not a highly populated area so strolling on the beach will seldom be noisy and finding a spot that is crowded will never happen. Palm trees

line the beach and nature lovers will find it easy to get around to spot birds and reptiles. The beach beside the hotel goes out a long, long way before it starts to get deep. This is a great value.

Hotel Playa Giron, Playa Giron, ☎ 45/9-4118, $$, has 290 rooms in cabins that are interspersed throughout the gardens with plenty of space between them. Each cabin is air-conditioned, with private bathroom, a fridge, barbeque pit, and cable TV. The floors are tiled and there is a wooden table and kitchen chairs in each room. A pool and restaurant are also on the property. You can rent a bike or motor scooter to visit surrounding areas.

Guama, Laguna del Tesoro (reached by boat from La Boca), ☎ 45/9-5515, $$, has 50 cottages with thatched roofs dotted around a well-kept garden. They are air conditioned, with private baths and cable TVs. Bring lots of mosquito repellent as Guama is near a swamp. Guama is actually 12 tiny islands connected by wooden bridges. On one island is Tainos Village and on another is a disco. The silence of the lake is swallowed at night by the music from the disco.

Odd and rustic is what I'd call this place, but you are here to see nature. As you scratch yourself to sleep, always remember that mosquitoes are part of that ecosystem. Boats cost $10 for a return trip from La Boca (where the road ends) or you can catch the regular boat that leaves at 10 am and noon daily.

Casas Particulares

There are a number of *casas* in the village of Buena-ventura, about a kilometer from the hotel at Playa Larga. Below I have profiled just a few, but when you get to either place, ask anyone for directions to the numerous other *casas*. The other option is to look for the blue triangular sign on the doors of the houses, indicating that this is a *casa*.

Hostal Luis, on the road to Cienfuegos, near Playa Giron (no phone), has rooms with air conditioning. Breakfast is included in the price. They can arrange offshore diving trips ($25 for one tank) and they offer great meals.

Miguel Padron, Playa Giron, ☎ 45/9-4100, has one room with air conditioning in a comfortable house.

Maritza Lopez, Apt. 21, Playa Giron, ☎ 45/9-4266, has one room. The phone number belongs to a neighbor, so Spanish is a must.

Mayra Otega, Apt. 19, Playa Giron, ☎ 45/9-4252, has two very clean rooms. The phone number belongs to a neighbor so, again, calling ahead would require some Spanish.

La Casa de Roberto Mesa, Playa Large, ☎ 45/9-7210, has two rooms, one that will hold two people and another that will hold four. The rates here include all meals.

■ Places to Eat & Party

Eat at the hotels, the *casas* or the restaurant at the cave. As for nightlife, if the disco isn't to your liking, you'll have to use your own creative imagination.

Cienfuegos

Located on the Bay of Jagua, the colonial city of Cienfuegos (100 fires), was founded by French colonists in 1819. Often overlooked, this beautiful city has some of the nicest colonial architecture in the country. The theater on the plaza offers first-class shows and the town itself takes a few days to explore. Close by on the water is an old fort protecting the entrance to the city. In the opposite direction is a botanical garden. Luxury seekers will appreciate Ciego Montero Spa, backset by the Escambray Mountains.

> **AUTHOR NOTE:** Graham Greene's agent Wormold said that Cienfuegos was "one of the quietest ports in the world."

■ History

The town, first called Fernandina de Jagua, was founded by the French and was later named after Camilo Cienfuegos, a revolutionary in the fighting days of Castro and Guevara. During a demonstration, when Cienfuegos was 23 years old, demonstrators were fired upon and he was hit in the leg with a bullet. During his hospital stay, he was cheered by hundreds of students much to the chagrin of Batista. Cienfuegos' popularity resulted in his becoming a captain of a platoon stationed near the mountains.

In the early days of the revolution, rebels seized the police station and the Batista military post and then stayed around to protect the city's civilians from the government troops. But Batista had more military power than the rebels. He sent B-26 bombers and tanks in and they captured and killed most of the rebels. Any who surrendered were buried alive. Cienfuegos was not captured. Instead, he was sent to lead his 700-man force to the battles near Camagüey and Las Villas.

After the revolution, Cienfuegos was flying from Camagüey to Havana when his plane disappeared. Although a search was conducted, his remains were never found. Some believed that Castro got rid of him because he was much too popular. In Cienfuegos, on October 28th – the day of his death – children of the area throw flowers into the sea to honor him.

■ Getting Here & Around

BY BUS: A collectivo taxi takes 3½ hours from Havana to Cienfuegos. The fare is $20 per person and the cab holds three people. There's no direct bus service from Varadero. However, you can jump on a bus going between Havana and Trinidad and get off at Cienfuegos. Buses leave Havana at 8 and 8:30 am and 4 pm daily and arrive 2½ hours later. The cost is $6 per person. The bus from Varadero to Trinidad, with stops in Santa Clara and Cienfuegos, leaves at 7:30 am from Varadero, 10:45 from Santa Clara.

The bus from Trinidad to Havana (not Varadero) with stops in Santa Clara and Cienfuegos, leaves Cienfuegos at 4 pm, Santa Clara at 5:25 pm and arrives in Havana at 8:40 pm. The fare from Varadero to Cienfuego is $10, and from Varadero to Santa Clara is $11.

You will find many people take a collectivo. The cost is the same as a bus and the travel time usually much shorter. Wait around the bus station and a driver will approach. If the bus comes before he can load his vehicle, you can quickly purchase a bus ticket.

■ Services

Post Office, Ave 56 and Calle 35, open Monday to Saturday, 8 am to 8 pm.

Etecsa Telephone Office, Calle 37 #4820, or Calle 31 between Ave 54 and 56, has Internet service for $3 for half an hour. There are five machines, you pay in advance, and you cannot save time for later use.

International Clinic, Calle 37 #202, has an attached drug store that is open 24 hours a day.

Police, ☎ 116

■ Festivals

Late August or early September, Cienfuegos hosts the Benny Moré Festival. Moré is a famous Cuban musician who once said, "Cienfuegos is the city I love most." The three-day event, held every other year on the odd-numbered year, features popular dance music and workshops on genres, styles and history of music in Cuba. At night the concerts include rap, rumba, son and mambo. The city really comes alive during the evenings, with many venues around town featuring famous Cuban groups.

■ Sightseeing

Cementario La Reina, Calle 7 between Ave 50 and 52, at the western end of the city, was opened in 1830. Inside, the most famous statue is *Bella Durmiente* (*Sleeping Beauty*), a white marble statue of a woman dressed in a long gown, leaning in sitting position against a cross. This was the city's first cemetery.

Cementario Tomas Acea, Ave 5 de Septiembre, was opened in 1926. This is the location of the monument to the Martyrs of the September 5, 1957 uprising. At the entrance is a replica of the Parthenon of Greece, probably the cemetery's most notable piece.

Castle of Our Mother of Los Angeles of Jagua, ☎ 41/9-6402, also known as the Jagua Castle, is a 250-year-old fort on the bay that was used to defend the area from marauding pirates and to protect sailors during storms. Today, regattas and races are held in the waters around the castle. The fort is interesting to walk around and has a tiny museum inside. However, the most interesting aspect is the "Lady in Blue," a ghost who apparently makes her presence known every now and then. I didn't meet her, but you might be lucky. The village of El Perché surrounds the castle. To get here you must take the small ferry that leaves from the corner of Calle 23 and Ave 46 at 8 am, 1 pm and 5:30 pm. It returns at 6:30 am, 10 am and 3 pm daily. Walk along the Prado to Calle 25 and then down to the water. There is a sign indicating where the boats leave from. The cost is in Cuban pesos and equivalent to 50 cents. It takes 45 minutes to reach the fort. There is a restaurant at the fort and another in the village.

Central Plaza

This is one of the nicest plazas in Cuba. So nice, in fact, that it's worth your time to go up the tower at the Palacio Ferrer to photograph the plaza. Sit at one of the restaurants under the colonial arches that surround the square or stroll through the center with its flower gardens and statues.

The plaza in Cienfuegos.

At one end of the plaza is **José Martí Park**, which has a granite compass indicating point zero of the city, the distance from which town measurements are taken. In front of that is the famous Arch of Triumph.

Cathedral of the Purist Conception, Ave 56 #2902 and Calle 29, at the same end as the Arc de Triumph, was built between 1833 and 1869 and is still in use today. Rather plain from the outside with only two large towers (one used for the bells), the building has 12 stained glass windows that are striking when the sun shines through.

Palacio Ferrer, Ave 54 and Calle 25, allows you to enter its tower for a view of the city. Built in the early 1900s, it is the present home of the Provincial Cultural Center. There is a $3 charge to go up the tower.

National Naval Museum, Ave 60 and Calle 21, ☎ 43/2-9143, is located at José Martí Park. It contains more documents and some information about the history of the navy in Cuba, especially since the Castro take-over. It also has some remnants of the rebel attempt to take over the city in 1957, like the blood-stained shirt of one of the revolutionaries. The museum is open daily from 8 am to 4 pm and costs $1 to enter.

Tomas Terry Theatre, Ave 56 #2703 and Calle 27, ☎ 43/2-3361, was built between 1886 and 1889 and is a must if there is a show on. I managed to take in a contemporary ballet and the production was superb, the atmosphere colonial and the acoustics perfect. It is worth the $5 just to see the inside of the building and to feel the elegance of sitting in one of its 900 seats, never mind enjoying quality entertainment. It costs $2 to tour the building, which is open daily from 9 am to 6 pm.

East of Havana

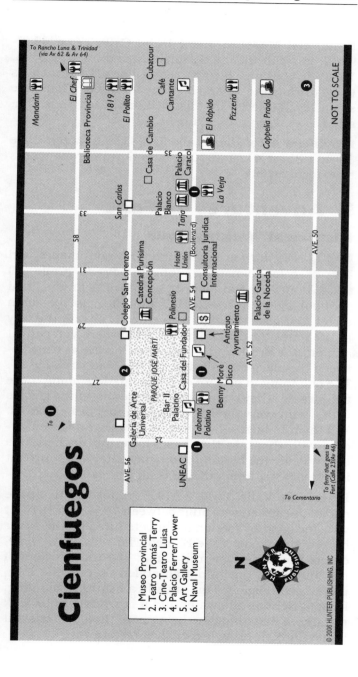

Cienfuegos

1. Museo Provincial
2. Teatro Tomás Terry
3. Cine-Teatro Luisa
4. Palacio Ferrer/Tower
5. Art Gallery
6. Naval Museum

© 2006 HUNTER PUBLISHING, INC

To Rancho Luna & Trinidad
(via Av 62 & Av 64)

Mandarin

El Chef

Biblioteca Provincial

1819

El Pollito

Cubatour

Café
Cantante

Casa de Cambio

Palacio
Caracol

El Rápido

Pizzeria

San Carlos

Palacio
Blanco

La Verja

Coppelia Prado

NOT TO SCALE

Taria
(Boulevard)

Colegio San Lorenzo

Catedral Purísima
Concepción

Hotel
Unión

Consultoría Jurídica
Internacional

Palacio García
de la Noceda

AVE. 50

Polinesio

AVE. 54

Antiguo
Ayuntamiento

AVE. 52

PARQUE JOSÉ MARTÍ

Galería de Arte
Universal

Bar II
Palatino

Casa del Fundador

Benny Moré
Disco

Taberna
Palatino

To

AVE. 56

UNEAC

To Cementerio

To ferry that goes to
Fort (Calle 23/Av 46)

N

HUNTER PUBLISHING

Provincial Museum, Ave 54 and Calle 27, ☎ 43/2-9722, is set in the old Spanish Casino built in 1896. Today it contains furniture and porcelain that was used during the Spanish reign in Cuba. There are some lovely pieces in this well-organized museum, and the cost to enter is a mere $2.

Provincial Art Gallery, Ave 54 #3310 between Calle 33 and 35, ☎ 41/9-3310, contains numerous works from local artists.

■ Adventures on Foot

Historical Walking Tour

Cienfuegos has numerous monuments and colonial houses along the **Prado** (Calle 37) and the **Boulevard** (Ave 54). The Prado, lined on both sides with colonial buildings, is the main street that goes through the center of city all the way to the water. At the end is a gazebo where you can sit and enjoy a drink and a rest. The Boulevard runs between the plaza on Calle 29 and the Prado at Calle 37. The one thing to beware of is the hustlers along these two streets. They imagine themselves as young gigolos with whom every foreign woman should be enamored. Tell them to buzz off, unless of course you are enamored with them. In that case, have fun! If there is a sign outside the building, you may enter and tour, but if not, viewing from outside is all you can do.

Palacio de Valle, Calle 37 (the Prado) #3501, at the end of the street, was built between 1913 and 1917. It was designed by foreign architects hired by the sugar baron, Acisclo del Valle Blanco who was, at the time, one of the richest men in Cuba. The three towers of the building, one Moorish-styled, represent love, power and religion. This is truly a beautiful building, located right on the water and it is a privilege to walk through. I can't imagine living here though. Today, it houses a high-class (expensive) restaurant.

Casa de los Leones, Calle 37, ☎ 41/9-5804 or 432-419-5808, is farther along the Prado, past the Palacio de Valle and closer to the gazebo.

Avenues 56 and 52 run along the side of the central plaza. **Casa Almacen José Garcia de la Noceda**, Ave 52 #2913-15; **San Lorenzo College**, Ave 56, between Calle 27 and 29; and **Casa del Fundador**, Calle 29 and Ave 54, are all close together and worth having a look at.

Casa de Vivienda del Antiguo Central, Ave Real #204, and **Antigua Ingenio Carolina**, along the Highway to the oil refinery, are a bit farther out. However, if you are traveling on these roads, keep an eye out for these two colonial buildings.

Caving

Martin Infierno Cave at Yaguanabo Beach, east of Cienfuegos but still on the bay, has gigantic stalactites that stand 60 meters/200 feet tall. One, the highest in the world, reaches 67 meters/220 feet. Two other notable towers in this cave are the Moon Milk and the Flores de Yeso. You must hire a guide from one of the tour agents in town to visit this cave. Even if you get there on your own, you can't enter without a guide. The cost for a tour is $20. That includes transportation and a guide – well worth the cost.

■ Adventures in Nature

Botanical Gardens, 15 km/nine miles along the highway to Trinidad is open daily from 9 am to 4 pm and costs $2.50 to enter. The park is maintained by the Ecological Institute of Cuba and the main attraction is the Royal Palm Highway, where these majestic trees line two sides of a walkway. Considering the condition of royal palms throughout the Caribbean, this is an impressive site. The two newer palms were planted in the late 1960s in honor of Richard Howard, a director of the Arnold Arboretum at Harvard University who came to the botanical gardens as a student in 1940. However, it was Edwin F. Atkins, a plantation owner living here, who put aside five hectares of land for sugarcane research. As time passed he added other plants to the area and by 1919 professors from Harvard University came to look at the newly developed tropical research station. After the revolution, the Cuban government took over the station and renamed it. The gardens are now the best in the country.

Located on 97 hectares, the gardens have over 2,000 varieties of plants, including a cactus garden, 200 varieties of palms and numerous orchids. The bamboo groves are impressive; some of them form a corral in which you can get shade in the hot season and protection from the rain during the wet season. The many trails in the park can be somewhat confusing and you may get slightly lost. There is a steam running through the property, crossed by bridges, to help you get back and forth. There is a restaurant.

To get here, take a bus going to Trinidad or a collectivo from town. The cost is $10 for up to six people in a collectivo. A Viazul bus goes past the gardens at 12:30 pm daily and costs $6 per person. To get back to town, walk back the two km/1.2 miles toward town and to the main highway and then hitch a ride. There is no bus.

El Nicho is in the Escambray Mountains and at the source of the Hanabanilla River, which flows into the bird-rich **Laguna de Guanaroca**. It is about 50 km/ 31 miles from the city on the road toward Trinidad and 150 meters/500 feet above sea level. There is a lovely waterfall, plus spectacular views of the country. Along the river are small pools in which you can swim. Birding is good; the lake is a nesting site for flamingos. The variety of plant species is staggering. I have had reports of up to 6,500 different species in this one small area. There is a restaurant at the waterfall, but prices are exorbitant. Bring food and drink with you!

To get here, you must either take your own car or hire a taxi. The cost of a taxi is more than renting a car for the day (cars cost $50). Or rent a motorbike for $20. You can also sign up for an organized tour arranged at El Union Hotel (see page 295) for $30 per person. This includes the trip, a guide and a meal.

■ Adventures in Water

Beaches

Rancho Luna Beach, just 18 km / 11 miles from Cienfuegos, is on a horseshoe-shaped beach with white sand and shallow waters that contain rich marine life. There are a number of hotels along the beach and a few along the road that leads to the beach. Swimming and some snorkeling are good here and, when not on the property in front of a hotel, it is a treat to be here. (The front of the property is crowded and workers don't really like non-guests to be there.) Buses run in the morning and evening taking workers to the hotels. Catch a bus or hire a taxi to take you out and another to take you back to Cienfuegos.

Scuba Diving

There are about 50 sites in the bay, some of which include sunken ships, colonies of coral and a huge number of fish such as grouper, tarpon, barracuda, snapper, grunt and angelfish. You may be lucky enough to see turtles, jewfish, spotted eagle rays and whip rays. Mid-winter brings whale sharks. The Pillar Coral site has been dubbed Notre Dame because of its gothic-looking towers, one of which is almost six meters/20 feet tall. Other popular sites in this bay are the Barreras Cove and Las Playitas. Check with the Whale Shark Scuba Dive Center, below.

Ciego Montero Spa, Palmira, 23 km / 14 miles north from the city, ☎ 43/2-0056, is perched on the slope of a mountain. It is known for its thermal baths, with temperatures up to 47°C/117°F). The mineral waters are said to cure arthritis and skin or bone disorders. Doctors have been studying the possibility of finding relief for fibromyalgia here also. The water is heated by an exothermic reaction between chloride and sodium with a little sulfur in the mix, so the odor is mild. A complete body massage will cost $5 and a taxi to the spa is $15. The marble pools are indoors. Attendants watch and advise you about bathing. There is a limit as to how long you can stay in the water as the temperature is so high it can cause problems instead of performing cures. The cost is $2 for a dip. Phone ahead or contact the tourist desk at your hotel for hours. The spas are generally open from 8 am to 5 pm.

■ Adventures of the Brain

Spanish School, 5059 St. Denis, Montreal, ☎ 888-691-0101, www.edutourstocuba.com, offers 62 hours of study that combines classroom work and excursions where Spanish must be spoken. The school has four levels of learning from beginner to advanced, all taught by skilled teachers. The options are studying in Cienfuegos (where you will have to practice the language) or in Havana (where you may find more English). This company only takes customers with bookings made ahead of time from Canada. It does not allow individuals to book lessons upon arrival.

■ Tour Operators

Cubatour, Calle 37 between Ave 54 and 56, ☎ 43/2-5-4785, offers excursions to most places around town and out to El Nicho for $30 or the Sugar Factory near Trinidad but often visited from Cienfuego, for $20.

The Whale Shark Scuba Diving Center at Rancho Luna Beach offers day and night dives and courses for beginners. At the marina where they are located, there is an immigration office and a spot for boats to moor.

EduTours, 5059 St. Denis, Montreal, ☎ 888-691-0101, offers a Spanish-learning, immersion tour that looks after everything for you, including your accommodations and airfare.

■ Places to Stay

Hotels

El Union, Calle 31 and Ave 54, ☎ 41/9-1204, $$, is a beautifully restored colonial building in the center of town. It has three dozen rooms with every luxury you could imagine, including air conditioning, hairdryers, cable TVs, mini bars, in-room safes and fine décor. The

PRICE CHART
Per room for two people, per day.
$. $25-50
$$. $51-75
$$$. $76-100
$$$$. $101-150
$$$$$. . . . . over $150

pool, the rooms, the restaurant and the building itself are immaculate. There is a Jacuzzi, a gymnasium, business center, two patios and a restaurant all serviced by friendly staff. Modern Cuban art decorates the walls. Bicycles or motorbikes are available for rent. I loved this place.

Amigo Faro de Luna, Carretera Pasacaballo, km 18, near Rancho Luna Beach, ☎ 43/3-5162, $$, is tucked into a small cove for privacy. The rooms, located in six-plexes, are large, and have balconies or patios, king-size beds, sitting areas, tiled floors and private bathrooms with hot water. You can opt to have meals included. There is a pool, although the hotel is just 300 meters/980 feet from the ocean. Because the diving is good in this area, there is a diving operator at the hotel. The Spanish school mentioned above is also centered at here.

Punta la Cueva Hotel, Km 3 on the Rancho Luna Road, ☎ 43/3-8703, $$, has cabins on a small private beach. Each cabin has air conditioning and cable TV, and some are wheelchair accessible. There is a coffee shop, disco and bar along with a pool and gift shop.

Yaguanabo Hotel, Km 55 on the road to Trinidad, $$, ☎ 49/6-6212, is at the mouth of the Yaguanabo River, where it flows into the ocean. The setting is both romantic and beautiful. The rooms are nothing to scream about, but for the price, you can't go wrong. They have air conditioning and private bathrooms with hot water, and are located in small cabins surrounded by jungle vegetation. Some are a bit musty. Horseback riding and boat rides can be arranged.

La Jagua Hotel, Paseo del Prado #416 between San Rafael and San Miguel, ☎ 41/9-3021, $$$, offers all the comfort of a first-class hotel. It has 150 rooms on seven floors. Each has air conditioning, private bathroom with hot water, tiled floors, 1950s décor, cable TV, mini-bar, small fridge, and a security box. Some rooms have balconies. There is a saltwater pool, a games room, tourist desk, salon, post office, laundry and safe car park. This is the town's most famous hotel.

Rancho Luna, Carretera Rancho Luna, ☎ 43/4-8120, $$$, is right on the beach. Its 225 air-conditioned rooms have private baths with hot-water showers and double beds, cable TVs and safe-deposit boxes. Although the rooms are not huge, they are clean and comfortable. There are two restaurants, two bars (one on the beach), a large saltwater pool, and a souvenir shop. You can sign up for an all-inclusive rate on longer stays or stay just a night without meals. Beginner diving lessons are offered from dive masters. You can also rent a motorcycle or use some of the non-motorized watersports equipment. Be aware that there are water fleas on this bay. They are usually in the water in the afternoon and blown back out to sea by the evening. I like this pattern.

Pasacaballos Hotel, Carretera Rancho Luna, ☎ 49/6-6013, $$$$, at the entrance to the bay and across the water from the fort, is a huge monstrosity that offers everything a first-class hotel could offer. The 200 rooms have color TVs, private bathrooms with hot water, rather odd décor, air conditioning, telephones and tiled floors. There is a small boat that goes back and forth across the bay between the fort and the hotel.

Casas Particulares

Bertha Linares Rodriguez, Calle 43 #3402, between Ave 34 and 36, ☎ 25/1-9926, berta@correosonline.co.cu, is near the point and the water. They have three rooms with a private bath each and hot water all day, air conditioning, tiled floors, and large closets. The entire house is immaculate and is located in a quiet neighborhood. One of the rooms has a tiny kitchenette, but I'd suggest eating with the family. Although I didn't stay here, the gal who recommended the house says the food was the best in Cuba and the portions are huge. I hated to argue with her (I thought I'd found the best in Cuba) so you shall have to decide. The hosts speak English, French and Italian. They can also recommend places to stay when you move on to your next destination.

Manuel Busto Solis, Ave del Golfo #11 (no phone), is 30 meters/100 feet from the beach. This lovely home can be reached from Cienfuegos by taxi for about $20. The room has a king-size bed, air conditioning and private bathroom with hot water. Private parking is available. There is a well-tended yard with a patio that catches breezes from the beach. English is spoken.

Casa Colonial, Calle Camilo Cienfuegos #213, between Francisco Cadahia and José Martí, ☎ 41/9-4140, has air-conditioned rooms with private bathrooms and parking. Of all the places I have stayed in Cuba, this is one place I would return to just for the meals. The pork-chop dinner is the Cuba's best.

"La Flor de Cuba," Ave 56 #4936 and Calle 51 (no phone), is near the bus terminal. The wooden colonial house is well maintained and has three rooms with shared bath, hot water all day and air conditioning in the rooms. There is safe parking available.

> **LOCAL TRIVIA:** Fidel Castro was arrested in La Flor de Cuba before the revolution, and the local police chief used to reside here.

Maria Nuñez Suarez, Ave 58 #3705 between Calle 37 and 39, ☎ 43/2-251-7867, has a room with private bath and hot water, air conditioning, and a place to park your car. This clean, secure place is popular with foreigners and is often full. The owners will direct you to another room if they don't have rooms available. The price includes breakfast.

Casa Hernandez, Calle 37 #4220, between Ave 42 and 44 (no phone), has one room with air conditioning and a private shower. Breakfast is not included. The room is clean and located in a quiet area.

Jorge & Ana Maria Miranda, Ave 58 #2725 between Calle 27 and 29, ☎ 43/2-251-7532, is in the center of the city and has two rooms, one with air conditioning and a less-expensive one without. The bathroom with shower and hot water is shared. You may also use the fridge. Meals and laundry service can be arranged.

Zoraida Machin, Ave 56 #4906, ☎ 41/9-3336, is next to the bus station. The rooms are basic but clean, with shared bathroom. The owner's daughter teaches Spanish to foreigners. Breakfast is extra but all meals can be arranged.

Mr. Manolito Lujan, Calle 39 #5019 and Ave 52 (downtown), ☎ 41/9-8676, has three rooms with air conditioning and private bathrooms. The owner can help you get a room in another city. Meals are not included in the price but this is one of the cheapest places in Cienfuegos. It has private parking.

Finca Neo Marisol, Km 14 on the Rancho Luna Road, ☎ 43/2-7630, is within a five-minute walk of Rancho Luna public beach and the hotels. The farm has two rooms, one with a double bed, the other with two twins. The rooms have a private bathroom with hot water all day, air conditioning and a fan, and one room has a fridge. The place is clean and quiet. You are welcome to join the family and use the dining room, kitchen or patio out back. The cook can prepare excellent meals upon request.

Casa Ana Maria, Calle 35 #20, ☎ 43/2-251-3269, has two rooms with air conditioning and shared (between guests) but private (from the rest of the house) bathrooms with hot water all day. The colonial house is near the water and La Jagua Hotel (page 296). Meals are available.

Osvaldo Beltran, Calle Miguel Calzada #111 between Ave Lino Perez and Camilo, ☎ 41/9-3940, has two rooms with air conditioning, hot water all day and a garage for parking a car.

■ Places to Eat

Restaurant El Chef, Prado and Ave 58, is in an old building that first opened in 1819. This is where most of the cakes served throughout the city are made. Take a look at the kitchen; although it has been redone, you can tell that it was built at a time when spaciousness was important. The fish dinner for $5 or the shrimp for $7 are both worth trying.

Restaurant Los Amigos, Calle 37 #4220 between Ave 42 and 44, has some good meals for about $8 per plate.

Polynesian Restaurant (no phone), on the plaza, has a dark and romantic atmosphere and is decorated in Polynesian style. There is entertainment nightly at the bar, or you can sit outside on the plaza. The price for a veggie stir-fry is about $6. The restaurant is a good one and conveniently located.

Tarja Restaurant, Boulevard between the plaza and the Prado (no phone), has an open-air patio and inside seating. This is a classy little place with bronze statues around the room, red tablecloths and good paintings on the walls. Meals run between $5 and $7 and are large for the price. There is also a bar.

Palacio del Valle, Ave 36 and Calle 2, ☎ 41/9-9651, is the place to go if you want to treat yourself to something expensive. Just to sit in the restaurant would be a delight. However, since I didn't treat myself, I can't say how good the food is. I have been told it isn't as good as the heavenly setting. They serve mostly seafood dishes that cost anywhere from $ 7-$17, except for lobster, which is $30.

■ Nightlife

 Bar Il Palatino, on the plaza, serves excellent mojitos, and there is live music in the afternoon and evenings. However, if you don't give them a tip when the hand comes out, they become outright rude. I was called a cheap bitch – in English.

LOCAL MUSICIANS

Carlos Rafael plays in the Cuiban band, IROSO OBBA. He was born in Cienfuegos and his band has performed in Spain, Italy, Japan and Canada and is often in the city. They play Afro-Cubano music and rumba with a funkiness and groove all their own. They are rapidly getting famous. Ask at the tourist office if they are in town while you are here; if you like them, find their CD at one of the stores.

Guanaroca Cabaret, in La Jagua Hotel, Paseo del Prado #416, between San Rafael and San Miguel, ☎ 41/9-3021, has live entertainment every night. The music is reminiscent of what was played when rich Americans came before the revolution.

Discoteca Benny Moré, Ave 54 #2709, between Calle 27 and 29, on the plaza at the José Martí end, offers Cuban music and lots of rap. There is a $3 cover charge and drinks are extra.

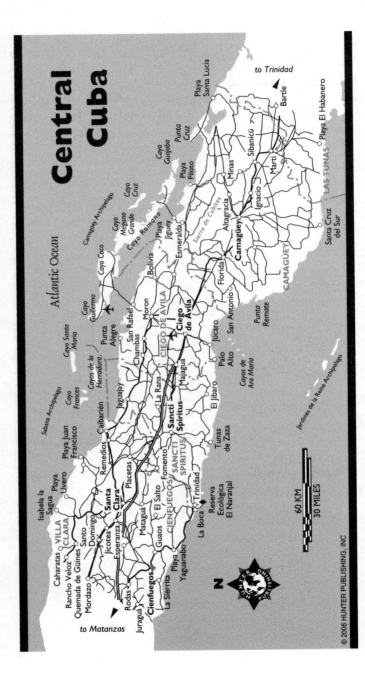

Central Cuba

© 2006 HUNTER PUBLISHING, INC

Central Cuba

Provinces of Sancti Spíritus, Ciego de Avila, Villa & Camagüey

Trinidad

Located in what is called the Valley of the Sugar Mills in Sancti Spíritus province, Trinidad is another great colonial city. It has a population of about 50,000, many of whom have Afro-Cuban roots. Trinidad is in hill country, just up from the ocean.

Its mild climate is a relief from the heat at sea level. Rarely does the temperature go higher than 33°C/86°F or below 12°C/54°F, and the humidity hovers around 75%. Usually, there is a nice breeze too.

The city is built on a limestone hill 120 feet above sea level and about four km/2.5 miles from the ocean. The **Guaurabo River** flows past the town down to La Boca on the Caribbean. The people are laid-back and fun to be with, often preferring to spend time talking to a foreigner than working in the fields or shops. There are many nice places to stay and lots to see.

■ History

1513. Diego Velazquez arrives and settles on Guaurabo River. He calls the town Manzanilla.

1514. Bartolome de las Casas holds the first mass and, shortly after, the town is renamed Trinidad.

1518. In addition to the local people, 60 to 70 Spanish families live here, mining gold.

1544. The gold mines exhausted, the Spanish migrate to Mexico. The locals become agrarian and raise cattle for commercial purposes.

1590. The Count of Rical was appointed by the King of Spain to be Lieutenant governor and war captain to protect the territory from pirates such as Drake.

1607. Growing of tobacco is outlawed for 10 years. Indians sell the plant on the black market (and probably make themselves far too rich).

1675. John Springer ransacks the city and makes away with a sack of loot.

1702. The last pirate attack, pulled off by Charles Grant, is so bad that Grant even takes the jewels from the church.

1755. Population is up to 5,840 and the city has 31 streets. There are 56 farms, 25 sugar mills, 105 ranches and 104 tobacco farms (now legal).

1772-1778. Slave uprisings are frequent.

1782. First newspaper, *Gazeta de la Habana*, is established

1790. Forty sugar mills produce 650-750 tons of sugar annually.

1801. Alexander von Humboldt, a German scientist, visits the area.

1827. Slave population reaches 11,697, with the majority being male. Foreigners number about 12,000. There are now about 1,300 buildings standing in the city.

1839. Sixteen sugar plantations are set on fire by rebellious slaves.

1842. First Philharmonic Society is established.

1855. Population grows and the village earns city status.

1895. Uprisings are common for those wanting independence from Spain.

1896. Trinidad is seized by mambí forces under the leadership of Colonel José Téllez Caballero.

1898. Spanish-Cuban-American war ends with US gaining control of Cuba.

1919. Railway is built connecting the city with others.

1954. Sanatorium for tuberculosis is built on the mountain outside of town.

1988. The city and its surrounding sugar mills are declared a UNESCO Heritage Site.

■ Getting Here & Around

 BY BUS: The bus station is on Calle Boca between Ave Gutiérrez and Gloria. Buses leave Cienfuegos for Trinidad at 12:30 and cost $6 per person. This is the same bus that leaves from Havana and goes to Cienfuegos. A taxi for four is $30.

Varadero to Trinidad with stops in Santa Clara and Cienfuegos leaves at 7:30 am from Varadero, 10:45 from Santa Clara, 12:15 pm from Cienfuegos and arrives in Trinidad at 1:55 pm.

Trinidad to Havana (not Varadero) with stops in Santa Clara and Cienfuegos leaves Trinidad at 2:45 pm, Cienfuegos at 4 pm, Santa Clara at 5:25 pm and arrives in Havana at 8:40 pm.

The cost from Varadero to Trinidad is $20, to Santa Clara is $11.

BY TAXI: Once in Trinidad, taking a local taxi is not expensive because the city is not large. It costs $5 to and from the farthest points. The bus station is a bit away from the center – about 20 minutes walking – so in the mid-day heat, a taxi may be in order.

■ Services

International Clinic, Ave Lino Perez #103 and Calle Reforma, ☎ 419/6492, has doctors, dentists and a drugstore open 24 hours a day.

Post Office, Ave Gutiérrez between Calle Colón and Rosario, 8 am to 6 pm daily except Sunday.

Telephone and Internet at ETECSA, Lino Perez and Parque Cespedes on the José Marti and Miguel Calzada side. They sell $15 Internet cards good for five hours. No refunds are given for unused amounts.

Police Station, Julio Cueva Diaz, ☎ 419/6330.

■ Festivals

Bird singing competitions occur between January and June, when bird breeders congregate at different locations. Be sure to watch for it. Judging relies on the intensity, frequency and duration of the song produced by the birds. Winning birds often sell for a large amount of money (in Cuban terms).

Recorrido del Via Cruses, or "Way of the Cross," is a catholic celebration that occurs each March, around Easter. Pilgrims carry crosses through the streets along a designated route. It is a colorful celebration, although a tad somber. It is worth seeing if you are in the country during this time.

Carnival is on the weekend between June 24 and 29.

There are **fiestas** on January 1, May 1, July 26 and October 10, during which hill farmers come on horseback to partake in or watch the dancing, parades, horse races and music (not to mention drinking!).

Copus Christi is actually the old carnival with a new name. Held during the week of Easter in the old days, it had the usual evil devils, half-snake-half-woman beings and fire-spitting creatures scaring the hell (literally) out of watchers. They had white devils and black devils, each with tails that they used to whip each other (signifying suffering). Back in 1772, the carnival was abolished but the spirit of the beliefs never died and in 1815 it was an approved celebration again. However, after the revolution, the government disapproved of the practice so they changed the dates (rather than the practices) attaching the celebrations to San Pedro, San Juan and San Pablo rather than directly with Christ.

■ Sightseeing

Plazas & Parks

Real del Jigue Plaza, Calle Peña and Desengaño, was where the first mass was held in Trinidad on December 25, 1513. **La Canchanchara** restaurant was the first building in the city. At the time, it was a shed. **El Jigue Restaurant** is in a colonial building and the House of Wheel (another building) was the venue for the famous music group Parranda de Perico Tellez. There is also the **Temple to Yemaya**, an African saint, on this plaza. She was originally the goddess of the Ogun River and has such large breasts because she gave birth to many Yoruba gods. Also known as Mama Watta, she is responsible for the waters of the world. She made new springs even when she slept. In Cuba, she looks after the sea, who can become violent and overpowering. She can be seen only in dreams.

The Searte Plaza, Calle Galdos and Ave Amargura, goes almost unnoticed except for the **House of Minstrels**, which was the home of the Machado Family prior to the revolution. On the alley of Galdos, which runs off the little plaza and at the street's end, is the **Borrell House**, which holds the restoration society's headquarters. It is known for its murals.

Santa Ana Plaza, Calle Santo Domingo and San Diego, is at the eastern end of the city and about half a kilometer from the main plaza. The restaurant on the plaza was once the city prison, constructed in 1844. Still inside are prison bars on some windows. Another building that has not been restored yet is the **Santa Ana Hermitage**, the main church for years. The original was destroyed by a storm and the present building was put up in 1812.

Plaza of Tres Cruces, Calle San Antonio and Ave Amargura, is in the city's northwest section and is recognized by the three wooden crosses that have stood since 1826. They were placed there to mark the Easter procession.

Carrillo Plaza, Ave Chunchiquira and Calle Procopio, holds the large yellow building that today is the city hall. At the other end of the plaza is **San Francisco de Paula Church**, with a hospital built beside it.

Cespedes Park, Calle San Procopio and Calle Jesus Maria, is where locals hang out to visit, discuss the latest soccer game, play dominoes and enjoy an ice cream cone (a stall just off the park sells them in Cuban pesos). Join the locals for a game or a discussion (if your Spanish is good enough). You will be welcome.

Museums

AUTHOR'S PICK

Romantic Museum, Calle Fernando Hecherri #53, between Rosario and Desengaño, ☎ 419/4363, on Central Plaza, is in Brunet Palace, built in 1808 by Count Brunet. It is one of the few two-storey homes in Trinidad. There are 14 rooms that display treasures such as antique furniture (some made by local cabinet makers), fine bone china dinner sets, Bohemian glassware, linens, ornamental gold and silver items, wood and marble carvings and paintings that once hung in the homes of the early sugar barons. The items are tastefully displayed and the museum gives a good idea of how rich these barons were. The museum is open 8:30 am to 5 pm every day except Monday. There is a $2 charge to enter.

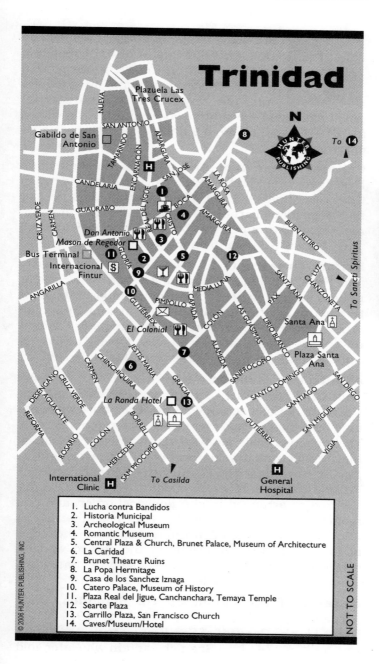

Trinidad

Central Cuba

1. Lucha contra Bandidos
2. Historia Municipal
3. Archeological Museum
4. Romantic Museum
5. Central Plaza & Church, Brunet Palace, Museum of Architecture
6. La Caridad
7. Brunet Theatre Ruins
8. La Popa Hermitage
9. Casa de los Sanchez Iznaga
10. Catero Palace, Museum of History
11. Plaza Real del Jigue, Canchanchara, Temaya Temple
12. Searte Plaza
13. Carrillo Plaza, San Francisco Church
14. Caves/Museum/Hotel

© 2006 HUNTER PUBLISHING, INC

NOT TO SCALE

AUTHOR'S PICK

Museum of Archeology, Calle Simón Bolívar #457 and Calle Desengaño, ☎ 419/3420, on Central Plaza in Don Pedron Palace. This is not an extensive museum. However, it does have an interesting bust of Alexander von Humboldt who visited in 1810. Open daily from 9 am to 5 pm. There is a $1 entry fee.

Cultural Museum of Art, on Real de Jigue and Desengaño, on Central Plaza in Casa de Alderman Ortis, was built in 1809. The gallery holds a permanent collection of art by Cuban painters such as Antonio Herr and Juan Olivia. Open daily from 8 am to 5 pm. There is a $1 fee to enter. No telephone.

History Museum, Calle Boca between Calle Cristo and Real del Jigue, was completed in 1827 and is housed in Cantero Palace. The most important part of this house are the murals painted by famous Italian artists of the day. There is also a three-story watchtower that gives a view of the city. Open Tuesday to Sunday, 9 am to 5 pm. There is a $2 fee to enter.

Architecture Museum, Calle Rispala #83, between Calle Cristo and Real de Jigue, ☎ 419/3208, on Central Plaza in Casa de Don Pedron. The house was originally two homes that were later joined to make one. The museum holds many items that give reference to the architectural development of the city. One notable piece is the engraving of the city by French painter, Eduard LaPlante. There are eight permanent exhibition rooms arranged in chronological order, and one room for temporary exhibits. The most interesting item here is the wooden-frame roof over the older house (built in 1738). Some of the carved wooden doors are also worth a look. Tuesday to Saturday, 9 am to 5 pm; $2 entry fee.

Museum of the Lucha Contra Bandidos, Calle Fernando Hernandez Hecherri #357, ☎ 419/4121, is located in the Convent of San Francisco de Assisi that was built in 1741 by a Spanish captain who later sold it to the Franciscan Fathers. The building was made into a school of philosophy and then served as the local church. Later, the Franciscans gave it to the government, who put it to use as an infantry barracks during the War of Independence. It became a museum in 1984 and holds yet more documents and photos about the revolution. The courtyard holds old trucks and a boat, all used in the latest struggle. If nothing else, Castro and his regime certainly did collect a lot of records. The two houses that make up this museum belonged to Alberto Delgado and Limones Cantero, both of whom were killed by American gangs in 1961 and are considered heros. Tuesday to Sunday, 9 am to 5 pm; $2 charge to enter.

La Casa de la Musica, Calle Francisco Javier Zerquera, ☎ 419/3640, shows the development of music in Trinidad with a special tribute to pianist Felo Bergaza and to Lico Himenez, director of the Hambourg Conservatory between 1890 and 1917. In the evenings there is often music being played in one of the halls or on the front steps. There is no charge to listen, but a donation is always welcome.

Dragones Garrison, or Caballeria, is on the southeast edge of the city on the road to the beach. The barracks was built in 1844 and is now the Provincial School of Art.

The **Museum of Speleology** (caves) is at Las Cuevas Hotel, Finca Santa Ana, two km/1.2 miles northeast of the city. The museum was erected in 1956 after the discovery of the spectacular Marvellosa Cave. You can hire a guide at the hotel here to take you through the cave, which is also a living museum. Some people opt to stay at the on-site hotel, while others prefer to stay in Trinidad and walk to the cave by following Calle San Propopio north out of town. It is not far. The hotel at the caves incorporates Disco Ayala, which is set in one of the caverns. Claustrophobic and noisy, I think, since rock does not absorb any sound.

The well-lit main cave, which is the museum, is 225 meters/700 feet long and open daily until 10 pm. The locals revered this cave because of its many calcium carbonate stalactites and stalagmites.

CAVE LEGEND

Legend says that, upon arrival in the area, Vasco Porcally de Figueroa fell in love with a beautiful Indian lady. But she was engaged to be married to another, so Figueroa had the man killed. When the maiden heard of this, she ran to the cave and hid, refusing to eat or drink, until she died. During a full moon, the ghost of the maiden can be seen at the mouth of the cave looking for her slain lover.

A fountain at the mouth of the cave was erected in her honor. If you wash in its waters you will find true love. If you already have it, the love will become even truer.

■ Adventures on Foot

Historical Sights

The center of Trinidad covers 55 blocks with 1,211 historical buildings, many of them mansions built by sugar barons of centuries past. Walking the narrow, cobbled streets is a visual smorgasbord. Knowing a little history adds to the meal.

Central Plaza is between Calles Desangaño and Rosario and Aves Real de Jigue and Cristo. It features the **Parochial Church of the Santisima Trinidad** that was originally a thatch-roof hut. By 1670 the building was erected complete with tile roof and glass windows. However, in 1812 a storm destroyed most of the city, along with much of the church, which wasn't rebuilt until 1892. The main altar is made of hardwoods collected and carved in the area. The dark glow of the wood is mystical. The lesser altar is made of Carrara marble and is dedicated to the Virgin de la

Misericordia. It is the only one like it in the country. On your visit, be sure to check out the **Milagroso Cristo de Vera Cruz**, a bow ornament taken from a Spanish ship in the early 1700s and stored in the church ever since.

The plaza itself was completed in 1857 and it looked like it does now with its decorative outer railings so rare in Latin America. The design was created by Julio Sagebien and the first two gardens were dug in 1868.

On the plaza are the **Brunet** and **Padron Palaces**, both museums. The Brunet Palace was constructed in 1808 by Count Casa Brunet, a wealthy businessman of that time. It now holds the Romantic Museum (page 308). The Palace of Don Padron holds the Museum of Archeology (page 310). Also on the plaza is a house built in 1809 called the **Casa de Alderman Otis**. It is the **Cultural Center**, which runs an art gallery. Beside the stairs leading to the church is the **House of Music**, which has recently been dubbed the House of the Hill. I don't know why.

La Casa de los Sanchez Iznaga is down Calle Desengaño and at the corner of Ave Gloria. It was built in 1820 and is now the Museum of Trinitarian Architecture. This building features one of the few portals of the city and has an exceptional interior courtyard.

Close by and still on Calle Desengaño is **Catero Palace**, built in 1827. Today it is the Museum of History. Farther north along this street is **Malibran House**. Owned by a sugar baron whose wife died at age 31, the house has been written about by local poets because of her tragic death.

On Gloria, between Desengaño and Boca, is **Antonio Mauri's** house, which has been turned into the Don Antonio Restaurant. Also in this section of town are the houses of **Miguel Suarez del Villar** and **Mauel Meyer**. All these men made their money in the sugar industry.

On Calle Cristo is the **House of the Conspirators,** where Alexander von Humboldt stayed when he came to the city. A block to the west along Calle Cristo is a house with a high tower. This is the home of the **National Museum of the Struggle Against Counterrevolutionary Groups** (not another!). Prior to its present prestigious position, it was the convent and church of San Francisco de Assisi, although all that remains of the church is the tower. The rest of the building was taken down in 1929 and replaced with a primary school. The tower is the best place to view the city – you can see all the way to the beach from here. Next to the tower is **Rodriguez Altunaga House**, which holds the city archives.

La Popa Hermitage, Calle Boca at the northeast end of the city, was built from 1710-1725 and had a hospital attached. It was set on the hill so it could be seen from the ocean. It is a lovely structure from the outside, but rather plain on the inside.

Brunet Theater Ruins, Ave Gutiérrez, and Calle Colón, was built on the site of a theater, which was destroyed by the famous storm of 1812. Aristocrats once performed in the living rooms of their mansions but, for Brunet, this didn't seem to fill the bill. He built this theater in 1840 to accommodate his needs and it became the center of Trinidad's culture until 1901, when its roof collapsed. During its day it hosted famous players such as the Armentas, Robreño, Adelina Valti and Juventino Rosas. The front still looks like a ruin, with bare red bricks and some arches filled in. However, the inside is still a cultural center of sorts, with Afro-Cuban musical shows in the evenings. It is open daily from 10 am to 10 pm. No phone.

MUSICAL TALENT POOL

Trinidad is well known for its contributions to Cuban culture as the Brunet Theater indicates. The following Cuban musicians all had some affiliation with the theater. In the 19th century, Lico Jimenez became the director of the Hamburg Conservatory of Music and in 1815 songwriter Santiago Fuentes Candamo composed music about the local history and people. Many were inspired to follow his style. Others who played here were Patricio Gascon (an improviser and director), Las Tonadas Trinitarias (folk musicians), Matilde Torrado, Felo Bergaza, Felix Reyna, Julio Cuevas, Rafael Saroza, Felo Pomares and Pedro Ganzalez. It must be the yellow clay found in the area that grows such great talent. The list is longer but my space is short.

Hiking

Manaca Iznaga Tower is in the **San Luis Valley**, about 12 km/seven miles from Trinidad and just a few feet off the main highway leading to Sancti Spíritus, where the many ruins of the sugar industry can be found. The tower is the most important site. It was built by Pedro Iznaga in 1816 so that he could watch the slaves (who worked in the scorching heat about 16 hours a day) and prevent their escape. The grueling days were marked by the ringing of a bell once every hour. The bell now sits on the ground beside the tower, along with numerous clotheslines where locals hang and sell their wares.

The tower is 45 meters/150 feet high and has 184 steps leading to the top. It is just a short distance from the main house, which can also be visited. There is a museum in the house and refreshments can be purchased. There is no charge to enter the tower or to look around the house. The restaurant is open from 9 am to 5 pm daily.

Besides visiting the tower and getting its wonderful views from the top, you can also visit the ruins at **Magua** and **Guarico**. At the height of the sugar production there were over 70 mills along this road between Trinidad and Sancti Spíritus. The ruins hold things like slave huts, farmers' houses, objects used in sugar production and items used in slave control.

On the road to Condado, north of the Iznaga Tower, is the farmhouse of **Guachinango**. It is 250 years old but very well preserved. It is still a functioning farm, and you can join the farmers in the cane fields, milk a cow or do other farming chores.

Visiting the San Luis Valley is an all-day excursion that can be done on a tour or with a rented vehicle. This tour is highly recommended and costs about $50 for the day. Tour offices in the main hotels in Trinidad offer this excursion.

Topes de Collantes National Park, ☎ 25/4-0219 or 25/4-0228, is 16 km/10 miles from Trinidad, along the main highway toward Cienfuegos, There are numerous hotels, and spending a few days here is not a bad idea. Within the park is the country's most important health spa. It was originally a tuberculosis sanatorium that was built in 1954; a few years later it became the cleanup headquarters for those fighting in the 1959 uprisings. Now it is one of the most important adventure tourist centers in the country, with hiking trails, waterfalls, caves and numerous hotels and restaurants.

The park and village site is on a 800-meter/2,600-foot hill that has a tropical forest surrounding it. The average temperature is 16°C/61°F) and the humidity is usually around 85%, with gentle ocean winds stirring the melting pot. This climate has created a rainforest that is home to many flowers and trees. There are about 15 species of pines, 12 eucalyptus and over 100 ornamental plants, including orchids, moss, lichen and tree ferns. There are carob, cedar, mahogany, magnolia and teak trees. The lush jungle also has numerous bird species. Common are parrots, trogons, bullfinches, hawks, woodpeckers and owls. Food for some of the bigger birds includes bats, quail and the Colin frog. You might spot white-tailed deer, wild boar, spiders and mollusks while walking on the trails. Because of Cuba's problems with the US and the lack of man-made drugs, many locals have gone back to using traditional herbal medicines for their ailments. This area is rich in such medicinal plants.

Caburni Falls can be reached from the end of the road where Villa Caburni Hotel is located. Follow the trail (not the paved road) for about 2.5 km/1.5 miles to the falls, which have been declared a national monument because of their beauty. Water drops about 60 meters/200 feet into a spring-fed pool. The trail has pines, eucalyptus, coffee plants and many types of ferns. South of the falls and along a similar trail are the **Vegas Grandes Falls**. To find the trailhead, go south past Kurhotel Escarbray, toward Casa de Horriedo. There is a marked sign and a marked trail from there leading to Vegas Grande Falls. There is a charge of $10 to enter this area.

A sign at the general "carpeta" or information center, which is across from the sundial, will show you the trails in the area. At the information center you can hire a guide or purchase maps that show the trails and photo-ops or lookout points.

Medicinal Trails are along the marked trail leading from the **Organoponico**, the restaurant and park center just beyond. When you come to the first fork in the trail, take the path to the right past the garden and coffee shop. Continue along to the medicinal plant section. You can go only a few kilometers before you reach the end, where you must pass through to the road in front of the Cultural center.

Codina Trail is about five km/three miles from the center of Topes de Collantes. Just over three km/1.8 miles long, it follows a horseshoe shape around a plantation, ending at the hacienda. There are ferns, orchids and medicinal plants along this trail. You can take a vehicle to the trailhead or you can walk from Topes park. To get there, follow the road toward Cienfuegos for three km/two miles. When you reach the top of a hill, you'll see the trail go off to the side. If you reach a fork in the main road, you've gone too far.

Guanayara Park is 15 km/nine miles from the center of Topes de Collantes, on the main road going north. The six-km/four-mile hiking trail starts at La Gallega Farm. There is a sign. It follows the river through a forest with 100-year-old trees. Along the way you'll see butterfly lilies, royal palms and giant reeds. The trail ends at Rocio Falls and Venado Pool, where you can swim. There is a restaurant. Tours can be arranged at the visitor center or the hotel in Topes de Collantes. This tour can also be booked in Trinidad.

■ Adventures in Nature

Javira Natural Preserve has short hiking trails and a great waterfall that empties into a pool where you can swim. Set on Guaurabo River, the park runs for two km/1.2 miles along both sides and features dense vegetation. The main reason to visit is the birds, some of them endemic. Behind the waterfall is a bat cave – excellent to explore. (These are fruit bats, so they won't bite.) Los Almendros Snack Bar and Restaurant is a good spot for a break.

BAT TRIVIA

Bats mate for life and become distraught when separated from their partners for too long. Mother bats become ill if something happens to their young. Bats can hibernate at will, especially during food shortages. When hunting, they can soar up to 3,000 m (10,000 ft).

Located just five km/three miles from town, you can take a taxi one-way to the park and walk back. If you opt to walk to the park, follow Calle Guarabo west and, at its end, go north toward Cienfuegos and Topes de Collantes. Occasionally, a horseman might be waiting at the edge of town ready to take you. He will say the cost is $20 round-trip (this is steep). If he tries to scam more (make sure he understands you) take a taxi. I have also heard that the horseman will try and get non-existent park fees from you. Beware!

■ Adventures on Water

Ancon Peninsula, south of town, has many resorts, some of which you can visit for the day. The beach is lovely, with shallow water going out for at least 100 meters/300 feet before it drops. This makes the water even warmer. There are a few hotels along the strip, but it hasn't yet been built up to gross proportions. If you go north of the peninsula you can visit La Boca at the mouth of Guarabo River to look for birds. Going south, you pass Punta Maria Aguilar and its hotels, and just beyond that are the Ancon Beaches. The peninsula also has a marina.

You can get here by local bus that goes to the hotels three times a day. It leaves from the bus station in Trinidad. A taxi will run about $7.

Scuba Diving & Snorkeling

Scuba diving along the **Casilda Coast**, along the southern shore of the island and south of Trinidad, will allow you to see a colony of black coral, the endangered species that grows less than half an inch every hundred years. The seabed is mainly sandy, with patches of coral and ridges about five meters/15 feet high. There are also some tunnels. Numerous sponges, sea fans and gorgonians live on the sea floor, and the site is, of course, dotted with colorful fish. Other dive sites are located at **Cayo Blanco** and **Macho Afuera Cay**.

Jardines de la Reina can also be reached from here, with time enough to do two dives. It is one of the last places in Cuba where turtles still lay eggs. However, it is better to visit the Jardines de la Reina from Ciego de Avila on the other side of the mountains. Blanco Cay International Diving Center on the peninsula can take care of all your needs. See below. There are a number of islands in this area, including Caballones, Anclitas, Piedra Grande and Cachiboca. The uneven bottom results in many species of fish, including sharks.

> **AUTHOR NOTE:** Snorkeling close to shore is not so good here because the water is shallow. Join one of the dive boats and go for the day.

■ Tour Operators

Cubatur, Calle Antonio Maceo and Ave Francisco Javier Zerquera, ☎ 419/6314, will take you anywhere in the valley. A second office is at Calle Juan Manuel Marquez #30 between Simón Bolívar and Jesus Menendez, ☎ 419/6302. A day-trip to Topes runs about $30.

Blanco Cay, Peninsula de Ancon, ☎ 419/6205, has an international diving center that rents equipment and will take you on a day or night dive for $50-$75, depending on where you go and when.

■ Places to Stay

Topes de Collantes

Kurhotel Escambray, ☎ 42/4-0219, $$$, looks like a huge Russian production, with 200 rooms on seven floors in a plain cement building. What adds to its overpowering appearance is its location, perched on a hill. Each room has private bath, color TV with VCR, and a mini-bar. The hotel has a warm-water pool, gym, beauty parlor, restaurant, bar, massage room, steam bath and sauna. For your health, you can have a special program drawn up to help with heart problems, hormone imbalance, stress-related disorders, orthopedic or neurological problems or geriatric complaints (I think this means they can get rid of wrinkles).

Los Helechos, ☎ 42/4-0227 or 42/4-0304, $$$, is a more aesthetically pleasing option. It has 48 sterile rooms, in cottages or apartment-like buildings, that have small sitting areas, fridges, bamboo furniture, writing desks, color TVs and double or twin beds. Some rooms have patios off the bedroom. There is a pool, a restaurant and a small disco – if that's too much, you can try lawn bowling. The hotel is most proud of using all natural-fiber products in its reception area. Getting to and from the hotel means walking up and down a hill, as it is perched on a little knoll.

PRICE CHART
Per room for two people, per day.
$ . . . . $25-$50
$$ . . . . . . $51-$75
$$$ . . . . $76-$100
$$$$ . . . $101-$150
$$$$$ . . Over $150

Villa Caburni, ☎ 42/4-0198, $$$, is a small place with just 12 rooms located in one- or two-storey air-conditioned cabins that have either two or four rooms each. The cabins have private baths, satellite TVs, mini-bars, and living rooms with fairly comfortable furniture. The reception area is away from the cabins and often full of guests sitting on the porch enjoying a drink and taking in the views. In my opinion, this is the best place to stay in the park, but it costs a bit more than others.

Camping is possible half a kilometer past Los Helechos. You can pitch a tent or hang a hammock. There is a fresh-water tap and the area is not subject to flooding during rainy season. The sites are fairly close together and patronized mostly by Cubans.

Trinidad Hotels

Hotel La Ronda, Calle Martí #238, ☎ 419/2248, $, costs about the same as a *casa*, and will give you a bit more privacy. This little hotel has 19 rooms with air conditioning, private baths and cable TVs. There is a restaurant on the premises but there are so many good ones in town you'll probably not have enough time to visit this one too. I really liked this little hotel, even though I didn't stay here. It is clean and not overly friendly or intrusive.

Hotel Las Cuevas, Finca Santa Ana (just outside Trinidad by two km/1.2 miles), ☎ 419/0139, $$, has 110 rooms in 60 little cottages with balconies, air conditioning and private bathrooms. The cottages are up-and-down duplexes with attractive stone siding, and the yard has lots of shrubbery, which attracts birds. There is a pool, tourist office, disco (in the cave) and restaurant. You can rent a car or motorcycle at the reception area.

Ma Dolores Farm, two km/1.2 miles from Trinidad on the highway to Cienfuegos, ☎ 419/6481, $$, has just under 50 rather basic but comfortable air-conditioned rooms in a farm environment. Meals are included; roasted pig cooked on a spit could be served for dinner. They encourage you to take part in some of the farm chores, or at least visit the river at the spot where Don Diego Velazquez first arrived. There is dancing and singing in the evenings. You can ride a horse or the newer type of *caballo*, called a moped.

Meson de Regedor, Calle Simón Bolívar, ☎ 419/6572, $$, is a restored mansion with two comfortable rooms furnished with restored furniture. Both rooms have balconies and two beds, plus the use of a bathroom that is shared only between the two guest rooms. The owners speak English and an excellent breakfast is included in the price (I've been told that the lobster dinner can be a bit tough). Beer is only $2 per cold bottle. This is a great place to stay.

Trinidad Casas Particulares

Hostal Coatzacoalcos, Camilo Cienfuegos #213, between Francisco Cadahia and José Martí, ☎ 419/4140, has three rooms in a lovely old mansion. They have air conditioning and a bathroom with hot water available all day. The rooms are clean, there is safe parking and the garden is a bonus. Antiques in the house add to the ambiance. Note that one room is a bit smaller and thus cheaper. Meals are extra. The owners also have a *casa* in Havana, in Miramar subdivision.

Carlos Gil Lemes, Ave José Martí #263, between Ave Colón and Francisco J. Zerquera, ☎ 419/3142, is another colonial home. It has one of the nicest gardens in Trinidad. The room has private bath and air conditioning and the place is clean.

Mabel Oritz Duran, Calle Francisco Javier Zerquera #360, between Calle Ernesto V. Muñoz and Gustavo Izquierdo, ☎ 419/2220, is a colonial house with two rooms. The private bath has hot water 24 hours a day. It is very secure.

Isobel Mendez Gil and N. Gil Rodriguz, Calle Custavo Izquierdo #28, between Ave Colón and Francisco Javier Zerquera, ☎ 419/3229, has a large room with a private bath and hot water all day. There is a lovely patio and private parking available. Clean.

Casa Pompi, Calle Miguel Calzada #111 between Lino Perez and Camilo Cienfuegos, ☎ 419/3940, has two rooms. One is new, tiled and with a private bath. The second room is small. The house has a sitting room and kitchenette area that all guests can use. Casa Pompi is clean and secure and about a 10-minute walk from the main plaza. Meals are average.

Hostal Don Juan Medinilla Ortiz, Calle Gustavo Izquierdo #128 between Piro Guinart and Simón Bolívar, ☎ 419/3342, has two rooms in a comfortable house with private bathrooms, air conditioning and hot water all day.

Casa Muñoz, José Martí #401, between Fidel Claro and Santiago Escobar, ☎ 419/3673, trinidadjulio@ yahoo.com, is a lovely old mansion (again) with two rooms for rent, both with air conditioning and private bathrooms. There is a splendid inner courtyard plus a rooftop terrace. However, this house is mostly for animal lovers (I'm one). Rosa, the wife, loves horses and has one on the premises. To keep the horses company they have two dogs, one a Dalmatian. Her husband is a photographer and can arrange workshops. What a place to practice!

Nancy Ortega Lopez, Calle Manuel Solano #17, between Francisco Zerquera and Patricio Lumumba, ☎ 419/3734, has a house in the downtown area of the city with air conditioning and a lovely patio out back. She can arrange excursions or set up Spanish lessons while you stay in the city.

Casa Font, Gustavo Izquierdo #105, between Piro Guinart and Simón Bolívar, ☎ 419/3683, has one room with air conditioning in a colonial house that is clean as a whistle. Antiques are what the family loves and there are many to look at (and use, of course). The house is close to the bus station and meals are possible. There is also a patio for guests use.

Casa Meyer, Gustavo Izquierdo #111, ☎ 419/3444, is just up the street from Casa Font and has two rooms, one in the house and one out back in the garden. Both Casa Meyer and Casa Font are excellent.

Casa Machin, Calle Francisco Javier Zerquera #159 between Frank Pais and Francisco Peterson (no phone), is another clean, friendly and accommodating place. It is just three blocks from Santa Ana Plaza and church and the prices here are a tad lower than at many of the others.

Hotels on the Beach

Costasur Hotel, Playa Maria Aguilar, ☎ 419/6172, $$, is 12 km/eight miles from Trinidad. It has 130 rooms with air conditioning, private bathrooms, and cable TVs. There's a restaurant, bar, nightclub, swimming pool and motorcycle rentals. The restaurant overlooks the beach and is surrounded by flowering trees. The pool is lovely, but you will find the beach far nicer. They prefer to do all-inclusive stays, but will rent the room only if you insist.

Hotel Ancon, Peninsula Ancon, ☎ 419/4011, $$, is 12 km/eight miles from Trinidad. The five-story building has large rooms with balconies, air conditioning, private bathrooms with hot water, twin beds, and cable TVs. The buildings are not as attractive as Brisas Trinidad (below), but the hotel is almost as large. There is a pool, safe deposit desk, baby-sitting services, café, bar and free parking. This hotel also prefers to book all-inclusive packages.

Brisas Trinidad del Mar, Peninsula Ancon, ☎ 419/6500, $$$, is an all-inclusive hotel set right on the beach. Its 200-plus rooms surround the swimming pool. All have air conditioning, cable TV, safe deposit boxes, and private baths. There is a business office, drugstore, laundry service and tour desk. You can rent a car, moped or bicycle. Because it is an all-inclusive, you also get your entertainment arranged for you. Non-powered water vessels are available for paying guests. Last but not least is the old karaoke bar that I am told is popular.

Casas on the Beach

Hospedaje Vista al Mar, Calle Real #47, Playa La Boca, ☎ 419/3716, operated by Manolo Menendez, is the only place I know that is near the ocean. There are two rooms (one is especially suited for a family) with shared bathroom, hot water all day, and secure parking. Meals are optional. There are many draws to this place. The front porch overlooks the ocean. The house is just four km/three miles from the city center and eight km/five miles from the main area of Ancon beach.

■ Places to Eat

Trinidad

 Restaurant Polibalente, Plaza Santa Ana, Ave José Mendoza, ☎ 419/6423, was one of Batista's favorite old prisons. It has been tastefully restored and now operates as a restaurant that can hold almost as many guests as before, about 200. Some of the tables are set around an arched patio, while others are in a dining hall. The specialty of the house is steak, done to perfection ($12). Open from 9 am to 11 pm daily.

Restaurant Trinidad Colonial, Calle Gutiérrez #402 and Ave Colón, ☎ 419/6473, is in an old restored house. The best dish is Creole fish ($8 per serving) accompanied by a beer and eaten on the patio. You do need time though, as the service is slow.

Restaurant Meson del Regidor, Calle Simón Bolívar #424, ☎ 419/6456, was first opened in 1801 as a Spanish inn. It still looks like an inn, with wooden shelves displaying ceramic dishes and local artwork on the walls. There are lots of wine choices. Lobster seems to be the best offering, but I liked the fish with rice ($9 a serving). Open 9 am to 10 pm every day.

Via Reale, Calle Ruben Martinez Villena #74 (no phone), has the pizza you may have been craving. It is the chef's special and a meal is under $5 per person.

Restaurant El Jigue, Calle Ruben Martinez Villena #69 and Piro Guinart, ☎ 419/6476, is on Plaza Jigue and in a house decorated with blue painted tiles. The best meal here is chicken with rice ($7). There is often live music playing during the day and evenings. Open from 10 am to 11 pm daily.

Don Antonio, Calle Gustavo Izquierdo #112, ☎ 419/6548, has a number of different rooms decorated with rattan furniture and local artwork on the walls. Seafood is good with paella (about $8). The food is okay, but not very spicy – even the *ceviche* is mild. Open from noon to midnight every day.

At the Beach

Restaurant Grill Caribe, Peninsula Ancon, ☎ 419/ 6241, is the original restaurant opened along this strip of beach. It is a palapa hut that can hold about 50 people. Seafood is, of course, their specialty. The service is relaxed and the prices are a bit higher than you would find in Trinidad. The beach is great.

La Boca Beach Shack Snack Bar (say that after a couple of beers!), La Boca, has lots of snacks. However, they claim that their paella ($7) is the best meal.

■ Nightlife

 Casa de la Trova Jazz Bar translates as the Troubadors House, Calle Fernando Echerri #29, ☎ 419/6445, is the best known jazz bar in town. It's located in a modern building with a huge patio out back. There is a $1 cover charge and remember, it is not only jazz they play. The entertainment includes salsa, son and cha-cha. Open daily from 11 am to midnight.

Taberna la Canchanchara, Ave Real del Jigue between Ave Boca and San José (no phone), is named after the cocktail made from honey, lime juice and sugarcane liquor. This is a lovely patio bar with vines as the roof. Most tour groups visit this tavern. Drinks are not cheap. The building dates from 1723 and still has its original cedar roof, which to me is far more interesting than the drink.

Carlos de Ayala Disco, Las Cuevas Hotel, ☎ 419/ 6133, just a few kilometers from town, is the cave disco. It is fun and popular with the younger crowd with hearing that can still afford to be damaged by the loud music. The drawback is that you must get back to the city once the dancing is over. If there is a group,

by all means stagger home. But don't do it alone.
Taxis are hard to come by at this time of night.

■ Shopping

 Trinidad is known for its yellow clay, from
which some of the best pottery and roof tiles
are made. Generations of potters have
passed down the art of making jugs, plates, bowls,
etc, all decorated with unique designs.

The other popular craft items are embroideries and
cotton tablecloths. Most are a non-bleached white
with hand-stitching for decorations. They are not expensive and can be purchased at the open-air markets on and around the Plaza Central.

Casa de Material, Calle Rosario #369, has lovely tablecloths with fine-quality embroidery for $20-$40.
They are all made from handwoven cotton. The owner
also offers crocheted articles and some unique
blouses that are different from those in the market.

House of Cigars, Calle Franciso Javier Zerquera and
Ave Luis Diaz, ☎ 419/6149, has – you guessed it –
cigars.

Drum-maker's shop, Trinidad.

Sancti Spiritus

This is a spread-out city with the bus station a long way from the center. Unless you have a special interest in quiet colonial cities, you may not want to stop. I found it a wonderful place to stay, with good food and friendly people who are unaccustomed to hordes of tourists. I also enjoy the colonial buildings.

■ History

Fourth of the original seven villas of Cuba founded by Diego Velazueza in 1514, Sancti Spíritus was located on Tuinucu River. The other cities included in this "first seven" are Baracoa, Santiago de Cuba, Havana, Trinidad, Camagüey and Bayamo. Sancti Spíritus' original population was 36 lonely souls who tried to eke out a living here. In the mid 1500s, Friar Bartolome de las Casas arrived at the village and denounced the Spanish treatment of the local Indians.

In 1522, the city was moved to its present location on the banks of the **Yayabo River** because the people felt the land was better. It took 60 years, until 1580, to build the first church in the city. Not much else happened until 1822, when the King of Spain allowed the city to have its own banner. Three years later, the famed bridge over the Yayabo River was constructed, and 50 years after that, the village became a city.

Sancti Spíritus remained rather tranquil, growing quietly until 1895 when Maximo Gómez and Antonio Maceo joined forces and continued to fight in a westerly direction on the island in an attempt to gain self-rule for Cuba.

During the latest revolution, Che Guevara led some troops through the mountain passes and set up a revolutionary front in the city. He got support from the local people when they held a general strike in protest of Batista's rule.

Sancti Spíritus has returned to being a tranquil town, busy at building its cultural centers, like the library and the museum of colonial art, and maintaining the bridge and the church as national monuments.

■ Getting Here & Around

 BY BUS: The bus from Trinidad arrives about 12:30 pm and costs $6. A shared taxi to town costs $30. Little moto-taxis run from the bus station into town for $5.

BY PLANE: There is a tiny airport near the city but flight schedules are non-existent. To find out if any planes are coming here, talk to a hotel travel office.

BY CAR: The best way to get around is to rent a car. **Transtur Car** rental on Plaza Serafin Sanchez (close to the library), ☎ 41/2-8533, offers great deals for cars that are in excellent shape. The cost for a small- to medium-sized car is about $50 per day, including insurance. They will also give you convoluted information on how to navigate the ring roads of the town (they literally go in circles) and onto the main highway. My advice: Don't bother asking. The roads are so confusing that you must ask someone at every corner until you are out of the city.

■ Services

Cubatur, Plaza Serafin Sanchez near Maximo Gómez, ☎ 41/2-8518, is a helpful and friendly office where you can get information about hotels and transportation.

Immigration, Independencia #107, between Calle Frank Pais and Cruz Perez, is open Monday to Thursday, 7 am to 3 pm, and Friday until noon.

Central Cuba

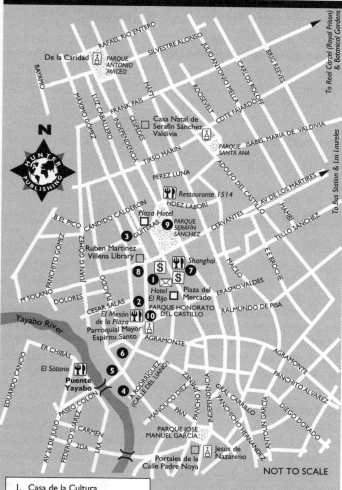

1. Casa de la Cultura
2. Casa de la Trova
3. Conrado Benítez Cinema
4. Rumbos
5. Teatro Principal
6. Colonial Art Museum
7. Oscar Fernandez Morera
   Art Gallery
8. Museum of Natural History
   & Museum of History
9. Museum Sera Fin Sanchez
10. Community Center

Sancti Spíritus

© 2006 HUNTER PUBLISHING, INC

Post Office, Ave Independencia #8, between the Plaza and Calle Honorato, is open Monday to Saturday, 8 am to 6 pm.

Police, Plaza Serafin Sanchez, ☎ 614 (for emergencies only).

ETECSA office on the plaza and is open daily, 7 am until 6 pm. They have one computer that can be used for Internet access at a rate of $5 an hour.

Medical Service, Clinico Quirurgico Camilo Cienfuegos, Calle Bartolome Maso, ☎ 41/2-4017.

■ Sightseeing

Ruben Martinez Villena Library, Calle Maximo Gómez #1 and Manolo Solano, on the plaza, ☎ 41/2-3133, is the lovely colonial building with Doric columns; the one that looks like it should be in Greece rather than here. The dome on top is gold and many of the decorations on the inside are covered in gold leaf. The staircase is of marble and the wall murals are original. In the old days, the educated class met here to discuss whatever men of letters discuss. If you see nothing else in Sancti Spíritus, this building is worthwhile. There is no charge to enter and it is open during regular business hours.

Community Center, Calle Cervantes #9 and Maximo Gómez, ☎ 41/423-7772, is where Che Guevara spoke over the radio to the people of Sancti Spíritus on Christmas day 1958. This was after the revolutionaries had won the battle against Batista and just before they took control of Havana. The house originally belonged to a lawyer who became famous trying to defended seven students accused of desecrating a tomb in Havana. He failed in his defense and the students were shot. Today the building is used as an art center.

The **Yayabo River Bridge** is the only bridge of its kind in the country. It is made of bricks, sand and lime obtained from the area. Its mortar is known as Roman cement, a style imported from Europe that was supposed to be made with blood or goat's milk. Construction took place between 1817 and 1835, and was according to the design of Domingo Valverde and Blas Cabrera. Most of the labor was done by black slaves. Recently, the government started referring to these slaves as prisoners. The building cost at the time was 30,000 Cuban pesos. An attractive bridge, set across the slow-moving river, it is surrounded by greenery and is still used.

MUSICAL CLAIM TO FAME

The city is the birthplace of two important musicians; Miguel Companioni, who composed the music of *Mujer Perjuria*; and Rafael Gómez Teofilito, a singer, songwriter and author of *Pensamiento*.

Museums

Museum of History, Calle Maximo Gómez #3, ☎ 41/2-7435, is set in a colonial house that was built in 1740. The house once belonged to Captain Pedro de Castañeda and Gregoria de Ranzoli. It underwent some remodeling in 1843 and then again in modern times when it was modified to accommodate the museum. Here you will find many items related to the slave trade during the early years of Spanish rule. Open every day except Monday from 8:30 to noon and 1 pm to 5 pm. The cost to enter is $1.

Museum of Colonial Art, Calle Placido #74 and Ave Jesus Menendez, ☎ 41/2-5455, is also called the House of a Hundred Doors. It reflects 19th-century architectural style with lots of balconies, stained-glass windows and wrought-iron grills. I am told that there are over 100 windows and doors in this building. It was the first two-storey structure in the city. The woodwork, using local hardwoods, is still in excellent shape. The house was originally owned by the Iznaga family, a sugar baron from Trinidad. It was built to sit ostentatiously between the main church and the Yayabo Bridge; probably to remind the less fortunate of what can happen if one works hard and diligently. Today the exhibition halls are decorated with the treasures from the homes of many old sugar barons and cattle ranchers from a century past. Inside are Sevres porcelains, crystal lamps, Swiss engravings and oil paintings. Most objects belonged to the last owner of the house, although there are items left by some of the previous owners, and from other houses in the city. One known artist with work in the building is Oscar Fernendez Morera, who was born in the city in 1880 and became known for his urban landscapes. The furnishings are carved from local hardwoods. Museum closed Monday, open every other day, 9 am to 5 pm, with lunch from noon-1 pm.

Museum of Natural History, Calle Maximo Gómez #2 and Ave Cadena, ☎ 41/2-6365, is in a building that is itself more interesting than the museum's treasures. The house was built in 1812 as the marriage home of Felix Ramon de Camino and Mariane de Jesus Marin Cancio, wealthy residents of the city. The wall murals are original. The museum's collections, most of which are from the area, were donated by Dr. Carlos de la Torre y Huerta in 1986. However, the museum itself wasn't opened until 1992. The permanent exhibits contain minerals, petroglyphs, plant and flower specimens from the valley, and some insects. Open 9 am to 5 pm, daily except Monday. The cost is $1 to enter.

Museum of Serafin Sanchez, Calle Cespedes #112, ☎ 41/2-2779, was the home of Sancti Spíritus's most famed independence fighter, Serafin Sanchez Valdivia. Born in the city in 1846, Sanchez became the Inspector General of the Liberation Army while fighting for Cuban independence in the 1800s. He died at the Battle of Las Damas beside the Zaza River at the age of 50. Sanchez was the second child of Isabel Maria de Valdivia Salas and José Joaquin Sanchez Marin. The house itself was built almost 50 years before Sanchez's birth. In the museum is a large collection of books on the war of independence – they are available to anyone. Other notable objects include the saddle that Sanchez used when riding into battle on the last day of his life. The town's main plaza, inaugurated on October 10, 1904, is named after Sanchez.

Plazas & Parks

Plaza Serafin Sanchez has the **Church of Espiritu Santo** at one end. Its construction was started in 1680 and it took almost a hundred years to finish. The original building, which was moved from the Tuinucu River when the town decided to change locations, was made of palm fronds, straw and adobe bricks and even after being moved in 1522, this humble building served the people well until the new one was started. The first public clock was put into the church in 1771 and the garden at the back was used as a cemetery until the middle 1800s.

The central part of the square, paved in 1911, features a statue of Rudesindo Antonio Garcia Rijo, who was a doctor, scientist and benefactor of the city. He was murdered a year after his statue was erected (by some jealous failing artist no doubt).

■ Adventures in Nature

 Botanical Gardens, 1.5 km/one mile from the center on Calle Frank Pais. This is a quiet park that was first opened in 1996 with the idea of adding a new section every few years. When it opened, there were some ornamental and medicinal plants. In 1998, the gallery forest was completed. It now has plants of economic significance such as mahogany, tobacco and sugarcane. The most important addition was the herbarium, which, when completed, will contain over a thousand plants that can be found around the province. A section containing plants threatened by extinction is partially completed and open to the public. The gardens are well maintained and worth a walk. The trumpet bushes (highly poisonous) are my favorite, but the calabash and mahogany specimens are also quite impressive. These gardens will be used for educational purposes in the future. There is a small fee ($1) to enter.

■ Places to Stay

Hotels

Plaza Hotel, Calle Independencia #1, ☎ 41/2-7102, $$ on the side of the plaza, is designed in traditional colonial style and has 29 air-conditioned rooms with high ceilings, cable TVs, private bathrooms and blue-tiled floors. If you are into historic buildings, you

PRICE CHART
Per room for two people, per day.
$. $25-50
$$. $51-75
$$$. $76-100
$$$$. $101-150
$$$$$. . . . over $150

may want a night or two here. Originally a family mansion, it was built in 1843 and later became a cafeteria, cake shop and hotel. It was totally rebuilt in 1996 to its present state. There are stone sculptures in the halls, antique furniture in the reception area and lots of paintings on the walls. There is a rooftop bar, restaurant and tourist desk in the hotel, plus access to the Internet even for non-guests. This is a lovely place.

Hotel El Rijo, Calle Honorario del Castillo #12, ☎ 41/2-8588, $$$, is an upscale rendition of the home that was originally owned by Rudesindo Garcia Rijo, a local doctor. Constructed in 1827 and remodeled in the 1990s, this tiny place has only 16 large rooms, all large in size, with high ceilings and tiled floors. The patio has a fountain, lots of plants and sitting spots.

Villa San José del Lago, Calle Antonio Guiteras, Mayajigua, Yaguayjay, ☎ 41/5-6108, $/$$, is on the main road going north toward Remedius. This is a wonderful little place with 50 air-conditioned buildings that hold up to eight apartments, each with private bath, tiled floors, double and/or single beds and daily maid service. There is a little lake, a thermal pool and a large pool where locals swim, drink and have fun. The gardens are well kept and full of tropical plants. There is safe parking and a restaurant that serves mostly Creole foods. I loved this place.

Villa Hatuey, Central Carretera, Km 383, ☎ 41/2-8315, $$$, is two km/1.2 miles from the edge of Sancti Spíritus. It offers lovely one- and two-story cottages around a central pool. They have TV, private bath and air conditioning; some are wheelchair accessible. There is an Internet center, games room, restaurant, bar and disco. The surroundings – distant mountains and the hotel's verdant grounds – are the draw.

Zaza Hotel, Finca San José, ☎ 41/2-8512, $$, is five km/three miles from town and three km/two miles off the main road. It sits by the manmade Lake Zaza, where fishers drop their lines for some pretty large fish. Rods and lines can be rented, along with a boat and guide, at the hotel. The best fishing season is November to April and bigmouth black bass is the trophy, weighing up to eight kilos/18 lbs. Eighty rooms set in older buildings have air conditioning, balconies and cable TV, while the amenities include a cool and breezy swimming pool, games room, bar, restaurant and disco. If this isn't enough, hunters can go out and bag a quail, pigeon, dove or guinea fowl in the preserve near by. The more conservative can go horseback riding. The place is very pretty, with many birds in the trees around the hotel property.

Casas Particulares

Tomas Dias, Maximo Gómez #9, between Plaza Serafin Sanchez and Ave Honorato, ☎ 41/2-7626, has a room with private bath in a cottage at the back of the property. A very well-prepared breakfast is included. The owner, Tomas, loves filtered coffee – take some paper filters.

Keep an eye open for the fruit bats that live in the building next door. At dusk, you can see them. The bats alone make it worth staying here. If Tomas is full, go upstairs to #9A or #11, which has two comfortable rooms that are often patronized by Italian travelers (who are great fun).

Osmaida, Calle Maceo #4, and Garcias, ☎ 41/2-4336, has comfortable rooms and gracious hosts.

Anais y Cayuco, Calle Piro Guinart #254, between Gómez Toro and Ruben Villena, ☎ 41/2-3462, has two air-conditioned rooms with private bath in a colonial mansion close to the center of town.

■ Places to Eat

I suggest eating either at the hotel or *casa* where you are staying. I didn't find many places worth recommending.

AUTHOR NOTE: The casa I stayed in served *bonisto hervido*, a sweet, potato-like substance. Ask for it.

El Meson de la Plaza, Maximo Gómez #34, ☎ 41/2-8546, is on the plaza and serves Cuban food that's nothing to write home about.

■ Nightlife

Principal Theatre, Calle Jesus Menendez #102, ☎ 41/2-5755, was built in 1839 and has been a theater, a hospital, a military barracks and a meeting place for rebels. Built by the same designers as the city's famous bridge, the building has hosted many foreign and local artists. They have plays, operas and musical productions throughout the year; check at the tourist office to see if a performance is on while you are in town.

Troubadours' House, Calle Maximo Gómez #26, ☎ 41/2-6802, is another old mansion that was restored in 1980. It offers music performances (classical and modern) during the day and at night. Check at the theater or at the tourist office about tickets.

Ciego de Avila

There is no reason to go into the village of the same name as the province. However, visiting the towns of Moron, the beaches at **Cayo Coco** and **Cayo Guillermo**, stopping at **Laguna de la Leche** or seeing the **Pueblo Holandes** are fun things to do. For the most part, you need a car to get around.

Entering Ciego de Avila, follow Ave Independencia, the main street along which the **Teatro Principal** is located. It is a beautiful old building that has the best acoustics of all the theaters in Cuba. Continue to José Martí Park, named after the famous poet and activist for independence. Finally, you will see the **San Eugenio de la Palma Church**. St. Eugenio is the patron saint of the city.

■ Services

? **ETECSA**, Plaza José Martí, open 8 am to 5 pm daily. There is one machine that can be used for Internet in the little office.

General Hospital, Maximo Gómez #257, ☎ 33/422-2429.

Post Office, Calle Chicho Valdes and Ave Marcial Gómez. Open Monday to Saturday, 9 am to 5 pm.

Tourist Office, Maximo Gómez Oeste #82, open 9 am to 5 pm daily except Sunday.

■ Sightseeing

Museums & Galleries

 Provincial Museum, José Antonio Echevarria #25, ☎ 33/412-8128, has primarily items of interest to the fans of the Castro revolution. This means it is full of documents and memorabilia found in the mountains after the revolution. Open from 10 am to 3 pm, Tuesday to Saturday.

Provincial Art Gallery, Independencia, between Maceo and Honorato del Castillo, ☎ 33/412-3900, has a small collection of paintings, some sculptures and some pottery. Open 10 am to 4 pm daily except Mondays.

■ Places to Stay

Hotels

 Hotel Ciego de Avila, Carretera de Ceballo, Km 2.5, ☎ 33/412-8013, $$, seems to cater more to the hunter/fisher than the eco-tourist. You can get guns, jeeps, shotguns, cartridges, fishing gear and guides, plus a room. Your meals at the Trucha restaurant here include lots of meat. The 150 or so large, clean rooms all have cable TVs and private baths. There is a pool and safe parking, and room service is available.

Casas Particulares

I don't have the names of *casas* in this town but there are three near the bus station. Look for the inverted blue triangle on the door and you will find one. If you go accept the assistance of a *jinatero*, he or she will, of course, want a commission.

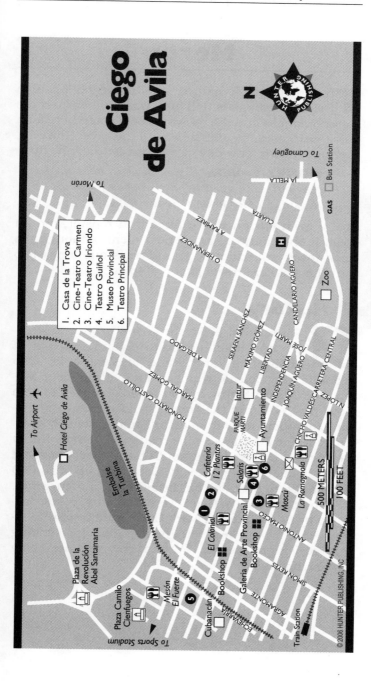

Ciego de Avila

1. Casa de la Trova
2. Cine-Teatro Carmen
3. Cine-Teatro Iriondo
4. Teatro Guiñol
5. Museo Provincial
6. Teatro Principal

Central Cuba

© 2006 HUNTER PUBLISHING, INC

Moron

This interestingly-named small town (in Spanish the word means "small hill") was built around the sugar business and the railway. People stop here for a quick visit, usually on their way to the cays. However, staying in town for a day or two can actually be fun.

MONEY SAVER: *If you want to visit the cays but don't want to pay the price for a hotel, stay in Moron and do day-trips.*

At the town entrance is a huge iron rooster, mouth open. It once crowed, but is now silent, although the clock tower still chimes. The town is one long strip with the smaller streets going off to each side.

■ History

Founded in 1750, the area was once the center of Cuban agriculture, and remains of sugar mills still stand at Venezuela, Ciro Redonda and Bolivia, which are all vilages near Moron. The Jucaro-Moron military road was built to help move troops across the country and prevent the Cuban Liberation Army from getting to the island's western end. The 70-km/43-mile road goes from Moron in the north to Jucaro in the south had military posts at every kilometer along the way. Some had up to 10,000 men posted to them, all on the lookout for insurgents. At important points there were listening posts protected by tons of barbed wire. These were communication centers supplied with heliographs for sending and receiving messages. Parts of the road are being reconstructed.

THE HELIOGRAPH

The heliograph is a mirror with a machine that is able to make dots and dashes reflect on the mirror. The mirror faces a receiving heliograph about a kilometer away and the message is decoded. It is basically a visual Morse code.

It wasn't until 1977, long after the commies took power, that Ciego de Avila became a province. Prior to that it was part of Camagüey Province.

Because of the sugar production and the growth of pineapple and citrus fruits, the railway has a large station here. It's worthwhile having a look. Beside agriculture, the fishing industry is big. It was started by men fishing from dinghies to feed their families. Now they fish from large boats to feed the tourists.

■ Getting Here & Around

 BY CAR: You can hitchhike here, but having a car will make it convenient to visit places nearby. Buses go to and from the city of Ciego de Avila five times a day from the train station (times change often, so check at the station).

BY TRAIN: You could take the slow, crowded and cumbersome train from Ciego de Avila to Moron. This is not advisable.

The nicest thing about Moron is its size; you can walk anywhere in town or take a horse-drawn cart; there are tons around the train station.

■ Services

 Post Office, Colonial Española Building, on Calle Castillo, the main street going into town. Monday to Saturday, 8 am to 6 pm.

Telephone office, in the same building as the post office, open 8 am to 10 pm daily.

■ Sightseeing

 The **Train Station** is a huge round building constructed at the turn of the last century. It has archways inside and out and decorative wrought iron on all the doors and windows. The original counters and benches are still in use. Train schedules are printed on a blackboard to the side of the ticket booths. There are places where you can purchase a newspaper or soda.

> **AUTHOR NOTE:** Hundreds of birds nest in the rafters, so watch out.

The **Cock of Moron** is the big brass rooster that sits at the foot of the clock tower at the entrance to town. He is named after an event that took place in the city. There was a greedy tax collector who levied unfair taxes. He confiscated property and evicted the homeowners until the townsfolk rebelled and sent the tax collector running. They composed a song with the line, "the cock of the walk has been left plucked and crowing." The cock of Moron is the hero of the song. The clock tower has a mechanical crow twice a day, once at 6 am and once at 6 pm.

Municipal Museum, Calle Castillo #374, ☎ 33/5-4501, is in a restored colonial building and has a collection of artifacts, mostly from around the area. Open from Tuesday to Friday, 9 am to 5:30 pm with an hour for lunch at noon. Independent visitors are sometimes refused entry; it is best to come here with a tour group. The cost should be $1 per person.

The **Church** on the plaza across from the train station is the only church in the country featuring a tower where sentry can watch for danger. The building was used during the Guerra de la Chambelona (Lollipop War), the last battle fro independence fought in the area.

Directly in front of the church is where the country had its first bullfight. It occurred in 1851.

■ Adventures on Water

Laguna de Leche is just five km/three miles from Moron. It gets its name from the milk-colored stream laced with sodium bicarbonate that feeds the lake. There is abundant bird life around the reeds and bulrushes at the lake's edge.

Restaurant, Lago de Leche.

Seven kilometers farther along is **Laguna la Redonda**. The legend goes that some American fishers hooked 5,078 trout in five days while fishing on this lake. I wonder what they did with the fish? Laguna la Redonda hosts the international black bass fishing tournament every February. For details, ask at your hotel or at the tourist office in Ciego de Avila.

A great place to eat is the **Atarraya Restaurant**, which overlooks the lake and has a large wrap-around porch. If it is too cold or breezy, sit inside, where wrap-around windows allow great views. This restaurant's best meal is fish.

■ Adventures in Culture

Holandes de Turiguano is past Laguna la Redonda and on the way to Bolivia. This is an odd village that stands out as really different from the rest of Cuba. The village was a poor cattle-raising swamp before the revolution. When the owners of the farms fled, the government built new homes for the locals. Celia Sanchez, one of Castro's closest companions (Cubans will not openly admit whether they think she was his lover during the revolution, but they do often wink and smile when asked) designed the buildings. Sanchez had been in Holland prior to the revolution and decided to build the houses in Dutch-country style. The village still raises cattle – mostly to feed the tourists.

■ Adventures in Nature

Loma de Cunagua is past Turiguano on the road to Cayo Coco. Turn left at the big yellow sign and follow the road through a farm area to a gate, where they expect you to pay a dollar to enter. Unless you are a very avid bird watcher, I wouldn't bother. If they let you in for nothing, then you could eat at the restaurant or stay at the basic hotel. However, paying to drive a road and then walk a path, even if it has got a lot of vegetation and some nice birds, is taking the exploitation of the tourist a bit far. On the way to the hill, at the village of **Las Palmas**, is a picnic area. There is lots of vegetation and bird life here and, at this writing, it was free. Foreigners don't get much for nothing in Cuba, so take advantage of it.

■ Places to Stay

Hotels

Hotel Moron, ☎ 33/5-3901, $$, on the highway coming from Ciego de Avila, at the edge of town, is a huge modern building with Russian influence in its design. It has 144 rooms with air conditioning and private bathrooms. The décor is okay and the rooms, although not huge, are also acceptable. The price is right and meals can be included if you wish. There is a pool, restaurant, bar, beauty salon and secure parking.

PRICE CHART
Per room for two people, per day.
$. $25-50
$$. $51-75
$$$. $76-100
$$$$. $101-150
$$$$$. . . . . over $150

La Casona de Moron, Calle Cristobal Colón #41, ☎ 33/5-2236, $$$, is not really a hotel nor is it really a *casa*. It has only seven rooms, all tucked into a yard surrounded by lush vegetation. The rooms are large and clean with tiled floors and high ceilings. There is cable TV, air conditioning and a mini-bar in each room and a tiny swimming pool out back for guests. This place caters mostly to the fishing/hunting crowd.

Casas Particulares

Margarita Sierra, Calle Jas #89 between Ave Martí and Castillo, ☎ 33/5-3798, has a lovely large room with private bathroom off a nice patio. There is always cold beer in the fridge and a meal can be arranged. Some English is spoken and the hosts can't do enough to make you welcome. There is also secure parking in the yard. This would be my first choice in town.

Casa Carmen, General Peraza #38, between Ave Filipe Poey and Carlos Manuel de Cespedes, ☎ 33/5-4181, is near the train station and has two rooms with air conditioning. The house is lovely, with antique furnishings and friendly owners. Meals can be arranged.

Juan Perez, Castillo #189, between San José and Serafin Sanches, ☎ 33/5-3823, close to the center, has two rooms with private bath and air conditioning. Juan is far more pleasant than his rooms.

Cayo Coco & Cayo Guillermo

To reach these cays you must cross two manmade causeways. It is 27 km/17 miles to Cayo Coco. If you drive the length of the cay you will then come to more causeway over shallow water and mangroves to Cayo Guillermo. It costs $2 each way per car to cross and everyone must show their passport. Only foreigners and those working on the islands have access to this area.

There are 22 km/14 miles of flour-sand beaches along the north shore of the islands and not too many people on them. You can visit the beaches at any of the cays' hotels, but usually you must pay anywhere from $4 to $40 for the day. The advantage is you can also book a dive or snorkel trip from the hotels.

Driving the causeway is worth the $2. You must be off the island before 9 pm, or spend the night.

As you approach the cays the water becomes shallow and clumps of new mangrove is seen. The colors are a combination of turquoise blue, white, green and gold.

Called the **Garden of the Queens**, this area – which includes the entire Archipelago of Camagüey – covers 91,000 acres, half still in its natural state. The bird life is phenomenal. You'll see cormorants, woodpeckers, flamingos, spoonbills, mockingbirds and so many pelicans they become almost ho-hum. You might also see deer, wild pigs, crabs and iguanas. Take your time.

Cayo Guillermo has the highest sand dune in the Caribbean. It stands at 15 meters/45 feet. The cay is where Hemingway came to fish. According to him, Playa Pilar, at the end of this cay, is the nicest in Cuba. There are five beaches on this island. Just one kilometer from shore is a coral reef.

ENVIRONMENTAL DAMAGE

Wildlife suffered when the causeway was built without a sufficient number of culverts under the road to let the water and wildlife flow/swim back and forth. The ramifications haven't totally been appreciated yet. (The second causeway was built to Cayo Santa Maria has culverts.) There are plans to build causeways to the islands of Providencia and Caoba in the near future. More damaging than the causeways, of course, are the huge hotels.

■ Adventures on Water

Scuba Diving & Snorkeling

There are about 32 km/20 miles of coral reef along this archipelago, providing a home to parrotfish, snappers, grunts, yellowtail snappers and angelfish. This is one of the last places in the Caribbean where sea turtles still come to nest. Because the sea bottom is flat, many larger fish such as tarpons, bonefish and barracuda can be seen swimming around the sharks. Cubans claim that there are 50 species of coral, 200 species of sponges and 500 species of tropical fish in and around this reef. There are also 27 sunken ships, among them the *Galeon of Fernando Estela*, the *Mortera* and the *Nuevo Mortera*, which were built in Liverpool in the late 1800s.

TOP DIVE SPOTS

- The Black Coral
- The Deer's Horn
- Bride's Bouquet, with its purple, orange and yellow

Diving costs anywhere from $40 for a one-tank dive to $450 for 20 dives. Guides take anywhere from 15-30 divers per boat. Lessons cost about $200 for easy dive courses, $300 for open-water courses and $250 for advanced open-water dives. Trying for a dive master certificate will take eight days and cost $550. This includes your boat, belt, weights, tank and the qualified English-speaking instructor certified in ACUC, CMAS AND SNSI systems. Dive masters are located at Melia, Sol Club and Melia Tryp hotels on Cayo Coco.

■ Places to Stay

 There are no *casas* on the islands and the hotels are mainly all-inclusive, so they take care of everything from drinking water to transportation and entertainment to babysitting. They are best for people who need a resting vacation, rather than an exploring adventure. I offer basic comments about the hotels. Unless you get a good deal with your agent, all hotels are $100-$150+ per night.

All-Inclusives

Villa Cojimar, ☎ 33/0-1712, Cayo Coco, has over 200 rooms. It is quiet and adequate, without ostentatious luxury. In fact, the place is a bit shabby and the yards are not as nice as the other hotels. Rooms are in brightly painted cabins and have TVs, private baths, air conditioning and tiled floors. There are three restaurants, three bars, an outdoor pool, tennis courts, massage parlor and a gym.

Melia Cayo Guillermo, ☎ 33/0-1680, is for adults only and is popular with the diving crowd. You are looking at a hefty bill here, as rooms seldom go for less than $250 a day. The hotel has 250 rooms with balconies, air conditioning, two full-size beds, full bathrooms with hairdryers, satellite TVs, in-room safes and mini-bars.

There are four restaurants, one outside grill area, and bars at the pool and the billiard tables. There is a dress code for à la carte restaurant meals. Amenities include Internet access, outside sports court and a massage parlor. They offer weddings and vow-renewal services and if you come with 17 people and stay for six days, you will get a discount (I should hope so!). The property is luxurious, with lots of private beach area and hammocks set in shady places. It also has one of the nicest beach areas of all the hotels.

Blau Colonial, Cay Coco, ☎ 33/01-1311, allows kids under 12 to stay and eat free of charge with two full-paying adults. This monster of a hotel has 450 rooms with balconies or patios. Each room has a king-size bed or two three-quarter ones (between a twin and a full-size), full bathroom, air conditioning, hair dryer, cable TV, stocked mini-bar, coffee maker, in-room safe, iron and ironing board. Bathrobes are provided.

The hotel has six restaurants. However, all breakfasts and lunches are served at the buffet. If you prefer to have supper in one of the restaurants, you must book as soon as you arrive. They will not take bookings for your whole stay – you must book day-by-day. Lobster and shrimp cost extra unless they are served at the buffet. Snacks are available all day. There is a dress code. Numerous bars are located throughout the building.

There is a fitness center, children's playground, tour desk, car rental agency, whirlpool, laundry service. For use on the beach are small catamarans, paddle boats, sail boats, windsurfing boards, and plastic canoes. Aqua-fit lessons are offered, or you can enjoy French bowling, archery, volleyball, tennis courts, a gymnasium, a games room and bicycles. Bicycles can be used for two hours per day per person.

El Senador, Cayo Coco, ☎ 33/0-1490, is a favorite with Canadians. Some of the 700 rooms are built on stilts over a lagoon and painted bright Latin colors. The pool is up from the lagoon and the beach is beyond. Like Blau Colonial, this place does not charge for non-guests to visit and children are welcome (those under age three stay free; up to age 12, stay free only in specific seasons). Some of the draws are a Jacuzzi, showers on the beach and private sunbathing (don't know how they arrange that when there is a possibility of 1,400 guests at any one time!). The property has seven restaurants, eight bars – including one at the pool and one at the beach – two pools for adults and one for kids, plus an extra area for aqua-fit programs. Kids' games are all arranged for them. This is a splendid place to stay, although it is very big.

Iberostar Daiquiri, Cayo Coco, ☎ 33/0-1650, has 300 rooms in colonial-style apartment buildings, three levels high, placed around a huge pool. The gardens are very well kept and their walkways are melodious with bird songs. Each plain but spacious room has a balcony or a patio plus twin beds, full bathroom, air conditioning, cable TV, hairdryer, mini-bar and in-room safe.

Watersports include snorkeling, kayaking, and windsurfing. For these you must book your times. There is also table tennis, a pool, aerobics, a disco and nightly entertainment. There are three restaurants and four bars, a babysitting service and a car rental desk.

Tryp Cayo Coco, ☎ 33/0-1031, has over 500 rooms, each with a balcony or patio, double bed, full bathroom, safe, air conditioning, and cable TV. The more expensive rooms have hairdryers and mini-bars. They take kids, but give discounts only at specific times of the year. There are five restaurants, two outside BBQs, six bars and a few children's playgrounds. Massages are extra, whirlpools are free. Trying to overcome complaints about people not being able to get into the à la carte meals, the hotel guarantees four reservations per week.

Sol Cayo Guillermo, Cayo Guillermo, ☎ 33/0-1760, is a small hotel with a beautiful reception area. Its lovely painted cabins feature bright rooms that have double, triple or quadruple accommodations. The cabins are two-story buildings with balconies or patios off each room. They have open-beam ceilings and marble bathrooms, rattan furniture and constantly stocked mini-bars. What really makes this a great place is that the cabins give privacy so if you want to stay up late, you won't be bothering anyone except those sharing the building.

The shall beach with fine white sand is good for children.

There are three restaurants, four bars, rental bicycles and muscle-powered watercraft. These must be booked and have time limits. A pool, a disco bar and a Jacuzzi are available. Laundry, babysitting and massage parlor are included in the cost. The meals are the usual rather bland type so common in Cuba, but the yogurt, fruits, fish and cheeses are excellent. They even have deep-fried bananas. What a treat.

Santa Clara

For Che Guevara fans, Santa Clara is the place to pay homage. The gigantic **Plaza of the Revolution**, with its Russian-sized statue of Che, is where his ashes are buried and an eternal flame glows in his memory. Except for the few pilgrims, the plaza is generally empty.

The town itself is busy, with narrow streets and many students rushing about to get to classes in the third-largest university in the country.

■ History

Prior to the revolution, Santa Clara was a commercial city where products like sugar and citrus were loaded onto the train and sent to Havana or to other seaports for export. When the revolution was at its peak, Batista sent a train loaded with ammunition and arms to Santiago de Cuba, but as it passed Santa Clara, it was derailed. The revolutionaries, under the leadership of Che Guevara, overtook the military that was on the train and confiscated the weapons. This act changed the direction of the revolution and Guevara and Castro won.

■ Getting Here & Away

BY BUS: The Terminal de Omnibus is at Carretera Central and Oquendo, at the edge of the city. A taxi to the center will cost $5.

BY CAR: Santa Clara sits in a bit of a depression and a perimeter highway goes around it. You will not see a sign for Revolution Plaza from the highway, but you will see the road that leads there. It is obvious.

BY TAXI & CARRIAGE: Going into the city with its narrow streets is best done by taxi, moto-taxi or horse-drawn carriage. The cost to get around is about $3 anywhere within city limits.

■ Services

Medical Clinic, Serafin Garcia Oeste #167, ☎ 42/222-2720.

Post Office, Calle Colón #10, is open Monday to Saturday, 9 am to 5 pm.

Telephone/Internet, Calle Cuba and Ave Eduardo Machado, is open every day from 9 am to 5 pm.

Police, Colón #222 and Serafin Garcia, ☎ 42/221-2623

■ Festivals

Known as the country's best-dressed city, Santa Clara puts on a regal **fashion show** each May when the best designers and models from around the country come to show their stuff. There were some uniquely designed and painted garments draped on sexy Cuban females (and males!), who seem to exude sensuality from the moment they open their eyes in the morning. One of the shows was held in Leoncio Vidal Park – a red carpet went down the center. It was quite a spectacle.

Participating artists and designers sell their hand-painted swimsuits, dresses and blouses at the studio at Calle Julio Jover #6 between Ave Maximo Gómez and Juan Bruno, ☎ 42/229-1429.

■ The Life of Che Guevara

You can't visit Santa Clara without knowing a little about Che, shown at right, age three.

Che Guevara was born in 1928 in Argentina. All his life he suffered from asthma. Because of his ailment, he was unable to participate in many children's games, so he read from his father's collections of Marx, Engels and Freud instead. As a university student, Che became anti-Perón, although he never participated in the demonstrations that called for Perón's fall.

Guevara studied medicine, specializing in dermatology in general and leprosy in particular. But he was a restless sort with socialist ideals so, in 1949 he took his famous motorbike trip north, working along the way at everything from ditch digging to practicing physician in specialized clinics for leprosy. In 1951 he arrived in the United States.

He came to Bolivia in 1952 to be part of the revolution that was occurring at the time. But he found it an opportunists' revolution (not pure enough) and refused to participate. Instead, he went to Guatemala, where he earned a living writing travel articles. At that time he became an even purer socialist and rejected most forms of communism. He lived with Hilda Gadea, an Indian and Marxist who helped Che with his indoctrination. She also married him.

In 1954, Che met Raul and Fidel Castro in Mexico City and followed them to Cuba, where he studied guerrilla warfare. He became ruthless in his methods of ruling, shooting without question those who turned against the Batista regime to join Castro. He hated a turncoat. He also hated cowards and shot them too. With this type of dedication, it didn't take long for Che to become Fidel's top man.

After the success in Cuba, restlessness and desire for revolution continued to drive Che. He divorced Hilda and married a lady named Olidia. Together they visited the Congo in Africa before arriving in Bolivia. Che believed that the country, because of its poverty, was ripe for insurrection. Bolivia also bordered five countries so he believed the spread of the revolution would be easy. Che entered Bolivia on November 1, 1966. The miners were on strike but he failed to see this as the place to start. Instead, he formed a guerrilla training camp in Santa Cruz that attracted a few men but got no sympathy or support from the locals. In the meantime, the US, still smarting about the Cuban Revolution and the Bay of Pigs, was tracking Che. CIA agent Felix Rodreguez worked with the Bolivian army in the hunt. In order to get support of the locals, the first thing they did was drop pamphlets from the air saying they would pay $4,200 for the capture of Guevara. Rodrequez then led a 650-man battalion into the area near Vallegrande.

Between March and August 1967, Che and the Bolivian military had skirmishes, but nothing serious happened until August 31 when the army killed about one third of Che's men. They also captured Che's best soldier, Paco. Che retreated south, and then his asthma started up, causing him great discomfort. During his retreat, on a trip to Alto Seco to buy food and spend the night, Che learned that one of the locals had gone to inform the military of his presence. So Che and his men changed their plans and went to Loma Larga, a ranch between Alto Seco and La Higuera. The peasants living there fled. Che continued on to Vallegrande, but he found that there, too, most of the villagers were absent. Shots could be heard in the distance and Che quickly surmised that they meant the Bolivian military was hot on his tail. He and his men moved toward Valle Serrano, south of the Rio Grande. He thought that if he got across the border into Paraguay he would be okay.

The group was camped on the River Yuro when an old lady passed by. Che paid her to keep quiet about their presence. However, it was an old woman who told the military that she heard voices of men on the Yuro River near San Antonio. It has never been confirmed that it was the same lady.

The final battle started along river. Che was shot in the leg and, as he retreated, he was hit several more times. His follower, Sarabia, picked him up and ran. Che lost his hat. Sarabia sat down in an open area and tried to defend Che. They both shot at the military but the army circled them, filling Che with bullets. He could no longer hold his gun and fire at the same time. At one point, Che shouted that he was worth more alive than dead. He surrendered. The battle ended at 3:30 pm with Che being taken prisoner.

Carried on a stretcher to La Higuera, Che was placed in a school house where he lay in the dirt, arms and legs tied, hair matted, clothes torn, bullet wounds all over. He was also having trouble breathing due to asthma. Rodriguez arrived in a helicopter. He took some photos of Che (the

one above is an official CIA record) and of his diary and then, against the advice of his bosses, gave the orders to execute Guevara. Rodriguez also warned the firing squad not to shoot Guevara in the face because he wanted it to look like Guevara had been killed in battle. As Che stood facing the firing squad his last words were, "Know this now, you are killing a man."

After Che died, Rodriguez took Che's Rolex watch and later showed it to newspaper reporters. He stored the body in the laundry room of the hospital. When journalists wanted proof that Che was still alive, the military men brought the body out and held Guevara up so he looked like he possibly could be alive. His eyes were still open. The journalists took their photos.

However, when reports went into the Pentagon, there were discrepancies. The pentagon wanted Guevara alive and journalists reported that he was alive. If he had died in battle – as Rodreguez told the Pentagon – he should have been dead 24 hours before the time indicated on his death certificate. Rodriguez tried to cover his tracks. In doing this, he had Che's hands cut off then buried his remains in an unmarked grave under the tarmac of the airport at Vallegrande.

■ Sightseeing

Plaza of the Revolution, Rafael Trista and Carretera Central, ☎ 42/221-5878, takes up a few city blocks in its expanse. The plaza itself features red bricks laid in a pleasing design and covers a huge area on different levels. At the head is a gigantic statue of Guevara dressed in military uniform, hat perched on head, rifle in hand. Below are the words, *Hasta La Victoria Siempre*, which mean, "Always to the Victory." You will come across the phrase everywhere in Cuba, especially where Guevara's image is seen.

Under the statue of Guevara is a museum where the eternal flame burns in the center of a circle. Around

Santa Clara's impressive Plaza of the Revolution.

the edges are the tombs of several men who fell with Guevara during the revolution. There are also some softly lighted small cases that have stone plaques with images of heroes who died with Guevara. Once you have been through the mausoleum, you can go into the museum, which features photos, documents and other items from Che's life, including his beret.

The museum and mausoleum are open Tuesday to Saturday, 8 am to 9 pm, and Sunday until 5 pm. They allow only a few people in at a time and you must wait in line until your turn. A coffee shop and snack bar on the plaza sell refreshments. There is a parking lot.

Monument to the Train Wreck, road to Camagüey between Puente de la Luz and Linea, ☎ 42/222-2758, is the monument to the train that Guevara and his comrades managed to derail during the revolution. This was the turning point, when the revolutionaries were able to take control of the area (thanks to the ammunition and arms that were on the train). The five coaches here remain in the state they were when they derailed in 1958. You can enter for $1 and take photos for another buck. The train is open daily from 8 am to 7 pm, except Sunday when it closes at noon.

Cigar Factory, Calle Maceo #181, ☎ 42/220-2211, occupies a full city block and employs over 400 workers who hand-make Montecristos, Romeo and Julietas and other brands. You can enter on weekdays from 7 am to 4 pm, except for an hour from noon to 1 pm. A tour costs $5 per person and it is well worth it to see how the workers layer one slice of tobacco leaf over the shredded leaves to make the perfect smoke. Many workers who have smoked all their lives show missing teeth when they smile. It's more economical to come here and tour the factory than it is in Havana. You can buy high-quality cigars at the shop across the rod.

Palacio de Justica, on Plaza Leoncio Vidal, is the beautiful white stone building with high Doric columns and long narrow windows. It is a place you don't want to be forced to visit – passing for pleasure is much nicer. You can go inside and look around the main entrance but are not permitted to walk around on your own – you may be a spy! It is the nicest building on the plaza.

Museum of Decorative Arts, Calle Marta Abreu, Plaza Leoncio Vidal, ☎ 42/222-5368, is in a colonial building. Its rooms feature furniture from the 1800s, some of it quite dark and well carved while other pieces are wicker. Check out the crystal chandelier in the main living room. The museum is open odd hours; Monday, Wednesday and Thursday from 9 am to 6 pm, Friday and Saturday from 1 pm to 6 pm and Sunday from 2 pm to 10 pm. It costs $2 to enter and the same to take photos. I obviously have no photos of this place!

Teatro La Caridad, Plaza Leoncio Vidal and Luis Estevez, is the other old building on the plaza. This one is not very ornate on the outside but the inside is rococo. Built in 1885 by wealthy city dweller Marta Abreo Estevez, the building was restored after the revolution. Red velvet seats grace three levels, but the

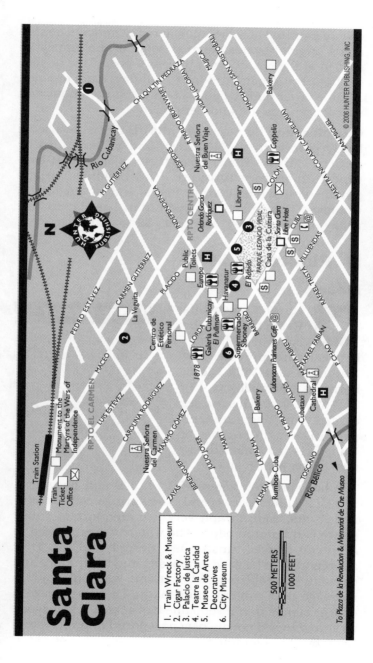

Central Cuba

Santa Clara

1. Train Wreck & Museum
2. Cigar Factory
3. Palacio de Justica
4. Teatre la Caridad
5. Museo de Artes
   Decoratives
6. City Museum

To Plaza de la Revolucion & Memorial de Che Museo

500 METERS
1000 FEET

© 2006 HUNTER PUBLISHING, INC

ceiling painting is what you will really notice. The theater's original owner donated some of the money he earned at the box office to the city's poor. This no longer happens. Open Tuesday to Sunday, 9 am to 5 pm; a guided tour (in English) will take about an hour and cost $1. Photos are another dollar.

City Museum, Boulevard #1 and JB Zayas, has some lovely porcelain vases, dishes, and oil paintings by modern Cuban artists. Also, there is some last-century 19th-century furniture. The building itself is grand, with white marble floors and stained-glass windows. The museum is open from Tuesday to Saturday, 9 am to 5 pm, and costs $2 to enter.

■ Places to Stay

Hotels

 Hotel Elguea Spa Resort is on the coast at the border between the provinces of Matanzas and Villa Clara, north of Corralillo, ☎ 42/368-6292, $$$. This is a secluded and hard-to-reach place. The main purpose of being here is to take advantage of the health spa.

PRICE CHART
Per room for two people, per day.
$. $25-50
$$. $51-75
$$$. $76-100
$$$$. $101-150
$$$$$. . . . . over $150

The hot spring is about 45°C/113°F and flows at a rate of 25 liters per second. The springs contain bromide salts, sodium and very low amounts of sulfur (there is minimum odor). The waters are supposed to keep you relaxed, unstressed, fit and vitalized. They are reported to be good for obesity and respiratory and circulatory problems. While there you can enjoy a massage or a mineral mud bath. The gentleman in charge claims that if someone has a facial, they'd look so young they'd need a new passport. I'm pretty skeptical, but I am tempted.

The gym is spacious and people dressed like doctors will make certain that you are doing the best exercises. From there you can have a dry sauna and then lie in the thermal springs before having your blood pressure checked. If you have any physiotherapy, a trained nurse will monitor your body's reaction to the workout. The indoor pool is luxurious, as are the rooms, with soft lights and tasteful décor. All have air conditioning, cable TV and private bathrooms. The garden is well kept and clean. There are the usual amenities like a games room, souvenir shop, restaurant, beauty salon and tennis courts. You can opt to have meals included.

Hotel Los Caneyes, Ave de los Eucaliptos and the perimeter highway, ☎ 42/222-8140, $$$, has rooms in circular thatch-roof huts. It is believed by many cultures that round huts stay cooler than those with corners. Although Los Caneyes is a bit out of town, it is by far the most comfortable choice. There is a restaurant, bar, swimming pool, gift shop and souvenir shop. Some rooms are wheelchair accessible.

Santa Clara Libre, Plaza Leoncio Vidal #6, between Calle Trista and Padre Chao, ☎ 42/222-7548, $$, is definitely central and within easy walking distance of all sights. The rooms are small and some need perking up, but all are comfortable enough. A 12th-floor restaurant overlooks the city. Even if not staying here, have a beer up top for the views.

Casas Particulares

Omelio Moreno Lorenzo, Calle E. Machado #4 between Ave Cuba and Colón, ☎ 42/221-6941, is very close to the central plaza. The two rooms are clean, the food is good and the rooms are comfortable. Enjoy a cold beer from your in-room fridge; they use the honor system. Omelio speaks English and French; if his *casa* is full, he will recommend another.

Olga Rivera, Calle Evangelista #20 between Calle Rodriguez and Maximo Gómez, no phone, has a room with double bed, private bath with hot water, cable TV and air conditioning. The biggest draw is the patio, which has plants everywhere and a few exotic birds too. The price of the room includes your breakfast. Good deal!

Villa El Renacer, Calle Marta Abreu #105, between Juan Bruno Zayas and Rafael Lubian, ☎ 42/220-5470, is owned and operated by Maria Matilde Morales. She has a room with a double and single bed (good for three people) private bath, air conditioning and color TV. There is also safe parking. Another house with an inner courtyard is well decorated with tons of plants and a few birds. Hospitality is the big thing here.

■ Places to Eat

El Castillo, Calle 9 de abril #9 between Ave Cuba and Villuendas, is a peso place. It serves Moors and Christians with all its meals that cost next to nothing.

Colonial 1878, Maximo Gómez between Marta Abreu and Independencia, serves international food like chicken, pork or beef with Moors and Christians.

Eat either at your hotel or *casa* – the *casas* in Cuba are the very best for food.

■ Nightlife

Santa Clara Libre, Plaza Leoncio Vidal #6, between Calle Crista and Padre Chao, ☎ 42/222-7548, has a popular disco that starts at 11 pm and goes until dawn. This is definitely for the young. There is live salsa music at the **Primavera** on Maximo Gómez #51.

Remedios

This is another pretty little colonial town with little to do. What there is to do, though, is pleasant. There is a cathedral, a museum, a place to eat and nice streets to walk around. Because there aren't many tourists in the area, the locals are anxious to meet you, help you, befriend you. If Cayo Santa Maria is a destination, this is a good base. I thought that Remedios was a much nicer place to stay than Caibarein, although some disagree.

■ History

Remedios was originally established during the 1500s. It was constantly being attacked by pirates, so some people decided to move the town to the location of Trinidad, while others wanted to stay. Those wanting to move burned the town to the ground, but the stubborn ones decided to stay and rebuilt. By early 1700s, Remedios was an established community.

■ Getting Here & Away

BY BUS: The bus station, on the highway between Calle Pichardo and Ampara, is a 15-minute walk from Plaza Martí in the center. Two buses arrive every day from Santa Clara, one in the morning and the other later in the day.

BY CAR: It is best to have a car. To park on the plaza will cost you $1. I believe this is a "watching" fee, whereby the person will keep an eye on your vehicle.

■ Services

Post Office, Ave José Antonio Peña and Calle Antonio Romero, is open Monday to Saturday, 9 am to 6 pm.

■ Sightseeing

Iglesia de San Juan Bautista, on the plaza, is a colonial church. The original was built in the 1600s. The newer structure has been here only since the late 1800s, even though it looks a lot older. It wasn't until the 1940s that philanthropist Eutimio Falla Bonet paid for the restoration and it became the showpiece you see today. The inside has a lot of gold and carved wood collected from other parts of Cuba. To enter the church you must knock on the back door to have someone let you in. Open to the public 10 am to 4 pm, $1.

Museums

Museum Alejandro Garcia Catur, on the plaza and Ave Ayuntamiento, is named after Cuba's most famous musician and composer who played with the Havana Philharmonic Orchestra. He was also a lawyer and was killed by a man whom he was going to prosecute the following day. This happened in 1940. There are many items pertaining to music, plus Catur's study, on display. The museum is open Monday to Friday, 9 am to noon and 1 pm to 6 pm; Saturday 2 pm to 10 pm; and Sunday, 9 am to 1 pm. The entry fee is 50¢.

Portales de la Plaza is next door to the museum. It was built in 1875 and has great old tiled floors and crystal chandeliers. The antiques around the room are also from that era and are well preserved.

Museo de las Parrandas, Calle Maximo Gómez #71 and Ayuntamiento, just a block from the plaza, is where you will find a mish-mash of photos and memorabilia from the December 24 event that is called the Parrandas – the parade reminiscent of Carnival in places like Brazil or Bolivia. The colorful floats and costumes are creative and expensive.

vious page: San Francisco de Paula Cathederal, Trinidad's famous church.
Above: Horse and carriage, Moran.
Opposite: Statue at Remedios.
Below: River flowing out of Lago de Leche.

Above: Causeway to Cayo Coco.
Opposite: Plaza in Camagüey.
Below: Luxury, all-inclusive hotel on Cayo Coco.

Above: New mangrove trees near the cays.

Opposite: Dock at Hotel Colony, Isla de la Juventud.

Below: Che Guevera memorial, Santa Clara.

Above: Cathedral, Santiago de Cuba.

Below: Musicians in Santiago de Cuba.

AUTHOR NOTE: The hawk you see around town is the symbol of El Carmen and the rooster, also seen around town, is the symbol of El Salvador, the two areas of town that compete for the best float during this celebration.

If you are lucky, you will be taken upstairs to view the mask collection. If you are even luckier, you may be able to try one on. They are very heavy. The museum is open Tuesday to Saturday, 9 am to 5 pm with an hour off for lunch at noon. There is a $1 entrance fee.

Museum of History, Calle Maceo #58, between General Carrillo and Fe del Valle, just at the plaza, has a collection of papers and photos displaying the town's history. The furniture in the museum is more interesting than the documents. There is a $1 fee to enter.

■ Trip to Cayo Santa Maria

 Cayo Santa Maria is part of King's Garden Archipelago, about 40 km/25 miles from the Remedios on the mainland. It has an airport and is also connected to the mainland by causeway ($2 per car, you must show your passport). This causeway winds above the water and around mangrove trees that hold plenty of birds. There are two hotels (profiled below) and more being built. Both can be visited, but I'd stay away from Hotel Sol Cayo Santa Maria unless you feel very charitable.

Hotel Sol Cayo Santa Maria, ☎ 33/235-1500, is an all-inclusive resort that charges $40 for non-guests to visit. For that price I'd suspect they were doing something pretty special.

As an all-inclusive guest who has arrived in Havana and is being transported to the hotel, you will not be checked in at the front desk but rather as you are driving along the causeway. You will get your identity bracelet, hotel passport that gives you access to beach towels, key card for your room and your registration card. This is efficiency at its best.

The hotel has 29 two-story cabins and six one-story cabins. Most have four rooms in them and a few have two rooms. Some are wheelchair accessible. There are also a few luxury suites that have a Jacuzzi and separate living rooms. All rooms have huge beds, private bathrooms with hairdryers, mini-bars, safes, cable TV and either a balcony or patio. You can rent a car or motorbike to tootle around the island or use any of their muscle-powered water vessels. You can swim in a pool with water jets, play volleyball, go to the gym or soak in the sauna (costs extra!).

There is an Italian restaurant, a Creole restaurant, a barbecue snack bar and buffet service plus a swim-up bar and a piano bar.

Villa Las Brujas, ☎ 42/220-4199, has two-dozen little cabins bordered by white sand on one side and jungle on the other. Isolation is the selling point for this luxurious place. The rooms are standard and lunch, served in one of the uninteresting restaurants, is nothing special (mine was a slice of cheese slapped onto two slabs of white bread). The cabins are clean, with tile floors and sitting areas. For less than $100 a day, this is a good deal.

Visitors pay $4 to enter the property and with that you get a sandwich and a soda – served rather grudgingly. The beach is pretty and backed by wild vegetation. If you try to enter without paying, the guards along the beach will accost you.

■ Adventures on Foot

On Cayo Santa Maria, at the end of the main road, (the only road on the island), a six-km/four-mile hiking trail. Officially, it is open from 9 am to noon and 1 pm to 4 pm, Tuesday and Friday only, and you may not go along it without a guide

($2). However, I went there during "open" hours and no one was around so I walked it by myself. The trail is clear and points of interest – such as the tiny cenote at one spot and a bird's nest at another – are marked. Wear good shoes as the trail is along volcanic rocks.

■ Places to Stay

Hotel Mascotte, Plaza Central, ☎ 33/9-5327 , $$, has only 10 rooms, all set on the second floor around the central patio. This hotel is where one of the documents was signed in 1899 freeing Cuba from Spanish rule. Unknown to the Cubans at the time, this docu-

PRICE CHART
Per room for two people, per day.
$. $25-50
$$. $51-75
$$$. $76-100
$$$$. $101-150
$$$$$. . . . over $150

ment put the island under American rule. The hotel has been totally renovated so everything old remains with all new amenities. The hotel's restaurant is the only place to eat in town. The staff is wonderful, the prices are low (dinner about $6), and the meals are large.

Tours of the sugar mills by steam engines in the Valle de Los Ingenios are the most popular excursions from Remedios. The trip can be arranged at your hotel. The day-trip will cost $15 per person.

Hostel El Patio, Calle José Antonio Peña #72, between Garcia and Antonio Romero, ☎ 33/9-5220, is owned by Elsa Valdez Martinez. She has an independent room with private bath and air conditioning. Although I never stayed here, El Patio comes highly recommended – the food has a good reputation too.

Central Cuba

Caibarien

This tiny little fishing village, spread across a lot of land, is interesting for a day or so. Locals walk the long sea wall in the evenings when things cool off, and it's here that you'll find fresh seafood always available.

Windsurfing is the sport of the area and you will see locals playing for hours on the bay.

SAFETY FOR WINDSURFERS

- If you fall off your board, stay with it. Your board floats.
- Never sail alone.
- Know the national distress call.
- Know your wind directions. Only very skilled surfers can go against the wind to get back to shore. The idea is to travel sideways against the wind.
- Watch for boat traffic and avoid heavily used areas.

The town is noisy. You will see dogs, cats and roosters strutting around competing to see who can make the most noise. Then the stereos and TVs kick in. As supper approaches, mothers can be heard calling for their kids who answer with the same gusto. Finally, the hawkers arrive selling cakes, breads, ice cream, milk, chicken or fresh vegetables. It's quite a show.

If the scene from your balcony or front steps gets boring, walk the malecón, stop at a restaurant along the way for a beer and watch the people.

■ Getting Here & Away

BY BUS: Buses come and go three times a day to and from Remedios. They stop at the train station. Check times at the Remedios bus station or the train station in Caibarien.

BY CAR: Once in Caibarien, it is a long walk from one end of town to the other. For exploring the town and the surrounding area, a car is best.

■ Places to Stay

Casas Particulares

Eladio Herrada Bernabea, Ave 35 #1016B, between Calle 10 and 12, ☎ 33/6-4253, has two air-conditioned rooms with fans, soft beds and hot water. The windows are covered with heavy wool blankets so the street noise is muffled and you can sleep past the 5 am hawker's calling time. Breakfast is exceptional. There is safe parking. The owner is known as "Yayo" – call him that and he will be pleased. If his place is full, he will take you to rooms on Ave 37, a block away.

THE TOWN OF "FLORIDA"

Florida at Carretera, Km 536, ☎ 33/5-3011, is marked on the map as a city. Although there seems to be some scattering of houses around, there is no city, not even a town. Florida is actually a moderately sized hotel, with 75 rooms, a restaurant, a nearby lake and a pool. If you are driving between Camagüey and Sancti Spíritus or Ciego de Avila, you may want to stop for the night or for a meal. Rooms are $30 for a double and they have air conditioning, private bath and TV. The grounds are really nice and the lake is good for birding.

Central Cuba

Camagüey

This is one colonial city that (unlike some in the eastern part of the island) is a delight. It has not been over toured so the locals are still eager to have visitors. The city has beautiful plazas, confusing, narrow streets, lots of entertainment and things to see. Plus, it is just 30 km/19 miles from beaches that still haven't been discovered by the big hotel chains.

■ History

 Named Santa Maria of Puerto Principe in 1514 when it was founded, the city wasn't renamed until the 1900s, when it was given the local name of Camaguayo, Guaimaro or Camaguebax. Because of its original proximity to the ocean, the area became a favorite raiding place of Henry Morgan. The city was moved inland to the Caonao River and, finally, to the spot the Indians called Camaguayo. It was the raids of Morgan that inspired Silvestre de Balboa, a Camagüey native, to write his epic poem, *Espejo de Pacencia* (Mirror of Patience), in 1608. The writing is about a bishop who was captured by a pirate. The poem is still recited and studied in the universities of Cuba today. One of the reasons the city streets are so narrow and winding is that they were built to confuse pirates when a chase was on.

When the wave of independence-fighting started, Camagüey was one of the first places to see aggressive fighting. Francisco Velazco, a noted rebel, was executed by the Spanish here in 1826. In 1851, after some independence was won, the first draft of the Constitution was drawn up here. Later, during the war of 1895, many military campaigns were planned or took place near the city. After the Americans were relieved of their responsibilities of ruling Cuba, the cattle industry in the area became a huge part of the economy.

From early days the city was called the City of the Tinajones (large clay jars used to gather water). Today, the jars are found throughout the city, decorating patios and gardens.

■ Getting Here & Away

 BY PLANE: Planes from Havana arrive daily at the airport about eight km/five miles from the center of town. Check with **Cuban Air**, ☎ 7/33-4949, for schedules, which change often.

BY BUS: The bus station is about three km/two miles out of the center and, unless you want to walk in the heat, a taxi or moto-taxi will take you to and from. Buses go as follows:

Trinidad to Santiago de Cuba with stops in Sancti Spíritus, Ciego de Avila, Camagüey, Las Tunas, Holguin, and Bayamo. The bus leaves Trinidad at 8:15 am, Santi Spíritus at 9:45 am, Ciego de Avila at 11:15 am, Camagüey at 1:50 pm, Las Tunas at 3:50 pm, Holguin at 5:05 pm, Bayamo at 6:25 pm.

Santiago de Cuba to Trinidad with stops in Sancti Spoiritus, Ciego de Avila, Camagüey, Las Tunas, Holguin and Bayamo. The bus leaves Santiago de Cuba at 7:30 pm, Bayamo at 9:40 pm, Holguin at 11 pm, Las Tunas at 12:15 am, Camagüey at 2:15 am, Ciego de Avila at 4:15 am, Sancti Spíritus at 5:35 am and arrives in Trinidad at 7 am.

The cost from Trinidad to Sancti Spíritus is $6, to Ciego de Avila is $9, to Camagüey is $15, to Las Tunas is $22, to Holguin and to Bayamo is $26, to Santiago de Cuba is $33.

BY CAR: Travel by car is by far the easiest way and the one that will give you the most experiences because you cover more territory, but it is also isolating. Hitching is fun. Most Cubans hitch, but it takes time.

BY TAXI: Use the metered taxis or the moto-taxis to take you anywhere in town for about $5. They are parked outside the bus station whenever buses arrive and depart.

■ Services

Post Office, Ave Agramonte #461, open from 8 am to 6 pm daily except Sunday.

Telephone office, Avellaneda #308, between Calle Lopez Recio and Independencia, has both phone and Internet service. Open 7 am to 9 pm daily.

Medical Clinic, República #211 between Calle Gómez and Castellano, ☎ 32/229-7810, has some doctors that can speak English.

Immigration, Ave Ignacio Agramonte #421, ☎ 32/225-4785, at the Cubatur office.

Internet access is available at a place just off the plaza beside the Islazul Office. They take your money, book you in – if the machine doesn't work, it's your loss. They won't tell you which machines work. Avoid this place unless you can't live without Internet regardless of cost.

■ Festivals

The International Theatre Festival held in Havana has some events performed here and hosted by the **Ballet of Camagüey**. This festival each year has a different theme, such as the 150th anniversary of the theater in Havana or the celebration of composers or musical styles. It is held in late October or early November. Check with the tourist office at your hotel for information if you are around at that time. If planning a trip, go to www.balletcuba.cu and click on Festivals for the latest information.

The **Festival of San Juan** is Carnival in Camagüey. It consists of a week of dancing and parades starting on June 24. Every street corner has a pot of soup boiling or a roast pig spinning on a spit. Everyone is welcome to eat, dress in costume, drink, sing and dance, but it is the Folklorico dancers, a young group of 16 artists, who are the biggest draw.

■ Sightseeing

Plazas & Parks

Agramonte Park, Calle Martí and Ave Ignacio Agramonte, was first paved in 1528 as the Plaza de Armas, with the Iglesia Mayor majestically flanking its one side. Later, in 1850, the theater was built, adding even more splendor to the plaza. The park was renamed Ignacio Agramonte, after a lawyer born in Camagüey who, in 1868, took part in the uprising against Spanish rule. He became secretary to the provisional government and, later, a member of congress. A short peace came and he became one of the signers of the declaration to free slaves. He died in battle, at Jimaguayd, in 1873, as Major General of the local forces who were now trying to win independence for the island. In the park's center is a bronze statue of Agramonte standing in front of a modern stone carving of horses and soldiers.

Flanking one side of the plaza is the **Santa Iglesia Catedral Nuestra Señora de la Candelaria**, an 18th-century stone church that, from the outside, appears austere and off-putting. The inside has a large collection of porcelain statues of Christian saints, some of which are exceptional.

San Juan de Dios Plaza and Hospital, Calle San Juan de Dios y San Rafael, features the Church of San Juan de Dios and the museum of the same name. The church was built in 1728 and retains its original brick floor. The dark wooden pews face an ornate altar, and the short bell tower outside is painted in colors that match the homes surrounding the plaza. The hospital next door is where Agramonte was laid to rest after he was killed. The Spanish burned and buried him without allowing Cubans to pay their last respects. Today, the hospital has been turned into a museum. There isn't much to see in the hospital, but you can tour the building. It is open Tuesday to Saturday, 9 am to 5 pm and costs $1 to enter (this includes a guide).

Parque de los Trabajadores, Ave Ignacio Agramonte, between Calles Independencia and Cisneros, has Iglesia Nuestra Señora de la Merced on one side and the birthplace of Ignacio Agramonte (see below) on the other. **Iglesia Nuestra de Señora de la Merced** holds the Holy Sepulcher, a highly ornate coffin made of silver, which cost one believer 23,000 gold coins. The donor was in mourning for his son, who was killed in a duel, and his wife, who died a few months later. The man joined the monastery and donated his wealth to the church. The sepulcher was made in readiness for himself. A portion of his donations have recently been used to buy paint for the church.

The rooms to the side of the altar, set around a small patio, were originally built in 1747 as a convent, and are still being used as such. Having many lives, the church was rebuilt in the 1800s and again in the early 1900s. What you see now has lasted over a hundred years, which seems to be a record. There are high vaulted ceilings and a crypt under the altar.

Plaza del Carmen, Ave Hermanos Agüero between Honda and Carmen, is the prettiest plaza in the city. The most notable parts, gated off by low chain fences, are the bronze statues standing beside or sitting on the benches placed around the cobbled passages. They feature workers selling water from large clay jugs and women sitting on benches like welcoming committees. This lovely plaza is surrounded by brightly painted one-story houses with geraniums blooming in their windows.

Other Sights

Casa Natal de Ignacio Agramonte, Ave Ignacio Agramonte #459, between Calles Independencia and

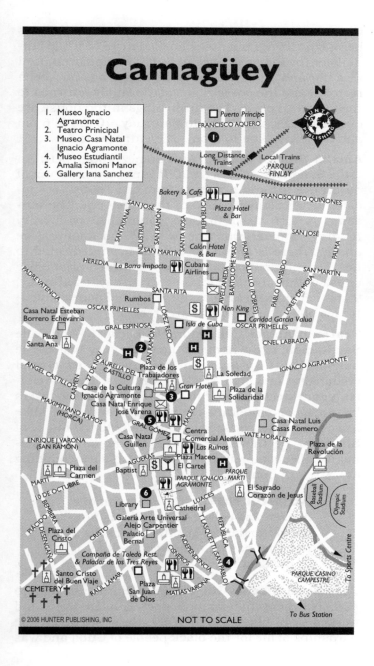

Camagüey

1. Museo Ignacio Agramonte
2. Teatro Prinicipal
3. Museo Casa Natal Ignacio Agramonte
4. Museo Estudiantil
5. Amalia Simoni Manor
6. Gallery Iana Sanchez

Puerto Principe
FRANCISCO AQUERO
Long Distance Trains
Local Trains
PARQUE FINLAY
FRANCISQUITO QUIÑONES
Bakery & Cafe
SAN JOSÉ
Plaza Hotel & Bar
SANTAYANA
INDUSTRIA
SAN RAMÓN
SANTA ROSA
REPÚBLICA
SAN JOSÉ
SAN MARTIN
Colón Hotel & Bar
PADRE OLALLO (POBRES)
PABLO LOMBIDO
LORETO DE MOJA
PALMA
HEREDIA
La Barra Impacto
Cubana Airlines
SAN MARTIN
PADRE VALENCIA
SANTA RITA
BARTOLOMÉ MASO
AVELLANEDA
Rumbos
Casa Natal Esteban Borrero Echevarria
OSCAR PRIMELLES
Nan King
Caridad García Valua
OSCAR PRIMELLES
Plaza Santa Ana
GRAL ESPINOSA
Isla de Cuba
CNEL LABRADA
ANGEL CASTILLON
2
SAN RAMÓN
LÓPEZ RECIO
IGNACIO AGRAMONTE
27 DE NOV
CARMEN
AURELIA DEL CASTILLO
Plaza de los Trabajadores
La Soledad
MAXIMITIANO RAMOS (HORCA)
Casa de la Cultura Ignacio Agramonte
3
Gran Hotel
Plaza de la Solidaridad
Casa Natal Enrique José Varena
5
ENRIQUE J VARONA (SAN RAMÓN)
GRAL GÓMEZ
MACEO
Casa Natal Guillen
Centra Comercial Alemán
Las Ruinas
VATE MORALES
Casa Natal Luis Casas Romero
Plaza de la Revolución
AGUERAS
Plaza del Carmen
Baptist
Plaza Maceo
El Cartel
PARQUE IGNACIO AGRAMONTE
PARQUE MARTI
El Sagrado Corazón de Jesus
Baseball Stadium
MARTI
10 DE OCTUBRE
6
Library
LUACES
REPÚBLICA
T. LASQUETTI (SAN PABLO)
Olympic Stadium
BEMBETA
PLÁCIDO
DESENGAÑO
CRISTO
Cathedral
Galería Arte Universal Alejo Carpentier
Palacio Bernal
Plaza del Cristo
Compaña de Toledo Rest. & Paladar de los Tres Reyes
CISNEROS
INDEPENDENCIA
4
PARQUE CASINO CAMPESTRE
Santo Cristo del Buen Viaje
RAÚL LAMAR
Plaza San Juan de Dios
MATÍAS VARONA
CEMETERY
To Bus Station
© 2006 HUNTER PUBLISHING, INC
NOT TO SCALE

Central Cuba

Cisneros, is the home of Camagüey's most famous hero, Ignacio Agramonte, who died in 1873 while battling for the independence of Cuba. Having been used as a bar and a marketplace, the house has now been restored and the possessions of the family returned to their rightful place. The furnishings in the house are exquisite. Open Tuesday to Saturday, 10 am to 6 pm and Sunday, 1 am to 6 pm. The entry fee is $2.

Amalia Simoni Manor, Ave Gómez #608, between Calle Simoni and Plaza de la Havana, is a museum of decorative art and furniture from the 1800s. It is located in a colonial house of the same era. The museum is also used to hold contemporary literary reading. Simoni was the wife of Agramonte (see above). There is also a hospital in town dedicated to her. For information on events, visit the tourist office or ask at the museum. It is open Tuesday to Saturday, 9 am to 5 pm with an hour off at noon. There is an entry fee of $1, but readings are free.

Teatro Principal, Calle Padre Vallencia #64 and Calle San Ramon, is the home of the Camagüey ballet. The building adds splendor to the city with its crystal chandeliers and stained-glass windows. There are often youngsters learning to be ballerinas or teenagers learning contemporary dance. Boys and girls alike learn the minuet or the old time waltz to the music of Straus or Beethoven. However, the home of the famous ballet company is now located at a new building at Carretera Central #3331.

> **AUTHOR NOTE:** The most famous dancer was called **Alicia**. She is now too old to dance, but the town sells a perfume named after her. Look for it in the shops.

Casa Natal Nicolás Guillén, Calle Hermanos Agüero #58, is where the famous poet Guillén lived and worked until his death in 1989. He wrote about the hardships of life for the black people of Cuba and was also a promoter of the arts. He started the National Union of Writers and Artists in Cuba and was awarded the Lenin Peace Prize for his efforts. The house is nothing special but the broadsides hanging on the walls are worth looking at. The house is open Tuesday to Saturday, 9 am to 4:30 pm, with an hour off at noon. There is a $1 charge to enter.

Iglesia de la Soledad, Calles Maceo and República, is the location of those tall white steeples you can see from anywhere in town. This is the church where the town hero, Agramonte was baptized and married. The present building was constructed in 1758. There is a legend attached to the church, in which a priest was stuck in the swamp nearby and screamed for days for help. Finally, he managed to climb out by himself but he was carrying a cross. As he hit high ground, the church appeared to him in a vision. It was later built on the same spot.

■ Adventures on Foot

Old Villa of Santa Maria del Puerto del Principe is an area of town southwest of Plaza of San Juan de Dios on Calle San Juan de Dios y San Rafael. This is the oldest section of town and it contains the old cemetery, built in 1814, on Plazuela de Cristo. The cemetery houses some of the independence fighters who died in the last 200 years. Cemeteries are often interesting. This one has some attractive mausoleums. On the tiny plaza is the church of Santo Cristo del Buen Viaje (Christ of the Good Travels), which may be of interest to some travelers. Also in the old town is the Funda del Catre, or Bed Cover Alley. It measures 2.2 meters/7.2 feet wide and 77 meters/253 feet long and was one of the alleys constructed to cause problems for pirates who were chasing locals for the purpose of robbery. The narrowness of the alley would not permit two horses to pass each other so the robber couldn't overtake the victim.

Central Cuba

■ Adventures on Water

Scuba Diving & Snorkeling

 Cayo Sabinal and **Santa Lucia** are the best and closest places but, at present, the road leading to them is impassable. However, you can go to Cayo Coco and Cayo Guillamo and hire a boat from one of the hotels to take you to this area. See page 348.

JINATERO TROUBLE

Be aware that Camagüey has one of the worst reputations for *jinateros* bothering tourists. They stalk and follow foreigners unmercifully, and have even been known to swarm. The purpose of swarming is to create an environment where the tourist can be robbed. One day, a local man about 85 years old approached me and aggressively insisted I give him money. He finally left me alone when I told him that I was Cuban.

■ Tour Operators

 Cubatur, Ave Agramonte between Solidad and Iglecia de la Merced, is open from 9 am to 6 pm. This is what the sign on the door said, but I never found them open. Across the road is a camera shop with some old projectors, including one from the Ukraine. While you are waiting for the tour office to open, walk over and enjoy the cameras.

■ Places to Stay

Hotels

 Camagüey Hotel, Carretera Central, Km 4.5, suburb of Jayamá, ☎ 32/8-7267, $$, has small but clean rooms with tiny balconies. The hotel is in a four-storey Russian-styled building

that contains 150 rooms altogether. There is a pool
and safe parking. The
drawback is the location,
away from the center.

Hotel Colón, Calle República #472, between San
José and San Martín, ☎ 32/
8-3368, $$, has the most
character of all hotels in the
city. It was built in the

PRICE CHART

*Per room for two
people, per day.*

$. $25-50
$$. $51-75
$$$. $76-100
$$$$. $101-150
$$$$$. . . . . over $150

1920s and has maintained its old-day elegance. To
add to its attraction are the recent renovations. The
entrance has a lovely stained glass window of Colum-
bus arriving in Cuba. Just beyond that is a marble
staircase. The rooms are small (minuscule actually),
but they have old-fashioned furniture too, so it looks
like it should. The tiled floors brighten the rooms and
the bathrooms are tiled too. Breakfast, included in the
price, is served as a buffet in the main patio area.

Plaza Hotel, Calle Van Horne #1 between Ave
República and Avellaneda, ☎ 32/8-2413, $$, has 29
rooms in a freshly painted colonial building close to
the old train station. The moderately-sized rooms
have private baths with hot water all day, air conditioning, mini-bars and soft beds.

Gran Hotel, Calle Maceo #64, between Ignacio
Agramonte and Calle Gómez, ☎ 32/9-2093, $$$, was
for the longest time the best hotel in town, but the
Colón is now giving it some competition. Rooms here
are larger than at the Colón, and are set around a cen-
tral courtyard complete with an attractive fountain.
They also have all the amenities common with better
hotels, including beautifully tiled floors and rich
décor. There is a lovely outdoor pool with a bar close
by and the dining room on the top floor is elegant.

Central Cuba

Casas Particulares

Casa One, Hospital #193, between Calle Martí and 20 de Mayo (no phone), close to Plaza del Carmen. This *casa* has clean, comfortable rooms and friendly owners. The location of this house is the biggest draw.

Casa Two, Calle Martí #424, between Barcelo and Plaza del Carmen (no phone), is another house in a good location. The rooms have air conditioning and a private bathroom for the two rooms.

Casa Lucy y Ivan, Calle Alegria #23, between Agramonte and Montera, ☎ 32/8-3701, has lovely rooms in an immaculately kept colonial house decorated with tons of valuable antiques. The place is quiet, but they charge far too much for their meals.

Caridad Garcia Valera, Oscar Primelles #310, between Bartolome Maso and Padre Alallo, ☎ 32/9-1554, is a house of musicians who treat their guests like family. There are two large, bright rooms with private bathrooms, comfortable beds and air conditioning. The garden is well tended and a delight to use. The friendly owners will get you another place if they are full. Meals can be arranged and you will at last get something delicious that is not chicken! This place comes highly recommended.

Manolo Banegas Misa, Independencia #2551 and Plaza Maceo, ☎ 32/9-4606, has three large rooms in an apartment building overlooking the main plaza. The place is full of antiques and the rooms are exquisitely decorated. The owner, Manolo, and his brother, Hector, are both friendly, although neither speaks English.

■ Places to Eat

The best places to eat are usually in your hotel or *casa,* and this is especially true in Camagüey. It is difficult to find a really good restaurant.

Gran Hotel Snack Bar, Calle Maceo #64, between Ignacio Agramonte and Calle Gómez, is excellent and cheap and a great competition to some overpriced casas. A good burger and fries will run about $2.50 and fried eggs with bacon, toast and potatoes is about $1.25.

Campaña de Toledo, Calle San Juan de Dios #18, between Ramón Pinto and Pedro Olallo, on Plaza San Juan de Dios, has an uncommon house specialty: beef stuffed with ham. It costs $10, and a beer costs another convertible peso. It is so good to have something different. The terrace in the back is an excellent place to sit and enjoy an afternoon refreshment.

La Barra Impacto, Calle República #358, ☎ 32/8-6339, serves snacks and is often patronized by locals. This is a good sign. However, I did not eat here.

Las Ruinas, Calle Independencia and Hermanos Agüero, by Plaza Maceo (no phone), serves burgers and sandwiches for about $3 a meal.

Nan King, Calle República #222, ☎ 32/9-5455, serves Chinese dishes that are a great relief from the standard fare. The food is not the best Chinese food I've ever tasted, but a full meal shouldn't cost more than $5 per person.

Paladar de los Tres Reyes, Calle San Juan de Dios #18, ☎ 32/229-5888, serves great local cuisine. Chicken anyone? This restaurant is next door to the Campaña de Toledo and has food that is equally as good, but the atmosphere is not as nice.

■ Nightlife

The bar in **Hotel Camagüey**, Carretera Central, Km 4.5, suburb of Jayamá, ☎ 32/8-7267, is one of the best places to whoop it up while in town. The disco/bar usually starts to swing around 9 pm and goes until 2 am.

1920 Piano Bar, Gran Hotel, Calle Maceo #64, between Ignacio Agramonte and Calle Gómez, is a seedy little place with a piano, dim lighting and cheap drinks. It is quiet.

Gallery Colonial, Calle República #472, between San José and San Martín, in the Colonial Hotel, is a quiet little piano bar that has nightly entertainment.

Saturday nights along the streets are where you can get authentic Cuban nightlife. Walk anywhere in the downtown area. You will hear music, take in the aroma of food cooking, and see people dancing and having fun. They will welcome you to join them.

■ Shopping

 Gallery of Iana Sanchez and Joel Jover, Calle Martí #154 between Ave Independencia and Cisneros, ☎ 32/229-2305, is an art studio that sells the works of many local artists. However, it is the owners who have some incredible pieces. Joel studied photography at the university and sells his photos. His wife, Iana, does contemporary painting. She has been painting for 25 years and has had work displayed in numerous countries, including France. Just going into the gallery with its stained glass windows and collection of religious statues is worth the time.

Southeast Cuba

Provinces of Holguin, Las Tunas & Guantanamao

L as Tunas is a quiet farming district. There are places to stay, places to eat, but this is not a tourist area and the Cubans here have not been affected by tourism like those in Havana, Varadero or Santiago. Las Tunas town is pretty and your stay here will most likely be pleasant. Moving away from the capital city, you will find sugarcane fields, cattle farms and virgin beaches, some with just one hotel on them.

Las Tunas

■ History

The village of Las Tunas was established in 1759, but it wasn't until the last half of the 1800s that people started moving here in large numbers. Originally, the town was called Victoria de las Tunas. No one was interested in using such a huge handle, so they started calling it Las Tunas.

■ Services

Post office, Parque Vicente Garcia #6, is open 9 am to 6 pm, Monday to Saturday.

Telephone Office, Guardia off Parque Vicente Garcia, has one computer hooked to Internet.

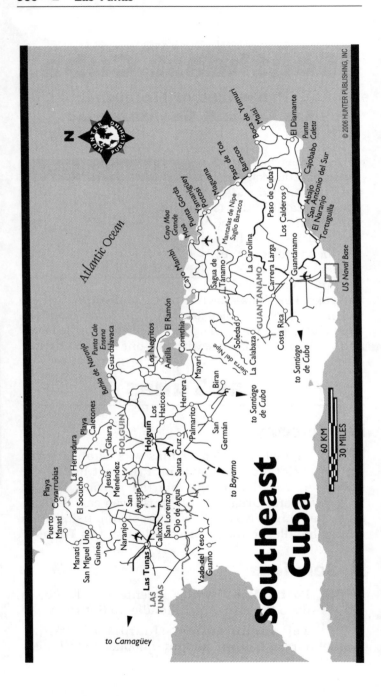

© 2006 HUNTER PUBLISHING, INC.

Che Guevara Hospital, Ave CJ Finlay and 2 de Diciembre on the road toward Holguin, ☎ 31/4-5012.

■ Festivals

Festival de Decima Cucalambeana takes place at the end of June or beginning of July. It hosts a competition where poets from many different countries, including places like Germany and Peru, come to read their work. Competitors start by swearing their allegiance to the former Decima King and poet, Juan Cristóbal Napoles Fajardo or El Cucalambre. They then recite an original 10-line stanza, which they have created. Adolfo Alfonso is the current honored winner of the contest. After the competitions, there is a traditional festival with music, dancing, food and plenty of booze.

■ Sightseeing

Museo Provincial, Ave General Vicente Garcia and Calle Franciso Varona, ☎ 31/4-8201, is open daily except Monday from 10 am to 7 pm. There is a $1 entry fee. I did not have time to visit this museum.

■ Adventures on Water

Beaches

There are 35 beaches along the 265 km/165 miles of coastline in this province. Most of them are undeveloped.

Villa Covarrubias Beach Resort, Playa Covarrubias, ☎ 31/4-6231, $$$$, part of the Gran Caribe chain, on the northern shore of the province, is an all-inclusive. It has a number of two-story cabins located either on the beach or around the pool. The cabins have porches and the colors are stereotypically Caribbean; bright pinks, blues, and yellows. The large rooms

have bathrooms with hot water, cable TVs, air conditioning and mini-bars. The hotel has volleyball courts,
tennis courts and pool tables. You can swim, walk
along the beach or get one of their famous mud baths.
If that doesn't cure your ailments, try some acupuncture. You can go for a pedal-boat ride or snorkel for a
few hours, get sun burned and then require the mud
bath or the acupuncture for pain relief. Dance lessons
and introductory Spanish lessons are offered, all included in the price of your stay.

A six-km/four-mile **coral reef** is the longest continuous stretch of reef near the island, just 1.5 km/one
mile from shore. More interesting than the reef is
Laguna Real, a pink-water lake that is home to many
birds, including the pink flamingo that actually gets
its color from the organism living in the water.

Nightly entertainment can be found at a disco located
on a man-made island near the resort. You know how
sound travels over water! Or you can go into Puerto
Padre by cab (26 km/16 miles) for a quieter visit to the
bars and restaurants. The taxi will cost $15 each way.

Although this is an isolated resort, you should know
that they are #1 for returnees of the 85 hotels belonging to the Gran Caribe chain. That is just about all the
recommendation you need if you are looking for this
type of vacation. It is a "Garden of Eden" with or without the mud baths.

■ Adventures on Wheels

The village of **Puerto Padre** holds little for the
tourist except a change of pace from the
beach. One of the largest sugar mills in the
country was built near here in 1860, but the town
wasn't founded until 1869. It became important for its
strategic position during some of the significant battles of the Ten Years War for independence from
Spain. There are claims that the town's name was on

maps as early as the 16th century, but this doesn't agree with the town's founding date.

Emiliano Salvador, a musician, pianist, and composer was from this village. He died in 1992 at the age of 41. He was a famous jazz musician who played Afro-Cuban music. His CD, which is for sale in the village, features a song called *Puerto Padre*. The CD makes a unique souvenir.

El Fuerte de la Loma, Calle 25 de Diciembre in Puerto Padre, was built by the Spanish to hold off the Cuban army (mambises) fighting for independence. It sits on a hill that rises about 35 meters/100 feet above the town. The fort is open daily except Monday, 10 am to 4 pm.

To get here you must travel 50 km/33 miles north from Holguin or 25 km/16 miles south from the beaches. The cost of a taxi should not be more than $15 convertibles, each way.

A **monument** to Juan José Napoles Fajardo, or El Cucalambe as he was commonly called, is in the town plaza. He was a poet who cultivated the *espinela* (the 10-line stanza), which has since been accepted as one of the more disciplined poetical styles and one that is often emulated by other Cubans. Below is Fajardo's most famous stanza.

> *Oh, come to Las Tunas*
> *My fellow countrymen.*
> *Here the swallows fly at dawn*
> *Over the lagoons.*
> *Come to listen to the notes*
> *Of my crude song, and with my lyre,*
> *In the blossoming plains,*
> *Say how fortunate is he*
> *Who witnesses the return of the sun.*

Fajardo was born in Las Tunas in 1829, the son of a sugar baron from El Cornito. His father and one of his brothers were also scribes; the brother was a poet. El

Cucalambre wrote plays, too, the most famous of which, *Consequences of a Misdeed*, has a moral message. El Cucalambre left for Santiago de Cuba in 1861 to write, and mysteriously disappeared.

■ Places to Stay

Hotels

 Hotel Las Tunas, Ave 2 de Diciembre, ☎ 31/4-5014, $$, is located on a hill overlooking the town. It is a huge, 1960s-styled hotel complete with swimming pool and game arcade. All rooms have private bathrooms, air conditioning and TVs. Rates include breakfast. This is the only hotel in town taking foreigners at present.

PRICE CHART
Per room for two people, per day.
$ . . . . $25-$50
$$ . . . . $51-$75
$$$ . . . . . $76-$100
$$$$ . . . $101-$150
$$$$$ . . Over $150

Casas Particulares

Casa Rodrigo y Yosi, Ave Coronel Reyes #41 and Gonzalo de Quesada, ☎ 31/4-1153, has one large and clean room with air conditioning and hot water. Meals are available and I recommend you take up this offer as I couldn't find one restaurant worthy of a recommendation.

Roberto Rabert, Calle Joaquin Agüero #124, between 13 de Octobre and 24 de Febrero (no phone), also has one room with air conditioning and private bath. I liked staying here.

Holguin

I first stopped at Holguin (the city located in the province of the same name) to break up the trip between Santiago and Havana. I soon learned that the city had lots to offer, so I stayed longer than just overnight.

The cobblestone plaza is a great place to enjoy a beer. During my visit, there were no *jinateros*, the climate was warm and tempered by trade winds, and the city appeared to be clean. As I started talking with people, I learned that there are mountains with caves, 34 rivers altogether and six waterfalls (one of which, Guayabo, is the largest in Cuba). Beach- and sun-lovers also get what they want here, as some of the biggest luxury resorts in the country are located near the city. As a bonus, the people are cooperative and ready to share their city and province with foreigners.

■ History

 Christopher Columbus landed in Gibara along the coast near Holguin and declared that it was the most beautiful land ever seen by human eyes. Obviously, the indigenous people thought this too because there is evidence of their presence for about 10,000 years. After the Spanish arrived, the first Indian rebellion, headed by a Taino Indian chief named Hatuey, ended in disaster for the Indians. Hatuey was born on the island of Hispañola and made Cuba his home as an adult. He hated the Spanish because of what they had done to his home country, so when they started moving through Cuba, Hatuey tried to discourage them. He used a unique method of warfare, one that was unknown to the Spanish. Hatuey would attack and then retreat to the hills. When least expected, he would attack and retreat again. However, the Spanish had superior weapons and eventually captured Hatuey and put him to the stake. Hatuey's followers were then subdued. Before he was set afire, a priest offered Hatuey his life if he took the Christian god as his own, but Hatuey couldn't swear allegiance to a god who allowed the Indians to suffer. He died a hero to his own people and is the first martyr to give his life for Cuba's independence.

By 1863 Holguin had become a large farming province with 76 sugar mills and 750 tobacco plantations. From this, the population grew to 228,000 today.

■ Getting Here & Around

 BY BUS: Buses that go from Trinidad to Santiago de Cuba stop in Sancti Spíritus, Ciego de Avila, Camagüey, Las Tunas, Holguin, and Bayamo. The bus leaves Trinidad at 8:15 am, Sancti Spíritus at 9:45 am, Ciego de Avila at 11:15 am, Camagüey at 1:50 pm, Las Tunas at 3:50 pm, Holguin at 5:05 pm, and Bayamo at 6:25 pm.

Buses go from Santiago de Cuba to Trinidad with stops in Sancti Spíritus, Ciego de Avila, Camagüey, Las Tunas, Holguin and Bayamo. They leave Santiago de Cuba at 7:30 pm, Bayamo at 9:40 pm, Holguin at 11 pm, Las Tunas at 12:15 am, Camagüey at 2:15 am, Ciego de Avila at 4:15 am, Sancti Spíritus at 5:35 am and arrive in Trinidad at 7 am.

The cost from Trinidad to Sancti Spíritus is $6, Ciego de Avila is $9, Camagüey is $15, Las Tunas is $22, Holguin and Bayamo is $26, Santiago de Cuba is $33.

BY TAXI: There are taxis in town, but if you telephone for one, you will wait a long time. It is best to hail a cab when you see one.

BY HORSE & CART: Horses and carts are available for travel within the town. The cost from the center to the bus station is $5.

■ Services

Post office, Calle Maceo #114 on Parque Cespedes, is open from 8 am to 6 pm daily except Sunday.

Telephone, ETECSA, Calle Martí #122 between Ave Gómez and Martires, ☎ 24/6-1102, is open daily from 8 am to 9 pm. Internet service is available.

Medical service can be found at **Hospital Lenin**, Ave Lenin, ☎ 24/2-5302.

■ Festivals

Romarius is the biggest celebration in Holguin. The festival has occurred every May 3 since 1950. During this celebration, locals raise the city flag on Loma de la Cruz (Hill of the Cross), location of the Ax of Holguin. The axe was found at the archeological site in Banes where the first island Indians are believed to have lived. It has become the symbol of the city because of its suggestion of rebellion.

■ Sightseeing

Plaza Calixto Garcia, has an art deco theater, an art gallery, the Museo Provincial and the cathedral around its perimeter. A statue of Garcia himself graces its center. Garcia's grandfather was the first in the family to choose a military life. He fought with the Spanish at the Battle of Carabobo in Venezuela in 1821. He changed allegiance and became aligned with those who wanted reforms for Cuba. One of their goals was to achieve freedom for slaves. For this, he was imprisoned. The younger Garcia followed his grandfather's desire for fairness and freedom and fought against the Spanish from 1868 to 1898. After the war he moved to Washington, where he died of natural causes at the age of 59. He was buried in Arlington National Cemetery.

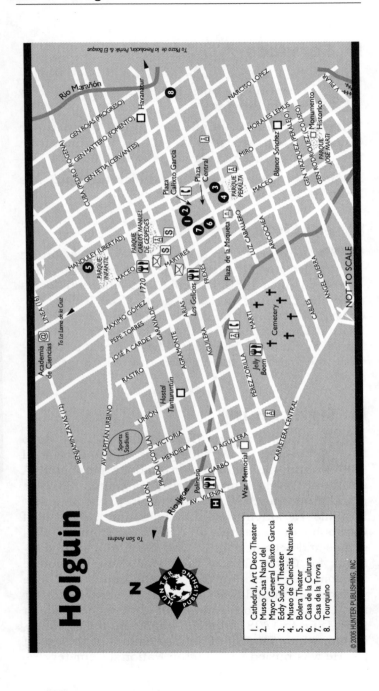

Holguin

To Plaza de la Revolución, Pernik & El Bosque

Río Marañón

Havanatur

GEN ROJAS (PROGRESO)

GEN MATTERO (FOMENTO)

GEN FETIA (CERVANTES)

CUBA (PEDRO ROGENA)

MANDULEY (LIBERTAD)

NARCISO LOPEZ

Plaza
Calixto García

Plaza
Central

MORALES LEMUS

PARQUE
PERALTA

MIRO

MACEO

Blanca Sánchez

GEN VÁZQUEZ (PERALEJO)

GEN RODRÍGUEZ (COLISEO)

PARQUE
JOSÉ MARTÍ

Monumento
Historico

Y PILAR

PARQUE
CARLOS MANUEL
DE CÉSPEDES

Plaza de la Maqueta

LUZ CABALLERO

ARICOCHEA

MARTIRES

FREXES

Academia
de Ciencias

LINEA (16)

To La Loma de la Cruz

PARQUE
INFANTIL

MAXIMO GOMEZ

PEPE TORRES

JOSÉ A CARDET

1720

MACEO

Los Gallcias

ARIAS

AGUILERA

ANGEL GUERRA

CABLES

NOT TO SCALE

RASTRO

GARAYALDE

AGRAMONTE

MARTÍ

Cemetery

BENJAMIN ZAYAS (12)

Hostal
Tunturuntún

PEREZ ZORILLA

Jelly
Boom

AV CAPITÁN URBINO

UNION

Sports
Stadium

PRADO (COYULA)

VICTORIA

MENDIELA

D AGUILERA

War Memorial

CARRETERA CENTRAL

COLON

Río Jigoe

GARBO

AV. VILENIN

Polimiesio

To San Andres

N

HUNTER PUBLISHING

© 2006 HUNTER PUBLISHING, INC.

1. Cathedral, Art Deco Theater
2. Museo Casa Natal del
   Mayor General Calixto García
3. Eddy Suñol Theater
4. Museo de Ciencias Naturales
5. Bolera Theater
6. Casa de la Cultura
7. Casa de la Trova
8. Tourquino

Eddy Suñol Theatre, Calle Martí #123, between Ave Libertad and Calle Maceo (no phone), is the home of the **Rodrigo Pratts Opera Company**. Check at the hotel tour offices to see if there is anything playing while you're here. If not, visit the building anyway for the pleasure of seeing its beautiful design.

Provincial Museum of History, Calle Frexes #198, between Calle Manduley and Maceo, ☎ 24/6-3395, was nicknamed the Periquera (bird cage), but was originally and officially named after the colors of the uniforms worn by the colonial soldiers stationed here when Spain was in power. The museum contains many archeological items, including an axe carved with the face of an Indian idol. There are
also, of lesser inter-
est, numerous histor-
ical documents,
weapons and items
from the many wars of
independence. The
museum is open
Monday to Saturday,
noon to 7 pm. There is a $1 entrance fee.

Carlos de la Torre Natural History Museum, Calle Maceo #129, between Ave Martí and Luz Caballero, ☎ 24/2-3935, has a large collection of stuffed birds and animals. One of the most important is the royal woodpecker, almost extinct today although there are rumors of one family living somewhere in the Sierra Maestras. There is also the carcass of a manatee stuffed for posterity. These creatures were hunted unmercifully for centuries and used as food because it was easy to lure them near the boat and kill them. Today around Belize, the population is again rising. This museum is open from Tuesday to Saturday, 8 am to 6 pm, and Sundays until noon. There is a $1 entrance fee.

THE MANATEE

The manatee, or sea cow, is a favorite attraction for tourists. This gentle aquatic animal weighs about 180 kg/400 lbs and is two meters/seven feet long, although some large males have been known to weigh 680 kg/1,500 lbs. The 11 teeth on the manatee's bottom jaw rotate. As the front two wear out, they drop off and the entire row moves forward. In the space where the very back molars were located, a new set develops.

Now protected, the manatee was hunted as food for centuries. Apparently, its meat is deep red and quite rich. People used to consider this animal a fish, so it was eaten by Christians on Fridays and during Lent. It has since been learned that they are mammals.

Mausoleum and Forest of the Heroes, Ave Aniversario de la Victoria, ☎ 24/2-5578, has a mausoleum with a frieze on it that depicts the struggle of the Cuban people. In the forest section of the park monuments have been erected in memory of those who lost their lives during the bloody Easter battle of the revolution. These include Lucia Iñguez and Jesus Menendez.

■ Adventures on Foot

Loma de Cruz has a paved walkway leading to 450 stone steps. These go to the top of the hill where you will find a spectacular view of the city, the surrounding green countryside, and the El Jigue and El Marañon rivers. On the way up are some benches and viewpoints. The top is crowned with a roundhouse featuring four different gateways symbolizing the original Christian cross raised on this hill on May 3, 1790. That cross could be seen from all four approaches to Holguin. Now, each May 3, the flag of Holguin, which has the image of the ax found at the burial site in Banes, is raised here. This event is accompanied with celebrations of drinking, dancing, and music.

■ Places to Stay

Hotels

Pernik Hotel, Ave Jorge Dimitrov and Calle Aniversario, ☎ 24/8-1011, $$, on the plaza, has over 200 rooms in a 10-storey building with elevators that work. The rooms are small but adequate, with air conditioning, private baths, cable

PRICE CHART
Per room for two people, per day.
$. $25-50
$$. $51-75
$$$. $76-100
$$$$. $101-150
$$$$$. . . . . over $150

TVs and carpeted floors (not so good). The price of the room includes breakfast. (If you are leaving early to catch the bus to Havana, they will be upset if you don't eat – make certain you get up early enough to enjoy their breakfast offering.) The Internet service is excellent, with four fast machines, $6 an hour.

Mirador de Mayabe, Km 8 from Holguin, on Mayabe Hill, ☎ 24/2-2160, $$, is famous for its Burrito named Pancho, who likes a few *chicharrones* (pork rinds) with his beer. He brays loudly if ignored. A shuttle bus makes the run up the hill (1.5 km/one mile) for $1. There's a restaurant, bar and pool and the views here are as good as from Loma de Cruz. Rooms have the usual amenities that come with a three-star hotel in Cuba – nothing special, but clean and comfortable. This is a cozy little place with just two-dozen rooms.

Villa El Bosque, Ave Jorge Dimitrov and Calle 9, in the Pedro Diaz Cuello district, ☎ 24/8-1012, $$/$$$, is a bit farther from the center than the Pernik. It has a pool and a well-tended garden. The rooms have air conditioning, private baths, cable TVs and mini-bars.

There is a restaurant and the bar by the pool comes recommended.

Casas Particulares

Juan Figueiras, Calle Narciso Lopez #81, between Agramonte and Garayalde, ☎ 24/2-4585, has two bedrooms with private bathroom and a private entrance. The place is clean and comfortable, but meals are not available.

Casa Lilita, Agramonte #108 Altos, between Calle Fomento and Cervantes, ☎ 24/2-2649, has a plain, clean room with a private bath. There is a fan as well as air conditioning. Guests can use the dining room and patio, and meals can be arranged.

Aimee Leyva Torres, Calle Cuba #145, between Ave Fomento and Progreso, ☎ 24/2-2842, is just four blocks from the central plaza. There is one room with air conditioning, private bath and private entrance. Guests have use of the kitchen and fridge, and parking is available. This is a comfortable, classy place that convenient and safe.

Luis Borrego Mas, Calle Cervantes #205, between Arias and Agramonte, ☎ 24/2-2062, is just five blocks from the center. It comes highly recommended by a Canadian friend of mine, who says there is a private entrance, air conditioning, and a shower with tons of hot water. The owners are hospitable and will do everything in their power to make your stay enjoyable.

Guardalavaca

Guardalavaca has one of the most famous beaches in Cuba. It offers visitors coral reefs and mountains with steep cliffs as a backdrop. Thick jungle vegetation, housing many birds, covers the mountains. The beaches are covered with crushed shells. Guardalavaca is not far from Gibara, the place where Colón first landed in Cuba.

The drive from Guardalavaca to Banes, where the country's most important archeological site is located, is the most scenic in the province. If you wish to stay in a *casa*, you will have to stay in Holguin, as the government has forbidden any *casas* to open near the all-inclusive resorts.

■ Sightseeing

 Museum Indocubano Bani, Calle General Marrero #305, between Calle Cespedes and Martí, Banes, ☎ 24/8-2487, is the best museum in the province. It contains many Indo-Cuban artifacts, labeled and well organized. Among the thousands of pieces is a Mesoamerican sculptured gold piece – its body is that of a female, with huge ears, a thick nose and thick lips. In another room is a skull with a hole in it. No one knows for certain what caused the hole. The museum is open daily from Tuesday to Saturday, 9 am to 5 pm and Sundays until 1 pm. The $3 fee includes entrance to the archeological site (see below).

While in Banes, you should see the archeological site at Chorro de Maita on Cerro de Yaguajay, where the museum pieces were found. This is the most important and largest aboriginal archeological site in Cuba. Late last century, an aboriginal cemetery was discovered with 108 human bodies, some with their arms crossed over their chests indicating European influence. To substantiate this, skeleton #57 turned out to be a male Caucasian, buried around 1500, about the time the first Europeans arrived. The gold piece at the museum was found here. The reconstruction of an Indian village complete with burial site is on display. The site is open daily from Tuesday to Saturday, 9 am to 5 pm and Sundays until 1 pm.

■ Adventures on Foot

Las Guanas Path hiking/nature trail at the west end of Esmeralda Beach takes about an hour and a half to complete. Snails, crabs and lizards crawl beside clay reproductions of Indians in traditional costume (mostly naked). The trail is 1. 5 km/one mile walkway. The best part is the cave at the trail's end, which features some early paintings. Getting into the cave is a bit of a challenge, as the steps and entrance platform are made of thin, wobbly sticks lashed together, and they wobble when you walk on them. But it is safe enough if you have good walking shoes.

Punta Lucrecia Lighthouse is close to Banes at the eastern end of Playa Largo between the Port of Naranjo and the Bay of Nipe. Construction was started in 1861. Its purpose was to help ships navigate through dangerous waters that were so booby-trapped with coral reefs that even small vessels had a hard time passing. The building was started when Francisco Serrano Dominguez became Cuba's governor. The lighthouse was called "Serrano," but because Cubans have always frowned upon buildings being named after politicians, the Royal Order of Cuba changed the name back to it original, Punta Lucrecia.

Inside the conical building, the first 33 stone steps (up to 121 meters/400 feet) were constructed by prisoners. The remaining steps are made of cast iron; they lead to the light room where a modern light now beams 60 km/42 miles out to sea, flashing every five seconds. Inside the keeper's quarters is a small museum where documents, photos and pieces of equipment used in construction are on display.

The lighthouse was attacked by independence fighters who destroyed the light, so that the Spanish navy couldn't see to navigate.

■ Adventures in Nature

Cayo Saetia, Bay of Nipe, is a 42-square-km/16-square-mile island where the largest wild animals in the country can be found roaming freely throughout thick jungle vegetation. A vast array of buffalo, antelope, deer, ostrich, peacocks, zebras and wild hogs can be hunted with a camera. Hunting with a rifle was permitted at one time as the area was originally a private game reserve, but this has changed. One side of the island features limestone cliffs that stand 25 meters/75 feet high and make a beautiful backdrop to the wildlife preserve.

Because 30% of Cuba's endemic plant species can be found here, together with hundreds of migratory birds, the area is under constant care.

> **AUTHOR NOTE:** Cayo Saetia is where Fidel and his brother Raul came for R&R during the heavy fighting days of the revolution.

A small hotel open for tourists has just 12 air-conditioned rooms with private baths. This is a lovely, quiet place, great for those who want isolation and wildlife in a tropical setting. There's a restaurant and bar, and Jeep or horse safaris can be arranged. To get to the hotel on your own is pretty hard as the road is almost impassable. However, Gaviota Tours in Guardalavaca, ☎ 24/2-5350, offer day tours that include some time snorkeling. They can also book rooms. The cost of a double room is in the $$$$ category.

■ Adventures on Water

Naranjo Bay Aquarium is a fenced-in ocean aquarium a few kilometers from the mainland, just west of Guardalavaca. Boat tours are offered by government tourist offices located in all the larger hotels. On a tour you will see a dolphin

Southeast Cuba

show plus, for extra bucks, be able to swim with them. For even more bucks, you can have your photo taken with a dolphin. Trying to horn in on the popularity of the dolphins is Vita, the sea lion who puts on a good show. This is a popular tour, especially for kids. It costs $75 per person.

Scuba Diving & Snorkeling

Eagle Ray Scuba Diving Center, ☎ 24/3-0185, located in the Guardalavaca Beach Hotels, will take you to the 22 sites close to town. All dive masters are ACUC certified, and the five instructors can take up to 30 divers per trip. Prices include all equipment except a wetsuit and night diving lights. The cost is $75 for a full day of diving (two tanks), $60 for a night dive, and $35 for a single daytime dive. Per-dive rates drop to $25.55 when 20 dives are booked and paid for. Dives go from five-40 meters/ 16-131 feet and feature reefs, sunken ships, caves, crags, vertical walls and tunnels.

POPULAR DIVE SITES
■ Tanques Azules (a series of flooded caves)
■ Jardin del Coral (coral garden)
■ Cueva Uno (first cave)
■ El Salto (waterfall)
■ Cañon de los Aguajíes (grouper canyon)
■ Pesquero de Esponjas (cage of sponges)

■ Places to Stay

Castro's goal in 1996 was to have 5,000 luxury rooms available in this area by 2003. He succeeded, and this is now the hottest destination in Cuba. Most hotels offer all-inclusive packages in their five-star accommodations. Trying to describe them is difficult, so I have put only a few details down for a few hotels. For the most part, you will have to make your booking through your travel agent. The Cuban workers might get frustrated and would probably refuse you entry if you showed up asking for a room. However, it has been done by a few persistent tourists with good Spanish and lots of patience.

All-Inclusives

Playa Pesquero, Guardalavaca Beach, www.cuba.tc/ playpesquero.html, $$$$, is a fairly new all-inclusive with rooms that have tiled floors, small foyers, sitting areas, queen-sized beds and balconies or patios. The entrance is decorated in Oriental style complete with a fishpond and soft lights. There are numerous restaurants and bars, plus an ice-cream parlor, beer garden, pool bar and snack bar. The usual array of fitness rooms, saunas, swimming pools and tennis courts are available. You can send your kids to toddler or teenage events (I like that service) organized by trained personnel. You also have the option of mountain biking, snorkeling, kayaking, or salsa dancing. Room service is 24 hours and costs $5 per service (it is not part of the all-inclusive price). This is a Gaviota Hotel. They can be contacted in Holguin, Carretera de Guardalavaca, Playa Estero Ciego, ☎ 24/3-0139.

Brisas Guardalavaca, Calle 2, Guardalavaca, ☎ 24/ 3-0218, $$$$, is an all-inclusive with huge rooms, air conditioning that works well, clean tiled floors and large bathrooms. There are two large pools and well-kept gardens that are full of butterflies, birds and lizards. The food is good, but not superb. There are buffet meals and small snack or grill bars where you can get foods such as pizza.

Club Amigo Atlantico, Banes, ☎ 24/3-0180, $$$, is a monstrosity with 750 standard rooms in bungalows interspersed around the resort. The bungalows are clean and have private baths, cable TVs, hairdryers, mini-bars and patios or balconies. The air conditioning has remote control! There are actually four sections to the resort. The Guardalavaca section is the oldest and the Villa section is the newest. Guests have access to all sections. All are well maintained, and each has its own pool, restaurants and bars. Especially nice was a little tea garden where tea is served all day. Massages cost about $25 for a complete pounding and $15 for a half-session. Tours are offered to other areas of the peninsula or to Havana.

Paradisus Rio de Oro, Playa Esmeralda, ☎ 24/3-0090, $$$$, specializes in weddings. They have a co-ordinator who handles details that you cannot, such as flowers, photos (with some free ones included), and videos of the ceremony if you wish. Wedding guests not staying at the hotel must pay for a day pass ($25).

Paradisus has numerous restaurants. **Restaurant El Patio** serves international dishes of set meals (you can't choose). They serve (for example) lobster on Monday, pork on Tuesday and veal done in a straw-berry sauce on Wednesday. **El Bohio** is a Cuban res-taurant that specializes in chicken, salad with prawns and, for dessert, fried bananas. **The Tsuru** is a Japa-nese restaurant where the chef cooks the food at your table. Tempura prawns and beef teriyaki are the rec-ommended dishes. **Mediterraneo** serves things such couscous and babaganush (eggplant with tons of gar-lic). There are also places where you can get pizza, pasta, sandwiches and more. The food is varied and delicious. The hotel in general is spacious and well or-ganized. Regardless of how heavily booked they are, you should never feel crowded.

Beach equipment, included in the price of your room, consists of snorkeling gear, pedal boats, and sun loungers. A large pool has different sections for volley-ball or aerobics; there is a separate children's pool. The Jacuzzis are on all day and a champagne bar is close by. Some may prefer the ocean to the pool as the ocean water is warmer. Both the beaches and the pool at Paradisus are surrounded with lounge chairs and gazebos. The beach isn't as nice as the one at Sol Club Rio de Luna/Mar.

Bicycles are available. A favorite activity is to have a massage in the glass-floored hut. While you are pounded, you can watch the ocean pound away beneath you. There are no standard rooms, just junior suites. These are huge, some are split into two levels.

Paradisus was the first hotel in Cuba to win the Holly Award given by the German Tour Operator, TUI, for the best 100 hotels in the world. This is a world-class, luxury hotel.

Sol Club Rio de Luna/Mar, Playa Esmeralda, ☎ 24/3-0030, $$$, is a huge complex with over 300 large double rooms plus a few junior suites. The buildings are in two sections – the Luna and the Mar, with the Mar being in better repair. If you can get a deal, go for it, but it is not worth the non-discounted price.

The restaurants serve good meals that include everything from pizzas and burgers to roast and ribs. Bars are interspersed around the property and getting a drink never seems to be a problem.

As for things to do, there is archery, volleyball, shooting, horseback riding, snorkeling, JetSkiing, tennis, miniature golf and basketball. The 10-acre garden has a swimming pool and a kids play area.

Gibara

This tiny colonial village, similar to Baracoa, is known as the White City of Crabs. It is the only city aside from Havana that has protective stone walls built around it. If you need a rest from the hubbub of bigger places, you may want to chill out here.

■ History

Gibarans claim that Columbus landed here (rather than in Baracoa). Whether that is true or not is hard to prove, but it is known that he was here for two weeks during a bad storm.

After colonization, the town was subject to many pirate attacks so, like Havana, the residents built a wall and the Bateria Fernando Septimo Fortress.

This tiny village gives claim to being the birthplace of G. Cabrera Infante, a film and literary critic who has lived in London for 30 years. His parents were on the founding committee of the Communist Party of Cuba.

■ Getting Here & Away

Road surfaces are horrid in this area but hopefully, by the time this book gets to print, they will have been resurfaced. Unless you fly in, hitching or hiking are your only options.

■ Festivals

At the end of June, Gibara hosts the **International Poor Cinema Festival**. The films are low in budget, but the event is high in spirit. The best two-dozen films entered in the festival are sent around the country for viewing. In 2006, 40 countries participated in this event.

■ Around Town

Loma de la Vigia, behind the village, can be climbed. Remains of the wall and fort are at one end of the town.

The **central park**, named after Calixto Garcia, was once the military parade grounds.

Museum of Natural History, Calle Independencia #23, ☎ 44/3-4222, is open Tuesday to Saturday, 9 am to 6 pm, with an hour off for lunch. It has stuffed critters and charges a dollar to enter.

■ Places to Stay

Casa Particular

Juan Provenza, Calle Aguera #96, between Ave Cespedes and Mora, has one room. The place is clean and has a garden for guests to use. If Juan is full, he will direct you to other places.

Guantanamo

You are not permitted near the prison owned by the Americans, so don't even think about it. You'd never get past the security and, even if you did, you'd be in sorry shape by the time you got out. However, for the curious, there is a lookout point in the city that offers views of the prison seven miles away.

Guantanamo itself is a large bustling city by Cuban standards, but it doesn't hold much for the visitor. However Baracoa, a picturesque colonial town with beaches and hiking, is just an hour away. There are beaches and a good park where hiking is made interesting by the impressive wildlife.

■ History

The most interesting history occurred after Cuba gained independence. As part of the agreement, the US retains a lease on Guantanamo Naval Base, built in 1903, at a cost of $2,000 per year. It covers just under 30,000 acres, or 45 square miles, of land and includes water up to three miles from shore. The original lease stated that the land was to be used only as a naval base and for coaling (refueling). A supplemental agreement signed by Theodore Roosevelt later that year said the US would pay Cuba $2,000 in gold yearly for use of the land and that lawbreakers would be turned over to their respective governments. The US agreed that Cuban vessels would be granted permission (for no charge) to use the bay and harbor.

In 1934 the treaty was again amended and signed, giving the US a perpetual lease on the land. The agreement could be cancelled only by mutual agreement.

With World War II the terms of the agreement were again modified. The bay was to be used only as a "Naval Defensive Sea Area" and a "Naval Air Space Reservation." This means that all commercial shipping and air traffic was barred except vessels engaged in Cuban trade. The base flourished. The US built a water reservoir and buildings for government operations.

After the revolution, Castro denounced the treaty on the grounds that Cuba had been coerced into signing. The logic, as far as Castro is concerned, falls under article 52 of the Vienna Convention on Law of Treaties that states treaties are invalid if threats are used. The Cubans claim that the US would not leave Cuba unless the US got the leased land. The US claims that the older agreement has little to do with the later agreement signed after WW II. The latest dispute between the US and Cuba over Guantanamo is the use of the land to hold prisoners. Recently, the Bush administration gave contractor Halliburton $30 million to build another detention facility and to secure the perimeter of the base over 500 prisoners, mostly Afghanistan. The UN published a report requesting the US to close the facility.

The most interesting part of this legal quagmire is that Guantanamo prisoners are entitled to all the legal privileges of the US court system. This was tested in the American Supreme Court and upheld. However, prisoners captured from non-US soil (Afghanistan) can only be classified as prisoners of war. If they are not so classified, they are considered kidnapped. This means they are being held illegally.

Human rights abuses have been reported by Amnesty International. Three British and one Swede, who were detained for three years each, made public statements attesting to the tortures. One man, Mr Begg, in his first interview after his release, claimed that "I witnessed two people get beaten so badly that I believe it caused their deaths."

This saga will continue.

■ Getting Here & Around

 BY BUS: Buses are infrequent. They go from Santiago de Cuba to Baracoa with a stop in Guantanamo, leaving at 7:45 am and arriving at 12:35 pm.

Buses from Baracoa to Santiago de Cuba leave at 2:15 pm and arrive in Santiago de Cuba at 5 pm.

The fare is $15 between Santiago de Cuba and Baracoa, $6 to Gunatanamo from Santiago de Cuba.

BY TAXI: Once in Guantanamo or Baracoa, take a taxi or cyclo-taxi as the bus stations are a long way from the center.

BY AIR: There are five flights a week to Guantanamo. They leave Havana on Sunday, Monday, Wednesday, Friday and Saturday. Check for times with the tour desk at your hotel. There is a public bus from the airport to the town center.

■ Services

International Hospital, Carretera de El Salvador, ☎ 21/235-5450, in front of Hotel Guantanamo, is open 24 hours a day. Some English is spoken.

ETECSA office, Calle 15 Norte and Ave Ahogados, is open from 8 am to 10 pm daily. It has one machine offering Internet access at a cost of $6 per hour. There is a second office at Calle Aguilera between Los Maceos and Calixto Garcia. It has the same operating hours.

Post Office, Calle Pedro A Perez on Parque Martí, is open Monday to Saturday, from 8 am to 6 pm with an hour off at lunch.

Immigration, Calle 1 Oeste between Ave 14 and 15 Norte, is open Monday to Friday, 9 am to 4 pm, with two hours off at noon for lunch.

Southeast Cuba

■ Sightseeing

 Parque Martí is surrounded by the highly poisonous but beautiful laburnum trees, also called golden-chain trees, that come into full bloom in March. They have beautiful yellow flowers that produce a gray, furry seedpod. It is the seedpods and seeds that are most dangerous – their poison is enough to kill a child. The leaves and roots also contain some poison.

The cream-colored **Iglesia Santa Catalina de Ricci**, built in 1836, is at one end of the plaza. It was here that the area's first teacher gave lessons. The building was soon found to be too modest so, in 1847, it was expanded. Shortly after the expansion, the congregation grew to over 1,000 people.

In the center of the plaza is a monument of **General Pedro A Perez**, a friend of José Martí and Antonio Maceo, who helped keep Yatera trackers from working with the Spanish. There is also a bust dedicated to the mothers of the world. Both are carved from white marble. The bandstand in the plaza often has live music.

GUANTANAMERA

Guantanamera is the best-known/most-sung (by foreigners) song in Cuba. The lyrics are taken from a poem written by José Martí and adapted by Julian Orban. The music was written by Fernandez Dias.

Casa Natal de Regino Boti, Ave Bernabe Varona #815 between Ave José Martí and Pedro Agustin, is the birthplace of the poet of Guantanamo who died in the US in 1958 at the age of 80. The Instituto Cervantes of Spain dedicated the memorial to him. When he died, Boti was just becoming internationally famous for his poetry, historical essays and paintings. His best poems are collected in the anthology called *Visit of the Gods*, printed 127 years after his birth. There is a $2 fee to enter the house, which is open Tuesday to Friday, 10 am to 4 pm.

Mariana Grajales Square, Calle 11 between Ave 2 and 3 West, is a large plaza with gigantic granite pillars and posts that are a tribute to the heroes of the revolution. The piece is called the Monument to the Heroes. The square is a lovely place to sit.

Stone Zoo is 40 km/25 miles north of the city on the road going through El Salvador and to Sagua de Tanamo. The "zoo" has about 400 animal sculptures made by a local farmer, Angel Inigo Blanco. He sculpted these creatures from rocks in his fields. There are carvings of animals from around the world and their size is determined by the stone, rather than the animal. For an example, a giraffe is three feet high while a fox is seven feet high. The farm has trees and coffee plants with walking trails winding through. It is open from 9 am to 6 pm and costs $1. This park is considered eco-art at its finest.

■ Adventures on Wheels

Mirador de Malones is 30 km/19 miles from Baracoa, on the east side of the bay. A restaurant at the top of a hill here offers a distant view of the American Naval base with its 7,000 or so American servicemen, its own TV and radio stations, water desalination plant, medical building and recreational facilities. This is truly a tiny piece of America in Cuba. However, don't bother trying to get onto American soil. The Mirador has binoculars set up so you can see the base better – but it is seven kilometers away so you know that you won't see the hazel eyes of the Afghans in prison. There is a $5 charge to enter the viewing platform (the Cubans never miss a trick) and this includes a drink.

> **AUTHOR NOTE:** There are places to stay in Guantanamo, but I recommend you stay in Baracoa.

Baracoa

Baracoa, sitting on Honey Bay, was the first settlement in Cuba. Development of the townsite started in 1512 under the directorship of Diego Velazquez and has been continuous since then. Shadowed by the flat-topped and anvil-shaped Mount Yunque, the city sits between it and the El Toa river. Because of the lush vegetation, it is often called the City of Wood, Chocolate and Fruits.

■ Getting Here & Around

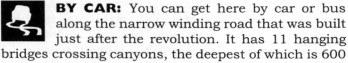

BY CAR: You can get here by car or bus along the narrow winding road that was built just after the revolution. It has 11 hanging bridges crossing canyons, the deepest of which is 600 meters/2,000 feet. It is one of the most beautiful roads in the country, but it is also one of the slowest.

BY BUS: Buses go from Santiago de Cuba to Baracoa with a stop in Guantanamo. It leaves at 7:45 am and arrives at 12:35 pm.

Buses from Baracoa to Santiago de Cuba leave at 2:15 pm and arrive in Santiago de Cuba at 5 pm.

The fare is $15 between Santiago de Cuba and Baracoa and $6 from Santiago de Cuba to Gunatanamo.

BY TAXI: Once in Guantanamo or Baracoa, I recommend taking a taxi or cyclo-taxi as the bus stations are a long way from the center.

■ Services

Medical, Calle Martí #427, ☎ 21/244-2162, is a clinic open 24 hours a day.

Post Office, Calle Maceo #286, is open from 9 am to 6 pm daily except Sunday.

ETECSA, Calle Maceo, next door to the post office, is open from 8 am to 10 pm daily.

■ Sightseeing

 Our Lady of Assumption Church, Ave Maceo #152, on the plaza, has one of the 29 wooden crosses left by Columbus during his first voyage. Called the Parra Cross, it is made from uvilla wood, a light and coarse wood. Uvilla is also known as the Amazon Grape Plant that grows up to 50 feet in height. The cross was constructed in Europe and is the only one left of the original 29. It got its name from the parra tree under which it sat. It stayed there for centuries but because fishers were taking pieces of the cross as good luck charms, priests placed it in a glass case beside the altar in their church. Carbon tests on the wood show that it was growing before 1492, but the scientists who tested the tree also said that it was grown in the Caribbean. The story may need some adjusting.

The **Municipal Museum** is in Fort Matachin on the southeast end of the malecón. The one-story building was constructed over 200 years ago of adobe brick and is now whitewashed to a glitter. It has thick walls, red-tiled roofs and cannons around the yards. Inside are some archeological exhibits found in the Baracoa area and other items relating to local history. The founder of the museum was Miguel Angel Castro Machado, a historian and ecologist who still lives in Baracoa. His book about the town, called *Baracoa: Where Cuba Begins*, is a 96-page production with 80 color plates of the author's paintings. The descriptions are mostly poems or quotations from other famous artists. It sells for $20 – quite a deal.

At **Finca Duaba**, six km/four miles on the Rio Toa Road, you can watch the making of chocolate, from the plant to the sweet stuff. The tour includes a Creole lunch and costs about $10 per person. The *finca*, or farm, is open Tuesday to Sunday, noon to 4 pm. Note the obelisk, which was placed at the farm by Antonio Maceo y Grajales, an activist for independence.

You can visit the farm only with the Cuban tour company. Often, a trip here is combined with a visit to Yumuri River. Rates are $25 per person for the two destinations. Book at Hostal La Habanera, at the Rumbos Office, ☎ 21/4-5155, rcubar@enet.cu.

Punta de Maisi, with a lighthouse that was built in 1861, sits at the very eastern point of Cuba. On the way, you will pass under the wedge of Mt Los Alemanes, a mountain that is split down the middle. The lighthouse is a cylindrical tower, 35 meters/115 feet high, with an automatic light flashing. You can climb the lighthouse (there is no charge for entering – yet) for an excellent view on a clear day.

The vegetation in this dry climate is called cactus scrub. The mountains protect the point from getting northern rains. Precipitation is usually 800 mm per year, most of which falls within one to two months. The average temperature is 16°C/61°F. These conditions are perfect for cactus scrub and this area offers the best example on the island. Here the cacti can grow up to six meters/20 feet in height.

■ Adventures in Nature

 Mount Yunque de Baracoa is about eight km/five miles west of the town center. This is a tropical rainforest. Mount Yunque is 590 meters/1,900 feet high and flat on top, except for an anvil-shaped hump. A marked trail takes about three hours to ascend and two to descend. The views en route are good. Vegetation includes banana trees, coconut trees and medicinal plants (ask your guide to point them out). There are also maiden ferns and some new fern species that have yet to be identified by scientists. To get to the trailhead, take a taxi to El Yunque Campismo, eight km/five miles from town on the road to Moa. Follow the marked trail. The entry fee is $20 if going on your own. If you hire a guide, it is $40. Go to Hostal La Habanera, to the Rumbos Office, ☎ 21/4-5155, rcubar@enet.cu, for information.

Alejandro Humboldt National Park is 40 km/25 miles northwest of Baracoa on the Bay of Taco. Named after the German scientist who crossed the island in 1800-1801, this park is one of the most interesting in the country, with fantastic plant species and interesting geological formations. Mangroves near the water are home to both endemic and migratory birds. Farther from shore are rocks that are toxic to plants, so some unique adaptions can be seen.

UNESCO AWARD

Many things are considered before an area is dedicated a UNESCO preserve. At Humboldt, one important fact was that 70% of the 1,302 spermatophytes (plants that produce seeds), from a total of 1,800-2,000 in the Western Hemisphere, are endemic to the park.

Geological formations are of karst, serpentine, peridotite and pseudokarst and the mountains hold a large number of endemic animals, both vertebrates and invertebrates.

ROCKY ROOTS

Serpentine rock is light green to black in color and is often mottled with lighter specs. Karst rock is made of limestone that has greater solubility than other rocks. Karst formations are usually associated with caves. Pseudokarst looks like karst but has far less solubility. (We, as laymen, cannot tell the difference.) Peridotite includes hard rock like granite. Diamonds from South Africa are formed in mica-rich peridotite.

You can hire an English-speaking guide at the park's information center to take you on one of three treks. The longest is five km/three miles and goes uphill to some caves (always a draw for me). The two-km/1.3-mile trek is not challenging but is the best place to see medicinal plants. A third includes a short walk and a trip around the bay by boat. Hikes cost $10-$15.

You can drive to the park or hire a Cuban tour company, located at Hostal La Habanera, to the Rumbos Office, ☎ 21/4-5155, rcubar@enet.cu.

■ Adventures on Water

Beaches

 Managua Beach, the most popular with tourists and locals, is 20 km/12 miles northwest of the city center. To get there, follow the road to Moa. It will cost about $25 for a taxi both ways, plus waiting time. Your other option is to rent a motorbike or hitch a ride; the second is not recommended. Motorbikes can be rented in town for about $25 a day.

There are many eateries along the beach, all of which will be playing local music. There is also a small hotel that can be booked from Hotel Porto Santo in Baracoa. Rooms cost about $50 for a double.

Rivers

Chuchillas del Toa park is 10 km/six miles northwest of Baracoa. A large park, it is home to the ivory-billed woodpecker that, until recently, was believed to be extinct. It also has the *solenodon*, the world's smallest frog, and Cuban land snails. There are over 900 species of plants here. The carnivorous dragon tree, almost extinct, is one. This tree can withstand long periods of drought, and it produces an edible fruit and the sap has medicinal properties. It is endangered because many birds that ate the seeds and passed them through their intestinal tract (necessary for germination) are also extinct.

You can take a whitewater rafting trip down the Tao River, the largest in Cuba, or a slower boat trip where you can get off and look at things. Go to Hostal La Habanera, to the Rumbos Office, ☎ 21/4-5155, rcubar@enet.cu, or visit the Parques Naturales de Baracoa office, Calle Martí #207, ☎ 21/4-3665, for more information.

The **Toa River** is big. It is located 10 km/six miles from the city center in the direction of Moa. You might find local women washing clothes in the river or having a quiet lunch beside it. The jungle vegetation is good for birders. Transportation for this trip, done through the tourist office, will cost about $10 each way. Go to Hostal La Habanera, to the Rumbos Office, ☎ 21/4-5155, rcubar@enet.cu, for more information.

The **Yumuri River** is 30 km/20 miles southeast of Baracoa on the eastern road to Maisi. This spectacular river should be explored by boat. It passes through a canyon with high walls covered in vines and thick vegetation. Swimming holes offer a chance for a refreshing dip. At the mouth of the river is a little village where meals are available. The area is known for its *jinateros*, so be aware. You could take a bus to this village and then a water taxi ($1) upstream to do some quiet birding or swimming. Go to Hostal La Habanera, to the Rumbos Office, ☎ 21/4-5155, rcubar@enet.cu, for more information if you do not want to travel on your own.

The **Miel River** can be reached on foot. Leave town and head toward Guantanamo; turn right at the service station. At the next junction, turn right again and continue along the malecón until you come to the statue of Christopher Columbus. Go down to the beach and walk east to the river's mouth. Follow the river upstream. This is a popular spot for locals on weekends as there are numerous swimming holes.

■ Places to Stay

Hotels

 El Castillo Hotel, Calle Calixto Garcia, ☎ 21/4-2125, $$, was once the Sanguily Fort. It is perched on a hill overlooking the bay. Sitting at the pool, you face the opposite direction, taking in El Yunque. The rooms have air conditioning, cable TVs, private baths, mini-bars and safe deposit boxes (cost extra if used). There is a pool, disco, restaurant, taxi service, laundry service and a games room. Motorcycles are available for rent. Working out of this hotel is the best guide in Baracoa. His name is Tony Mas Gamez and he can arrange a car or scooter rental, plus he can guide you on hiking/touring trips. This hotel is the most popular in town.

PRICE CHART
Per room for two people, per day.
$. $25-50
$$. $51-75
$$$. $76-100
$$$$. $101-150
$$$$$. . . . . over $150

Hotel Porto Santo, Airport Road, ☎ 21/4-5106, $$, is near the airport and overlooks a small unattractive beach. It is a ways from town so not very convenient, but it does have a decent pool. The rooms and bathrooms are tiny, but each room has a balcony, cable TV, air conditioning and mini-bar. There is a restaurant and a couple of bars (one is at the pool).

Casas Particulares

Marlin Noa Hernandez, Calle Ciro Frias #18 between Calle Martí and Maceo (no phone), has the best rooms in town. Each has a private bath and air conditioning. The food is delicious and the place is spotless. Recommended.

Ana Torres, Calle Calixto Garcia #162, between Ave Cespedes and Coroneles Galano, ☎ 21/4-2754, has two rooms with fans and private bathrooms. This is a clean place and it is recommended to eat all meals with her.

Birtha Barbon Matos, Reparto Paraiso #2, ☎ 21/4-3217, is on the edge of town and has a room with a fan and a private bath. Meals can be arranged. Breakfast is not included.

Edda and Alexis, Ave Flor Crombet #115, ☎ 21/4-3429, has a secure apartment with two large rooms, air conditioning and a private bath with a shower. Breakfasts are excellent, although not included in the price; dinners can be arranged.

Alex Gonzales, Ave Roberto Reyes #20, between Calle Martí and Maceo, ☎ 21/4-2175, has two rooms on the second floor with air conditioning. There is a large balcony. The bathroom is shared between the two rooms and guests have limited use of the kitchen. Meals can be arranged. Alex speaks English and is willing to help with your travel plans.

■ Places to Eat

Hotel Castillo Restaurant, Calle Calixto Garcia, ☎ 21/4-2125, offers food not usually found in Cuba. The owners come from the Haitian culture that influenced Cubans in culinary creations before the revolution. Their meals are from that culture. The fish with coconut milk (called *fufu*) is one of the recommended dishes. It costs $14 for a large meal.

BARACOA DELICACY

The delicacy of Baracoa is a sweet called *cucurucho*. It is made with coconut, sugar and guava or orange, wrapped in a banana leaf and eaten like ice cream. Sweet! Purchase some at Casa de Chocolate on Maximo Gómez Street.

Southeast Cuba

Paladar el Colonial, Calle Martí #123, has a lovely atmosphere and food to match. A meal will cost about $10 per person and beer is $1 per small bottle. I recommend the pork – mine was done to perfection.

■ Nightlife

 Saturday night in Baracoa is a must. There is dancing on the streets and everyone seems to enjoy a drop or two of rum while barbecuing pork. Locals bring their ghetto blasters and stereo speakers, and the conflicting songs seem to blend into one harmonious racket. The rum helps. I met one lady who ended up spending three months in Baracoa just because she loved the Saturday night entertainment.

Casa de la Trova, Ave Maceo #149 and Maximo Gómez, has nightly live entertainment, usually salsa that starts around 9 pm. There is a $2 cover charge.

La Terraza, Calle Maceo #120, is an open-air disco on the roof of the building. There is always live entertainment and you are expected to participate in dancing, drinking and laughing. The cover charge is $2 for ordinary nights and more when special bands play. Music usually starts at 9 pm and goes until long after midnight.

Southern Cuba

Provinces of Granma & Santiago de Cuba

Santiago de Cuba

Santiago de Cuba, known as the capital of the Caribbean, is almost a different country than the rest of Cuba. Al-

though the buildings are colonial, the people are happy and full of music. The Sierra Maestra Mountains separate the western and eastern areas like a border. The general atmosphere of the city is for those with time to enjoy life. The people, mostly descendants of the slave trade, will make you welcome if you have the same appreciation for life as they do.

There is plenty to do in and around Santiago. Just exploring the city could take you a week or more, without enjoying some of the nightlife (music is one of the main reasons people come to Santiago, so check out the *Nightlife* section, page 445). Those wanting adventure in music should spend their entire vacation either here or in Havana. Hiking in the mountains is the best in the country.

■ History

Diego Velazquez arrived at Baracoa, just a short way from Santiago de Cuba, in 1514, and colonization of the island began. Because the Spanish exterminated most of the local Indians, they had no laborers to work the coffee plantations and gold mines and load the boats, so the

Spanish imported slaves. Most were brought to the Santiago de Cuba region.

To protect themselves from the pirates that roamed the seas for the next few hundred years, Castillo de San Pedro de la Roca, commonly called **El Morro**, was built. The **Castillo de la Estrella** and **La Socapa** were added later, making it one of the strongest fortifications in the country.

There was resistance by the slaves but by 1818, after the English had captured Havana and been thrown out again, the Spanish encouraged more trade and development. They put down any discontent and also brought in more slaves. By the mid-1800s, the slaves could no longer take the "development." They rebelled and were brutally suppressed by the Spanish, causing more dissension, which led to more rebellions.

Finally in 1886, slavery was abolished, Chinese labor was no longer imported and by 1893 civil status for blacks and whites was proclaimed equal. That, of course, didn't happen. There is still discrimination against blacks in Cuba, although it is far more covert now that the communists have taken over.

As dissension in the country increased, men like José Martí, a writer, helped stir the people to revolt. He is buried in Santiago, in the Santa Ifigenia Cemetery.

From 1952 through to 1959, revolts in the mountains and eastern provinces resulted in communist control. The US opposed this, and in 1961 the famous Bay of Pigs battle took place. The communists took many prisoners, whom they traded later for aid money. Santiago de Cuba has always been, since the first slaves were mistreated, a place where rebellion brewed.

■ Getting Here & Around

BY AIR: Flights from Havana into Santiago's airport take one hour and cost $125 one way, which beats the 16-hour bus ride.

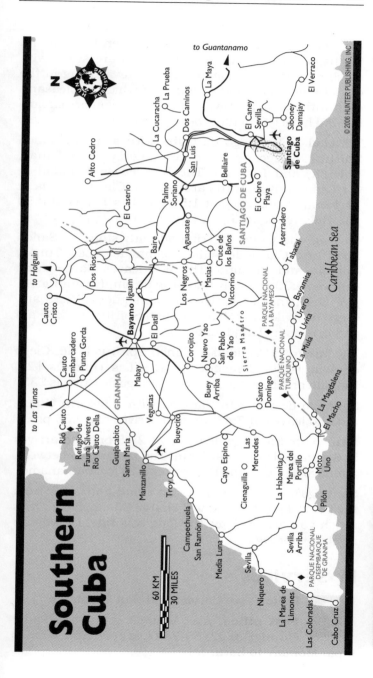

Southern Cuba

to Guantanamo

La Maya
La Prueba
El Caney
Sevilla
Siboney
Damajay
El Verraco
La Cucaracha
Dos Caminos
Santiago
de Cuba
Alto Cedro
La Maya
San Luis
Bellaire
El Cobre
Playa
El Caserio
Palmo
Soriano
SANTIAGO DE CUBA
Aserradero
Baire
Aguacate
Cruce de
los Baños
Tabacal
Dos Rios
Los Negros
Matias
Victorino
PARQUE NACIONAL
LA BAYAMESO
Bayamita
La Urrero
Cauto
Cristo
Bayamo
Jiguam
El Datil
Corojito
Nuevo Yao
San Pablo
de Yao
Sierra Maestro
PARQUE NACIONAL
TURQUINO
La Uvita
La Mula
Cauto
Embarcadero
Punta Gorda
Mabay
Buey
Arriba
Santo
Domingo
La Magdalena
Rio Cauto
GRANMA
Veguitas
Bueycito
La Macho
Refugio de
Fauna Silvestre
Rio Cauto Della
Guajacabito
Santa Maria
Cayo Espino
Las
Mercedes
Moto
Uno
Manzanillo
Troy
Cienaguilla
La Habanita
Marea del
Portillo
Pilón
Campechuela
San Ramón
Media Luna
Sevilla
Sevilla
Arriba
PARQUE NACIONAL
DESEMBARQUE
DE GRANMA
60 KM
30 MILES
Niquero
La Marea de
Limones
Las Coloradas
Cabo Cruz

to Holguin

to Las Tunas

Caribbean Sea

© 2006 HUNTER PUBLISHING, INC

BY BUS: It is 16 hours by bus between Havana and Santiago – a long, arduous trip. You are stuck with catching a very early morning bus or arriving in the city at a very late hour, neither of which is pleasant, even with a stop part-way. However, if you are exploring and have lots of time, below are the bus schedules:

Trinidad to Santiago de Cuba with stops in Sancti Spíritus, Ciego de Avila, Camagüey, Las Tunas, Holguin, and Bayamo. The bus leaves Trinidad at 8:15 am, Santi Spíritus at 9:45 am, Ciego de Avila at 11:15 am, Camagüey at 1:50 pm, Las Tunas at 3:50 pm, Holguin at 5:05 pm, Bayamo at 6:25 pm.

Santiago de Cuba to Trinidad with stops in Sancti Spoiritus, Ciego de Avila, Camagüey, Las Tunas, Holguin and Bayamo. The bus leaves Santiago de Cuba at 7:30 pm, Bayamo at 9:40 pm, Holguin at 11 pm, Las Tunas at 12:15 am, Camagüey at 2:15 am, Ciego de Avila at 4:15 am, Sancti Spíritus at 5:35 am and arrives in Trinidad at 7 am.

The fare from Trinidad to Sancti Spíritus is $6, Ciego de Avila is $9, Camagüey is $15, Las Tunas is $22, Holguin and Bayamo is $26, Santiago de Cuba is $33.

Santiago de Cuba to Baracoa with a stop in Guantanamo leaves at 7:45 am and arrives at 12:35 pm.

Baracoa to Santiago de Cuba at 2:15 pm and arrives in Santiago de Cuba at 5 pm. The fare is $15 between Santiago de Cuba and Baracoa and $6 to Guantanamo.

Santiago's bus station is about a half-hour walk from the central park. A taxi will charge $5, no matter how much you argue. After the long bus ride, I'd walk to stretch your legs.

■ Services

Police, Ave Corona and San Geronimo.

Post office, Ave Aguilera and Calle Padre Quiroga. ☎ 22/65-2397, is open from 8 am to 6 pm Monday to Saturday.

ETECSA, Calle Heredia #156 on Parque Cespedes, 7 am to 9 pm daily. There is **Internet** access ($5/hour) at Hotels Casa Granda and Santiago. The Libertad had the fastest machine and the Granda had the slowest.

Tourist Office, #5 Perez Carbo (Plaza de Marte), ☎ 22/62-3302.

Medical care is offered at the International Clinic Pharmacy, Ave Raul Pujol and Ave 10, Parque Ferreiro, ☎ 22/ 64-2589, and the Institute of Medical Sciences of Santiago de Cuba, Ave de las Americas and Calle J, ☎ 22/62-6679, part of the university.

> **AUTHOR NOTE:** Santiago de Cuba is reputed to be the wildest city for pickpockets and *jiniteros*. I found even yelling didn't get rid of them. One old man just yelled back at me! Carry cash in your money belt, and wear your daypack in front. Leave jewelry at home and stay out of crowds. If you put down your pack in a public place, place the shoulder strap around your ankle.

■ Festivals

Fiesta del Fuego, Casa del Caribe, Calle 13 and 8, Vista Alegre, ☎ 22/64-2285. Fire Festival organizers and the Ministry of Culture host this event every year in July, before Carnival. It honors an event, like the Bicentennial of Independence for Haiti (for the 2004 celebrations). After the opening speeches at Teatro Heredia, the celebrations take place in over 40 different venues. Organized events include dance and music performances by artists from around the world. Parades and street parties, that go on for the entire week, compel everyone to dress in bright Caribbean costumes. Bring your own drinking vessel – rum and beer flow as freely as the music and sensuality.

Music festivals occur around the province. Palma Soriano, a suburb of Santiago, has the **National Orchestra of Charangas** in November and city center has the International **Matamoros Son festival** in September. For details, contact the Tourist Office.

On July 26 1953, Castro led an ill-fated assault on the Moncada Barracks in Santiago in an attempt to overthrow Batista. The date was chosen because it was the 100th anniversary of the writer and activist José Martí's birth. The attack failed, but July 26 remains an important date in the most recent revolutionary history. It is a huge celebration throughout the country and Santiago is where the biggest parties occur. Placards, posters and banners are strung up throughout the city and it is part of the Carnival celebrations that are precluded by the Fiesta del Fuego.

A month of partying Cuban-style will make any foreigner want to go home and wring out his/her liver.

■ Sightseeing

Castillo de San Pedro de la Roca, or **El Morro** as it is commonly called, is 15 km/10 miles from the city center at Santiago Bay, ☎ 22/69-1669. Take a bus or taxi to Ciudamar and the walk the short distance to the fort, which was built to protect the city from invading pirates. Standing on a rock overlooking the ocean, it is one of the best examples of European Renaissance military engineering in the Caribbean. It was designed in 1638 by Italian architect Juan Bautista Antonelli, who also claims the castle in Havana.

The huge interior features the **Pirate's Museum**, ☎ 22/69-1569, a fine collection of weapons, swords, muskets and other paraphernalia used by pirates. The museum is open Tuesday to Saturday, 9 am to 5 pm and costs $5 to enter. To get here you will need to take a taxi ($30 for four people) or a truck (that could take all day) to Ciudamar.

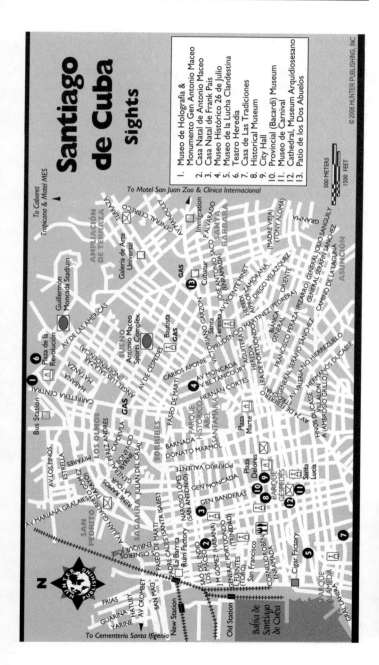

Santiago de Cuba Sights

To Cabaret Tropicana & Motel MES

To Motel San Juan Zoo & Clínica Internacional

1. Museo de Holografía & Monumento Gen Antonio Maceo
2. Casa Natal de Antonio Maceo
3. Casa Natal de Frank País
4. Museo Histórico 26 de Julio
5. Museo de la Lucha Clandestina
6. Teatro Heredia
7. Casa de Las Tradiciones
8. Historical Museum
9. City Hall
10. Provincial (Bacardi) Museum
11. Museo de Carnival
12. Cathedral, Museum Arquidiosesano
13. Patio de los Dos Abuelos

© 2006 HUNTER PUBLISHING, INC

500 METERS
1500 FEET

Southern Cuba

Caridad el Cobre, 18 km/11 miles from Santiago in El Cobre, is Cuba's most famous church. It holds the Virgin of El Cobre, robed in rich brocade embroidered with gold threads, sitting on a silver moon-shaped stand that is decorated with precious stones. The black virgin, the protector of Cuba, is holding the Christ child and both are capped with golden crowns inlaid with more precious stones. The virgin stands about 15 inches high and the Christ child holds a golden globe. The halo around the virgin's delicate face is of solid gold, inlaid with yet more stones. Her counterpart in Afro-Cuban worship is Ochun, goddess of femininity. When you are approaching El Cobre town, which is tucked in the Sierra Maestras near old copper mines (also visible), the triple-domed church looms into view long before you arrive. Hawkers show up quickly, selling everything from miracle stones to sunflowers.

THE LEGEND

The legend is that three fishers were bobbing in an ocean storm, facing certain of death, when they found the virgin. She was made of wood and had a sign in her hand that said she was the virgin of charity. Clinging to the statue, the men made it to shore safely.

Pilgrims come in September (mostly) to pray. Often they do the last part of their journey on their knees. Once at the church, they leave offerings in thanks for those who the virgin has helped. Because of her miracles, the virgin was declared the patron saint of Cuba in 1916, by Benedict XV. In 1977, the church was raised to the status of Basilica and when Pope John Paul II came in 1998, he crowned the virgin. This was her second crowning.

When mass is held, the virgin, who sits in a glass case on the second level of the church, is turned to face the congregation. Her feast day is September 8.

Parks & Plazas

Parque Cespedes, Ave Aguilera and Enramada, is a fairly large plaza with the **Cathedral de la Asuncion** at one end and **City Hall** at the other. City Hall, built in 1950, was where Castro made his first speech after the revolution. **Gran Hotel Santiago** is located on another of the park's corners, with a large balcony where locals and foreigners alike sit and enjoy the ever-changing scenes. The park was first called the Plaza des Armas and was built in 1516. It was one of the first seven built in the country. The **Governor's House**, also called **Casa de Don Diego Velazquez** (the first Governor of Cuba), is now a museum.

Plaza de la Revolución, Ave de las Americas and Los Desfiles, features a huge marble statue designed by Alberto Lezcay of General Antonio Maceo on his horse, front hooves in the air, surrounded by 23 machetes that represent the weapons used by farmers fighting for independence.

> **AUTHOR NOTE:** The machetes required 90,000 tons of bronze to complete and the marble was brought from quarries in Isla de Juventud.

Maceo, known as the Bronze Titan, led most of the fighting between 1868 and 1878 when the Cubans were fighting for independence and again for the three years beginning in 1895 when the Cubans wanted freedom from the United States. This is the plaza where Pope John Paul II spoke in 1998. Below the statue is a small museum, ☎ 22/882-0906, open Tuesday to Saturday from 9 am to 5 pm, $5. It has a few objects like first editions of Maceo's works, some maps, and other objects that are a reminder of the hero's life. It's best to take photos outside and forget donating another $5 to the Castro establishment.

Plaza de Dolores, Calle Enramada and Ave Aguilera (the main streets in town), is a two-block-long park surrounded by trendy restaurants and shaded by old trees. It's a lively park, and getting a seat on one of the benches is often difficult. This is the place to people-watch and photograph. There are signs saying the park is only for tourists, but you will see drunks and hawkers everywhere while the police watch. You will also see kids in baggy pants playing hacky sack or just shoving each other around, alongside a tradition-ally costumed African woman selling her best cakes. You can have your photo taken with her for a buck. Older residents come to sit in the shade and read newspapers and workers from the area often bring their bag lunches. The monument in center is dedi-cated to those who fought for freedom. This is where the Spanish executed troublemakers. The hat on the top of the monument is called a *gorro frigio* and is the symbol of Cuban independence, a replica of the hat Romans gave slaves who had been freed. Head to the bakery at the southeast to purchase some "real" Cu-ban baking and/or fresh bread.

Museums

The Provincial Museum, also called the **Bacardi Museum**, Calle Pio Rosado and Aguilera, ☎ 22/62-8402 is the second-oldest museum in the country and has a collection of colonial paintings dating back 200 years, plus an impressive collection of antiques. The man-sion housing the museum was not completed until af-ter Emilio Bacardi's death. His wife felt that his artifacts, collected from around the world, should be housed in a fitting place, so she oversaw the completion. After the revolution, the family was re-lieved of their wealth. They left for the United States and continued producing the famous rum. The origi-nal Cuban Bacardi rum factory is down by the water, in the French quarter.

The museum has two floors. The first one displays ob-jects, particularly weapons, used by the colonists when they came to Cuba. Some of the weaponry is in-teresting, but the pieces used on slaves give rise to feelings of horror and shame. I really didn't feel like taking photos – which cost a dollar. The displays are well done, not overcrowded. The rest of the floor is dedicated to island history, with more weapons and some personal items connected to Cuban heroes, like a pen that once belonged to Martí. When I was there, the mummies and Egyptian collections were at the back of the museum.

The second floor holds colonial and contemporary art, which includes oil paintings, watercolors, sculptures and a few pieces of old furniture. This floor is really the best part of the building. It has some great portraits done by José Joaquín Tejada Revilla (1867-1943). My favorite portrait of his was called *Catalan o Borracho* (Spaniard or drunk). Interestingly, not one piece of art in this collection is by a woman.

The museum is open from Tuesday to Saturday, 9 am to 6 pm and Sunday until 1 pm. There is a $2 entry fee and a charge of $1 per photo. Forget the photos and buy a book when you get back home.

Museo de Carnaval, Calle Heredia #301 and Ave Carniceria, ☎ 22/62-6955, is located in a dimly lit clapboard house and offers the history of Santiago's Carnival. There are masks and costumes, some richly decorated with sequins and glittery threads. The masks are every size up to the huge parade-leading renditions. Photos show Carnival before the communists took over. Seems like more money was spent on revelry in those days. The museum is open Tuesday to Saturday, 9 am to 6 pm and Sundays until 1 pm. There is a $2 entry fee and photos cost extra.

Museo de la Lucha Clandestina, Calle Rabi #1 between Ave Santa Rita and San Carlos, ☎ 22/62-4689, located on the Loma del Intendente. This museum describes the underground movement against the Batista regime. It features newspaper articles and photographs, some items of clothing, and equipment used by rebels. There's even a clipping announcing the death of Castro published by the Batistas. It is similar to Havana's revolutionary museum, but smaller, with an account of the events leading to the takeover. The museum is open Tuesday to Sunday, 9 am to 5 pm, and costs $3 to enter.

Historical Museum, also called Museum of Ambiente Cubano, Calle Santo Tomas #612 and Ave Aguilera, ☎ 22/65-2652, is just off Parque Cespedes. The building has ancient wooden balconies on its second floor and was once the residence of Diego Velazques, the original conqueror of Cuba. The furnishings are breathtaking, made of carved woods, some with inlay. One interesting room has the Pollo de la Ventana

(chicken window), which overlooks another part of the house and look like the windows used by harems in Arabia. If you are visiting only one colonial house museum in the country, make it this one. It has a great collection of porcelain, crystal and glassware. The house is most notable for the Moorish décor in the halls and some rooms. It is open Monday to Saturday, 9 am to 5 pm and Sunday until 1 pm. There is a $2 entry fee; photos are $1 extra.

Balcon de Velazquez, corner of Calle Heredia and Corona, was originally built as fort and lookout, with cannons pointing over the bay. But the fort deteriorated and a house was built on the site. That too, fell into disrepair and the city decided to rebuild it in honor of Velazquez. You can enter the lookout daily from 7 am to 8 pm (free) and enjoy one of the better views of the city. This is not a museum.

Granjita Siboney, Carretera de Siboney, Km 13.5, ☎ 22/63-9168, is the farm house where the revolutionaries hid while planning to attack Moncada Garison on July 26, 1953. Inside the museum are clothes, shoes, rifles and other personal objects belonging to the rebels who lost the battle but won the war. The items of interest are well displayed, although a tad uninteresting. The museum is closer to the beach and Hotel Siboney than it is to Santiago, and you must be really interested in the revolution to make a trip out here. It is open from Tuesday to Saturday, 9 am to 5 pm. There is a $2 fee to enter.

Museum of 26th of July, Calle General Portondo and Moncada, ☎ 22/62-0157, is in the Moncada Garrison, that was attacked by troops headed by Fidel Castro when he fought against the Batista military stationed in Santiago. Inside are pictures, documents and uniforms worn by those who fought this battle. The revolution of Cuba has to be the most documented event in history. Here you will find even more stuff, like photos of atrocities and blood-stained uniforms. The barracks are impressive and worth looking at; they are painted the same color as the prison that held Castro on Isla de le

Juventud. Open Tuesday to Saturday, 9 am to 6 pm and Sunday until 2 pm. Entry fee is $5 per person.

Casa Natal de Antonio Maceo, Calle Los Maceos #207, between Ave Corona and Rastro, ☎ 22/62-3750, is another monumental attempt to show appreciation for the leadership of this military leader commonly called the Bronze Titan. The museum features a number of posters and photos of Maceo, plus other memorabilia from his life.

The city also has **Casa Natal de José Maria Heredia**, Calle Heredia #260, between Pio Rosado and Hartman, and **Casa Natal de Frank Pais Garcia**, Calle General Banderas #226 between Ave Habana and Maceo. If you are a "birthplace museum" collector, these are interesting. They are open from Tuesday to Saturday, 10 am to 4 pm and cost $3 to enter.

Cementerio Santa Ifigenia, Calzada Crombet, holds the remains of José Martí, Carlos de Cespedes and Emilio Bacardi, plus some revolutionary martyrs. The gargantuan monument to Martí is hexagonal, with windows on each side so that the embalmed body, which lies in a coffin, always has the sun shining on him. There is a marble statue of him sitting in the thinker's position. Martí died in combat in 1895 at Dos Rios near Santiago. The cemetery is not as large as the one in Havana, but some of the mausoleums are worth seeing. There is a $1 fee to enter.

Museum Arquidiosesano, Calle Heredia and Santo Tomas, in the cathedral on Plaza Cespedes, ☎ 22/62-2143, was built in 1528 but had to be rebuilt numerous times due to human destruction and earthquakes. The cathedral, completed in 1818, has five naves and is covered with an impressive dome originally (or finally) built in 1922. Much of the furniture and altars are made from hardwoods found in the area. Take note of the magnificent pipe organ and the center altar, made of marble. On the other side of the church is a small chapel dedicated to the Virgin of Caridad.

> **AUTHOR NOTE:** The greatest story attached to the cathedral is that the body of Diego Velazquez is somewhere in or under the building.

The museum has paintings, furniture and religious objects, such as frescoes painted by the Dominican friar Desangles. It is open from 8 am to noon daily, except Tuesdays. There is no charge to enter. You may attend mass offered daily at 6:30 pm.

LIFE IN CUBA

It is normal for men to whistle and jeer at women in Cuba. It is also normal for the woman to make sharp remarks back.

■ Adventures on Foot

Loma de San Juan, Ave de Raul Pujol and the Carretera de Siboney, is two km/1.2 miles from the center of town, next to Hotel San Juan. This is the famous hill that Teddy Roosevelt and his Rough Riders stormed to defeat Spanish troops in 1898 during the Spanish-American War. When fighting broke out between America and Spain, Roosevelt formed a regiment of volunteers and called them the Rough Riders. When they were leaving New York for battle, under the command of Leonard Wood, there was a lot of confusion, which resulted in some of the men and all the horses being left behind. The soldiers who did make it to Cuba had to run up the hill on foot. The battle took one day. Roosevelt was nominated for the Congressional Medal of Honor but the nomination was rejected. Crushed, Roosevelt went on to become the governor of New York the following year and then put himself in line for Vice President. When the president was killed in 1901, Roosevelt fell into the presidency.

A block or so away from the hill is **Santiago's Zoo**, definitely not the best place for captured animals to be living. The zoo charges a dollar to enter.

La Gran Piedra, Carretera de la Gran Piedra, 25 km (15 miles) east of town in the Sierra Maestras, is a giant rock standing 1,214 meters/3,700 feet high. It weighs 70,000 tons and is in the *Guinness Book of World Records* as the third-largest solid rock in the world. After climbing from the parking lot up the 425 steps to the top, you can see all of Sanitago de Cuba and across the Caribbean to Jamaica (on a clear day).

Southern Cuba

It is best to go in the morning; in the afternoons, cloud cover and mist can hamper your views. There is an admission fee of $1 per person and admittance is permitted from 9 am to 6 pm (unless staying at the hotel, page 440, in which case you can go up at night).

Often, taxis will refuse this trip because the road is so steep. If they do take you, the fare is $15 each way. There is no reliable bus. It is best to take a tour, unless you have your own car or can share a taxi.

Isabelita Plantation Museum, one km before the rock, shows items used to control slaves. The shackles and whips alone are worth the viewing, if for no other reason than to know we don't want slavery. There is a $2 entry fee and the museum is open from 9 am to 5 pm every day except Monday.

Pico Turquino is the highest mountain in Cuba at 1,974 meters/6,475 feet. The top is crowned by a bust of José Martí, donated in 1953 by Dr. Manuel Sanchez Silvera and Cecilia Sanchez Manduley (Cecilia of Castro fame). The bust was made by Jilma Madera, who also created the great white Christ in Havana. Pico Turquino is now a national park.

The hills in this area feature 17 peaks that rise above 1,300 meters/4,265 feet. At the top of Pico Turquino it can be quite cold, even in dry season, so carry a few items of extra clothing, like a jacket and long pants. You must have good walking shoes. The best time to go is during dry season from October to the end of April. In rainy season, parts of the trail can be quite slick and clouds can cause limited visibility, making the climb hardly worth the effort.

To get to the mountain, take a private taxi/public bus (unreliable – I could not get info on this) or drive to La Mula where there are some cabins for rent. Stay that day (take your time getting to La Mula) and start your ascent early in the morning. From La Mula, it is 12 km/seven miles to La Cueva, where the foot of the mountain is located. If you hire a car from Santiago and the driver stays at the cabins in Mula with you, expect to pay no more than $60. You will also have to pay your driver's food and lodging. A shelter at 600 meters/2,000 feet has a campsite for those carrying tents; there's another shelter at 1,500 meters/5,000 feet. Shelters offer very basic dorm rooms.

Once at Pico Turquina, you must pay $20 to enter, plus the cost of the guide. Each person pays the same, even if you have only one guide between you. You climb 6,000 feet within 10 km/six miles of trail to reach the top. The trail is clear and well maintained, with steps on some of the steeper parts. This is a very important historical area for the present government in Cuba, the place where Guevara and Castro made their hideout while fighting Batista.

You can opt to go down the other side of the peak to Alto del Naranjo in Granma province, but then you will have to arrange transportation from there back to Santiago. Inform park rangers at the station if you would like to do this – they are usually opposed to this option because the guides must get back to their place of origin. Some have been left in Granma with no choice but to walk the entire way. However, if you can arrange for your guide to come back to the park (and pay for all this) then it might work. The most common and easiest option is to come down the same way you went up. This makes about a 10-hour day of hiking, never mind birding, photographing, stopping to breathe and drink water.

These mountains hold the smallest toad in the world – it measures under half an inch. In contrast, spectacular giant ferns found on the mountain stand anywhere from 12 to 20 feet high. You'll see many birds hiding in this rainforest.

> **AUTHOR NOTE:** Humans use only 7,000 of the 75,000 known edible plants found in the rainforests around the world.

■ Adventures in Nature

 The **Botanical Gardens** are two km/1.2 miles before the Gran Piedra steps. Along the highway is a nursery. This is called a botanical garden (in this case anyway). Here, they charge the foreigner $1 to enter and see plants growing in flowerbeds rather than in a tended garden. There are some lovely tropical plants such as orchids (in season) and birds of paradise. However, if you have been anywhere in the jungle, you'll know that this is really a Cuban moneymaker rather than a tourist attraction.

Great National Park of Baconao, 25 km/15 miles southeast of Santiago, is an area with coffee plantations and a wildlife reserve, plus the Promenade of Sculptures – 170 concrete animals and people representing creatures dating back to the Jurassic period. Some stand two or three meters (seven-10 feet) high. The area has beaches backed by wooded areas, but be aware that there is little transportation to most places in the park, and travel is difficult unless you go with a government tour company or have your own car. If driving, travel east on Ave Raul Pujol and follow the coast toward Bacanao. There are signs. You will pass the museum at Siboney (see page xx). You will not be permitted to go farther than the village of Bacanao. Taking a taxi will run about $75 converted pesos for the day. It is almost 100 km/60 miles, one way.

The **Jardin Ave de Paraiso**, in town, which dates back to the mid-1800s, is a well-kept garden featuring some exotic plants. Birds? I hardly saw any, although I may have come at a very bad time of year.

■ Adventures on Water

 You can reach **Cayo Granma** by taking a truck or bus to Ciudamar, where a ferry runs once every hour on the hour over to the little island. Island restaurants offer refreshments. Your visit shouldn't take more than two hours; half an hour to walk around, half an hour waiting for food, half an hour to eat and half an hour to enjoy a beer.

Playa Siboney is just 20 km/12 miles from Santiago on the Bay of Santiago. Along this strip of land that juts out just a bit, are a few hotels and restaurants, but it is best to have your own car. Just beyond Siboney are **Playa Daiquiri, Playa Bucanero** and **Sierra Mar**, all inviting beaches. Check with the tour desk at a big hotels in order to dive or snorkel. See below for places to stay.

■ Places to Stay

Hotels

 Casa Granda, Ave Heredia #201 on Plaza Cespedes, ☎ 22/68-6600, $$$$, is a hangout for foreigners. Built in 1914, this 60-room hotel has been kept up so all the conveniences of modern-day life are available (like a hair dryer, hot-water showers and quality furniture), but the elegance

PRICE CHART

Per room for two people, per day.

$	$25-$50
$$	$51-$75
$$$	$76-$100
$$$$	$101-$150
$$$$$	Over $150

of the early 1900s remains. The location is the best draw and the patio restaurant and roof bar are second to none in Santiago. I loved this place.

Hotel Libertad, Calle Aguilera #658, Plaza de Marte, ☎ 22/62-7710, $$, is in a quieter area of town. Everything is clean and updated, with modern conveniences, although the rooms are just up from basic. The private bathrooms are small but functional. I have heard that some rooms do not have windows – ask for a room with a window. Rates, which include breakfast, are comparable to those at more expensive *casas*, so if you need some privacy, try them instead.

There is a restaurant and a business center with fast Internet for $4 per hour. The staff is pleasant.

Hotel Santiago de Cuba, Ave Los Americas and Calle M, ☎ 22/64-2634, $$$$, is a huge modern building about two km/1.2 miles from the town center. It was built in 1991. The rooms are large and each one has two double beds, sitting areas, cable TVs and writing desks. The bathrooms have hot-water showers and all the amenities needed to make your stay comfortable. A large pool can be visited by non-guests for a fee of $10. There's an Italian restaurant and a rooftop bar that offers an excellent view of the city.

Hotel San Juan, Carretera de Siboney Km 1.5, ☎ 22/68-7200, $$$, is four km/2.5 miles from the city center, within view of Loma San Juan and next door to the zoo. There are about 100 decent-sized rooms, some in cabins, others in hotel buildings. Adults can enjoy the large pool, and there's also a children's pool close by. The gardens have winding walkways that are trimmed with flowering bushes and shaded by lush tropical vegetation. Meals are good at the restaurant and the cabaret at night was worth visiting.

Hotel la Gran Piedra, Carretera Gran Piedra Km 28, ☎ 22/68-6147, $$, is close to the huge rock mountain of the same name. If you like hiking and mountain scenery, this is a good base. It has 22 double rooms in private cabins, each with cable TV, private parking and a shower. This is a very quiet place overlooking the mountains and surrounded by old coffee plantations. There is a restaurant, bar and disco. It costs $15 for up to four people to get here by cab from town.

Hotel Bucanero, Arroyo la Costa, Km 4 (Carretera de Baconao), ☎ 22/268-6363, is as good as the beer after which it is named. If you like rugged rocky coastlines, jungle-covered mountains and seclusion, this is a great place. The hotel is an all-inclusive only because it is four km/2.5 miles (a one-hour walk) to the nearest village and a $20 for a cab to Santiago. The 200 rooms, perched on a cliff, are clean. They are painted rather odd colors, but nothing unbearable. The pool overlooks the ocean and the service is excellent, although the food is rather bland and the menu monotonous. While at the Bucanero, you can kayak, sail, ride horses, ride motorbikes, cycle, and scuba dive.

The beach is very small and rocky, but the cliffs around the hotel have caves and depressions worth exploring. There's even a rope ladder to climb down. Be certain to take water and a guide (who will help you in getting down), and be prepared to spend a lot of energy as this is a tough hike/climb. If you prove yourself on this one, the guides will take you even farther into the jungle. You will see iguanas, crabs and hummingbirds among other wildlife. The beach undulates with crabs during a full moon. You should bring good walking shoes for the jungle and good water shoes for the beach as it is rocky and there are sea urchins. A lagoon close to the hotel is where most people go snorkeling, especially when the ocean is a bit choppy.

Hotel El Salta, Cruce de los Baños, ☎ 22/26-1175, $$, is tucked into the Sierra Maestra Mountains, surrounded by jungle vegetation. A waterfall on the property offers swimming in the little pool at its base. In addition, there are barbeque pits for cooking and palapa huts for shade.

The Salta health spa is reputed to help relieve stress, allergies, neuralgia, dermatitis, arthritis or respiratory infections. The staff will help with a workout program for these ailments. However, the hiking is what draws people. The local guide – who I am told can speak English, French and German (I don't really believe this) – will take you on a tour of the mountains where trails lead to small waterfalls. There are coffee, banana and cacao plantations to visit.

Unless you have your own car, you must book through Cubanacan in Santiago – their minivan can transport you to and from the hotel. There are no buses except for the odd tour bus that stops for lunch; hitching would be difficult. It is actually cheaper to

Southern Cuba

book through Cubanacan than it is to show up and take the price the hotel offers.

Rooms have cable TV, air conditioning, private bathrooms, and mini-bars. Although small, they are clean and bright. You will need mosquito repellent for the evenings. Available are all the services you will need to make your stay comfortable, as well as a disco, restaurant, massage parlor, and fitness center. They also provide live entertainment.

Casas Particulares

Casa Doris Gonzalez, Calle Corona #608, between Ave Heredia and Aguilera, ☎ 22/62-2161, has a very large clean room in a colonial building. The ceilings feature the original wood and the room has two beds, table, fridge, chairs, air conditioning and private bath. Breakfast (included) is good, although not large. Doris or her family can help you do anything from finding the best Cuban music to hiking in the country.

Ana Delia Villalon, Calle B Masso #172 between Corona and P. Pico, 2nd floor, ☎ 22/65-1191, has a lovely room with air conditioning and private bathroom. The owner was very pleasant and made me feel like I was part of the family.

Ana Rosa Lopez, Calle José Saco, between Ave Reloj and San Agustin, ☎ 22/62-3312, has a very clean room in a small house near Plaza Dolores. Breakfast can be negotiated.

Ana Irma Verzant, Calle San Carlos #308, Apt 2, between San Felix and San Pedro, ☎ 22/64-8445, has one room with air conditioning, private bath and lots of hot water. Very comfortable.

Casa de Edelio, Calle Herederia #57B, between Padre Pico and Corona, ☎ 22/65-4928, has a private room (away from the house) with a deck attached where you can sit and watch things going on in the yard next door. The room is drab, but the visiting hairless dog is a delight. There is air conditioning and a private bathroom with hot water.

Lopez Paneque, Ave Santa Lucia #478, between Reloj and Calvario, ☎ 22/62-0258, has two rooms with private bath. They cook Creole food that is excellent.

Martin and Esperanza, Calle Portuendo #604, between Pio Rosado and Moncada near the Inglesia de la Santisima Trinidad, ☎ 22/62-7608, has a clean room and a comfortable house. The house came recommended, although I did not stay here.

Vilma Aranguren Logas, Calle Terraza #158, between Ave 5 and 7, ☎ 22/624-1295, has two rooms with air conditioning and fan. One has a private bathroom, the other is shared. Neither room has a private entrance, but the place is clean and just two blocks from the Santiago Hotel. Meals can be arranged.

Angel Pimentel Iglesias, Ave Aguilera #1374, between Calle Anacaona and Gallego, ☎ 22/64-2818. There is one double room with private shower, air conditioning and hospitable hosts. If they are full, they will help you find another room. There is an excellent *paladar* close by – ask your hosts for directions

Juana Isabel Hernandez Verastequi, Calle L #203, between Ave 4 and 5, ☎ 22/62-7477, has one room with air conditioning and private bathroom. The house has a patio with lots of plants. Meals can be arranged. Juana speaks some French and English.

Raimundo Ocaña y Bertha Peña, Ave Heredia #308, between Ave Rosado and Porfirio Valiente, ☎ 22/62-4097, has two double rooms close to the center. They have air conditioning and private bathrooms. Meals are not included, but the hostess will make you coffee. This is a very nice place.

Rafael Gonzalez, Ave Raul Pujols #251, between Calle 9 and 11, ☎ 22/64-4140 has two large rooms with air conditioning, private entrance, kitchenette, private bath and terrace. The house is close to the zoo.

Southern Cuba

Ernesto and Alfredo, Ave Serrano #43, between Calle 4 and 5, Playa Siboney, ☎ 22/63-9324, $$, have a two-bedroom house for rent that includes a living room, kitchen, two bathrooms, private parking and a covered terrace with views of the sea. The living room can also be used as a bedroom. Meals can also be arranged.

▪ Places to Eat

By all means eat at your hotel or *casa*, but also try any restaurant that seems popular. An empty restaurant usually means a bad stomach, but one that is full of locals is always a draw. You might be lucky and get to pay in pesos too.

Matamoros Restaurant, Calle Calvario, between Aquilera and Enramadas on Plaza Dolores, is a quiet and comfortable, with good food in small portions. Chicken, pork or beef dishes cost about $3. Lobster and shrimp, however, run around $19 per serving.

Café Isabelica, Ave Aguilere on Plaza Dolores, is a good place for a strong coffee or a cold beer, which is what dominates the menu. The restaurant is named after the French lady who emigrated from Haiti and started a mountain *finca* (now a museum) that specialized in coffee. Open from 10 am to 8 pm.

Santiago 1900, Ave San Bacilio #354 between Calles Bartolomé Maso and Hartmann, is an elegant restaurant that looks expensive, with a large dining room and well-set tables. However, pizza costs about $5 and a beef-steak dinner runs $8. Thankfully, they have managed to get their hands on some spices so the food has flavor! This could be because it is part of a cooking school. Open from 1 to 3 pm and 6 pm to midnight, Tuesdays to Sundays.

Hotel Granda, Plaza Cespedes, is a must. The food is good and not expensive, and the atmosphere delightful. If you have one meal here, you are sure to return.

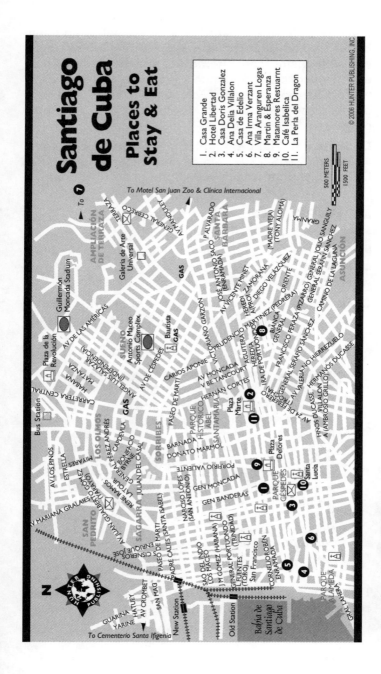

Santiago de Cuba

Places to Stay & Eat

1. Casa Grande
2. Hotel Liberdad
3. Casa Doris Gonzalez
4. Ana Delia Villalon
5. Casa de Edelio
6. Ana Irma Verzant
7. Villa Aranguren Logas
8. Martin & Esperanza
9. Matamores Restuarnt
10. Café Isabelica
11. La Perla del Dragon

© 2006 HUNTER PUBLISHING, INC

ZunZun, Ave Manduley #159, ☎ 22/64-1528, is the place to go for a special night out. It's set in an older house that has a porch with elegantly set tables (there are table inside, too, should the weather be unpleasant). Tablecloths and candles grace the tables and the waiters are not intrusive. A good meal of garlic shrimp or lobster with cilantro will cost about $15. Add a bit of wine and an appetizer!

La Perla del Dragon, Aguilera, between Calvario and Reloj, ☎ 22/65-2307, offers ample portions of good Chinese food for under $10. Open noon until 9 pm.

■ Nightlife

The music in Santiago de Cuba is second only to that in Havana. If you find Havana is a bit too much, come to smaller Santiago, where musicians specialize in trova-style music.

Casa de la Trova, Calle Heredia behind Parque Cespedes, became important during the last century when popular Cuban music, which later was known as trova, became recognized internationally.

TROVA BEGINS

Some of it started here in Santiago de Cuba with the principal styles being what is now known as son, bolero and huarache made famous by musicians such as Manuel Corona, Pepe Sanchez and Nico Saquito. The musicians, to begin with, called themselves *cantadores* (singers), rather than *trovadores* (troubadours), a term that became popular in the 1930s when soloists like Guyun and Codina appeared on the scene. However, *cantadores* soon picked up a shorter name, "trova," short for *trovadores*.

This house was opened so that the Santiago citizens could wile away the hours listening to music, joining in a song, and dancing.

Today, the house opens in the afternoon and musicians play all day and night. It costs $2 to get in (day or night) and drinks run about the same. If you have even a minor interest in Cuban music, stop here.

Casa de las Tradiciones, Calle General Lacret #651, has a back yard and a small balcony where you can escape the general group that goes to Trova. Although the premises are a bit smaller, the patrons love to sing and dance. The group Sol y Son plays here on a regular basis, and is well worth hearing. There is a small ($1-2) cover charge; drinks are comparable in price.

Patio de los Dos Abuelos. Perez Garbo #5 between Ave Garzon and Escario, ☎ 22/62-3302, is a lovely patio where you can enjoy a beer, soda or rum or stay for a full meal of fish, chicken or pork. A meal will cost about $5 and drinks are about $1 (cocktails run a bit more). It is the live entertainment people come for.

■ Shopping

 Secondhand Shop, Calle Heredia #305, across from La Trova, is a crowded shop that offers, among other things, peso bills with Che Guevara's signature on them. They cost about $5 per bill. There are also old books, magazines (some from the 1850s) and music records. Even if you don't buy, it is interesting to go inside and talk with the owners.

Fondo Cubano de Bienes Culturales, Calle Heredia and General Lacret, ☎ 22/6-502-358, has some good quality musical instruments with better prices than the shops on Plaza Cespedes. Drums are probably the best buy here in Santiago.

Bayamo

Located just 100 km/62 miles from Santiago, this town of 200,000 people is a quiet retreat after the buzz of the city. The places to stay are clean and comfortable and the food is passable. There are a few museums to visit and parks that can be reached from here, but there isn't too much to keep you here for long. Enjoy the peace for a day or so and then move on to brighter lights.

One bad thing about Bayamo is that you can't walk around un-hassled by local *jinateros* and drunks, all of whom are obnoxious.

■ History

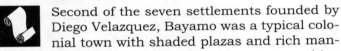 Second of the seven settlements founded by Diego Velazquez, Bayamo was a typical colonial town with shaded plazas and rich mansions until a fire in 1869 took almost everything except the cathedral. But before the fire, Bayamo, being close to the ocean, was rich from trading with slave traders and European smugglers trading contraband goods. During the struggles for independence, Francisco Vincente Aguilera, a rich landowner, and Pedro Figueredo, a musician, led underground movements.

Bayamo was proclaimed the "Birthplace of Cuba" on October 20, 1868 and the first Cuban National Anthem was sung here on that day. Just two months later, when the Spanish were invading during the Ten Years War, locals burned the city to the ground rather than let the enemy have it. This is also the town where national hero, Carlos Manuel Cespedes was born.

■ Services

Hospital Carlos Manuel Cespedes, Carretera Central, ☎ 23/42-5012.

ETECSA, Ave Cespedes and Calle Maceo, has one computer for Internet. 9 am to 10 pm daily.

Post office, Calle Maceo and Plaza Cespedes, is open from Monday to Saturday, 8 am to 6 pm.

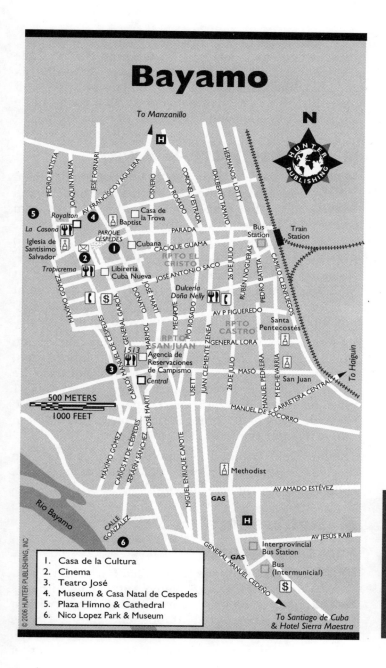

Bayamo

To Manzanillo

To Haiguín

To Santiago de Cuba
& Hotel Sierra Maestra

1. Casa de la Cultura
2. Cinema
3. Teatro José
4. Museum & Casa Natal de Cespedes
5. Plaza Himno & Cathedral
6. Nico Lopez Park & Museum

© 2006 HUNTER PUBLISHING, INC

Internet access is available at **Granma IDICT**, Calle General Garcia #58, just off the plaza, which has six good machines at a rate of 10 cents per minute – a bit high. But this is a private company so a good one to support. They are open from 8 am to 8 pm daily.

■ Getting Here & Away

 BY BUS: Bayamo is 2½ hours from Santiago de Cuba, on the same bus line from Havana and other places west, and 4½ hours from Camagüey. Bus schedules are as follows:

Trinidad to Santiago de Cuba with stops in Sancti Spíritus, Ciego de Avila, Camagüey, Las Tunas, Holguin, and Bayamo. The bus leaves Trinidad at 8:15 am, Sancti Spíritus at 9:45 am, Ciego de Avila at 11:15 am, Camagüey at 1:50 pm, Las Tunas at 3:50 pm, Holguin at 5:05 pm, Bayamo at 6:25 pm.

Santiago de Cuba to Trinidad with stops in Sancti Spiritus, Ciego de Avila, Camagüey, Las Tunas, Holguin and Bayamo. The bus leaves Santiago de Cuba at 7:30 pm, Bayamo at 9:40 pm, Holguin at 11 pm, Las Tunas at 12:15 am, Camagüey at 2:15 am, Ciego de Avila at 4:15 am, Sancti Spíritus at 5:35 am and arrives in Trinidad at 7 am.

The fare from Trinidad to Sancti Spíritus is $6, Ciego de Avila is $9, Camagüey is $15, Las Tunas is $22, Holguin and Bayamo is $26, Santiago de Cuba is $33.

■ Sightseeing

Parks & Museums

 Plaza Cespedes (also called Revolution Park) is the center of Bayamo and seems to be its society magnet. The plaza is large, with a Perucho Figueredo bust at one end and a Carlos Manuel de Cespedes statue at the other. Words of the national anthem are inscribed under the bust of Figueredo.

FIGUEREDO'S NATIONAL ANTHEM

Born in 1818 in Bayamo, Pedro Figueredo is accredited with writing the music of the national anthem. Lawyer, landowner, poet and musician, he first performed this piece of music for the public in 1868. Figueredo fought in the battle of Bayamo, part of the Ten Years War when the Cubans were trying for independence from Spain. Two years after the battle, he was captured and executed by the Spanish. The anthem was adopted in 1940. The words to this piece are below, translated by Lorraine Noel Finley.

Come, O Bayamese, rush to the battle,
All our proud country's enemies defying
Do not fear valiant men for dying
For our fatherland's sake, there is life
Come, O life.
Better death than a life bound by chains,
With contempt and opprobrium surrounded
When the clarion trumpet is sounded,
Rise to arms, and take part in the strife,
Better strife.

At the far end of the park where the pharmacy is located is the spot where the soldiers started the fire of 1869.

Casa Natal de Cespedes, Calle Maceo #55 (next to Hotel Royalton), ☎ 23/42-3864, is one of the few homes that wasn't destroyed in the fire of 1869. Cespedes was a wealthy man who got caught up in the desire for Cuban independence. He freed his slaves and got his army of less than 150 ready for battle. His enthusiasm and charismatic personality soon raised the number to 12,000 men who quickly captured both Bayamo and Holguin from the Spanish. They held those places for three months before the Spanish were able to regain the territory.

Southern Cuba

Each room in this lovely old house is displayed well. One room is dedicated to Mother Cespedes and it has some fine hand-made lace. The kitchen has an old-fashioned water filtering system. Some of the furniture too is worth noting, as are the personal things like the ceremonial sword owned by Carlos. The house is open Tuesday to Friday, 9 am to 5 pm; Saturday, 9 am to 2 pm and 8 pm to 10 pm; Sunday from 10 am to 1 pm. Entry fee is $1. When I was here, the upper floor was not open.

Himno Plaza is home to the Cathedral of Bayamo (San Salvador), Calle Joaquin Palma #130. This church was burned during the famous fire but has been rebuilt and restored. Although not too impressive inside, the most amazing part of this church is the painting over the altar that depicts the priest blessing the rebel's flag. It was here that the first national anthem was sung. Since that event, the plaza has been called the Plaza of the Hymn. Next to the cathedral is the Chapel of the Lady of Sorrows, which was built in 1740. Its ornate altar is the draw. The church is open 9 am to noon and 1 pm to 3 pm daily.

Nico Lopez Park/Museum, Ave Abihail Gonzalez (no phone), is a lovely botanical garden with palm trees and bougainvillea decorating the pathways. Inside the grounds is the Bayamo Barracks, built in 1973 to replace the original officers' club of the Cespedes Barracks. This one was dedicated to Lopez, who died in 1956. He led the battle here while other revolutionaries were fighting for the Moncada Barracks in Santiago. Lopez escaped from Cuba after the attack and lived in Guatemala. He met Che Guevara and introduced him to Castro. The museum has a few items relating to the attack, mostly paper documents. Tuesday to Saturday, 9 am to 5 pm; $1 entry fee.

Casa Natal de Celia Sanchez, Raul Podio #111, between Ignacio Perez and E. Basterrechea, in Manzanillo, ☎ 23/59-3476, is where the revolutionary fighter Celia was born on May 9, 1920. She was a constant companion to Fidel Castro during the revolution and led demonstrations demanding his release when he was imprisoned. She spent time in Batista's prisons for these acts. The museum has some personal items and documents relating to her part in the revolution. You must take a local bus to Manzanillo in order to see this museum. Closed Mondays; $1 to enter.

■ Adventures on Foot

La Desembarco National Park is a UNESCO preserve that covers over 100 square miles of land and water. It's along the ocean section of this park that revolutionaries, including Castro, landed aboard the boat *Granma*, after making their way across the Caribbean from Florida in 1956. The one-km/.6-mile trail down to Playa las Coloradas, where the boat landed, goes through mangrove jungle and ends at the Monument of Liberty. You must pay $2 for a mandatory guide. At the site is a replica of the boat and a museum with maps, photos and clippings of revolutionaries.

Far more interesting is **El Guafe walk**, a four-km/2.5-mile circular trek (you must take a paid guide) into the mountains where small caves feature petroglyphs. If you want to go beyond the trail, hike to the **Hole of Marlotte**, a sunken cave 75 meters/250 feet deep and 50 meters/165 feet wide. The other interesting destination is **Fustete Cave**, which also has petroglyphs.

The park has over 200 plant species, 10 of which are endemic. Some forest area near Royal Cove, by the beach, has never been cut and the birding there – and in the entire park – is the best in the area.

Cabins near the beach are clean and comfortable, with air conditioning and hot-water showers. There is a restaurant, bar and TV room. Cabins cost about $40 per day for two people. To get here and book your cabin, you need to contact Cubamar Colorada, ☎ 23/42-4807, or Cubamar Viajes, Calle 3 between the malecón and 12, Vedado, Havana, ☎ 7/66-2523, www.cubamarviajes.cu. They will arrange a van to the cabins plus other activities. They can make custom arrangements for any portion of your vacation.

> **AUTHOR TIP:** If coming to the park, plan to stay awhile. A day-trip from Bayamo would leave you cramped for time.

■ Adventures on Water

Scuba Diving

Marea del Portillo Beach is a black-sand beach two-km/1.2 miles long. It's set at the foothills of the Sierra Maestras, in an area that has 17 accessible dive sites. One of the sites has an old Spanish ship with 36 canyons and their metal "bullets." The virgin reef here has a terrace effect associated with karst development and is one of the reasons the area was declared a UNESCO site. Colonies of black coral inhabit the reef. There are also some caves, canals and walls. El Albacora Diving Center has an office at both the local hotels (Marea del Portillo and Farallon). They have two dive masters that can take 10 divers on each trip. Most dives go 10-35 meters/30-100 feet down and are about 25 minutes by boat from shore. The *Columbus* (sunken boat) is a 57-km/35-mile drive from the center, then just 10 meters/33 feet from the point of entry.

Snorkeling

Cayo Blanco is just 500 meters/1,500 ft from shore – almost swimming distance. The snorkeling here is very good. Gear can be obtained from the hotels and is part of your package if you are staying at an all-inclusive.

■ Places to Stay

The two hotels on the caye (The Portillo and Farallon) almost always operate on an all-inclusive basis. They have about 130 rooms each. There have been many complaints lately about the Portillo being overbooked. If you chance it, be aware that the place

PRICE CHART
Per room for two people, per day.
$. $25-50
$$. $51-75
$$$. $76-100
$$$$. $101-150
$$$$$. . . . over $150

has nothing more than the regular amenities and poor food.

Hotels

Royalton Hotel, Calle Maceo #53, between General Garcia and José Palma, $$, ☎ 23/42-2290, was constructed in the 1940s and all of its original charm remains. The rooms are small and a bit drab due to the poor lighting, but there is air conditioning, cable TV, a small fridge and a private bathroom with modern tiles. However, the bar downstairs on the street leaves you victim to every drunk, hawker, *jinetero* and psycho in the city.

Hotel Sierra Maestra, Carretera Central, ☎ 23/48-1013, is eight km/five miles from the center of town and is a huge place with swimming pool, lovely gardens, restaurants, souvenir shop, car rental and beauty parlor. The 120 rooms have cable TV and tiled bathrooms. Being so far from the center makes it hard to get around unless you have a car.

Casas Particulares

Siomara Milian Montalvo, Ave Francisco Vincent Aguilera #18, between Calle Marmal and J.J. Palma, ☎ 23/42-2996, has lovely rooms with bath and air conditioning. The lady is hospitable, the place is clean and the meals delicious. There is a patio.

Villa RoseMary, Calle Pio Rosado #22, between Ramirez and Ave Franco Aguilera, ☎ 23/42-3984, has two rooms with air conditioning and private bathrooms. The cost of the room includes breakfast. This is a very popular place.

Sr. Guido Raul Santiesteban Borges, Calle, J Estrada #76, between Ave Capote and Juan Rodriguez, ☎ 23/42-3029, has two rooms with private bath, air conditioning, hot water and private parking. The price includes breakfast.

Villa Coral, Calle Ruben Nogeras #22, between Casique Guama and José Antonio Saco, ☎ 23/42-3165, is a lovely house with people to match. The rooms are Ave and have private bathrooms. This is a #1 option.

Daniel León Tamayo, Ave Hermanos Lottis #121, between Calle Parada and Capote, ☎ 23/42-3822, is about 10 minutes walking from the center. There is air conditioning, shared bath and friendly hosts. The rate is lower than many places because of the shared bath, but a good breakfast is included.

Lydia and Rio, Ave Donato Marmol #323, between Calle Figueredo and Lora (no phone). is very close to the center. The house is comfortable and guests can use the kitchen and a large inner patio. The small, clean room has a good bed, a dresser and all linen, including towels, is provided. There is a private bath, air conditioning, and hot water all day.

Appendix

Recommended Reading

Purchase all books before going to Cuba as there are few for sale in the country and those that are available do not include things like bird or nature guides.

Che, A Revolutionary Life, Jon Lee Anderson, Grove Press, New York, 1997. Although intimidating, this tome is an excellent read and gives a full account of Che's life. If this is too much, at least see the movie or read the book, *Motorcycle Diaries*, an account of Che's trip through Latin America that changed his life. The movie is very well done.

Cuba, A Concise History For Travellers, Alan Twigg, Harbour Publishing, Canada, 2005, is a readable history of the country from the time of Columbus to Castro's love life to the latest CIA hit and miss list.

Hemingway in Cuba by Norberto Fuentes, Lyle Stuart Inc. Secaucus, NJ, 1982.

Old Man and The Sea, Hemingway. This has had numerous publications and should be hunted down in a second hand store.

Field Guide to the Birds of Cuba by Lester Short, Orlando H Garrido, Arturo Kirkconnell, Comstock Publishing, 2000, $20. Features 144 maps that show regional boundaries and 662 photos showing male, female and juvenile plumages.

Natural Cuba, Alfonso Silva Lee, Pangaea, 1996, St. Paul Minnesota, $17, is written both in Spanish and English and covers plants and animals of the island. It is very well written and entertaining. The photography of this book is exceptional.

Bird List

Bird	Date & Location
❑ Acadian flycatcher	
❑ American avocet	
❑ American bittern	
❑ American coot	
❑ American golden plover	
❑ American kestrel	
❑ American oystercatcher	
❑ American redstart	
❑ American robin	
❑ American white pelican	
❑ American widgeon	
❑ Anhinga	
❑ Antillean black swift	
❑ Antillean nighthawk	
❑ Antillean palm swift	
❑ Audubon's shearwater	
❑ Bachman's warbler	
❑ Bahaman mockingbird	
❑ Baltimore oriole	
❑ Bananaquit	
❑ Bank swallow	
❑ Bare-legged owl	
❑ Barn owl	
❑ Barn swallow	
❑ Bay-breasted warbler	
❑ Bee hummingbird	
❑ Belted kingfisher	
❑ Bicknell's thrush	
❑ Black rail	
❑ Black skimmer	
❑ Black tern	
❑ Black vulture	
❑ Black-and-white warbler	
❑ Black-bellied plover	
❑ Black-bellied whistling duck	

- Black-billed cuckoo
- Blackburnian warbler
- Black-capped petrel
- Black-cowled oriole
- Black-crowned night heron
- Black-faced grassquit
- Black-necked stilt
- Blackpoll warbler
- Black-throated blue warbler
- Black-whiskered vireo
- Blue-gray gnatcatcher
- Blue-headed quail dove
- Blue-winged teal
- Blue-winged warbler
- Bobolink
- Bonaparte gull
- Bridled tern
- Broad-winged hawk
- Brown booby
- Brown noddy
- Brown pelican
- Brown thrasher
- Buff-breasted sandpiper
- Burrowing owl
- Canada warbler
- Canvasback
- Cape May warbler
- Caribbean coot
- Caspian tern
- Cattle egret
- Cave swallow
- Cedar waxwing
- Cerulean warbler
- Cervera's rail
- Cervera's wren
- Chestnut manikin
- Chestnut-sided warbler
- Chimney swift
- Chipping sparrow
- Chuck-will's-widow

- ☐ Cinnamon teal
- ☐ Clapper rail
- ☐ Cliff swallow
- ☐ Common black hawk
- ☐ Common ground dove
- ☐ Common loon
- ☐ Common moorhen
- ☐ Common nighthawk
- ☐ Common snipe
- ☐ Common tern
- ☐ Common yellowthroat
- ☐ Connecticut warbler
- ☐ Crescent-eyed pewee
- ☐ Crested caracara
- ☐ Cuban blackbird
- ☐ Cuban bullfinch
- ☐ Cuban crow
- ☐ Cuban emerald
- ☐ Cuban gnatcatcher
- ☐ Cuban grassquit
- ☐ Cuban green woodpecker
- ☐ Cuban kite
- ☐ Cuban martin
- ☐ Cuban palm crow
- ☐ Cuban parakeet
- ☐ Cuban parrot
- ☐ Cuban pygmy-owl
- ☐ Cuban solitaire
- ☐ Cuban tody
- ☐ Cuban trogon
- ☐ Cuban vireo
- ☐ Dickcissel
- ☐ Double-crested cormorant
- ☐ Eastern kingbird
- ☐ Eastern meadowlark
- ☐ Eastern phoebe
- ☐ Eastern wood-pewee
- ☐ European starling
- ☐ Fernandina's flicker
- ☐ Forster's tern

- Fulvous whistling-duck
- Gadwal
- Giant kingbird
- Glossy ibis
- Golden-winged warble
- Grasshopper sparrow
- Gray catbird
- Gray kingbird
- Gray-cheeked thrush
- Gray-headed quail dove
- Great blue heron
- Great crested flycatcher
- Great egret
- Great lizard cuckoo
- Greater Antillean grackle
- Greater Antillean nightjar
- Greater Antillean pewee
- Greater flamingo
- Green heron
- Green-winged teal
- Gull-billed tern
- Gundlach's hawk
- Helmeted guinea fowl
- Herring gull
- Hooded merganser
- Hooded warbler
- House sparrow
- Hudsonian godwit
- Indigo bunting
- Ivory-billed woodpecker
- Kentucky warbler
- Key West quail dove
- Killdeer
- King rail
- La Sagra's flycatcher
- Laughing gull
- Leach's storm-petrel
- Least bittern
- Least grebe
- Least sandpiper

- ☐ Least tern
- ☐ Lesser scaup
- ☐ Lesser yellowlegs
- ☐ Limpkin
- ☐ Lincoln's sparrow
- ☐ Little blue heron
- ☐ Loggerhead kingbird
- ☐ Long-billed curlew
- ☐ Long-eared owl
- ☐ Louisiana water thrush
- ☐ Magnificent frigate bird
- ☐ Magnolia warbler
- ☐ Mallard
- ☐ Mangrove cuckoo
- ☐ Marbled godwit
- ☐ Masked booby
- ☐ Masked duck
- ☐ Merlin
- ☐ Mourning dove
- ☐ Neotropic cormorant
- ☐ Northern bobwhite
- ☐ Northern flicker
- ☐ Northern harrier
- ☐ Northern jacana
- ☐ Northern mockingbird
- ☐ Northern parula
- ☐ Northern pintail
- ☐ Northern rough-winged swallow
- ☐ Northern shoveler
- ☐ Northern water thrush
- ☐ Nutmeg manikin
- ☐ Olive-capped warbler
- ☐ Oriental warbler
- ☐ Osprey
- ☐ Ovenbird
- ☐ Painted bunting
- ☐ Palm warbler
- ☐ Parasitic jaeger
- ☐ Peregrine falcon
- ☐ Philadelphia vireo

- Pied-billed grebe
- Pine warbler
- Piping plover
- Plain pigeon
- Prairie warbler
- Prothonotary warbler
- Purple gallinule
- Purple martin
- Red knot
- Red-billed tropicbird
- Red-breasted merganser
- Reddish egret
- Red-eyed vireo
- Red-footed booby
- Redhead duck
- Red-legged honeycreeper
- Red-legged thrush
- Red-shouldered blackbird
- Red-tailed hawk
- Ring-billed gull
- Ring-necked duck
- Roseate spoonbill
- Roseate tern
- Rose-breasted grosbeak
- Royal tern
- Ruby-throated hummingbird
- Ruddy duck
- Ruddy quail dove
- Ruddy turnstone
- Sanderling
- Sandhill crane
- Sandwich tern
- Savannah sparrow
- Scaly-naped pigeon
- Scarlet tanager
- Semipalmated plover
- Semipalmated sandpiper
- Sharp-shinned hawk
- Shiny cowbird
- Short-billed dowitcher

- ☐ Short-eared owl
- ☐ Smooth-billed ani
- ☐ Snail kite
- ☐ Snowy egret
- ☐ Snowy plover
- ☐ Solitary sandpiper
- ☐ Sooty shearwater
- ☐ Sooty tern
- ☐ Sora
- ☐ Spotted rail
- ☐ Spotted sandpiper
- ☐ Stilt sandpiper
- ☐ Stygian owl
- ☐ Summer tanager
- ☐ Swainson's thrush
- ☐ Swainson's warbler
- ☐ Swallow-tailed kite
- ☐ Tawny-shouldered blackbird
- ☐ Tennessee warbler
- ☐ Thick-billed vireo
- ☐ Tree swallow
- ☐ Tricolored heron
- ☐ Turkey vulture
- ☐ Upland sandpiper
- ☐ Veery
- ☐ Virginia rail
- ☐ West Indian whistling-duck
- ☐ West Indian woodpecker
- ☐ Western sandpiper
- ☐ Western stripe-headed tanager
- ☐ Western wood-pewee
- ☐ Whimbrel
- ☐ Whip-poor-will
- ☐ White ibis
- ☐ White-collared swift
- ☐ White-crowned pigeon
- ☐ White-crowned sparrow
- ☐ White-eyed vireo
- ☐ White-tailed tropicbird
- ☐ White-winged dove

- ❑ Willet
- ❑ Willow flycatcher
- ❑ Wilson's plover
- ❑ Wilson's storm-petrel
- ❑ Wilson's warbler
- ❑ Wood duck
- ❑ Wood stork
- ❑ Wood thrush
- ❑ Worm-eating warbler
- ❑ Yellow-rumped warbler
- ❑ Yellow warbler
- ❑ Yellow-bellied flycatcher
- ❑ Yellow-bellied sapsucker
- ❑ Yellow-billed cuckoo
- ❑ Yellow-breasted chat
- ❑ Yellow-breasted crake
- ❑ Yellow-crowned night heron
- ❑ Yellow-faced grassquit.
- ❑ Yellow-headed warbler
- ❑ Yellow-throated vireo
- ❑ Yellow-throated warbler
- ❑ Zapata sparrow
- ❑ Zenaida dove

Appendix

Index